SEP 1 3

THE
unofficial GUIDE®
TO Disneyland
2014

Other titles in this series:

THE *unofficial* GUIDE®
TO Disneyland*

2014

BOB SEHLINGER, SETH KUBERSKY, and LEN TESTA

*Disneyland® is officially known as the Disneyland Resort®.

keen
communications

Please note that prices fluctuate in the course of time and that travel information changes under the impact of many factors that influence the travel industry. We therefore suggest that you write or call ahead for confirmation when making your travel plans. Every effort has been made to ensure the accuracy of information throughout this book, and the contents of this publication are believed to be correct at the time of printing. Nevertheless, the publishers cannot accept responsibility for errors or omissions, for changes in details given in this guide, or for the consequences of any reliance on the information provided by the same. Assessments of attractions and so forth are based upon the author's own experience; therefore, descriptions given in this guide necessarily contain an element of subjective opinion, which may not reflect the publisher's opinion or dictate a reader's own experience on another occasion. Readers are invited to write the publisher with ideas, comments, and suggestions for future editions.

Published by:
Keen Communications, LLC
PO Box 43673
Birmingham. AL 35243

Cover design by Scott McGrew

Text design by Vertigo Design and Annie Long

For information on our other products and services or to obtain technical support, please contact us from within the United States at 888-604-4537 or by fax at 205-326-1012.

Keen Communications, LLC, also publishes its books in a variety of electronic formats. Some content that appears in print may not be available in electronic formats.

ISBN: 978-1-62809-004-8; eISBN: 978-1-62809-005-5

Manufactured in the United States of America
5 4 3 2 1

CONTENTS

LIST *of* MAPS

ACKNOWLEDGMENTS

A BIG SALUTE TO OUR WHOLE UNOFFICIAL TEAM, who rendered a Herculean effort in what must have seemed like a fantasy version of Jean-Paul Sartre's *No Exit* to the tune of "It's a Small World." We hope you all recover to tour another day.

Special thanks to Disney historian Jim Hill; cartoonist Tami Knight; Unofficial Guide research director Len Testa; child psychologist Karen Turnbow, PhD; Unofficial Guide statistician Fred Hazleton; "Unheralded Treasures" writer Lani Teshima; and Unofficial friends Genevieve Bernard, Mike Scopa, David Swanson, and Guy Selga.

Amber Kaye Henderson, Marie Hillin, Annie Long, Ritchey Halphen, and Holly Cross all contributed energetically to shaping this latest edition. Much appreciation also goes to editorial-production manager Molly Merkle, cartographer Steve Jones, and indexer Ann Cassar.

—*Bob Sehlinger*

INTRODUCTION

∎ WHY "UNOFFICIAL"?

DECLARATION OF INDEPENDENCE

THE AUTHORS AND RESEARCHERS OF THIS GUIDE specifically and categorically declare that they are and always have been totally independent of the Walt Disney Company, Inc., of Disneyland, Inc., of Walt Disney World, Inc., and of any and all other members of the Disney corporate family.

The material in this guide originated with the authors and researchers and has not been reviewed, edited, or in any way approved by Walt Disney Company, Inc., Disneyland, Inc., or Walt Disney World, Inc.

This guidebook represents the first comprehensive *critical* appraisal of Disneyland. Its purpose is to provide the reader with the information necessary to tour the theme parks with the greatest efficiency and economy and with the least amount of hassle and standing in line. The researchers of this guide believe in the wondrous variety, joy, and excitement of the Disney attractions. At the same time, we realistically recognize that Disneyland is a business, with the same profit motivations as businesses all over the world.

With no obligation to toe the Disney line, we represent and serve you, the reader. The contents were researched and compiled by a team of evaluators who are completely independent of the Walt Disney Company, Inc. If a restaurant serves bad food, if a gift item is overpriced, or if a ride isn't worth the wait, we say so. And in the process, we hope to make your visit more fun, efficient, and economical.

DANCE TO THE MUSIC

A DANCE HAS A BEGINNING AND AN END. But when you're dancing, you're not concerned about getting to the end or where on the dance floor you might wind up. In other words, you're totally in the moment. That's the way you should be on your Disneyland vacation.

You may feel a bit of pressure concerning your vacation. Vacations, after all, are very special events, and expensive ones to boot. So you work hard to make your vacation the best that it can be. Planning and organizing are essential to a successful Disneyland vacation, but if they become your focus, you won't be able to hear the music and enjoy the dance.

So think of us as your dancing coach. We'll teach you the steps to the dance in advance so that when you're on vacation and the music plays, you will dance with effortless grace and ease.

THE IMPORTANCE OF BEING GOOFY

SMEDLEY PLOTZ, principal of the Disney Characters Junior Academy, is busy being bureaucratic when his secretary, Miss Nowitol, announces, "Wendy and the Lost Boys are here to see you, sir."

Plotz straightens his tie and draws himself up in his chair. "Very well. Send them in."

A modest procession pads in and stands sheepishly facing his desk. "You've been missing for three days!" Plotz exclaims. "We couldn't reach anybody in Never Land, and no one knew where you were! When you didn't show up for class, we immediately issued an APB for Hook, Smee, and the crocodile thinking that they had something to do with your disappearance."

"They all had verifiable alibis," Miss Nowitol volunteers. "Hook and Smee were booked at Chippendales, where the captain was taking tips on his hook between bumps and grinds. The croc was at the dentist for laser whitening."

"For *three days*?" the principal interjects.

"Lots of teeth, sir," Miss Nowitol advises. "Crocodiles are distinguished from alligators by the fourth tooth of the lower jaw protruding over the upper lip," she adds, apropos of nothing.

"Oh, Miss Nowitol, whatever would I do without you and your pointless factoids? Anyway . . . *you* there—start explaining."

"It was my fault," says Lost Boy Cubby. "Wendy wanted to go to Never Land by the usual route—you know, 'left at the North Star and straight till morning.' But I wanted to try out the GPS on my new iPhone, so we used that instead."

"I *told* you to get an Android, but *noooo!*" interjects Lost Boy Nibs.

Plotz gives Nibs a withering look before resuming his interrogation. "Cubby . . . you were saying?"

"I didn't know it, but I only had North America, South America, Central America, and Europe loaded on the GPS, so we ended up in La Tierra Nunca, off the coast of Honduras, by way of London. Every time we tried to head for the North Star, the GPS said, 'Please turn around as soon as possible. After the roundabout, please take Exit 3, La Tierra Nunca.' "

As if competing on a quiz show, Miss Nowitol blurts out, "La Tierra Nunca is Spanish for 'Never Land!' "

"Yeah, yeah, yeah—*then* what?" grouses the principal, clearly exasperated.

"Well," Cubby continues, "we stayed in London for a day and a half while I downloaded the entire known universe into the GPS software. Then I programmed Never Land as our destination, but the GPS said to go to Pluto—"

"Pluto? How did *he* get mixed up in this?

"Not Pluto the dog, Pluto the planet."

"Pluto is *not* a planet," Miss Nowitol smugly states. "According to astronomers, it's just a big ball of ice."

"Miss Nowitol, *please*!" Plotz entreats, his patience fading fast.

"But it has five moons," Wendy retorts.

"I mooned Ursula the Sea Witch last week," offers Lost Boy Slightly.

"ENOUGH ABOUT PLUTO AND MOONS!"

"I asked the GPS for an alternate route," Cubby resumes, "but when it was recalculating, it showed that there were tolls involved somewhere between the Milky Way and Andromeda. We didn't have much money; plus we weren't sure whether we needed exact change."

"And we didn't know what currency they take," Wendy adds.

"So we made it back to Earth and went to the bank around the corner from the school to sort it all out," Cubby concludes. "Pete"—the academy's truancy officer—"nabbed us once we got outside."

"This is a most egregious breach of the code of conduct," Plotz declares gravely. "Until I determine a suitable punishment, I'm taking away your phone."

"We don't have it," Wendy replies. "We loaned it to Alice, who gave it to the White Rabbit. He said he was late. For a very important date. With Hannah Montana."

And so it goes . . .

The Death of Spontaneity

One of our all-time favorite letters is from a man in Chapel Hill, North Carolina. He writes:

Your book reads like the operations plan for an amphibious landing: go here, do this, proceed to Step 15. You must think that everyone is a hyperactive, type-A theme park commando. What happened to the satisfaction of self-discovery or the joy of spontaneity? Next you will be telling us when to empty our bladders.

As it happens, we at the Unofficial Guides are a pretty existential crew. We are big on self-discovery when walking in the woods or watching birds. Some of us are able to improvise jazz without reading music, while others can whip up a mean pot of chili without a recipe. When it comes to Disneyland, however, we all agree that you either need a good plan or a frontal lobotomy. The operational definition of self-discovery and spontaneity at Disneyland is the "pleasure" of heat prostration and the "joy" of standing in line.

It's easy to spot the free spirits at Disneyland Park and Disney California Adventure, particularly at opening time. While everybody else is stampeding to Splash Mountain or Radiator Springs Racers, they're the ones standing in a cloud of dust puzzling over the park map. Later, they're the folks running around like chickens in a thunderstorm trying to find an attraction with less than a 40-minute wait. Face it: Disneyland Resort is not a very existential place. In many ways it's the ultimate in mass-produced entertainment, the most planned and programmed environment imaginable. Self-discovery and spontaneity work about as well at Disneyland as they do on your tax return. One mother of two young boys had this to say about our book:

> *Your book was invaluable in giving us the tools to plan a great day. . . . We had a magical day thanks to being able to prioritize our goals. Thank you for the full descriptions of rides—with only one day, you really need to pick your battles.*

We're not saying that you can't have a great time at Disneyland. Bowling isn't very spontaneous either, but lots of people love it. What we *are* saying is that you need a plan. You don't have to be inflexible about it. Just think about what you want to do—before you go. Don't delude yourself by rationalizing that the information in this modest tome is only for the pathological and superorganized.

HOW *This* GUIDE WAS RESEARCHED *and* WRITTEN

WHILE MUCH HAS BEEN WRITTEN CONCERNING Disneyland Resort, very little has been comparative or evaluative. In preparing this guide, nothing was taken for granted. The theme parks were visited at different times throughout the year by a team of trained observers who conducted detailed evaluations, rating the theme parks along with all of their component rides, shows, exhibits, services, and concessions according to formal, pretested rating criteria. Interviews with attraction patrons were conducted to determine what tourists of all age groups enjoyed most and least during their Disneyland visit.

Although our observers are independent and impartial, we do not claim special expertise or scientific background relative to the types of exhibits, performances, or attractions viewed. Like you, we visit the Disneyland parks as tourists, noting our satisfaction or dissatisfaction. Disneyland offerings are marketed to the touring public, and it is as the public that we have experienced them.

The primary difference between the average tourist and the trained evaluator is that the latter approaches attractions equipped with professional skills in organization, preparation, and observation. The trained evaluator is responsible for much more than simply observing and cataloging. While the tourist is being entertained and delighted by the *Enchanted Tiki Room*, the professional evaluator seated nearby is rating the performance in terms of theme, pace, continuity, and originality. The evaluator also checks out the physical arrangements: is the sound system clear and audible without being overpowering; is the audience shielded from the sun or rain; is seating adequate; can everyone in the audience clearly see the stage? Similarly, detailed and relevant checklists are prepared by observer teams and applied to rides, exhibits, and concessions, as well as to the theme park in general. Finally, observations and evaluator ratings are integrated with audience reactions and the opinions of patrons to compile a comprehensive profile of each feature and service.

In compiling this guide, we recognize the fact that a tourist's age, gender, background, and interests will strongly influence his or her taste in Disneyland offerings and will account for his or her preference of one ride or feature over another. Given this fact, we make no attempt at comparing apples with oranges. How, indeed, could a meaningful comparison be made between the serenity and beauty of the Storybook Land Canal Boats and the wild roller coaster ride of California Screamin'? Instead, our objective is to provide the reader with a critical evaluation and enough pertinent data to make knowledgeable decisions according to individual tastes.

The essence of this guide, then, consists of individual critiques and descriptions of each feature of the Disneyland parks, supplemented with some maps to help you get around and several detailed touring plans to help you avoid bottlenecks and crowds. Because so many Disneyland guests also visit Universal Studios Hollywood, we have included comprehensive coverage and a touring plan for that park as well.

A WORD TO OUR READERS
ABOUT ANNUAL REVISIONS

SOME OF YOU WHO PURCHASE EACH NEW EDITION of *The Unofficial Guide to Disneyland* have chastised us for retaining examples, comments, and descriptions from previous years' editions. This letter from a Grand Rapids, Michigan, reader is typical:

> Your guidebook still has the same little example stories. When I got my [new] book, I expected a true update and new stuff, not the same old, same old!

First, *The Unofficial Guide to Disneyland* is a reference work. Though we are flattered that some readers read the guide from cover to cover, and that some of you find it entertaining, our objective is fairly straightforward: to provide information that enables you to have the best possible Disneyland vacation.

Each year during our revision research, we check every attraction, restaurant, hotel, shop, and entertainment offering. Although there are many changes, much remains the same from year to year. When we profile and critique an attraction, we try to provide the reader with the most insightful, relevant, and useful information, written in the clearest possible language. It is our opinion that if an attraction does not change, then it makes little sense to risk clarity and content for the sake of freshening up the prose. Disneyland guests who try the Mad Tea Party, Peter Pan's Flight, or the *Enchanted Tiki Room* today, for example, experience the same presentation as guests who visited Disneyland in 2007, 1990, or 1986. Moreover, according to our extensive patron surveys (about 1,000 each year), today's guests still respond to these attractions in the same way as prior-year patrons.

The bottom line: We believe that our readers are better served if we devote our time to that which is changing and new as opposed to that which remains the same. The success or failure of this Unofficial Guide is determined not by the style of the writing but by the accuracy of the information and, ultimately, whether you have a positive experience at Disneyland. Every change to the guide we make (or don't make) is evaluated in this context.

WE'VE GOT ATTITUDE

SOME READERS DISAGREE with our attitude toward Disney. One, a 30-something woman from Golden, Colorado, lambasted us, writing:

I read your book cover to cover and felt you were way too hard on Disney. It's disappointing, when you're all enthused about going, to be slammed with all these criticisms and possible pitfalls.

A reader from Little Rock, Arkansas, also took us to task:

Your book was quite complimentary of Disney, perhaps too complimentary. Maybe the free trips you travel writers get at Disneyland are chipping away at your objectivity.

And from a Williamsport, Pennsylvania, mother of three:

Reading your book irritated me before we went because of all the warnings and cautions. I guess I'm used to having guidebooks pump me up about where I'm going. But once I arrived, I found that I was fully prepared and we had a great time. In retrospect, I have to admit you were right on the money. What I regarded as you being negative was just a good dose of reality.

A Vienna, Virginia, family chimed in with this:

After being at Disney for three days at the height of tourist season, I laughed out loud at your "Death of Spontaneity" section. We are definitely free spirit types who don't like to plan our days when we are on vacation. A friend warned us, and we got your guidebook. After skimming through it before we left, I was terrified that we had made a terrible mistake booking this vacation. Thanks to your book, we had a wonderful time. If it had not been for the book, we definitely would have been trampled by all the people stampeding to Space Mountain while we were standing there with our maps.

Finally, a reader from Phoenixville, Pennsylvania, prefers no opinions at all, writing:

Although each person has the right to his or her own opinion, I did not purchase the book for an opinion.

For the record, we've always paid our own way at Disneyland Resort: hotels, admissions, meals, the works. We don't dislike Disney, and we most definitely don't have an ax to grind. We're positive by nature and much prefer to praise than to criticize. Personally, we have enjoyed the Disney parks immensely over the years, both experiencing them and writing about them. Disney, however, as with all corporations (and all people, for that matter), is better at some things than others. Because our readers shell out big bucks to go to Disneyland, we believe that they have the right to know in advance what's good and what's not. For those who think we're overly positive, please understand that *The Unofficial Guide to Disneyland* is a guidebook, not an exposé. Our overriding objective is for you to enjoy your visit. To that end we try to report fairly and objectively. When readers disagree with our opinions, we, in the interest of fairness and balance, publish their point of view right alongside ours. To the best of our knowledge, the Unofficial Guides are the only travel guides in print that do this.

THE SUM OF ALL FEARS

EVERY WRITER WHO EXPRESSES an opinion is quite accustomed to readers who strongly agree or disagree. It comes with the territory. Troubling in the extreme, however, is the possibility that our efforts to be objective have frightened some readers away from Disneyland, or stimulated in others a state of apprehension. For the record, if you enjoy theme parks, Disneyland and Walt Disney World are as good as they get: absolute nirvana. They're upbeat, safe, fun, eye-popping, happy, and exciting. Even if you arrive knowing nothing about the place and make every possible touring mistake, chances are about 90% that you'll have a wonderful time anyway. In the end, guidebooks don't make or break great destinations. They are simply tools to help you enhance your experience and get the most vacation for your money.

As wonderful as Disneyland is, however, it is nevertheless a complex destination. Even so, it's certainly not nearly as challenging or difficult as visiting New York, San Francisco, Paris, Acapulco, or any other large city or destination. And, happily, there are numerous ways, if forewarned, to save money, minimize hassle, and make the most of your time. In large measure, that's what this guide is about: giving you a heads-up regarding potential problems and opportunities. Unfortunately, some folks reading the *Unofficial Guide* subconsciously add up the various warnings and critical advice and conclude that Disneyland is altogether too intimidating or, alternatively, too expensive or too much work. They lose track of the wonder of Disneyland and become focused instead on what might go wrong.

Our philosophy is that knowledge is power (and time and money too). You're free to follow our advice or not at your sole discretion. But you'd be denied the opportunity to exercise that discretion if we failed to fairly present the issues.

With or without a guidebook, you'll have a great time at Disneyland. If you let us, we'll help you smooth the potential bumps. We are certain that we can help you turn a great vacation into an absolutely superb one. Either way, once there, you will get the feel of the place and quickly reach a comfort level that will allay your apprehensions, as well as allow you to have a great experience.

THE *UNOFFICIAL GUIDE* PUBLISHING YEAR

WE RECEIVE MANY QUERIES each year asking when the next edition of *The Unofficial Guide to Disneyland* will be available. Usually our new editions are published and available in the stores by late August or early September. Thus the 2015 edition will be on the shelves in the autumn of 2014.

WHERE'S THE INDEX?

TO ELIMINATE YOUR HAVING TO CARRY THIS TOME around the theme parks, we've created quite a few tear-out pages with touring plans at the end of the book. Consequently, we've moved the index from its usual position as the last thing in the book to immediately precede the tear-out pages.

LETTERS, COMMENTS, AND QUESTIONS FROM READERS

MANY OF THOSE WHO USE *The Unofficial Guide to Disneyland* write to us, asking questions, making comments, or sharing their own strategies for visiting Disneyland. We appreciate all such input, both positive and critical, and encourage our readers to continue writing. Readers' comments and observations are frequently used in revised editions of *The Unofficial Guide to Disneyland* and have contributed immeasurably to its improvement.

Reader Survey

Please fill out our reader survey online by visiting **touringplans.com /disneyland-resort/survey.** You can rest assured that we won't release your name and address to any mailing-list companies, direct-mail advertisers, or other third party. Unless you instruct us otherwise, we will assume that you do not object to being quoted in a future edition.

How to Contact the Author

Write to Bob Sehlinger at this address:

The Unofficial Guide to Disneyland
P.O. Box 43673
Birmingham, AL 35243

Or e-mail him at **unofficialguides@menasharidge.com.** When you write, put your address on both your letter and envelope; sometimes the two get separated. It is also a good idea to include your phone number and e-mail address. If you e-mail us, please tell us where you're from. Remember, as travel writers, we're often out of the office for long periods of time, so forgive us if our response is slow. Unofficial Guide e-mail is not forwarded to us when we're traveling, but we will respond as soon as possible when we return.

Questions from Readers

Questions frequently asked by readers are answered in an appendix at the back of this Unofficial Guide.

DISNEYLAND RESORT:
An OVERVIEW

IF YOU HAVEN'T BEEN TO DISNEYLAND for a while, you'll hardly know the place.

First, of course, there is **Disneyland Park,** the original Disney theme park and the only one that Walt Disney saw completed in his lifetime. Much more than the Magic Kingdom at Walt Disney World, Disneyland Park embodies the quiet, charming spirit of nostalgia that so characterized Walt himself. The park is vast yet intimate, steeped in the tradition of its creator yet continually changing.

Disneyland was opened in 1955 on a 107-acre tract surrounded almost exclusively by orange groves, just west of the sleepy and little-known Southern California community of Anaheim. Constrained by finances and ultimately enveloped by the city it helped create, Disneyland operated on that same modest parcel of land until 2001.

Disneyland Park is a collection of adventures, rides, and shows symbolized by the Disney characters and Sleeping Beauty Castle. It's divided into eight subareas, or "lands," arranged around a central hub. First encountered is **Main Street, U.S.A.,** which connects the Disneyland entrance with the central hub. Moving clockwise around the hub, the other lands are **Adventureland, Frontierland, Fantasyland,** and **Tomorrowland.** Two major lands, **Critter Country** and **New Orleans Square,** are accessible via Adventureland and Frontierland but do not connect directly with the central hub. Another land, **Mickey's Toontown,** connects to Fantasyland. All eight lands will be described in detail later.

Growth and change at Disneyland (until 1996) had been internal, in marked contrast to the ever-enlarging development of Walt Disney World near Orlando, Florida. Until recently, when something new was added at Disneyland, something old had to go. The Disney engineers, to their credit, however, have never been shy about disturbing the status quo. Patrons of the park's earlier, modest years are amazed by the transformation. Gone are the days of the "magical little park" with the Monsanto House of the Future, flying saucer–style bumper cars, donkey riders, and Captain Hook's Pirate Ship. Substituted in a process of continuous evolution and modernization are state-of-the-art fourth-, fifth-, and sixth-generation attractions and entertainment. To paraphrase Walt Disney, Disneyland will never stop changing as long as there are new ideas to explore.

Disneyland Park was arguably Walt Disney's riskiest venture. It was developed on a shoestring budget and made possible only through Disney's relationship with ABC Television and a handful of brave corporate sponsors. The capital available was barely sufficient to acquire the property and build the park; nothing was left over for the development of hotels or the acquisition and improvement of property adjoining the park. Even the Disneyland Hotel, connected to the theme park by monorail, was owned and operated by a third party until 1989.

Disneyland's success spawned a wave of development that rapidly surrounded the theme park with whimsically themed mom-and-pop motels, souvenir stands, and fast-food restaurants. Disney, still deep in debt, looked on in abject shock, powerless to intervene. In fact, the Disneyland experience was etched so deeply into the Disney corporate consciousness that Walt purchased 27,500 acres and established an autonomous development district in Florida (unaccountable to any local or county authority) when he was ready to launch Disney World.

Though the Florida project gave Disney the opportunity to develop a destination resort in a totally controlled environment, the steady decline of the area encircling Disneyland continued to rankle Walt. After tolerating the blight for 30 years, the Walt Disney Company (finally flush with funds and ready for a good fight) set about putting Disneyland Park right. Quietly at first, then aggressively, Disney began buying up the mom-and-pop motels, as well as the few remaining orange and vegetable groves near the park.

In June 1993 the City of Anaheim adopted a Disney plan that called for the development of a new Disney destination resort, including a second theme park situated in what was once the Disneyland parking lot; a Disney-owned hotel district with 4,600 hotel rooms; two new parking facilities; and improvements, including extensive landscaping of the streets that provide access to the complex. City of Anaheim, Orange County, and State of California infrastructure changes required to support the expanded Disney presence included widening I-5, building new interchanges, moving a major power line, adding new sewer systems, and expanding utilities capacity.

By the end of 2000, all of the changes, modifications, and additions were finished, and Disneyland began the new century as a complete multitheme park resort destination. The second and newest park, **Disney California Adventure** (or DCA to the initiated), celebrated its grand opening on February 8, 2001.

DCA is an oddly shaped park built around a lagoon on one side and the Grand Californian Hotel on the other, with one of Disney's trademark mountains, **Grizzly Peak,** plopped down in the middle. **Buena Vista Street,** an entranceway evoking 1920s Los Angeles, leads to seven "lands." Inside the front gate and to the left is **Hollywood**

Land (formerly Hollywood Pictures Backlot), a diminutive version of the Disney's Hollywood Studios theme park at Walt Disney World. Then there are **Condor Flats, Grizzly Peak,** and **Pacific Wharf,** a trio of mini-lands (originally known collectively as Golden State) celebrating California's industry, cuisine, and natural resources. Next is **a bug's land,** with characters and attractions based on the Disney-Pixar film *a bug's life*. **Cars Land** is dedicated to the desert town of Radiator Springs from Disney-Pixar's *Cars*. Finally, **Paradise Pier** recalls the grand old seaside amusement parks of the early 20th century. DCA is described in detail later in the guide.

The entrances to Disneyland Park and DCA face each other across a palm-studded pedestrian plaza called the **Esplanade,** which begins at Harbor Boulevard and runs west, between the parks, passing into **Downtown Disney,** a dining, shopping, entertainment, and nightlife venue. From Downtown Disney, the Esplanade continues via an overpass across Downtown Drive and past the monorail station to the **Disneyland** and **Paradise Pier Hotels.**

Sandwiched between the Esplanade and Downtown Disney on the north and DCA on the south is the 945-room **Grand Californian Hotel** and the 50-unit **Grand Californian Villas.** Designed in the image of rustic national park lodges, the Grand Californian supplants the Disneyland Hotel as Disneyland's prestigious lodging property.

North of the hotels and across West Street from Disneyland Park is a huge multistory parking garage that can be accessed directly from I-5. This is where most Disneyland guests park. Tram transport is provided from the garage, the adjacent oversize-vehicle lot, and from outlying lots to the Esplanade. Kennels are located by the parking garage. Ticket booths are situated along the Esplanade.

SHOULD I GO TO DISNEYLAND PARK IF I'VE SEEN WALT DISNEY WORLD?

DISNEYLAND PARK IS ROUGHLY COMPARABLE to the Magic Kingdom theme park at Walt Disney World near Orlando, Florida. Both are arranged by "lands" accessible from a central hub and connected to the entrance by a main street. Both parks feature many rides and attractions of the same name: Space Mountain, Jungle Cruise, Pirates of the Caribbean, It's a Small World, and Dumbo the Flying Elephant, to name a few. Interestingly, however, the same name does not necessarily connote the same experience. Pirates of the Caribbean at Disneyland Park is much longer and more elaborate than its Walt Disney World counterpart. Big Thunder Mountain is more elaborate in Florida, and *The Enchanted Tiki Room* is about the same in both places.

Disneyland Park is more intimate than the Magic Kingdom, not having the room for expansion enjoyed by the Florida park. Pedestrian thoroughfares are narrower, and everything from Big Thunder Mountain to the castle is scaled down somewhat. Large crowds are more taxing at Disneyland Park because there is less room for them to disperse. At Disneyland Park, however, there are dozens of little surprises, small

CRITICAL COMPARISON OF ATTRACTIONS FOUND AT BOTH PARKS

ADVENTURELAND

Enchanted Tiki Room About the same at both parks.
Jungle Cruise Updated audio-animatronic (robotic) animals and funnier narrators at Disneyland, but longer ride at Walt Disney World.

CRITTER COUNTRY

Splash Mountain Longer ride and a bigger drop at Magic Kingdom, but Florida's effects are more frequently broken.
The Many Adventures of Winnie the Pooh Longer and with more motion at the Magic Kingdom.

FANTASYLAND

Carrousels About the same at both parks.
Castles Far larger and more beautiful at Magic Kingdom; Disneyland has walk-through display.
Dumbo the Flying Elephant About the same, but WDW version has double the capacity and an interactive circus-themed queue.
It's a Small World Disneyland version is longer.
Mad Tea Party Disneyland's is open-air; otherwise the same at both parks.
Peter Pan's Flight Shorter but with better lighting effects at Disneyland.

FRONTIERLAND

Big Thunder Mountain Railroad About the same; sights and special effects are better at the Magic Kingdom.
Tom Sawyer Island Comparable, but a little more elaborate and with a pirate theme at Disneyland.
Various river cruises *(canoes, boats, and such)* More interesting sights at Disneyland, and only Disneyland offers canoes.

MAIN STREET, U.S.A.

WDW/Disneyland Railroad The Disneyland Railroad is far more entertaining by virtue of the Grand Canyon diorama and the primeval world components not found at the Magic Kingdom.

NEW ORLEANS SQUARE

The Haunted Mansion Longer ride and new finale effects give Magic Kingdom the edge.
Pirates of the Caribbean Far superior at Disneyland.

unheralded attractions tucked away in crooks and corners of the park, which give Disneyland Park a special charm and variety that the Magic Kingdom lacks. And, of course, Disneyland Park has the stamp of Walt Disney's personal touch.

A Minnesota couple who have sampled Disney both east and west offered this observation:

> *We have been to WDW in Florida several times. This was our first visit to Disneyland. For parents with children 10 years of age and*

**CRITICAL COMPARISON
OF ATTRACTIONS FOUND AT BOTH PARKS***

TOMORROWLAND

Astro Orbitor About the same at both parks, but much higher in the air at the Magic Kingdom.
Autopia/Tomorrowland Speedway Disneyland version is superior.
Buzz Lightyear More mobile guns and better game play at Disneyland.
Space Mountain Much better at Disneyland.

*It should be noted that several of the attractions at Disney California Adventure, such as The Twilight Zone Tower of Terror, *Disney Junior, It's Tough to Be a Bug!*, Toy Story Midway Mania!, *Turtle Talk with Crush*, and *Muppet-Vision 3-D*, appeared first at one of the Walt Disney World theme parks. Versions of Soarin' Over California and Ariel's Undersea Adventure have been exported to Walt Disney World. None of the remaining DCA attractions are found at Walt Disney World.

younger, I highly recommend Disneyland instead of WDW. Its size is much more manageable. You can stay within walking distance of the front gate. That makes it practical and easy to get to the gates early in the morning (an absolute imperative) and get away in the afternoon for a break (always helpful). The size and scale of WDW make this impractical.

A Salem, Massachusetts, family who had visited WDW three years prior to their Disneyland trip, agreed:

We heard from many that Disneyland was small and that the castle was underwhelming. But the Disney magic was there, and we had a great time exploring what was unique about each park. We spent three days at the parks and wished that we had planned to be there longer. The parks may be smaller, but there is still plenty to see and do.

Disneyland first-timers (along with honeymooners and birthday or anniversary celebrants) are rewarded with a special pin, as this Oregon mom relates:

When I went to pick up something at Town Hall on Main Street, I realized that they had pins to proudly announce it was a first visit to DL. I don't recall reading anything about this in your book and would have taken advantage of it with my older son's first visit. Fortunately, there is no date on it, so I got one for each son and told them that no one would know it was the older one's second time.

To allow for a meaningful comparison, we have provided a summary of those features found at Disneyland Park and not WDW's Magic Kingdom (listed alphabetically on the following page), accompanied by a critical look at the attractions found at both parks on the facing page and above.

ATTRACTIONS FOUND ONLY AT DISNEYLAND PARK

ADVENTURELAND

Indiana Jones Adventure | Tarzan's Treehouse

CRITTER COUNTRY

Davy Crockett's Explorer Canoes

FANTASYLAND

Alice in Wonderland | Casey Jr. Circus Train | Fantasyland Theatre
Matterhorn Bobsleds | Mr. Toad's Wild Ride | Pinocchio's Daring Journey
Sleeping Beauty Castle Walk-Through | Snow White's Scary Adventures
Storybook Land Canal Boats

FRONTIERLAND

Fantasmic! (at Disney's Hollywood Studios) | The Golden Horseshoe
Sailing Ship *Columbia*

MAIN STREET, U.S.A.

The Disneyland Story, presenting *Great Moments with Mr. Lincoln*

MICKEY'S TOONTOWN

Chip 'n Dale Treehouse | Gadget's Go Coaster | Goofy's Playhouse
Mickey's House | Minnie's House | *Miss Daisy,* Donald's Boat
Roger Rabbit's Car Toon Spin

TOMORROWLAND

Captain EO (at Epcot) | Finding Nemo Submarine Voyage
Innoventions (at Epcot) | *Jedi Training Academy* (at Disney's Hollywood Studios)
Star Tours: The Adventures Continue (at Disney's Hollywood Studios)

PART ONE

PLANNING *before* YOU LEAVE HOME

▌■ GATHERING INFORMATION

IN ADDITION TO THIS GUIDE, we recommend that you first visit our website, **touringplans.com,** which offers essential tools for planning your trip and saving you time and money. Our blog, **blog.touringplans .com,** lists breaking news for the Disneyland Resort and Disney theme parks worldwide.

The site also offers computer-optimized touring plans for Disneyland and DCA. With these, you choose the attractions you want to experience, including character greetings, parades, fireworks, meals, and midday breaks, and we'll give you a step-by-step itinerary for your specific dates of travel, showing you how to see everything with minimal waits in line. The touring plans can incorporate any Fastpasses you retrieve.

You can update the touring plans when you're in the parks, too. Let's say that your touring plan calls for riding The Haunted Mansion next, but your family really needs an ice cream break and 30 minutes out of the sun. Get the ice cream and take the break. When you're done, click the "Optimize" button on your plan, and it will be updated with what to do next. The ability to redo your plan allows you to recover from any situation while still minimizing your waits for the rest of the day.

Another really popular part of **touringplans.com** is our Crowd Calendar, which shows crowd projections for Disneyland and DCA for every day of the year. Look up the dates of your visit, and the calendar will not only show the projected wait times for each day but will also indicate for each day which theme park will be the least crowded. Historical wait times are also available, so you can see how crowded the parks were last year for your upcoming trip dates.

The website also has complete dining menus for every food cart, stand, kiosk, counter-service restaurant, and sit-down restaurant in the Disneyland Resort, including wine lists. The whole thing is searchable, too, so you can find every restaurant in DCA that serves steak (and its prices), or see which snacks are available in New Orleans

Square. Updated constantly, these menus represent the most accurate collection of Disney dining information available anywhere.

The touring plans, menus, Crowd Calendar, and more are available in Lines, our mobile application, which provides continuous real-time updates on wait times at Disneyland. Using in-park staff and updates sent in by readers, Lines shows you the current wait and Fastpass distribution times at every attraction in every park, as well as our estimated actual waits for these attractions for the rest of today. For example, Lines will tell you that the posted wait time for Space Mountain is 60 minutes, and that based on what we know about how Disney manages Space Mountain's queue, the actual time you'll probably wait in line is 48 minutes. Lines is the only Disney app that shows you both posted and actual wait times.

Lines also has an online chat feature, where folks can ask questions and give travel tips. Hundreds of "Liners" interact every day in discussions that stay remarkably on-topic for an Internet forum, and the group organizes regular in-park meets. We're thrilled with it.

Lines is available free to **touringplans.com** subscribers for the Apple iPhone and iPad at the iTunes Store (search for "TouringPlans"; requires iOS 4.3 or later) and for Android devices at the Google Play Store (requires Android 2.1 Eclair or later). Owners of other phones can use the Web-based version at **m.touringplans.com.**

As long as you have that smartphone handy while visiting the parks, we and your fellow Unofficial Guide readers would love it if you could report on the actual wait times you get while you're there. Run Lines, log in to your user account, and click "+Time" in the upper right corner to help everyone out. We'll use that information to update the wait times for everyone in the park, and make everyone's lives just a little bit better.

Much of our Web content—including the menus, resort photos and video, and errata for this book—is completely free for anyone to use. Access to part of the site, most notably the Crowd Calendar, additional touring plans, and in-park wait times, requires a small subscription fee (current-book owners get a substantial discount). This nominal charge helps keep us online and costs less than lunch at the French Market restaurant in Disneyland. Plus **touringplans.com** offers a 45-day money-back guarantee.

In addition we recommend that you obtain copies of the following publications:

1. DISNEY RESORT TRAVEL SALES CENTER CALIFORNIA BROCHURE This full-color booklet describes Disneyland in its entirety and lists rates for the Disneyland hotels. Also described are Disneyland package vacations with lodging options at more than 25 nearby hotels. The brochure is available from most full-service travel agents, or it can be obtained by calling the Walt Disney Resort Travel Sales Center at ☎ 714-520-5060, or get the e-brochure at **kingdommagictravel.com/disneyland.**

2. DISNEYLAND GUIDEBOOK FOR GUESTS WITH DISABILITIES If members of your party are sight- or hearing-impaired or partially or

IMPORTANT DISNEYLAND RESORT PHONE NUMBERS	
ANAHEIM TRAVEL INFORMATION	☎ 714-765-8888
ASK OTTO AUTOMATED ATTRACTION INFO	☎ 714-520-7090
DINING RESERVATIONS	☎ 714-781-3463, Option 4
DISNEY CRUISE LINE	☎ 800-951-3532
DISNEY GUIDED TOURS	☎ 714-781-8687
DISNEYLAND HOTEL	☎ 714-778-6600
DISNEYLAND RESORT ROOM RESERVATIONS	☎ 714-956-6425
DISNEYLAND VACATION PACKAGES	☎ 714-520-5060
FANTASMIC! BALCONY RESERVATIONS	☎ 714-781-7469
FOREIGN LANGUAGE ASSISTANCE	☎ 714-781-7290
GRAND CALIFORNIAN HOTEL	☎ 714-635-2300
LOST & FOUND	☎ 714-781-4765
PARADISE PIER HOTEL	☎ 714-999-0990

wholly nonambulatory, you will find this small guide very helpful. Disney does not mail them, but copies are readily available at the park. You can also download the guide at **disneyland.com** by clicking on "Guest Services" at the bottom of the page.

3. HOTELCOUPONS.COM SOUTHWEST GUIDE Another good source of lodging discounts throughout the state of California, the *HotelCoupons .com Southwest Guide* can be obtained by calling ☎ 800-222-3948, Monday–Friday, 8:30 a.m.–5:30 p.m. EST, or visiting **hotelcoupons .com.** The guide is free, but you will be charged $3 for postage and handling. Similar guides to other states are available at the same number.

Disneyland Main Information Phone and Website

The following phone numbers and website provide general information. Inquiries may be expedited by using phone numbers specific to the nature of the inquiry (other phone numbers are listed elsewhere in this chapter, under their relevant topics). If you don't mind interacting with an A.I., you can call ☎ 714-520-7090 and Ask Otto, Disneyland's new automated information hot line, about ride wait times and upcoming shows.

Disneyland Guest Relations
☎ 714-781-4565 for recorded information;
☎ 714-781-7290 for live operator; **disneyland.com**

The Phone from Hell

Sometimes it is virtually impossible to get through on the Disneyland information numbers listed above. When you get through, you will get a recording that offers various information options. If none of the recorded options answer your question, you will have to hold for a live person. Eat before you call—you may have a long wait. If, after repeated attempts, you get tired of a busy signal in your ear or, worse, 20 minutes' worth of singing mice warbling "Cinderellie" in alto falsettos while you are on hold, call the Disneyland Hotel at ☎ 714-778-6600.

RECOMMENDED WEBSITES

A NUMBER OF GOOD Disneyland information sources are on the Web. The following are brief profiles of our favorites:

BEST OFFICIAL THEME PARK SITES The official Disneyland website, **disneyland.com,** is so loaded with videos, photos, and gimmicks that it's slow to load and cumbersome to search unless you have a fast computer and high-speed Internet. For those who do, there's a ton of information to be had, but even so it usually takes a lot of clicks to find what you're looking for. While **disneyland.com** has been upgraded recently, it still lags behind its sister site, **disneyworld.com,** especially in the area of online dining reservations. The Universal Studios website is **universalstudios hollywood.com.** Like the Disneyland site, it has a lot of bells and whistles. As far as your computer's concerned, be new, be fast, or be gone.

BEST OFFICIAL AREA WEBSITE Anaheimoc.org is the official website of the Anaheim–Orange County Visitor & Convention Bureau. You'll find everything from hotels and restaurants to weather and driving instructions on this site.

BEST GENERAL UNOFFICIAL WEBSITES We recommend the following websites for general information related to the Disneyland Resort.

Mouseplanet.com is a comprehensive resource for Disneyland data, offering features and reviews by guest writers, information on the Disney theme parks, discussion groups, and news. The site includes an interactive Disney restaurant and hotel review page, where users can voice opinions on their Disney dining and lodging experiences. We particularly enjoy the weekly Disneyland update column.

Intercotwest.com (Internet Community of Tomorrow–West) is a website filled with detailed information on every corner of Disneyland Resort. Featured are frequent news updates and descriptions, reviews, and ratings of every attraction, restaurant, and shop at the resort.

Deb Wills's **allears.net,** which maintains a fantastic site for Walt Disney World, also has a growing Disneyland sister site. It includes extensive information about the Disney resorts and attractions, including reader reviews. The site is updated several times a week and includes Disney restaurant menus, ticketing information, maps, and more.

Wdwinfo.com has a vibrant Disneyland section that can be found at **wdwinfo.com/disneyland.** It includes up-to-date dining menus, attraction reviews, touring tips, and more.

BEST DISNEYLAND HISTORY WEBSITE At **yesterland.com** you can visit the Disneyland of the past, where retired Disneyland attractions are brought back to life through vivid descriptions and historical photographs. Yesterland attraction descriptions relate what it was once like to experience the Flying Saucers, the Mine Train through Nature's

Wonderland, the Tahitian Terrace, and dozens of other rides, shows, parades, and restaurants.

BEST WEBSITE FOR RUMORS AND THE INSIDE SCOOP Jimhillmedia.com is perfectly attuned to what's going on behind the scenes—Jim Hill always has good gossip. He works with The Unofficial Guides as our resident historian and contributes sidebars and anecdotes to our Disney titles.

BEST DISNEYLAND NEWS SITES Micechat.com, with a dedicated group of local editors, is the definitive on-the-ground coverage of the Disneyland Resort. Be sure to check out "Dateline Disneyland" and "In The Parks," two weekly columns that stay on the pulse of the parks, complete with photos. For official news, the Disney Parks Blog (**disney parks.com/blog**) covers news from all Disney resorts.

BEST MONEY-SAVING SITE Mousesavers.com specializes in finding you the deepest discounts on hotels, park admissions, and rental cars. MouseSavers does not actually sell travel but rather unearths and publishes special discount codes that you can use to obtain the discounts. It's the first place we look for deals when we go to Disneyland Resort.

BEST DISNEY DISCUSSION BOARDS The best online discussion of all things Disney can be found at **micechat.com/forums, mousepad.mouse planet.com,** and **disboards.com.** With tens of thousands of members and millions of posts, they are the most active and popular discussion boards on the Web. There is also a rousing chat room inside our own mobile application, Lines (learn more at **touringplans.com/lines.**)

BEST DISNEY PODCASTS Our favorite Disneyland-centric podcast is Mousetalgia, found at **mousetalgia.com,** which covers Disneyland, Disney California Adventure, and everything else Disney. The hosts appreciate the history of the resort while maintaining balanced coverage of new Disneyland developments. **Seasonpasspodcast.com** has breaking news and in-depth interviews with theme park designers and executives from Disneyland and parks around the world. Hosted by industry veterans (and fans!), the show provides detailed discussions about how and why theme parks work. And if you want warts-and-all tales from behind the scenes of Mickey's kingdoms, don't miss *The Unofficial Guide's Disney Dish with Jim Hill,* hosted by coauthor Len Testa.

BEST DISNEY TWITTER FEEDS If you want your Disney news and rumors in 140 character bites, follow these prolific park Tweeters: @disneyparks, @disneyland, @touringplans, @micechat, @dlandnews-live, @latimesfunland, @thedisneyblog, @dcatoday, @disneylandtoday, and @skubersky.

ADMISSION OPTIONS

THEME PARK ADMISSION OPTIONS ARE pretty straightforward at Disneyland Resort. You have only two things to decide:

1. How many days admission you'll need.
2. Whether you want to go to both Disneyland Park and Disney California Adventure on the same day. This is known as park hopping.

ADMISSION OPTIONS	ADULT*	CHILD*
One-Day, One-Park Ticket	$92	$86
One-Day Park Hopper	$137	$131
Two-Day, One-Park Per Day	$175	$162
Two-Day Park Hopper	$210	$197
Three-Day, One-Park Per Day with Magic Morning	$225	$209
Three-Day Park Hopper with Magic Morning	$260	$244
Four-Day, One-Park Per Day with Magic Morning	$250	$230
Four-Day Park Hopper with Magic Morning	$285	$265
Five-Day, One-Park Per Day with Magic Morning	$265	$244
Five-Day Park Hopper with Magic Morning	$300	$279
Southern California Select Annual Passport *(weekdays only; some blackout dates)*	$279	n/a
Southern California Annual Passport *(some blackout dates)*	$359	n/a
Deluxe Annual Passport *(some blackout dates)*	$499	n/a
Premium Annual Passport *(no blackout dates; parking included)*	$669	n/a
Disney Premier Passport *(no blackout dates; valid at all California and Florida parks)*	$979	n/a
*Adult (age 10 and up) *Child (ages 3–9)		

Multiday tickets expire 13 days after the first use, so you don't want to buy more days than you'll need. Needless to say, tickets expire after you've used the number of days purchased even if 13 days haven't passed yet.

*un**official*** TIP
The money you can save makes researching Disney's dizzying array of ticket options worthwhile.

All admissions can be purchased at the park entrance, at the Disneyland Resort hotels, from the Walt Disney Travel Sales Center, on the Disneyland website, and at most Disney stores in the western United States. One- and 2-year-olds are exempt from admission fees.

Admission Costs and Available Discounts

It's possible to obtain discounts on all multiday tickets, but only in the 1%–7% range. One place to purchase admissions at a discount is **disneyland.com,** where Disney sells tickets with Magic Morning Hours. These tickets, in addition to the dollar discount, allow you to enter only Disneyland Park on select days 1 hour earlier than the general public one time during your visit. The feature is offered only on three-, four-, and five-day tickets purchased in advance of your visit.

If you purchase tickets on the Disneyland website, you can choose between "hard" tickets, which will be shipped to you, or e-tickets, which can be downloaded as PDF files and printed at home. An e-ticket printed from your home computer will show two bar codes. A cast member will scan these at the turnstiles. Once the bar codes are read, the cast member can issue your actual ticket. You can also now purchase one-day tickets through your smartphone at **m.disneyland .com** without needing to print anything, but these passes don't include any discounts or bonuses.

The deepest discounts we've found are from **ARES Travel** (**ares travel.com**). ARES usually beats the Disney advance purchase price by $4–$6 per ticket and also includes the Magic Morning feature. Guests may pick up their tickets at any main entrance window; a $2-per-ticket convenience fee applies. You can order online or call ☎ 800-434-7894.

If you plan to visit other Southern California attractions in addition to Disneyland, you might want to consider a **CityPass**. CityPass includes a three-day Park Hopper for Disneyland Park and DCA, including early entry to Disneyland Park for one day. Also included are one day's admission each to Universal Studios Hollywood and SeaWorld San Diego. Costing $319 for adults and $279 for children ages 3–9, the pass is valid for 14 days from first use. If you plan to visit all these parks, it will save you about 25% on admissions. If you don't use all of the admissions, however, you will save little or nothing by purchasing the City-Pass. The pass does not include dining or shopping discounts. Details concerning other CityPass destinations are available at **citypass.com**.

Military discounts are available for all Disney theme parks, usually in the 7%–25% range. Check with your base Morale, Welfare, & Recreation office for info. Military ID may be required at the gate. Many readers report buying military tickets for friends and relatives who used them without problems.

Disneyland Resort and other area attractions sometimes offer discounted afternoon and evening tickets for convention goers. See **disneyconventiontickets.com**.

Admission prices increase from time to time. For planning your budget, however, the chart on the opposite page provides a fair estimate.

One-Day, One-Park Ticket

This pass is good for one day's admission at your choice of Disneyland Park or Disney California Adventure. As the name implies, you cannot "hop" from park to park.

Park Hopper Tickets

These are good for one, two, three, four, or five days, respectively, and allow you to visit both parks on the same day. These multiday tickets do not have to be used on consecutive days, but they do expire 13 days after their first use. The 13-day expiration is in marked contrast to similar passes sold at Walt Disney World for which you can purchase a No Expiration option. If you mistakenly bought multiday tickets because you were not aware of the 13-day expiration, call ☎ 714-781-7290 or ☎ 714-781-4565 and ask to be connected to Guest Communications, which has the authority to issue you a voucher for the unused days on your ticket.

Any time before a pass expires, you can apply the value of unused days toward the cost of a higher priced ticket. If you buy a four-day Park Hopper ticket, for example, and then decide you'd rather have an Annual Passport, you can apply the value of unused days on the former toward the purchase of the latter. Upgraded passes expire on the same 13-day deadline date as the original ticket; annual passes expire one year from the first usage of the original ticket. To restrict the reselling of half-used passes, Disneyland photographs every multiday pass holder upon first entry for identification purposes; be prepared to have your pass (and face) scanned shortly before passing the turnstiles.

Annual Passports

The Disneyland Resort offers several annual passports. The Premium Annual Passport is good for an entire year with no blackout dates and is the only Disneyland passport that includes

unofficial **TIP**
If you visit Disneyland five or more days each summer, an Annual Passport is a potential money saver.

parking. The pass costs $669 and is good for admission to both parks (excluding arcades) and up to 15% discounts at most resort dining and merchandise locations. Deluxe Passports ($499) are valid 315 days per year (after pre-selected peak season blackout dates) and offer

10% discounts. Southern California and SoCal Select Annual Passports, priced at $279–$359, provide admission to both parks for a year, excluding up to 195 preselected blackout dates. These are available to residents in zip codes 90000–93599. Prices for children are the same as those for adults on all annual passports. All of these passes are a good idea if you plan to visit Disneyland parks five or more days in a year. If you purchase your annual passport in July of this year and schedule your visit next year for June, you'll cover two years' vacations with a single pass.

Admission passes can be ordered by calling ☎ 714-781-4565 or visiting the Disneyland website. They can also be purchased in advance from Disneyland Resort hotels, Disney Stores in the western United States, and the Walt Disney Travel Sales Center at ☎ 800-854-3104.

Rides and Shows Closed for Repairs or Maintenance

Rides and shows at Disneyland parks are sometimes closed for maintenance or repairs. If there is a certain attraction that is important to you, call ☎ 714-781-7290 before your visit to make sure that it will be operating. We also maintain an unofficial schedule of current and upcoming closures at **touringplans.com/disneyland-resort/closures**. A mother from Dover, Massachusetts, wrote us, lamenting:

> *We were disappointed to find Space Mountain and the Riverboat closed for repairs. We felt that a large chunk [of the park] was not working, yet the tickets were still full price and expensive!*

TOP 10 AMERICAN THEME PARKS

THEME PARK	ANNUAL ATTENDANCE	AVERAGE DAILY ATTENDANCE
WALT DISNEY WORLD'S MAGIC KINGDOM	17.5 million	48,044
DISNEYLAND	16.0 million	43,734
WALT DISNEY WORLD'S EPCOT	11.1 million	30,310
WALT DISNEY WORLD'S ANIMAL KINGDOM	10.0 million	27,392
DISNEY'S HOLLYWOOD STUDIOS	9.9 million	27,156
UNIVERSAL ORLANDO'S ISLANDS OF ADVENTURE	8.0 million	21,866
DISNEY CALIFORNIA ADVENTURE	7.8 million	21,301
UNIVERSAL STUDIOS ORLANDO	6.2 million	16,973
UNIVERSAL STUDIOS HOLLYWOOD	5.9 million	16,197
SEAWORLD FLORIDA	5.4 million	14,679

Source: Themed Entertainment Association

HOW MUCH DOES IT COST TO GO TO DISNEYLAND FOR A DAY?

LET'S SAY THAT WE HAVE A FAMILY OF FOUR—Mom, Dad, Tim (age 12), and Tami (age 8)—driving their own car. Because they plan to be in the area for a few days, they intend to buy the three-day Park Hopper tickets. A typical day would cost $571.34, excluding lodging and transportation. See the chart below for a breakdown of expenses.

HOW MUCH DOES A DAY COST?

Breakfast for four at Denny's with tax and tip	**$40.00**
Disneyland parking fee	**$16.00**
One day's admission for four on a Three-Day Park Hopper Pass	**$341.34**
Dad: Adult three-day with tax is $260 divided by three days = $86.67	
Mom: Adult three-day with tax is $260 divided by three days = $86.67	
Tim: Adult three-day with tax is $260 divided by three days = $86.67	
Tami: Child three-day with tax is $244 divided by three days = $81.33	
Morning break (soda or coffee)	**$14.00**
Fast-food lunch (burger, fries, and soda), no tip	**$46.00**
Afternoon break (soda and popcorn)	**$26.00**
Dinner in park at counter-service restaurant with tax	**$50.00**
Souvenirs (Mickey T-shirts for Tim and Tami) with tax*	**$38.00**
One-day total (without lodging or transportation)	**$571.34**

* Cheer up—you won't have to buy souvenirs every day.

TIMING *Your* VISIT

SELECTING THE TIME OF YEAR FOR YOUR VISIT

CROWDS ARE LARGEST at Disneyland during the summer (Memorial Day–Labor Day) and during specific holiday periods throughout the rest of the year. The busiest time of all is Christmas Day–New Year's Day. Thanksgiving weekend, the week of Washington's birthday, spring break for schools and colleges, and the two weeks around Easter are also extremely busy. To give you some idea of what *busy* means at Disneyland, more than 88,000 people have toured Disneyland Park in one day! While this level of attendance is far from typical, the possibility of its occurrence should prevent all but the ignorant and the foolish from challenging this mega-attraction at its busiest periods. Historically, attendance at Disney California Adventure had been about one-third that of Disneyland Park, but since the debut of Cars Land, DCA's population has actually edged out its older sibling's on several days.

> *unofficial* **TIP**
> You can't pick a less crowded time to visit Disneyland than the period following Thanksgiving weekend and leading up to Christmas.

The least-busy time of all is from after Thanksgiving weekend until the week before Christmas. The next slowest times are September through the weekend preceding Thanksgiving, January 4 through the first week of March, and the week following Easter up to Memorial Day weekend. At the risk of being blasphemous, our research team was so impressed with the relative ease of touring in the fall and other off-season periods that we would rather take our children out of school for a few days than do battle with the summer crowds. Though we strongly recommend going to Disneyland in the fall or in the spring, it should be noted that there are certain trade-offs. The parks often close earlier on fall, winter, and spring days, sometimes early enough to eliminate evening parades, fireworks, and other live-entertainment offerings such as *Fantasmic!* Also, because these are slow times of the year at Disneyland, you can anticipate that some rides and attractions may be closed for maintenance or renovation. Finally, if the parks open late and close early, it's tough to see everything, even if the crowds are light.

> *unofficial* **TIP**
> In our opinion, the risk of encountering colder weather and closed attractions during an off-season visit to Disneyland is worth it.

Most readers who have tried Disney parks at varying times of the year concur. A wintertime visitor from Sacramento, California, agrees:

> *Although there was a torrential storm on two days of our four-day visit, I can safely say that I will never visit in high season again. Yes, we were wet. Yes, there were attractions and rides closed for refurb. BUT, the longest line we waited in was 25 minutes to see the princesses. There were characters EVERYWHERE, and access to them was easy as pie. There were no issues with heat or sunburn. And we saved a boatload of money.*

Anaheim Convention and Special Event Calendar

DATES	CONVENTION/ EVENT	NUMBER OF ATTENDEES
2013		
Oct 4–6	Gay Days	30,000
Oct 12–18	Educause 2013 Annual Conv.	6,500
Oct 20–25	Confidential Group	3,200
Nov 14–20	American Assn. for Respiratory Care Annual Conv.	6,000
Dec 8–15	The Milton H. Erickson Fdn.: Evolution of Psychotherapy	8,000
2014		
Jan 11–14	Craft & Hobby Assn. Conv. & Trade Show	12,000
Jan 23–26	The NAMM Show	94,000
Feb 11–13	UBM Canon Medical Design & Mfg. Expo	42,000
Feb 14–21	Confidential Group	2,600
Feb 19–Mar 1	Helicopter Assn. International: Heli-Expo 2014	18,000
Mar 2–11	Natural Products Expo West Trade Show	65,000
Mar 13–16	Religious Education Congress	40,000
Mar 28–30	United Spirit Assn.: Spirit & Dance/Drill	33,000
Apr 3–10	Confidential Group	9,500
Apr 11–13	American Championships/American Showcase	22,000
Apr 28–May 5	Oncology Nursing Soc. 39th Annual Congress	5,000
May 2–10	Confidential Group	6,500
May 16–18	California Dental Assn.: Art & Science of Dentistry	30,000
May 26–Jun 2	Confidential Group	3,000
Jun 2–10	Confidential Group	5,500
Sep 19–27	Confidential Group	5,000
Oct 8–12	Salvation Army Adult Rehabilitation Conference	5,000
Oct 12–21	Produce Mktg. Assn.: Fresh Summit International Conv.	20,000
Oct 22–30	American Soc. for Healthcare Risk Mgmt. Annual Mtg.	2,000
Nov 12–22	Rockwell Automation Fair	7,800
Nov 28–Dec 12	American Soc. of Health-System Pharmacists Annual Mtg.	20,000
2015		
Jan 10–13	Craft & Hobby Assn. Conv. & Trade Show	12,000
Jan 22–25	The NAMM Show	94,000
Feb 10–12	UBM Canon Medical Design & Mfg. Expo	42,000
Feb 13–24	North American Assn. of Food Equipment Mfg.	20,000

Not to overstate the case: We want to emphasize that you can have a great time at the Disneyland parks regardless of the time of year or crowd level. In fact, a primary objective of this guide is to make the parks fun and manageable for those readers who visit during the busier times of year.

Of course, crowds are not the only consideration when deciding what time of year to visit Disneyland. Holidays are celebrated at Disneyland like nowhere else, and the festive decor is almost worth the price of admission. The parks are decked out for Halloween from late September until the end of October. Be aware that after-hours extra-cost Halloween parties (tickets are about $60) cause Disneyland to close early to day guests on several evenings in the fall, as a Tucson, Arizona, family found:

> *The Halloween event from mid-September to the end of October changes the low season to a zoo. Every local with an annual pass showed up in the afternoon. The park closed early for this event, [and] DCA backed up because of the early closure of Disneyland [Park].*

*un**official* **TIP**
If it's not your first trip to Disneyland and you must join the holiday-weekend crowds, you may have just as much fun enjoying Disney's fantastic array of shows, parades, and fireworks as you would riding the rides.

Christmas trappings transform Disneyland Park from mid-November until after New Year's Day. There's also a Christmas parade, and several attractions such as The Haunted Mansion and It's a Small World offer a special holiday version. Some holiday entertainment (such as the special parade and fireworks) may require a special ticket to an after-hours event, similar to Orlando's popular Mickey's Very Merry Christmas Party, expected to be introduced in Anaheim in 2013.

THE SPOILER

SO YOU CHOOSE YOUR OFF-SEASON DATES and then find it almost impossible to find a hotel room. What gives? In all probability you've been foiled by a mammoth convention or trade show at the Anaheim Convention Center. One of the largest and busiest convention venues in the country, the convention center hosts meetings with as many as 75,000 attendees. The sheer numbers alone guarantee that hotel rooms will be hard to find. Compounding the problem is the fact that most business travelers don't have roommates. Thus a trade show with 8,000 people registered might suck up 13,000 rooms (including people who registered late)! The final straw as you might expect is that room rates climb into the stratosphere based on the high demand and scarcity of supply. In regard to increased crowds at the theme parks, it's estimated that less than 10% of convention attendees will find time to enjoy the parks. It's also true, however, that business travelers are more likely to bring their spouse and even kids to a convention held in Anaheim. The bottom line is that you don't want to schedule your vacation while a major event is going on at the convention center. To help you avoid major trade shows and conventions, we've created a calendar of meetings scheduled through February 2015, showing the number of expected attendees of each (see page 25).

SELECTING THE DAY OF THE WEEK FOR YOUR VISIT

THE CROWDS AT WALT DISNEY WORLD in Florida comprise mostly out-of-state visitors. Not necessarily so at Disneyland Resort, which, along with Six Flags Magic Mountain, serves as an often-frequented recreational resource for the greater Los Angeles and San Diego communities. To many Southern Californians, Disneyland Park and Disney California Adventure are their private theme parks. Yearly passes are available at less cost than a year's membership to the YMCA.

What all this means is that weekends are usually packed. Saturday is the busiest day of the week. Sunday, particularly Sunday morning, is the best bet if you have to go on a weekend, but it is also extremely busy.

During the summer, Monday and Friday are very busy, Tuesday and Wednesday are usually less so, and Thursday is normally the slowest day of all. During the off-season (September–May, holiday periods excepted), Thursday is usually the least crowded day, followed by Tuesday.

In Florida, there are four Disney theme parks with a substantial daily variance in attendance from park to park. At Disneyland Resort, Disneyland Park usually hosts crowds 50% larger than those at Disney California Adventure, but because DCA is smaller, crowd conditions are comparable. Expressed differently, the most crowded and least crowded days are essentially the same for both Disneyland parks. However, if you are ineligible for early admission (see below), we advise visiting the park that does not offer early entry, as the other will be busy by the time ordinary guests arrive.

EARLY ENTRY

ANYONE WHO BUYS in advance a three-or-more-day ticket with Magic Morning admission may enter Disneyland Park 1 hour before the park is opened to the general public on one morning of their vacation. You can exercise your early-entry privilege on Tuesday, Thursday, or Saturday. Guests at the Paradise Pier, Grand Californian, and Disneyland Hotels can also enter on any early entry day, as long as they have any valid ticket; this privilege is referred to as Extra Magic Hour. During this early-entry hour, most of the Fantasyland attractions—along with Space Mountain, Finding Nemo Submarine Voyage, Astro Orbitor, Buzz Lightyear, and Star Tours in Tomorrowland—will usually be open. The rest of the park's attractions (and all Fastpass machines) will remain off-limits until the official opening time. Disney California Adventure (DCA) also offers its own Extra Magic Hour exclusively for hotel guests, offering access to all of Cars Land, along with select attractions in Hollywood Land, Paradise Pier, and Condor Flats, on four mornings (Sunday, Monday, Wednesday, and Friday) or daily, depending on seasonal demand.

OPERATING HOURS

DISNEYLAND RESORT RUNS a dozen or more different operating schedules during the year, making it advisable to visit **disneyland .disney.go.com/calendar** or call ☎ 714-781-4565 the day before you arrive for exact hours of operation.

PACKED-PARK COMPENSATION PLAN

THE THOUGHT OF TEEMING, jostling throngs jockeying for position in endless lines under the baking Fourth of July sun is enough to wilt the will and ears of the most ardent Mouseketeer. Why would anyone go to Disneyland Park or DCA on a summer Saturday or during a major holiday period? Indeed, if you have never been to the parks, and you thought you would just drop in for a few rides and a look-see on such a day, you might be better off shooting yourself in the foot. The Disney folks, however, being Disney folks, feel kind of bad about those interminably long lines and the basically impossible touring conditions on packed days and compensate patrons with a no-less-than-incredible array of first-rate live entertainment and happenings throughout the park.

Throughout the day, the party goes on with shows, parades, concerts, and pageantry. In the evening, there is so much going on that you have to make some tough choices. Big-name musical groups perform on the Tomorrowland Terrace stage. Other concerts are produced concurrently at the Hyperion Theater at DCA. There are always parades and fireworks, and the Disney characters make frequent appearances. No question about it—you can go to the Disneyland parks on the Fourth of July (or any other crowded extended-hours day), never get on a ride, and still get your money's worth. Even on the busiest days, there are attractions at each park that rarely require more than a 15-minute wait: *Great Moments with Mr. Lincoln,* the *Enchanted Tiki Room,* the railroad and monorail, and Innoventions at Disneyland Park, as well as Disney Animation, Blue Sky Cellar, and the sourdough factory at DCA.

If you decide to go on one of the parks' big days, we suggest that you arrive 1 hour and 20 minutes before the stated opening time. Use the touring plan of your choice until about 1 p.m., and then take the monorail to Downtown Disney for lunch and relaxation. Southern Californian visitors often chip in and rent a room for the group (make reservations well in advance) at the Disneyland or Grand Californian Hotels, thus affording a place to meet, relax, have a drink, or change clothes before enjoying the pools at the hotel. A comparable arrangement can be made at other nearby hotels as long as they are within walking distance or furnish a shuttle service to and from the park. After an early dinner, return to the park for the evening's festivities, which really get cranked up at about 8 p.m.

▌ GETTING THERE

DISNEY PATRONS CAN drive directly into and out of parking facilities without becoming enmeshed in surface street traffic. To avoid traffic problems, we recommend the following:

1. Stay as close to Disneyland as possible. If you are within walking distance, leave your car at the hotel and walk to the park using the pedestrian entrance on the east side of the resort, along Harbor Boulevard between Disney Way and Manchester Avenue, or through the Grand Californian Hotel into

Downtown Disney if walking from the west side along Disneyland Drive. If your hotel provides efficient shuttle service (that is, will get you to the parks at least 30 minutes before opening), use the shuttle.

2. If your hotel is more than 5 miles from Disneyland and you intend to drive your car, leave for the park extra early, say 1 hour or more.

3. If you must use the Santa Ana Freeway (I-5), give yourself lots of extra time.

4. Any time you leave the park just before, at, or just after closing time, you can expect considerable congestion in the parking lots and in the loading area for hotel shuttles. The easiest way to return to your hotel (if you do not have a car in the Disneyland Resort parking lot) is to take the monorail to the Disneyland Hotel or walk to the Grand Californian Hotel, and then take a cab to your own hotel. While cabs in Anaheim are a little pricey, they are usually available in ample numbers at the Disneyland hotels and at the taxi stand in Downtown Disney behind ESPN Zone. When you consider the alternatives of fighting your way onto a hotel shuttle or trudging back to your hotel on worn-out feet, spending $5–$10 for a cab often sounds pretty reasonable.

5. The Orange County Transit District provides very efficient bus service to Disneyland with several different long-distance lines. Running about every 30 minutes during the day and evening, service runs 10 a.m.–midnight, depending on the season and your location. Buses drop off and pick up passengers at the east shuttle loop off Harbor Boulevard. From there, guests can walk to the park entrance. Bus fare is about $2 and children age 5 and under ride free. A bus day pass is available for $5; seven-day passes are $25. For additional information, call ☎ 714-636-7433 or visit **octa.net.** For public transportation in the immediate area surrounding Disneyland, see our discussion of the Anaheim Resort Transit (ART) system starting on page 34.

DISNEYLAND PARKING

DISNEYLAND HAS FOUR PARKING AREAS. The main parking facility, the Mickey & Friends parking garage, can be accessed directly from I-5, Disneyland Drive, or Ball Road. One of the largest parking structures in the world, the garage is connected to Downtown Disney and the theme parks by Disney tram. If you have a noncollapsible stroller that's not permitted on the tram, the walking distance to the park gates is just less than 1 mile along a paved outdoor path.

The secondary parking areas are the Simba lot behind the Paradise Pier Hotel, the Pumbaa lot off Disney Way across from the Anaheim GardenWalk, and the Toy Story lot south of the corner of Katella Avenue and Harbor Boulevard (a favorite of local pass holders and our top pick for the most convenient place to park). From Simba you can walk through Downtown Disney to the parks or alternatively walk to the Downtown Disney Monorail stop and take the monorail into Disneyland Park (not Disney California Adventure). Toy Story (and sometimes Pumbaa) offers shuttles to and from the bus loop east of the Esplanade, or you can walk (about 0.5 mile for each). The Pinocchio parking lot between the main parking structure and Disneyland Hotel is used for overflow and for oversize vehicles and buses. Parking fees for all lots are

Continued on page 33

Southern California at a Glance

Around Disneyland

W. Ball Rd.

Santa Ana Fwy.

5

S. Disneyland Dr.

Main Parking Garage

Pinocchio Parking

ART loading

S. Walnut Rd.

DISNEYLAND PARK

Magic Way

Disneyland Hotel Self-Parking

Downtown Disney Self-Parking and Valet

Harbor Blvd.

DOWNTOWN DISNEY

ART stop

hotel shuttle loading

main pedestrian entrance

Fantasy Tower

ART stop

GRAND CALIFORNIAN HOTEL

Adventure Tower

DISNEYLAND HOTEL

Grand Californian Hotel Self-Parking

DISNEY CALIFORNIA ADVENTURE

Frontier Tower

DISNEY'S PARADISE PIER HOTEL

S. Disneyland Dr.

Downtown Disney Parking

Katella Ave.

ANAHEIM CONVENTION CENTER

0   0.25 mi

0   0.25 km

N

Continued from page 29

$16 for cars, $21 for RVs and oversize vehicles, and $26 for buses and tractors with extended trailers. After parking your car, save yourself a frantic search at the end of your day by taking a digital photo of the lot name and section number.

Valet parking is available after 5 p.m. at Downtown Disney ($6 plus $6 per hour, up to $36 daily) or any time at the resort hotels ($22 plus $9 per hour, up to $58 daily). If you have money to burn, valet parking at the Grand Californian puts you closest to the parks.

unofficial **TIP**
Warning: Most shuttles don't add vehicles at park-opening or park-closing times. In the mornings, you may not get a seat.

TAKING A TRAM OR SHUTTLE BUS FROM YOUR HOTEL

TRAMS AND SHUTTLE BUSES are provided by many hotels and motels in the vicinity of Disneyland. Usually without charge, they represent a fairly carefree means of getting to and from the theme parks, letting you off near the entrances and saving you the cost of parking. The rub is that they might not get you there as early as you desire (a critical point if you take our touring advice) or be available at the time you wish to return to your lodging. Also, some shuttles are direct to Disneyland, while others make stops at other motels and hotels in the vicinity. Each shuttle service is a little bit different, so check out the particulars before you book your hotel. If the shuttle provided by your hotel runs regularly throughout the day to and from Disneyland and if you have the flexibility to tour the parks over two or three days, the shuttle provides a wonderful opportunity to tour in the morning and return to your lodging for lunch, a swim, or perhaps a nap; then you can head back to Disneyland refreshed in the early evening for a little more fun.

Be forewarned that most hotel shuttle services do not add more vehicles at the parks' opening or closing times. In the mornings, your biggest problem is that you might not get a seat on the first shuttle. This occurs most frequently if your hotel is the last stop for a shuttle that serves several hotels. Because hotels that share a shuttle service are usually located close together, you can improve your chances of getting a seat by simply walking to the hotel preceding yours on the pickup route. At closing time, and sometimes following a hard rain, you can expect a mass exodus from the parks. The worst-case scenario in this event is that more people will be waiting for the shuttle to your hotel than the bus will hold and that some will be left. While most (but not all) hotel shuttles return for stranded guests, you may suffer a wait of 15 minutes to 1 hour. Our suggestion, if you are depending on hotel shuttles, is to exit the park at least 45 minutes before closing. If you stay in a park until closing and lack the energy to deal with the shuttle or hike back to your hotel, go to the Disneyland Hotel and catch a cab from there. A cab stand is also behind the ESPN Zone in Downtown Disney and another is at the Grand Californian Hotel.

The shuttle-loading area is located on the Harbor Boulevard side of the Disneyland Park's main entrances. The loading area connects to a pedestrian corridor that leads to the park entrances. Each hotel's shuttle bus is color-coded yellow, blue, red, silver, or white. Signs of like color designate where the shuttles load and unload. You'll also find a passenger drop-off loop (parking strictly prohibited) off Harbor; taxis may deposit here, but they are not supposed to pick up. If you are staying near the corner of Harbor and Katella, you can walk into the Toy Story parking lot and use its park shuttle for free.

Anaheim Resort Transit

Anaheim Resort Transit (ART) provides shuttle service to the Disneyland Resort, GardenWalk, and the convention center. The service operates 18 routes designated 1–19 (excluding 13). There are just three to nine well-marked stops on each route, so a complete circuit on any given route usually takes about 20 minutes, but some take up to 1 hour. All of the routes originate and terminate at Disneyland's bus loop east of the Esplanade near Harbor Boulevard. There is also service from Disneyland to Knott's Berry Farm, Discovery Science Center, and Angels Stadium in case you want to catch an afternoon ballgame. To continue on to the convention center, you must transfer at Disneyland to Route 1, 3–6, 9, 12, or 17–19.

The colorful buses are wheelchair accessible. They ideally run every 10 minutes on peak days during morning and evening periods but can take up to 30 minutes when it's really busy, every 20 minutes during the less busy middle part of the day, and every 20 minutes all day long on off-peak days. Service begins 100 minutes before park opening and ends 30–90 minutes after park closing (may vary seasonally). If you commute to Disneyland on ART and then head to Downtown Disney after the parks close, you'll have to find your own way home if you stay at Downtown Disney more than 90 minutes. All shuttle vehicles and respective stops are clearly marked with the route designation.

Hotels served by ART vending kiosks sell one-day, three-day, and five-day passes for $5, $12, and $20, respectively. You'll also find an ART vending kiosk at the Disneyland bus loop. Children age 2 years and under ride free with a paying adult. Day passes for children can be purchased for $2, a three-day pass for $3, and a five-day pass for $5. Children must be taken out of strollers to ride. Passes cannot be purchased from the driver. For more information, call ☎ 888-364-ARTS (2787) or check **rideart.org.** Passes are also available at ART's website.

◗ *A* **WORD** *about* **LODGING**

TRAFFIC AROUND DISNEYLAND, and in the Anaheim–Los Angeles area in general, is so terrible that we advocate staying in accommodations within 2–3 miles of the park. Included in this radius are many expensive hotels as well as a considerable number of moderately priced establishments and a small number of bargain motels.

READERS' DISNEYLAND RESORT REPORT CARD

RELATIVELY NEW TO *THE UNOFFICIAL GUIDE TO DISNEYLAND* is the Readers' Disneyland Resort Report Card. Room quality indicates cleanliness, bed comfort, and room size. Check-in efficiency rates how quickly and accurately the hotel staff get you into your room. Quietness of room considers soundproofing from neighbors and exterior noise. The pool rating includes the size of the pool, how crowded it gets, and how clean the pool and pool area are. Hotel staff assesses how friendly and effective the staff are at handling problems and special requests. Our hotel dining rating applies to any on-site counter-service dining, and the overall rating is the summary for every category.

This year, readers rated Disneyland hotels better than neighboring hotels. (The same was also true this year for Disney's Orlando hotels.) One reason for this might be that Disney had the financial resources to keep up maintenance and refurbishment on its properties throughout the recession and slow recovery, while other hotels struggled to keep the lights on. Another reason may be that for Disney to charge a premium on its rooms, it needs to have a substantially better product because it's surrounded by competitors.

As far as off-site hotels go, most received an overall rating of B, with the hotel dining options typically receiving a C rating. However, a wide variety of breakfast, lunch, and dinner options are available within a short walk, so this should not prevent you from staying off-site. Among the off-site hotels, the Howard Johnson Anaheim gets the highest rating from readers.

Readers' Disneyland Resort Report Card

HOTEL	ROOM QUALITY	CHECK-IN EFFICIENCY	QUIETNESS OF ROOM	POOL	STAFF	HOTEL DINING	OVERALL RATING
DISNEYLAND HOTEL	A	B+	B	B	B	C+	B
DISNEY PARADISE PIER	B+	B	B	C–	B	C	B
DISNEY'S GRAND CALIFORNIAN	B	B–	B	B	B+	C	B

WALKING TO DISNEYLAND FROM NEARBY HOTELS

WHILE IT IS TRUE THAT MOST DISNEYLAND area hotels provide shuttle service, or are on the ART routes, it is equally true that an ever-increasing number of guests walk to the parks from their hotels. Shuttles are not always available when needed, and parking in the Disneyland lot has become pretty expensive. A pedestrian walkway from Harbor Boulevard provides safe access to Disneyland for guests on foot. This pedestrian corridor extends from Harbor Boulevard west to the

WALKING TIMES TO THE THEME-PARK ENTRANCES AND SWIMMING-POOL RATINGS

HOTEL	MAP NUMBER (PGS. 46–47)	OVERALL QUALITY RATING	COST ($=$50)	WALKING TIME	POOL RATING
Alpine Inn	2	★★½	$$	13:00	2
America's Best Value Fantasy Inn	5	★	$$−	15:15	2
The Anabella	6	★★★	$$$+	14:30	6
Anaheim Camelot Inn & Suites	7	★★★½	$$$	7:15	2
Anaheim Plaza Hotel & Suites	11	★★★	$$$−	11:00	7
Best Western Plus Anaheim Inn	16	★★½	$$$−	7:15	2
Best Western Plus Park Place Inn	17	★★★	$$$	5:45	2
Best Western Plus Stovall's Inn	20	★★★½	$$$−	15:00	6
Candy Cane Inn	22	★★★½	$$$	10:30	4
Carousel Inn & Suites	23	★★★	$$$	6:45	2
Castle Inn & Suites	24	★★★	$$$−	12:30	1
del Sol Inn Anaheim Resort	33	★★½	$$$$−	7:00	3
Desert Inn & Suites	34	★★★½	$$$	6:40	1
Desert Palms Hotel & Suites	35	★★★½	$$$$$−	13:00	2
Disneyland Hotel	36	★★★★	$ x 8 +	10:00 –12:00	10
Disney Paradise Pier Hotel**	37	★★★★	$ x 7 −	7:00	7
Disney's Grand Californian Hotel	38	★★★★½	$ x 10 −	4:00*	10
Fairfield Inn Anaheim Disneyland Resort	44	★★★½	$$$+	9:30	4
Holiday Inn Express	51	★★★	$$$+	15:00	2
Howard Johnson Anaheim Hotel & Water Playground	55	★★★½	$$$$−	10:15	8
Jolly Roger Hotel Anaheim	57	★★★	$$$−	16:30	4
Park Vue Inn	62	★★½	$$$+	6:40	6
Portofino Inn & Suites	64	★★★★	$$$−	16:30	7
Ramada Maingate at the Park	68	★★★	$$$	8:20	8
Ramada Plaza Anaheim Hotel	69	★★★½	$$$	14:30	2
Red Lion Hotel Anaheim	70	★★★★	$$$−	16:45	4
Sheraton Park Hotel at Anaheim	74	★★★★	$$$+	17:00	7
Super 8 Motel Near Disneyland	78	★★½	$$	15:30	2
Tropicana Inn & Suites	82	★★★	$$$−	6:15	3

* To Disneyland Park. The Grand Californian has an on-site entrance to DCA.
** Requires crossing Disneyland Drive and cutting though the Grand Californian Hotel.

Disneyland Hotel, connecting Disneyland Park, Disney California Adventure, and Downtown Disney.

Close proximity to the theme parks figures prominently in the choice of a hotel. Harbor Boulevard borders Disneyland Resort on the east, and Katella Avenue runs along the resort's southern boundary. The closest non-Disney hotels, and the only ones really within walking distance, are on Harbor Boulevard from just south of I-5 to the north to just south of the intersection of Katella Avenue, and along Katella Avenue near Harbor. Farther south on Harbor are some of the best hotels in the area, but they are a little far removed for commuting to the parks on foot. Additionally, these hotels are close to the Anaheim Convention Center and tend to cater, though certainly not exclusively, to business travelers. While the hotels near Disneyland Drive appear close to Disney property on a map, there is no easy pedestrian access to the park from the west. If staying along Katella Avenue, you can walk north on Disneyland Drive and cut through the Grand Californian Hotel. From West Ball Road, you can walk south on West Place (between the Rodeway and Best Western) through the Mickey & Friends garage, and take a tram to the park. Neither walk is particularly convenient, and we can't recommend it for families with children.

For families, a second important consideration is the quality of the hotel swimming pool. We mention this because, unfortunately, many of the non-Disney hotels closest to the theme parks have really crummy pools, sometimes just a tiny rectangle on a stark slab of concrete surrounded on four sides by a parking lot. To bring pool quality and proximity to the theme parks together, we've developed a chart (see opposite page) that lists the hotels, both Disney and non-Disney, within walking distance of the theme parks.

The chart shows the walking time from each hotel to the theme park entrances. The times provided are averages—a couple of fit adults might cover the distance in less time, and a family with small children will likely take longer. Also on the chart we rate the swimming areas of the hotels listed on a scale of 1–10, with 10 being best. As a rule of thumb, any pool with a rating less than 5 is not a place where most folks would want to spend much time. Any hotel not listed is, in our opinion, too far away for walking. Note that several non-Disney hotels are closer than the Disneyland Resort hotels, except for the Grand Californian.

The chart and the above discussion might lead you to wonder whether there's any real advantage to staying in a Disney-owned hotel. The Disney hotels, of course, are very expensive, but if you can handle the tariff, here are the primary benefits of staying in one:

1. You are eligible for early entry at Disneyland Park three days each week and DCA on the other four days.
2. Dozens of full- and counter-service restaurants are within walking distance.
3. The Disney hotels offer the nicest rooms of any of the hotels within walking distance.
4. The Disney hotels offer the nicest swimming pools of any of the hotels within walking distance.
5. Numerous entertainment and shopping options are in Downtown Disney.
6. It's easy to retreat to your hotel for a meal, a nap, or a swim.

7. You don't need a car.

8. You can charge purchases at most Disney-owned shops and restaurants to your hotel account, and have packages delivered to your room.

DISNEYLAND RESORT HOTELS

DISNEY OFFERS THREE ON-SITE HOTELS: the **Grand Californian,** the **Disneyland Hotel,** and the **Paradise Pier Hotel.** The Grand Californian, built in the rustic stone-and-timber style of the grand national park lodges, is the flagship property. Newer, more elaborately themed, and closer to the theme parks and Downtown Disney than the other two on-property hotels, the Grand Californian is without a doubt the best place to stay . . . if you can afford it.

The next most convenient is the sprawling Disneyland Hotel, the oldest, but most recently renovated, of the three. Comprising three guest-room towers, the hotel is lushly landscaped with a new vintage Disneyana theme and offers large, luxurious guest rooms. Walking time to the monorail station, with transportation to Disneyland Park, is about 3–6 minutes.

The east side of the third Disney hotel overlooks the Paradise Pier section of Disney California Adventure theme park, hence the name Paradise Pier Hotel. Although the guest rooms and public areas have a beach-and-boardwalk flavor, the hotel is not themed. The guest rooms here are large. Walking to the monorail station and Downtown Disney takes about 5–10 minutes.

Guests at all three Disney-owned hotels can use their keys to charge dining and shopping within the resort to their room. Third-party vendors (including most Downtown Disney restaurants) are excluded, and you'll need to show photo ID along with your room key.

Disney's Grand Californian Hotel & Spa

The Grand Californian Hotel is the crown jewel of Disneyland Resort's three hotels. With its shingle siding, rock foundations, cavernous hewn-beam lobby, polished hardwood floors, and cozy hearths, the hotel is a stately combination of elements from Western national park lodges. Designed by architect Peter Dominick (who also designed the Wilderness Lodge at Walt Disney World), the Grand Californian is rendered in the Arts and Crafts style of the early 20th century, with such classic features as "flying" roofs, projecting beams, massive buttresses, and an earth-tone color palette. We strongly encourage visitors with an interest in architecture to take the fascinating (and free) hour-long Art of the Craft walking tour of the resort, offered several times each week through the Guest Services desk. Most reminiscent of the Ahwahnee Hotel at Yosemite National Park, the Grand Californian combines rugged craftsmanship and grand scale with functional design and intimate spaces. Pull up a vintage rocker in front of a blazing fire, and the bustling lobby instantly becomes a snug cabin.

The hotel's main entrance off Downtown Drive is primarily for vehicular traffic. Two pedestrian-only entrances open into Downtown

Disney and DCA; this last makes it a cinch to return to the hotel from DCA for a nap, a swim, or lunch.

The features we like in the 751 guest rooms include excellent light for reading in bed, more than adequate storage space, a two-sink vanity outside the toilet and bath, and, in some rooms, a balcony. Views from the guest rooms overlook the swimming pool, Downtown Disney, or Disney California Adventure theme park.

Ranging $475–$980 per night, guest rooms are the most expensive at Disneyland Resort. The Grand Californian, like the other two Disney-owned hotels, charges guests $15 a day for self-parking (up to two vehicles, free for Disney Vacation Club members) or $22 for valet (☎ 714-635-2300). On the plus side, none of the hotels charge a resort fee, and all provide safes, mini-fridges, coffeemakers, and free Wi-Fi (supposedly high-speed, but don't plan on streaming Netflix) in rooms and public areas.

Disney's time-share condo enterprise, the Disney Vacation Club, premiered its first West Coast property as part of the 2009 expansion of the Grand Californian. The Villas at Disney's Grand Californian consist of 48 two-bedroom equivalent villas and two Grand Villas. Equivalent is the term used to describe single units that can be sold (or rented) as studio suites or combined to make two- and three-bedroom villas. All villas except studio suites include kitchens, living rooms, and dining areas, as well as washers and dryers. Master bedrooms offer a king bed, while other bedrooms provide two queen beds. Studio suites come with a single queen bed. All bedrooms have a flat-panel TV, private bath, and private balcony. Though studio suites don't have full kitchens, they do include a small fridge, a microwave, and a coffeemaker. Two-bedroom villas consist of a one-bedroom villa joined to a studio suite. Three-bedroom Grand Villas are two-story affairs with the living area, kitchen, and master bedroom on the lower level and two bedrooms on the upper level. Rates for various villas range from $359 for a studio suite during the off-season to $5,000 for a three-bedroom Grand Villa on New Year's weekend. Other elements of the Grand Californian include a swimming pool for the villas and an underground parking garage.

Inspired by Napa Valley cuisine, the Napa Rose restaurant is the Disneyland Resort's premier fine-dining venue. Situated in a stunning room overlooking DCA, Napa Rose is very expensive but still a very good value (see a full profile on page 191). Just a notch down in price and formality, but likewise located in an exceptionally lovely (albeit more rustic) room, is the Storytellers Café, which serves breakfast, lunch, and dinner (see a full profile on page 197). The restaurant's name is drawn from period murals depicting tall tales set in early California. The fare consists of house-specialty wood-fired pizza and hearty home-style comfort food.

The resort's pool complex, beautifully landscaped with rocks and conifers in a High Sierra theme, includes a lap pool, a Mickey-shaped pool, and a kids' pool with a 100-foot-long twisting slide. The on-site Mandara Spa is one of Disney's best, offering a wide selection of treatments and a state-of-the-art fitness facility. Rounding out the Grand Californian's amenity mix are two clubby lounges and a child-care center for children ages 5–12.

The Disneyland Hotel

Walt Disney barely managed to finance the construction of the Disneyland theme park. He certainly didn't have the funds to purchase adjacent property or build hotels, though on-site hotels were central to his overall concept. So he cut a deal with petroleum engineer and TV producer Jack Wrather to build and operate the Disneyland Hotel. The deal not only gave Wrather the rights to the Disneyland Hotel but also allowed him to build other Disneyland Hotels within the state of California until 2054. It always irked Walt that he didn't own the hotel that bore his name, but Wrather steadfastly refused to renegotiate the rights. After Jack Wrather died in 1984, the Walt Disney Company bought the entire Wrather Corporation, which among other things held the rights to the *Lone Ranger* and *Lassie* TV series and, improbably, the RMS *Queen Mary*, docked at Long Beach. By acquiring the whole corporation, the Walt Disney Company brought the Disneyland Hotel under Disney ownership in 1988.

The Disneyland Hotel consists of three towers facing each other across a verdant landscaped plaza, a swimming complex, restaurants, shops, and gardens. The hotel was originally connected to Disneyland Park by monorail, but a portion of the hotel was demolished during the construction of DCA and Downtown Disney, and the station was rebuilt on its original location. Guest registration for all three towers is situated in the Fantasy Tower (previously called the Magic Tower, and the Marina Tower before that), which is connected to the Disneyland Convention Center and Disneyland Hotel's self-parking garage. Though all three towers share restaurants, shopping, and recreational amenities, the Fantasy Tower is most conveniently located. It and the Adventure Tower (formerly Dreams, née Sierra) are closest to Downtown Disney and the theme parks. The Frontier Tower (formerly Wonder, formerly Bonita) is the farthest from the action.

Rack rates for the Disneyland Hotel range from around $410 for a city view in the off-season to more than $720 for a theme park view during holiday periods. The best views can be had from the east/west-facing Adventure Tower, which overlooks the hotel's inner plaza and pool area on the west and Downtown Disney and the theme parks to the east. The most lackluster views are the north-facing vistas of the Fantasy Tower.

In August 2009 the Disneyland Hotel embarked on an ambitious and long-overdue renovation that included major improvements to the guest rooms, as well as a modernization of the hotel's exterior. While the hotel was formerly essentially themeless, the renovation has embraced the retro-nostalgia of baby boomer Disneyland devotees and added decorative elements evoking the park's early years; look for 1950s-style signage outside each tower and a tribute to Frontierland's long-gone Old Unfaithful geysers. The redesigned main lobby evokes Mary Blair's It's a Small World designs, and features a blown-up fun map of the original park. The check-in area sports early attraction concept artwork and seating styled after the spinning teacups, whimsical touches that stand in stark contrast with the ultramodern sculpted steel behind the front desk. Peek inside the Frontier Tower lobby to see an amazingly detailed model of Big Thunder Mountain.

The refurbished rooms abandon the heavy blond traditional guest room furnishings and decor in favor of a sleek monochromatic contemporary look. Each room has one king-size or two queen-size beds, along with a pullout couch; one-bedroom suites with a wet bar and living room are also available. Features include a headboard with a carving of Sleeping Beauty Castle; fiber optics in the headboard create a skyline with fireworks (accompanied by a tinny rendition of "When You Wish Upon a Star") at the flick of a switch. Other decorative touches include black-and-white photography depicting the history of Disneyland and hidden Mickey designs in the carpet, though the overall feel is more business modern than Disney whimsy. Each room has a flat-panel HDTV, perfect for connecting a laptop or video game console. Other room amenities include mini-refrigerators, coffeemakers, safes large enough for laptops, and high-tech phone, cable, and wireless Internet connections. Plumbing, electrical, heating, and air-conditioning systems upgrades also were included in the project.

As part of the exterior modernization, large windows were added, giving the facade a glistening sky-blue tint. The windows, which are specially designed to filter outside noise, replaced the original 8-foot sliding doors and small balconies on all rooms (except for a handful of corner suites and penthouses in the Frontier Tower). On the upside, you get a few extra square feet of living space; on the downside, you can't enjoy outside fresh air (or smog) anymore.

The bathrooms (with newly upgraded tubs) are still small for an upscale hotel, but there is a sink and vanity outside the bathrooms. As in most family hotels built in the 1950s and '60s, a connecting door, situated by the closet and the aforementioned single sink, leads to an adjoining room. Soundproofing around the connecting doors is nonexistent, so be prepared to revel in the sounds of your neighbors brushing their teeth, coping with indigestion, and arguing over what to wear. Fortunately, these sounds don't carry into the sleeping area.

The original pool has been greatly expanded into an "immersive water play area." The new complex's centerpiece is a pair of waterslides (187 feet and 112 feet long, respectively) themed to resemble vintage monorail trains, topped by the classic Disneyland block-letter logo. There's also a 19-foot kiddie slide and bubble jets for the little ones. While the footprint of the 4,800-square-foot E-Ticket Pool (formerly known as the Never Land Pool) remains unchanged, a new 4-foot-deep pool has been added between it and the new waterslides, with a footbridge allowing easy passage from one side of the water to the other. Unfortunately, the adult-friendly quieter Cove pools were lost in the construction, reclaimed as a grassy space for special events. Though the rebuilt amenities are attractive, they still appear inadequate in light of the hotel's volume of visitors. On sunny days expect long inefficient lines for the slides, as well as a severe shortage of lounge chairs and elbow room.

Also destroyed were the fan-favorite tropical gardens with walking paths, waterfalls, and koi ponds. In their place is Tangaroa Terrace and Trader Sam's, a casual restaurant and bar that banks on fond memories of Adventureland's 1960s-era Tahitian Terrace dinner show. Disneyland Hotel's other restaurants include Steakhouse 55 and Goofy's Kitchen, the hotel's character-meal headquarters. (All Disneyland Hotel restaurants are profiled in full in Part Four.)

As concerns practical matters, parking is a royal pain at the Disneyland Hotel. The self-parking garage is convenient only to the Fantasy Tower, and even there you'll probably have a long walk. To reach the other two towers, you must pass through the Fantasy Tower and navigate across the hotel's inner plaza and pool area. The Frontier Tower on the southern end of the property has a small parking lot to the rear accessible via Downtown Drive and Paradise Way. Unfortunately, many of the already limited spaces are reserved for the adjacent Disney Vacation Club time-share sales office. Even so, if you're staying at the Frontier Tower, it's your best bet. If there's no room in the Frontier lot, you're better off parking in the Paradise Pier Hotel's lot than in the Disneyland Hotel parking garage. The only valet parking is at the Fantasy Tower, so even if you valet park, you'll still have to hoof it to the other towers.

A California family who didn't have a car to park thought the Disneyland Hotel especially convenient:

> I initially thought that staying at the Disneyland Hotel was a nice treat that we might do just this once. I now see it as an absolute necessity as it allows early entry and an easy midday retreat. That plus the great service there seals the deal.

Paradise Pier Hotel

Disney acquired the independent Pan Pacific Hotel just south of the Disneyland Hotel in 1997 and changed its name to the Disneyland Pacific Hotel. Just before Disney California Adventure opened in 2001, the hotel was rechristened as the Paradise Pier Hotel in recognition of the Paradise Pier district of DCA that the hotel overlooks.

The 481-room property makes a mostly successful attempt to merge the hotel's original South Seas flavor with a vintage seaside amusement theme inspired by the attractions across the street. Guest rooms are furnished with blond wood furniture and the usual Disney-pastel soft goods, including bedspreads with a hidden Mickey pattern. Somewhat more whimsical than rooms at the Disneyland Hotel or the Grand Californian, Paradise Pier rooms include accents such as Mickey Mouse table lamps, beach ball pillows, and seashell-patterned carpets. Guest room picture windows on the hotel's east side offer the best vistas of any of the Disneyland Resort hotels, with a perfect view of the lights and attractions of Paradise Pier inside DCA. From rooms on the other side of the hotel you can see, well, parking lots. Rates range $300–$410, depending on season and view.

For dining, the informal Disney's PCH Grill serves a breakfast (with characters) and dinner daily. Amenities include a fitness center and an often breezy rooftop pool complete with a waterslide (the view from the top of the slide is killer). Self-parking in Paradise Pier's on-site garage is fast and convenient. Somewhat isolated on the Disneyland Resort property, the hotel is a 14-minute hike to the theme park entrances, farther away than most non-Disney hotels lining Harbor Boulevard on the east side of the resort, if you walk through Downtown Disney. Crossing Disneyland Drive and going through Grand Californian Hotel cuts the walk in half, or even shorter if entering DCA.

HOW TO GET DISCOUNTS ON LODGING AT DISNEYLAND RESORT HOTELS

SO MANY GUEST ROOMS ARE in and around Disneyland Resort that competition is brisk, and everyone, including Disney, wheels and deals to keep them filled. The recession has only compounded this. It has led to a more flexible discount policy for Disneyland Resort hotels. Here are tips for getting price breaks:

1. DISNEYLAND RESORT WEBSITE Disney has become more aggressive about offering deals on its website. Go to **disneyland.com** and check the page for "Special Offers." When booking rooms on Disney's or any other site, be sure to click on "Terms and Conditions" and read the fine print *before* making reservations.

2. SEASONAL SAVINGS You can save $15–$60 per night on a Disneyland Resort hotel room by visiting during the slower times of the year. Disney uses so many adjectives (regular, holiday, peak, value, and such) to describe its seasonal calendar, however, that it's hard to keep up without a scorecard. To confuse matters more, the dates for each season vary from hotel to hotel. Our advice: If you're set on staying at a Disney hotel, obtain a copy of the "Disney Resort Travel Sales Center California Brochure," which is described on page 16.

If you have a hard time getting a copy of the brochure, forget trying to find the various seasonal dates on the Disneyland Resort website. Easier by far is to check them out on the independent-of-Disney **mouse savers.com** site described in tip four on the next page.

Understand that Disney seasonal dates are not sequential like spring, summer, fall, and winter. For any specific resort, there are sometimes several seasonal changes in a month. This is important because your room rate per night is determined by the season prevailing when you check in. Let's say that you checked in to the Disneyland Hotel on April 19 for a five-night stay. April 19 is in the more expensive peak season that ends April 20, followed by the less pricey regular season beginning April 21. Because you arrived during peak season, the peak season rate will be applied for your entire stay, even though more than half of your stay will be in regular season. Your strategy, therefore, is to shift your dates (if possible) to arrive during a less expensive season.

3. ASK ABOUT SPECIALS When you talk to Disney reservationists, inquire specifically about special deals. Ask, for example, "What special rates or discounts are available at Disney hotels during the time of our visit?" Being specific and assertive paid off for an Illinois reader:

> I called Disney's reservations number and asked for availability and rates. . . . [Because] of the Unofficial Guide warning about Disney reservationists answering only the questions posed, I specifically asked, "Are there any special rates or discounts for that room during the month of October?" She replied, "Yes, we have that room available at a special price. . . . " [For] the price of one phone call, I saved $440.

Along similar lines, a Warren Township, New Jersey, dad chimed in with this:

> Your tip about asking Disney employees about discounts was invaluable. They will not volunteer this information, but by asking we saved almost $500 on our hotel room using a AAA discount.

4. LEARN ABOUT DEALS OFFERED TO SPECIFIC MARKETS The folks at **mousesavers.com** keep an updated list of discounts for use at Disney resorts. The discounts are separated into categories such as "for anyone," "for residents of certain states," "for Annual Passport holders," and so on. For example, the site once listed a deal targeted to residents of the San Diego area published in an ad in a San Diego newspaper. Dozens of discounts are usually listed on the site, covering almost all Disneyland Resort hotels. Usually anyone calling the Disneyland Resort Reservations Office (call ☎ 714-956-6425 and press 1 on the menu) can cite the referenced ad and get the discounted rate.

You should be aware that Disney has moved away from room-discount codes that anyone can use. Instead, Disney is targeting people with pin codes in e-mails and direct mailings. Pin-code discounts are offered to specific individuals and are correlated with that person's name and address. Pin-code offers are non-transferable. When you try to make a reservation using the code, Disney will verify that the street or e-mail address to which the pin code was sent is yours.

unofficial **TIP**
For the best rates and least crowded conditions, try to avoid visiting Disneyland Resort when a major convention or trade show is in progress.

To enhance your chances of receiving a pin-code offer, you need to get your name and street or e-mail address into the Disney system. One way is to call the Disney Resort Travel Sales Center at ☎ 714-520-5060 and request that written info be sent to you. If you've been to Disneyland previously, your name and address will already be on record, but you won't be as likely to receive a pin-code offer as you would by calling and requesting to be sent information. The latter is regarded as new business. Or, expressed differently, if Disney smells blood, they're more likely to come after you. On the Web, go to **disneyland.com,** click on "My Disneyland," and sign up to have offers and news sent automatically to your e-mail address.

Mousesavers.com also features a great links page with short descriptions and URLs of the best Disney-related websites and a current-year seasonal rates calendar.

5. KAYAK.COM This search engine compares discounts offered by hotel chains and Internet travel sellers. With Kayak's help you can see photos and descriptions of Disneyland-area hotels and determine which seller is offering the best discounts.

6. ANNUAL PASSPORT HOLDER DISCOUNTS Annual Passport holders are eligible for discounts on dining, shopping, and lodging. If you visit Disneyland Resort once a year or more, or if you plan on a visit of five or more days, you might save money overall by purchasing Annual Passport. We've seen resort discounts as deep as 30% offered to Annual Passport holders. It doesn't take long to recoup the extra bucks you spent on an Annual Passport when you're saving that kind of money on lodging. Discounts in the 10%–15% range are more the norm.

7. TRAVEL AGENTS Travel agents are active players in the market and are particularly good sources of information on time-limited special programs and discounts. In our opinion, a good travel agent is the best friend a traveler can have. And though we at The Unofficial Guides know a thing or two about the travel industry, we always give our agent a chance to beat any deal we find. If our agent can't beat the deal, we let her book it if she can receive commission from it. In other words, we create a relationship that gives her plenty of incentive to really roll up her sleeves and work on our behalf.

As you might expect, some travel agents and agencies specialize, sometimes exclusively, in selling Disneyland and Walt Disney World. These agents have spent an incredible amount of time at both resorts and have completed extensive Disney education programs. They are usually the most Disney-knowledgeable agents in the travel industry. Most of these specialists and their agencies display the "Earmarked" logo indicating that they are Authorized Disney Vacation Planners. These Disney specialists are so good that we use them ourselves. They save us time and money, sometimes lots of both. The best of the best include **Sue Pisaturo,** whom we've used many times and who is a contributor to this guide **(sue@wdwvacations.com)** and **Tracy Desjardin (tdwdwtravel@comcast.net).**

8. ORGANIZATIONS AND AUTO CLUBS Disney has developed time-limited programs with some auto clubs and other organizations. Recently, for example, AAA members were offered 10%–20% savings on Disney hotels and discounts on Disney package vacations. Such deals

Continued on page 48

Disneyland-area Hotels

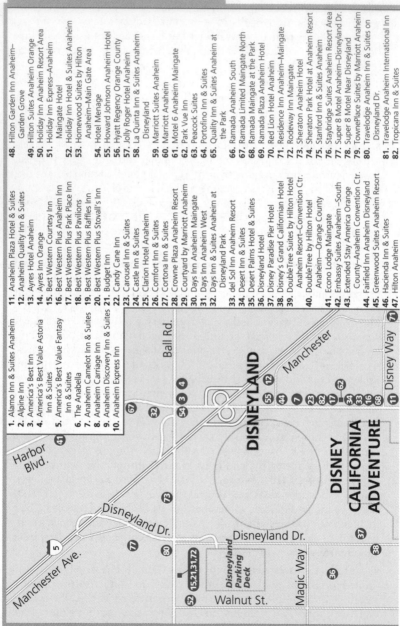

1. Alamo Inn & Suites Anaheim
2. Alpine Inn
3. America's Best Inn
4. America's Best Value Astoria Inn & Suites
5. America's Best Value Fantasy Inn & Suites
6. The Anabella
7. Anaheim Camelot Inn & Suites
8. Anaheim Carriage Inn
9. Anaheim Discovery Inn & Suites
10. Anaheim Express Inn
11. Anaheim Plaza Hotel & Suites
12. Anaheim Quality Inn & Suites
13. Ayres Hotel Anaheim
14. Ayres Inn Orange
15. Best Western Courtesy Inn
16. Best Western Plus Anaheim Inn
17. Best Western Plus Park Place Inn
18. Best Western Plus Pavilions
19. Best Western Plus Raffles Inn
20. Best Western Plus Stovall's Inn
21. Budget Inn
22. Candy Cane Inn
23. Carousel Inn & Suites
24. Castle Inn & Suites
25. Clarion Hotel Anaheim
26. Comfort Inn & Suites
27. Cortona Inn & Suites
28. Crowne Plaza Anaheim Resort
29. Courtyard by Marriott Anaheim
30. Days Inn Anaheim Maingate
31. Days Inn Anaheim West
32. Days Inn & Suites Anaheim at Disneyland Park
33. del Sol Inn Anaheim Resort
34. Desert Inn & Suites
35. Desert Palms Hotel & Suites
36. Disneyland Hotel
37. Disney Paradise Pier Hotel
38. Disney's Grand Californian Hotel
39. DoubleTree Suites by Hilton Hotel Anaheim Resort–Convention Ctr.
40. DoubleTree by Hilton Hotel Anaheim—Orange County
41. Econo Lodge Maingate
42. Embassy Suites Anaheim –South
43. Extended Stay America Orange County–Anaheim Convention Ctr.
44. Fairfield Inn Anaheim Disneyland
45. Greenwood Suites Anaheim Resort
46. Hacienda Inn & Suites
47. Hilton Anaheim
48. Hilton Garden Inn Anaheim– Garden Grove
49. Hilton Suites Anaheim Orange
50. Holiday Inn Anaheim Resort Area
51. Holiday Inn Express–Anaheim Maingate Hotel
52. Holiday Inn Hotel & Suites Anaheim
53. Homewood Suites by Hilton Anaheim–Main Gate Area
54. Hotel Menage
55. Howard Johnson Anaheim Hotel
56. Hyatt Regency Orange County
57. Jolly Roger Hotel Anaheim
58. La Quinta Inn & Suites Anaheim Disneyland
59. Marriott Suites Anaheim
60. Marriott Anaheim
61. Motel 6 Anaheim Maingate
62. Park Vue Inn
63. Peacock Suites
64. Portofino Inn & Suites
65. Quality Inn & Suites Anaheim at the Park
66. Ramada Anaheim South
67. Ramada Limited Maingate North
68. Ramada Maingate at the Park
69. Ramada Plaza Anaheim Hotel
70. Red Lion Hotel Anaheim
71. Residence Inn Anaheim–Maingate
72. Rodeway Inn Maingate
73. Sheraton Anaheim Hotel
74. Sheraton Park Hotel at Anaheim Resort
75. Stanford Inn & Suites Anaheim
76. Staybridge Suites Anaheim Resort Area
77. Super 8 Motel Anaheim–Disneyland Dr.
78. Super 8 Motel Near Disneyland
79. TownePlace Suites by Marriott Anaheim
80. Travelodge Anaheim Inn & Suites on Disneyland Dr.
81. Travelodge Anaheim International Inn
82. Tropicana Inn & Suites

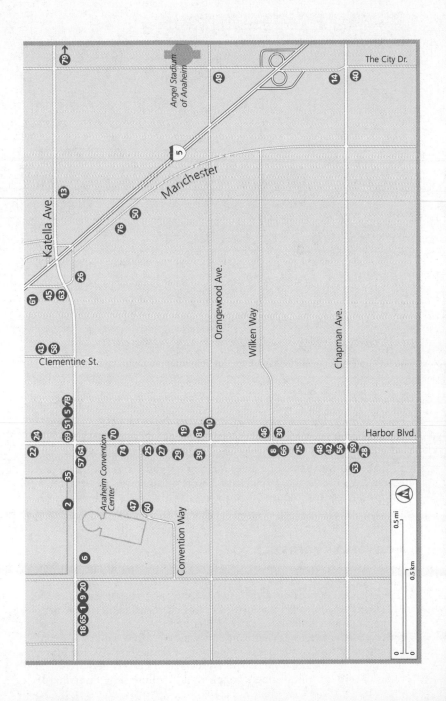

Hotels near Universal Studios

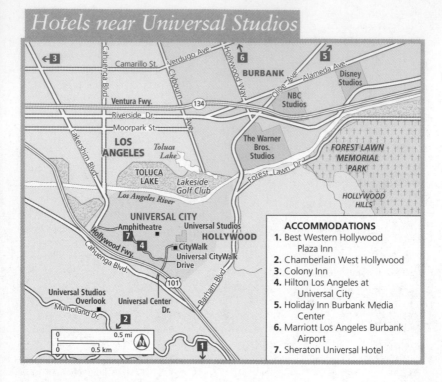

ACCOMMODATIONS

1. Best Western Hollywood Plaza Inn
2. Chamberlain West Hollywood
3. Colony Inn
4. Hilton Los Angeles at Universal City
5. Holiday Inn Burbank Media Center
6. Marriott Los Angeles Burbank Airport
7. Sheraton Universal Hotel

Continued from page 45

come and go, but the market suggests that there will be more in the future. If you're a member of AARP, AAA, or any travel or auto club, ask whether the group has a program before shopping elsewhere.

9. ROOM UPGRADES Sometimes a room upgrade is as good as a discount. If you're visiting Disneyland Resort during a slower time, book the least expensive room your discounts will allow. Checking in, ask very politely about being upgraded to a pool view room. A fair percentage of the time, you will get one at no additional charge.

NON-DISNEY HOTELS

WHEN WALT DISNEY BUILT DISNEYLAND, he did not have the funding to include hotels or to purchase the property surrounding his theme park. Consequently, the area around the park developed in an essentially uncontrolled manner. Many of the hotels and motels near Disneyland were built in the early 1960s, and they are small and sometimes unattractive by today's standards. Quite a few motels adopted adventure or fantasy themes in emulation of Disneyland. As you might imagine, these themes from five decades ago seem hokey and irrelevant today. There is a disquieting (though rapidly diminishing) number of seedy hotels near Disneyland, and even some of the chain properties fail to live up to their national standards.

If you consider a non-Disney-owned hotel in Anaheim, check its quality as reported by a reliable independent rating system such as those offered by the Unofficial Guides, AAA Directories, Mobil Guides, or Frommer's guides. Also, before you book, ask how old the hotel is and when the guest rooms were last refurbished. Be aware that almost any hotel can be made to look good on a website, so don't depend on websites alone. Locate the hotel on our street map (see pages 46–47) to verify its proximity to Disneyland. If you will not have a car, make sure that the hotel has a shuttle service that will satisfy your needs.

GOOD NEIGHBOR HOTELS

A GOOD NEIGHBOR HOTEL is a hotel that has paid Disney a marketing fee to display that designation. Usually there is a ticket shop in the lobby that sells full-price Disney tickets. Other than that, the Good Neighbor designation means little to nothing for the consumer. It does not guarantee quality. Some Good Neighbor hotels really aren't very nice, while others are excellent. Some are very close to Disneyland, while others are quite far away. Unlike at Walt Disney World, Disneyland does not require Good Neighbor hotels to provide free shuttle service to the park, though many do. The only dubious advantage to Good Neighbor hotels is that you can book them in a package with park tickets through the Walt Disney Travel Co.; prices are the same as if booked à la carte, though they toss in free on-attraction photo and some free collectible pins (woo-hoo). In our opinion, you shouldn't let the presence or absence of the Good Neighbor designation influence your hotel choice.

GETTING A GOOD DEAL AT NON-DISNEY HOTELS

FOLLOWING ARE SOME TIPS and strategies for getting a good deal on a hotel room near Disneyland. Though the following list may seem a bit intimidating and may refer to players in the travel market that are unfamiliar to you, acquainting yourself with the strategies will serve you well in the long run. Simply put, the tips we provide for getting a good deal near Disneyland will work equally well at just about any other place where you need a hotel. Once you have invested a little time and have experimented with these strategies, you will be able to routinely obtain rooms at the best hotels and at the lowest possible rates.

Remember that Disneyland Resort is right across the street from the Anaheim Convention Center, one of the largest and busiest convention centers in the country. Room availability, as well as rates, are affected significantly by trade shows and other events at the convention center. To determine whether such an event will be going on during your projected dates, check out the convention calendar on page 25.

1. MOUSESAVERS.COM is a site dedicated to finding great deals on hotels, admissions, and more at Disneyland Resort and Walt Disney World. The site covers discounts on both Disney and non-Disney hotels and is especially effective at keeping track of time-limited deals and discounts offered in a select market—San Diego, for example. However, the site does not sell travel products.

2. KAYAK.COM is a travel search engine that searches the better hotel-discount sites, as well as chain and individual hotel websites. Websites searched vary from destination to destination but do not include Expedia and Travelocity, which Kayak can optionally open in a separate window.

3. EXPEDIA.COM AND TRAVELOCITY.COM sometimes offer good discounts on area hotels. We find that Expedia offers the best deals if you're booking within two weeks of your visit. In fact, some of Expedia's last-minute deals are amazing, really rock-bottom rates. Travelocity frequently beats Expedia, however, if you reserve two weeks to three months out. Neither site offers anything to get excited about if you book more than three months from the time of your visit. If you use either site, be sure to take into consideration the demand for rooms during the season of your visit, and check to see if any big conventions or trade shows are scheduled for the convention center.

4. PRICELINE.COM allows you to tender a bid for a room. You can't bid on a specific hotel, but you can specify location ("Disneyland Vicinity") and the quality rating expressed in stars. If your bid is accepted, you will be assigned to a hotel consistent with your location and quality requirements, and your credit card will be charged in a nonrefundable transaction for your entire stay. Notification of acceptance usually takes less than an hour. We recommend bidding $35–$55 per night for a three-star hotel and $55–$80 per night for a four-star property. To gauge your chances of success, check to see if any major conventions or trade shows are scheduled during your preferred dates.

5. ENTERTAINMENT BOOKS are area-specific guides that contain discount coupons for hotels, restaurants, entertainment, shopping, and even car washes. The Anaheim version sells for about $40 at the beginning of the year but is discounted (up to $25 off) if you buy with only part of the year remaining. Sometimes the books sell out before summer. Unless you live in Orange County, you won't be able to use a lot of the coupons, but sometimes the savings on your hotel and dining will more than justify the purchase. To buy, or for additional information, visit **entertainment.com**.

6. HOTELCOUPONS.COM SOUTHWEST GUIDE is a book of discount coupons for hotels throughout California and is available free of charge at many restaurants and motels along the main interstates in and leading to California. However, because most folks make reservations before leaving home, picking up the coupon book en route does not help much. But for $3 ($5 Canadian) the company will mail you a copy, allowing you to examine the discounts offered before you make your reservations. The guide is free; the charge is for the postage. To order call ☎ 800-222-3948, Monday–Friday, 8:30 a.m.–5:30 p.m. EST. Or browse the guide for free at **hotelcoupons.com**.

7. SPECIAL WEEKEND RATES If you are not averse to about an hour's drive to Disneyland, you can get a great weekend rate on rooms in downtown Los Angeles. Most hotels that cater to business, government, and convention travelers offer special weekend discounts that range 15%–40% below normal weekday rates. You can find out about weekend specials by calling the hotel or by consulting your travel agent.

8. WHOLESALERS, CONSOLIDATORS, AND RESERVATION SERVICES Wholesalers and consolidators buy rooms, or options on rooms (room blocks), from hotels at a low negotiated rate. They then resell the rooms at a profit through travel agents, tour packagers, or directly to the public. Most wholesalers and consolidators have a provision for returning unsold rooms to participating hotels, but they are disinclined to do so. The wholesaler's or consolidator's relationship with any hotel is predicated on volume. If they return rooms unsold, the hotel might not make as many rooms available to them the next time around. Thus, wholesalers and consolidators often offer rooms at bargain rates, anywhere from 15%–50% off rack, occasionally sacrificing their profit margin to avoid returning the rooms to the hotel unsold.

When wholesalers and consolidators deal directly with the public, they frequently represent themselves as "reservation services." When you call, you can ask for a rate quote for a particular hotel or, alternatively, ask for their best available deal in the area where you prefer to stay. If there is a maximum amount you are willing to pay, say so. Chances are that the service will find something that will work for you, even if they have to shave a dollar or two off their own profit. Sometimes you will have to prepay for your room with your credit card when you make your reservation. Most often, you will pay when you check out. Listed below are two services that frequently offer substantial discounts in the Anaheim area.

ANAHEIM AREA WHOLESALERS AND CONSOLIDATORS

California reservations ☎ 800-780-5733   cheap-discount-hotels.com
hotels.com ☎ 800-246-8357   hotels.com

9. CLUBS AND ORGANIZATIONS If you belong to AAA, AARP, or a number of other organizations, you can obtain lodging discounts. Usually the discounts are modest, 5%–15%, but occasionally higher.

10. IF YOU MAKE YOUR OWN RESERVATION As you poke around trying to find a good deal, there are several things you should know. First, always call the hotel in question as opposed to the hotel chain's national toll-free number. Quite often, the reservationists at the national numbers are unaware of local specials. Always ask about specials before you inquire about corporate rates. Do not be reluctant to bargain. If you are buying a hotel's weekend package, for example, and want to extend your stay into the following week, you can often obtain at least the corporate rate for the extra days. Do your bargaining before you check in, however, preferably when you make your reservations. Work far enough in advance to receive a confirmation.

HOW TO GET THE ROOM YOU WANT

MOST HOTELS, INCLUDING DISNEY'S, won't guarantee a specific room when you book but will post your request on your reservations record and try to accommodate you. Our experience indicates that if you give them your first, second, and third choices, you'll probably get one of the three.

unofficial **TIP**
Request a renovated room at your hotel—these can be much nicer than the older rooms.

When speaking to the reservationist or your travel agent, it's important to be specific. If you want a room overlooking the pool, say so. Similarly, be sure to clearly state such preferences as a particular floor, a corner room, a room close to restaurants, a room away from elevators and ice machines, a nonsmoking room, a room with a balcony, or any other preference. If you have a list of preferences, type it up in order of importance, and e-mail or fax it to the hotel or to your travel agent. Be sure to include your own contact information and, if you've already booked, your reservation confirmation number. If it makes you feel better, call back in a few days to make sure that your preferences were posted to your reservations record.

About Hotel Renovations

We have inspected almost 100 hotels in the Disneyland Resort area to compile the lodging choices presented here. Each year we phone each hotel to verify contact information and inquire about renovations or refurbishments. If a hotel has been renovated or has refurbished its guest rooms, we reinspect that hotel along with new hotels for the next edition of this book.

Most hotels more than five years old refurbish 10%–20% of their guest rooms each year. This incremental approach minimizes disruption of business but makes your room assignment a crapshoot. You might luck into a newly renovated room or be assigned a threadbare room. Disney resorts will not guarantee a recently renovated room but will note your request and try to accommodate you. Non-Disney hotels will often guarantee an updated room when you book.

Our hotel ratings are provided starting on page 62.

TRAVEL PACKAGES

PACKAGE TOURS THAT INCLUDE lodging, park admission, and other features are routinely available. Some packages are very good deals if you make use of the features you are paying for.

Finally, here's a helpful source of regional travel information:

Anaheim–Orange County Visitor & Convention Bureau
☎ 714-765-8888; **anaheimoc.org**

How to Evaluate a Disneyland Travel Package

Hundreds of Disneyland package vacations are offered to the public each year. Some are created by the Disney Resort Travel Sales Center, others by airline touring companies, and some by independent travel agents and wholesalers. Almost all Disneyland packages include lodging at or near Disneyland and theme park admission. Packages offered by the airlines include air transportation.

Package prices vary seasonally, with mid-June to mid-August and holiday periods being the most expensive. During the off-season, forget packages; there are plenty of empty rooms, and you can negotiate great discounts (at non-Disney properties) yourself. Similarly, airfares and rental cars are cheaper at off-peak times.

Almost all package ads feature a headline stating "Disneyland for 3 Days from $298" or some such wording. The key word in the ads is *from*. The rock-bottom package price connotes the least desirable hotel accommodations. If you want better or more conveniently located digs, you'll have to pay more, often much more.

At Disneyland, packages offer a wide selection of hotels. Some, like the Disney-owned hotels, are very good. Others, unfortunately, run the quality gamut. Packages with lodging in non-Disney hotels are much less expensive.

When considering a package, choose one that includes features that you are sure to use. Whether you use all the features or not, you will most certainly pay for them. Second, if cost is of greater concern than convenience, make a few phone calls and see what the package would cost if you booked its individual components (such as airfare, rental car, and lodging) on your own. If the package price is less than the à la carte cost, the package is a good deal. If the costs are about the same, the package is probably worth it for the convenience.

If you buy a package from Disney, do not expect Disney reservationists to offer suggestions or help you sort out your options. As a rule they will not volunteer information but will only respond to specific questions you pose, adroitly ducking any query that calls for an opinion. A reader from North Riverside, Illinois, wrote to the *Unofficial Guide,* complaining:

> I have received various pieces of literature from [Disney], and it is very confusing to try and figure everything out. My wife made two telephone calls, and the [Disney] representatives were very courteous. However, they answered only the questions posed and were not very eager to give advice on what might be most cost-effective. The [Disney] reps would not say if we would be better off doing one thing over the other. I feel that a person could spend 8 hours on the telephone with [Disney] reps and not have any more input than you get from reading the literature.

If you cannot get the information you need from the Disney people, try a good travel agent. Chances are that the agent will be more forthcoming in helping you sort out your options.

Information Needed for Evaluation

For quick reference and to save on phone expenses, call the Disney Resort Travel Sales Center at ☎ 714-520-5060 and ask that they mail you a current "Disney Resort Travel Sales Center California Brochure" containing descriptions and room rates for all Disneyland lodging properties. In addition, ask for a rate sheet listing admission options and prices for the theme parks. With this in hand, you are ready to evaluate any package that appeals to you. Remember that all packages are quoted on a per-person basis, two to a room (double occupancy). Good luck.

ONE MORE THING

If your travel plans include a stay in the area of more than two or three days, lodge near Disneyland Resort only just before and on the days you visit the parks. The same traffic you avoid by staying close to the park will eat you alive when you begin branching out to other Los Angeles–area attractions. Also, the area immediately around Disneyland is uninspiring, and there is a marked scarcity of decent restaurants.

VACATION HOMES

SOME OF THE BEST LODGING DEALS in the Disneyland Resort area are vacation homes. Prices range from about $65 a night for two-bedroom condos and town homes to $200–$450 a night for three- to five-bedroom vacation homes.

Forgetting about taxes to keep things simple, let's compare renting a vacation home with staying at a three-star hotel near Disneyland. A family of two parents, two teens, and two grandparents would need three hotel rooms at the Fairfield Inn Anaheim Disneyland Resort. At the lowest rate obtainable, they'd be spending $134 per night per room, or $402 total. Rooms are 340 square feet each, so they'd have a total of 1,020 square feet. Each room has a private bath and a TV.

Renting at the same time of year, they can rent a 2,053-square-foot, three-bedroom, two-bath vacation home with a private pool within easy walking distance of Disneyland for $375—a saving of $27 per night over the Fairfield Inn rate. But that's not all: The home comes with a washer and dryer; an outdoor hot tub; a large, grassy play area; a barbecue grill; lounge chairs; a game room with pool table; a family room with a 52-inch high-definition TV, DVD player, and surround sound; a stereo system; a dining room with seating for eight, plus a covered patio dining area; and off-street parking. The only trade-off for our hypothetical family would be having two bathrooms instead of three.

You can see the specific home described above at **vrbo.com/175261.** VRBO stands for **Vacation Rental by Owner,** a listing service for owners of vacation properties nationwide. One thing we like about the VRBO website is that it offers detailed information, including a good number of photos of each specific home. When you book, the home you've been looking at is the actual one you're reserving. On the other hand, some vacation-home rental companies, like rental-car agencies, don't assign you a specific home until the day you arrive—these companies provide photos of a "typical home" instead of making information available on each of the individual homes in their inventory. In this case, you have to take the company's word that the typical home pictured is representative and that the property you'll be assigned will be just as nice.

Location is everything, especially in Southern California with its legendary traffic. Before renting a home, contact the owner and get the address. Then, using **google.com/maps,** obtain exact directions from the home to Disneyland. This will tell you how long and how complicated your commute will be. Avoid homes for which it's necessary to drive on a freeway for more than a couple of miles. Don't worry if the home isn't in Anaheim per se; it's the distance to Disneyland that counts.

The only practical way to shop for a rental home is on the Web. Going online makes it relatively easy to compare different properties and rental companies. The best sites are easy to navigate, let you see what you're interested in without having to log in or divulge any personal information, and list memberships in such organizations as the Better Business Bureau. Before you book, ask about minimum stays, damage deposits, cleaning charges, pets, and how any problems will be addressed once you're in the home.

■ HOTELS *and* MOTELS:
Rated and Ranked

WHAT'S IN A ROOM?

EXCEPT FOR CLEANLINESS, STATE OF REPAIR, and decor, most travelers do not pay much attention to hotel rooms. There is, of course, a discernible standard of quality and luxury that differentiates Motel 6 from Holiday Inn, Holiday Inn from Marriott, and so on. In general, however, hotel guests fail to appreciate that some rooms are better engineered than others.

Contrary to what you might suppose, designing a hotel room is (or should be) a lot more complex than picking a bedspread to match the carpet and drapes. Making the room usable to its occupants is an art, a planning discipline that combines both form and function.

Decor and taste are important, certainly. No one wants to spend several days in a room where the decor is dated, garish, or even ugly. But beyond the decor, there are variables that determine how livable a hotel room is. In Anaheim, for example, we have seen some beautifully appointed rooms that are simply not well designed for human habitation. The next time you stay in a hotel, pay attention to the details and design elements of your room. Even more than decor, these are the things that will make you feel comfortable and at home.

ROOM RATINGS

TO SEPARATE PROPERTIES ACCORDING to the relative quality, tastefulness, state of repair, cleanliness, and size of their standard rooms, we have grouped the hotels and motels into classifications denoted by stars. Star ratings in this guide apply to Anaheim properties only and do not necessarily correspond to ratings awarded by Mobil, AAA, or other travel critics. Because stars have little relevance when awarded in the

Disney Lodging for Less

Mary Waring, Webmaster at **mousesavers.com** (see page 44), knows more about Disney hotel packages than anyone on the planet. Here are her money-saving suggestions.

BOOK ROOM-ONLY. It's frequently a better deal to book a room-only reservation instead of buying a vacation package. When you buy a package, you're typically paying a premium for convenience. You can often save money by putting together your own package—just book room-only at a resort and buy passes, meals, and extras separately.

Disney now prices its standard packages at the same rates as if you had purchased individual components separately at full price. However, what Disney doesn't tell you is that components can usually be purchased separately at a discount—and those discounts are not reflected in the brochure prices of Disney's packages. (Sometimes you can get special-offer packages that do include discounts; see below.)

Disney's packages often include extras you are unlikely to use. Also, packages require a $200 deposit and full payment 45 days in advance; plus, they have stringent change and cancellation policies. Generally, booking room-only requires a deposit of one night's room rate with the remainder due at check-in. Your reservation can be changed or canceled for any reason until five days before check-in.

Whether you decide to book a Disney vacation package or create your own, there are a number of ways to save:

• **BE FLEXIBLE.** Buying a room or package with a discount code is a little like shopping for clothes at a discount store: If you wear size XX-small or XXXX-large, or you like green when everyone else is wearing pink, you're a lot more likely to score a bargain. Likewise, resort discounts are available only when Disney has excess rooms. You're more likely to get a discount during less-popular times (such as value season) and at larger or less-popular resorts.

• **BE PERSISTENT.** This is the most important tip. Disney allots a certain number of rooms to each discount. Once the discounted rooms are gone, you won't get that rate unless someone cancels. Fortunately, people change and cancel reservations all the time. If you can't get your preferred dates or hotel with one discount code, try another one (if available) or keep calling back first thing in the morning to check for cancellations—the system resets overnight, and any reservations with unpaid deposits are automatically released for resale.

absence of commonly recognized standards of comparison, we have tied our ratings to expected levels of quality established by specific American hotel corporations.

Star ratings apply to *room quality only* and describe the property's standard accommodations. For most hotels and motels, a standard accommodation is a hotel room with either one king bed or two queen beds. In an all-suite property, the standard accommodation is either a studio or one-bedroom suite. In addition to standard accommodations, many hotels offer luxury rooms and special suites that are not rated in this guide. Star ratings for rooms are assigned without regard to whether a property has a restaurant, recreational facilities, entertainment, or other extras.

In addition to stars (which delineate broad categories), we also employ a numerical rating system. Our rating scale is 0–100, with 100 as the best possible rating. Numerical ratings are presented to show the difference we perceive between one property and another. Rooms at the Desert Palms Hotel & Suites and Howard Johnson Hotel are both rated as three and a half stars (★★★½). In the supplemental numerical ratings, the Desert Palms is rated an 82 and the Howard Johnson a 76. This means that within the three-and-a-half-star category, the Desert Palms has slightly nicer rooms than the Howard Johnson.

OVERALL STAR RATINGS		
★★★★★	Superior rooms	Tasteful and luxurious by any standard
★★★★	Extremely nice rooms	What you'd expect at a Hyatt Regency or Marriott
★★★	Nice rooms	Holiday Inn or comparable quality
★★	Adequate rooms	Clean, comfortable, and functional without frills—like a Motel 6

HOW THE HOTELS COMPARE

COST ESTIMATES ARE BASED on the hotel's published rack rates for standard rooms. Each "$" represents $50. Thus, a cost symbol of "$$$" means a room (or suite) at that hotel will be about $150 a night (it may be less for weekdays or more on weekends).

On pages 68–70, we list a hit parade of the nicest rooms in town. We've focused strictly on room quality and have excluded any consideration of location, services, recreation, or amenities. In some instances, a one- or two-room suite can be had for the same price or less than that of a hotel room.

If you used an earlier edition of this guide, you will notice that many of the ratings and rankings have changed. In addition to the inclusion of new properties, these changes are occasioned by such positive developments as guest room renovation or improved maintenance and housekeeping. A failure to properly maintain guest rooms or a lapse in housekeeping standards can negatively affect the ratings.

Finally, before you begin to shop for a hotel, take a hard look at this letter we received from a couple in Hot Springs, Arkansas:

We canceled our room reservations to follow the advice in your book [and reserved a hotel highly ranked by the Unofficial Guide]. *We wanted inexpensive but clean and cheerful. We got inexpensive but dirty, grim, and depressing. I really felt disappointed in your advice and the room. It was the pits. That was the one real piece of information I needed from your book!*

Needless to say, this letter was as unsettling to us as the bad room was to our reader. Our integrity as travel journalists, after all, is based on the quality of the information we provide to our readers. Even with the best of intentions and the most conscientious research, however, we cannot inspect every room in every hotel. What we do, in statistical terms, is take a sample: we check out several rooms selected at random in each hotel and base our ratings and rankings on those rooms. The inspections are conducted anonymously and without the knowledge of the property's management. Although it would be unusual, it is certainly possible that the rooms we randomly inspect are not representative of the majority of rooms at a particular hotel. Another possibility is that the rooms we inspect in a given hotel are representative but that by bad luck a reader is assigned to an inferior room. When we rechecked the hotel that our reader disliked so intensely, we discovered that our rating was correctly representative but that he and his wife had unfortunately been assigned to one of a small number of threadbare rooms scheduled for renovation.

The key to avoiding disappointment is to do some snooping around in advance. We recommend that you ask to get a photo of a hotel's standard guest room before you book, or at least a copy of the hotel's promotional brochure. Be forewarned, however, that some hotel chains use the same guest room photo in their promotional literature for all hotels in the chain, and that the guest room in a specific property may not resemble the photo in the brochure. When you or your travel agent call, ask how old the property is and when the guest room you are being assigned was last renovated. If you arrive and are assigned a room inferior to that which you had been led to expect, demand to be moved to another room.

THE TOP 30 BEST DEALS

IN ADDITION TO LISTING THE BETTER ROOMS in town, we also take a look at the best combinations of quality and value in a room. The rankings are made without consideration of location or the availability of restaurants, recreational facilities, entertainment, or amenities.

The Disneyland Hotel, you may notice, is not one of the best deals. This is because you can get more for your money at other properties. The Disneyland and Grand Californian Hotels, however, are two of the most popular hotels in the area, and many guests are willing to pay a higher rate for their convenience, service, and amenities.

We once had a reader complain to us that he had booked one of our top-ranked rooms for value and had been very disappointed in the room. On checking we noticed that the room the reader occupied had a quality rating of ★★½. We would remind you that the value ratings are intended to give you some sense of value received for your lodging dollar spent. A ★★½ room at $35 may have the same value rating as a ★★★★ room at $85, but that does not mean that the rooms will be of comparable quality. Regardless of whether it's a good deal or not, a ★★½ room is still a ★★½ room.

Listed on pages 60–61 are the top 30 room buys for the money, regardless of location or star classification, based on rack rates. Note that sometimes a suite can cost less than a hotel room.

MAKING *the* MOST *of* YOUR TIME

ALLOCATING TIME

THE DISNEY PEOPLE recommend spending two to four full days at Disneyland Resort. While this may seem a little self-serving, it is not without basis. Disneyland Resort is *huge,* with something to see or do crammed into every conceivable space. In addition, there are two parks, and touring requires a lot of walking, and often a lot of waiting in line. Moving in and among large crowds all day is exhausting, and often the unrelenting Southern California sun zaps even the most hardy, making tempers short.

During our many visits to Disneyland, we observed, particularly on hot summer days, a dramatic transition from happy, enthusiastic touring on arrival to almost zombielike plodding along later in the day. Visitors who began their day enjoying the wonders of Disney imagination ultimately lapsed into an exhausted production mentality ("We have two more rides in Fantasyland; then we can go to the hotel").

OPTIMUM TOURING SITUATION

WE DON'T BELIEVE THAT THERE IS ONE IDEAL ITINERARY. Tastes, energy levels, and perspectives on what constitutes entertainment and relaxation vary. This understood, here are some considerations for developing your own ideal itinerary.

Optimum touring at Disneyland requires a good game plan, a minimum of three to five days on-site (excluding travel time), and a fair amount of money. It also requires a fairly prodigious appetite for Disney entertainment. The essence of optimum touring is to see the attractions in a series of shorter, less-exhausting visits during the cooler, less-crowded times of day, with plenty of rest and relaxation between excursions.

Because optimum touring calls for leaving and returning to the theme parks, it makes sense to stay in one of the Disney hotels or in one of the non-Disney hotels within walking distance. If you visit Disneyland during busy times, you need to get up early to beat the crowds. Short lines and stress-free touring are incompatible with sleeping in. If you want to sleep in *and* enjoy your touring, visit Disneyland when attendance is lighter.

THE CARDINAL RULES FOR SUCCESSFUL TOURING

MANY VISITORS DON'T HAVE THREE DAYS to devote to Disneyland Resort. For these visitors, efficient touring is a must. Even the most time-effective plan, however, won't allow you to cover both Disney theme parks in one day. Plan to allocate at least an entire day to each

The Top 30 Best Deals

RANK	HOTEL	MAP NUMBER (pgs. 46–47)	OVERALL QUALITY RATING	ROOM QUALITY RATING	COST ($ = $50)	PHONE
1.	Ramada Limited Maingate North	67	★★★½	78	$$–	714-999-0684
2.	DoubleTree by Hilton Hotel Anaheim–Orange County	40	★★★★	83	$$+	714-634-4500
3.	Extended Stay America Orange County–Anaheim Conv. Ctr.	43	★★★	69	$$–	714-502-9988
4.	Hyatt Regency Orange County	56	★★★★	89	$$$	714-750-1234
5.	Red Lion Hotel Anaheim	70	★★★★	85	$$$–	714-750-2801
6.	Portofino Inn & Suites	64	★★★★	83	$$$–	714-782-7600
7.	Staybridge Suites Anaheim Resort Area	76	★★★★	84	$$$–	714-748-7700
8.	Holiday Inn– Anaheim Resort Area	50	★★★½	80	$$+	714-748-7777
9.	DoubleTree Suites by Hilton Hotel Anaheim Resort–Conv. Ctr.	39	★★★★	86	$$$	714-750-3000
10.	Holiday Inn Hotel & Suites Anaheim	52	★★★½	82	$$$–	714-535-0300
11.	Crowne Plaza Anaheim Resort	28	★★★★	86	$$$	714-867-5555
12.	Sheraton Anaheim Hotel	73	★★★★	87	$$$+	714-778-1700
13.	Ramada Anaheim South	66	★★★	72	$$	714-971-3553
14.	Hilton Suites Anaheim–Orange	49	★★★★	86	$$$+	714-938-1111
15.	Ayres Hotel Anaheim	13	★★★★	85	$$$+	714-634-2106

park. If your schedule permits only one day of touring, concentrate on one theme park and save the other for another visit.

One-Day Touring

A comprehensive one-day tour of Disneyland Park or Disney California Adventure is possible, but it requires knowledge of the parks, good planning, and plenty of energy and endurance. One-day touring doesn't leave much time for full-service meals, prolonged shopping, or lengthy breaks. One-day touring can be fun and rewarding, but allocating two days per park, especially for Disneyland Park, is always preferable if possible.

Successful touring of Disneyland Park or Disney California Adventure hinges on three rules:

1. DETERMINE IN ADVANCE WHAT YOU REALLY WANT TO SEE What rides and attractions most appeal to you? Which additional rides and attractions would you like to experience if you have any time left? What are you willing to forgo?

To help you establish your touring priorities, we have described every attraction in detail. In each description, we include the author's critical evaluation of the attraction as well as the opinions of

The Top 30 Best Deals (continued)

RANK	HOTEL	MAP NUMBER (pgs. 46–47)	OVERALL QUALITY RATING	ROOM QUALITY RATING	COST ($ = $50)	PHONE
16.	Sheraton Park Hotel at the Anaheim Resort	74	★★★★	85	$$$+	714-750-1811
17.	Marriott Suites Anaheim	59	★★★★	85	$$$+	714-750-1000
18.	Best Western Plus Stovall's Inn	20	★★★½	82	$$$–	714-778-1880
19.	Greenwood Suites Anaheim Resort	45	★★★½	82	$$$–	714-808-9000
20.	Peacock Suites	63	★★★½	82	$$$–	714-535-8255
21.	La Quinta Inn & Suites Anaheim Disneyland	58	★★★½	76	$$$–	714-635-5000
22.	Embassy Suites Anaheim–South	42	★★★★	83	$$$+	714-539-3300
23.	Anaheim Camelot Inn & Suites	7	★★★½	80	$$$	714-635-7275
24.	Desert Inn & Suites	34	★★★½	81	$$$	714-772-5050
25.	Ramada Plaza Anaheim Hotel	69	★★★½	81	$$$	714-991-6868
26.	Candy Cane Inn	22	★★★½	78	$$$	714-774-5284
27.	Homewood Suites by Hilton Anaheim–Main Gate Area	53	★★★★	85	$$$$–	714-740-1800
28.	Travelodge Anaheim Inn & Suites on Disneyland Drive	80	★★★	65	$$+	714-774-7600
29.	Rodeway Inn Maingate	72	★★½	57	$$–	714-533-2500
30.	TownePlace Suites by Marriott Anaheim	79	★★★★	88	$$$$	714-939-9700

Disneyland Resort guests expressed as star ratings. Five stars is the highest (best) rating possible.

Finally, because Disneyland Resort attractions range in scope from midway-type rides and horse-drawn trolleys to colossal, high-tech extravaganzas spanning the equivalent of whole city blocks, we have developed a hierarchy of categories for attractions to give you some sense of their order of magnitude:

SUPER-HEADLINERS The best attractions that the theme park has to offer. They are mind-boggling in size, scope, and imagination and represent the cutting edge of modern attraction technology and design.

HEADLINERS Full-blown, multimillion-dollar, full-scale, themed adventure experiences and theater presentations. They are modern in their technology and design and employ a full range of special effects.

MAJOR ATTRACTIONS Themed adventure experiences on a more modest scale but incorporating state-of-the-art technologies, or larger-scale attractions of older design.

MINOR ATTRACTIONS Midway-type rides, small-scale dark rides (spook house–type rides), minor theater presentations, transportation rides, and elaborate walk-through attractions.

Continued on page 70

Hotel Information Chart

Alamo Inn & Suites Anaheim
★★
1140 W. Katella Ave.
Anaheim 92802
☎ 714-635-8070
thealamoinn.com

ROOM RATING	52
COST ($=$50)	$+
POOL	•
ON-SITE DINING	—

Alpine Inn ★★½
715 W. Katella Ave.
Anaheim 92802
☎ 714-535-2186
alpineinnanaheim.com

ROOM RATING	64
COST ($=$50)	$$
POOL	•
ON-SITE DINING	—

America's Best Inn ★★½
414 W. Ball Rd.
Anaheim 92805
☎ 714-533-2570
abianaheim.com

ROOM RATING	58
COST ($=$50)	$$$–
POOL	•
ON-SITE DINING	—

**Anaheim Camelot Inn
& Suites** ★★★½
1520 S. Harbor Blvd.
Anaheim 92802
☎ 714-635-7275
camelotinn-anaheim.com

ROOM RATING	80
COST ($=$50)	$$$
POOL	•
ON-SITE DINING	—

Anaheim Carriage Inn ★★½
2125 S. Harbor Blvd.
Anaheim 92802
☎ 714-740-1440
anaheimcarriageinn.com

ROOM RATING	63
COST ($=$50)	$$
POOL	•
ON-SITE DINING	—

**Anaheim Discovery Inn
& Suites** ★
1126 W. Katella Ave.
Anaheim 92802
☎ 714-533-4505
anaheimdiscoveryinn.com

ROOM RATING	34
COST ($=$50)	$$–
POOL	•
ON-SITE DINING	—

Ayres Hotel Anaheim ★★★★
2550 E. Katella Ave.
Anaheim 92806
☎ 714-634-2106
ayreshotels.com

ROOM RATING	85
COST ($=$50)	$$$+
POOL	•
ON-SITE DINING	—

Ayres Inn Orange ★★★
3737 W. Chapman Ave.
Orange 92868
☎ 714-978-9168
ayreshotels.com

ROOM RATING	69
COST ($=$50)	$$$
POOL	•
ON-SITE DINING	—

Best Western Courtesy Inn
★★½
1070 W. Ball Rd.
Anaheim 92802
☎ 714-772-2470
bestwestern.com

ROOM RATING	60
COST ($=$50)	$$$–
POOL	•
ON-SITE DINING	—

Best Western Plus Pavilions
★★½
1176 W. Katella Ave.
Anaheim 92802
☎ 714-776-0140
pavilionshotel.com

ROOM RATING	63
COST ($=$50)	$$$–
POOL	•
ON-SITE DINING	—

**Best Western Plus Raffles
Inn & Suites** ★★★
2040 S. Harbor Blvd.
Anaheim 92802
☎ 714-750-6100
bestwestern.com

ROOM RATING	67
COST ($=$50)	$$$–
POOL	•
ON-SITE DINING	—

Best Western Plus Stovall's Inn
★★★½
1110 W. Katella Ave.
Anaheim 92802
☎ 714-778-1880
stovallsinn.com

ROOM RATING	82
COST ($=$50)	$$$–
POOL	•
ON-SITE DINING	•

Castle Inn & Suites ★★★
1734 S. Harbor Blvd.
Anaheim 92802
☎ 714-774-8111
castleinn.com

ROOM RATING	66
COST ($=$50)	$$$–
POOL	•
ON-SITE DINING	—

Chamberlain West Hollywood
★★★½
1000 Westmount Dr.
West Hollywood 90069
☎ 310-657-7400
chamberlainwesthollywood.com

ROOM RATING	81
COST ($=$50)	$$$$$+
POOL	•
ON-SITE DINING	•

Clarion Hotel Anaheim ★★★
616 Convention Way
Anaheim 92802
☎ 714-750-3131
clarionanaheim.com

ROOM RATING	70
COST ($=$50)	$$$
POOL	•
ON-SITE DINING	•

America's Best Value Astoria Inn & Suites ★★½
426 W. Ball Rd.
Anaheim 92805
☎ 714-774-3882
anaheimastoriainn.com

ROOM RATING	61
COST ($=$50)	$$
POOL	•
ON-SITE DINING	—

America's Best Value Fantasy Inn & Suites ★
425 W. Katella Ave.
Anaheim 92802
☎ 714-776-2815
valueinnanaheim.com

ROOM RATING	38
COST ($=$50)	$$–
POOL	•
ON-SITE DINING	—

The Anabella ★★★
1030 W. Katella Ave.
Anaheim 92802
☎ 714-905-1050
anabellahotel.com

ROOM RATING	72
COST ($=$50)	$$$+
POOL	•
ON-SITE DINING	•

Anaheim Express Inn ★★½
620 W. Orangewood Ave.
Anaheim 92802
☎ 714-971-9000
anainn.com

ROOM RATING	57
COST ($=$50)	$$+
POOL	•
ON-SITE DINING	—

Anaheim Plaza Hotel & Suites ★★★
1700 S. Harbor Blvd.
Anaheim 92802
☎ 714-772-5900
anaheimplazahotel.com

ROOM RATING	65
COST ($=$50)	$$$–
POOL	•
ON-SITE DINING	•

Anaheim Quality Inn & Suites ★★½
1441 S. Manchester Ave.
Anaheim 92802
☎ 714-991-8100
anaheimqualityinn.com

ROOM RATING	57
COST ($=$50)	$$+
POOL	•
ON-SITE DINING	—

Best Western Hollywood Plaza Inn ★★½
2011 N. Highland Ave.
Hollywood 90068
☎ 323-851-1800
bestwestern.com

ROOM RATING	62
COST ($=$50)	$$$$$
POOL	•
ON-SITE DINING	—

Best Western Plus Anaheim Inn ★★½
1630 S. Harbor Blvd.
Anaheim 92802
☎ 714-774-1050
anaheiminn.com

ROOM RATING	61
COST ($=$50)	$$$–
POOL	•
ON-SITE DINING	—

Best Western Plus Park Place Inn & Mini Suites ★★★
1544 S. Harbor Blvd.
Anaheim 92802
☎ 714-776-4800
bestwestern.com

ROOM RATING	65
COST ($=$50)	$$$
POOL	•
ON-SITE DINING	—

Budget Inn ★★
1042 W. Ball Rd.
Anaheim 92802
☎ 714-535-5524
anaheim-budgetinn.com

ROOM RATING	50
COST ($=$50)	$$
POOL	•
ON-SITE DINING	—

Candy Cane Inn ★★★½
1747 S. Harbor Blvd.
Anaheim 92802
☎ 714-774-5284
candycaneinn.net

ROOM RATING	78
COST ($=$50)	$$$
POOL	•
ON-SITE DINING	—

Carousel Inn & Suites ★★★
1530 S. Harbor Blvd.
Anaheim 92802
☎ 714-758-0444
carouselinnandsuites.com

ROOM RATING	73
COST ($=$50)	$$$
POOL	•
ON-SITE DINING	—

Colony Inn ★★½
4917 Vineland Ave.
North Hollywood 91601
☎ 818-763-2787
colonyinn.com

ROOM RATING	60
COST ($=$50)	$$$–
POOL	—
ON-SITE DINING	—

Comfort Inn & Suites ★★★
300 E. Katella Way
Anaheim 92802
☎ 714-772-8713
comfortinnsuitesanaheim.com

ROOM RATING	69
COST ($=$50)	$$$–
POOL	•
ON-SITE DINING	—

Cortona Inn & Suites ★★★
2029 S. Harbor Blvd.
Anaheim 92802
☎ 714-971-5000
cortonainn.com

ROOM RATING	72
COST ($=$50)	$$$
POOL	•
ON-SITE DINING	—

Hotel Information Chart (continued)

Courtyard by Marriott Anaheim
★★★½
2045 S. Harbor Blvd.
Anaheim 92802
☎ 714-740-2645
courtyardanaheim.com

ROOM RATING	75
COST ($=$50)	$$$+
POOL	•
ON-SITE DINING	•

Crowne Plaza Anaheim Resort
★★★★
12021 Harbor Blvd.
Garden Grove 92840
☎ 714-867-5555
anaheim.crowneplaza.com

ROOM RATING	86
COST ($=$50)	$$$
POOL	•
ON-SITE DINING	•

Days Inn Anaheim Maingate ★★½
2200 S. Harbor Blvd.
Anaheim 92802
☎ 714-750-5211
daysinn.com

ROOM RATING	59
COST ($=$50)	$$
POOL	•
ON-SITE DINING	—

Desert Inn & Suites ★★★½
1600 S. Harbor Blvd.
Anaheim 92802
☎ 714-772-5050
anaheimdesertinn.com

ROOM RATING	81
COST ($=$50)	$$$
POOL	•
ON-SITE DINING	—

Desert Palms Hotel & Suites Anaheim Resort ★★★½
631 W. Katella Ave.
Anaheim 92802
☎ 714-535-1133
desertpalmshotel.com

ROOM RATING	82
COST ($=$50)	$$$$$–
POOL	•
ON-SITE DINING	•

Disneyland Hotel ★★★★
1150 W. Magic Way
Anaheim 92802
☎ 714-778-6600
disneyland.com

ROOM RATING	89
COST ($=$50)	$$$$$$$$$+
POOL	•
ON-SITE DINING	•

DoubleTree Suites by Hilton Hotel Anaheim Resort–Convention Center ★★★★
2985 S. Harbor Blvd.
Anaheim 92802
☎ **714-750-3000**
doubletree.com

ROOM RATING	86
COST ($=$50)	$$$
POOL	•
ON-SITE DINING	•

Econo Lodge Maingate ★★½
871 S. Harbor Blvd.
Anaheim 92805
☎ 714-535-7878
econolodge.com

ROOM RATING	57
COST ($=$50)	$$–
POOL	•
ON-SITE DINING	—

Embassy Suites Anaheim–South ★★★★
11767 Harbor Blvd.
Garden Grove 92840
☎ 714-539-3300
anaheimsouth. embassysuites.com

ROOM RATING	83
COST ($=$50)	$$$$–
POOL	•
ON-SITE DINING	•

Hacienda Inn & Suites ★★
2176 S. Harbor Blvd.
Anaheim 92802
☎ 714-750-2101
anaheimhaciendainn.com

ROOM RATING	46
COST ($=$50)	$+
POOL	—
ON-SITE DINING	—

Hilton Anaheim ★★★½
777 Convention Way
Anaheim 92802
☎ 714-750-4321
hilton.com

ROOM RATING	81
COST ($=$50)	$$$+
POOL	•
ON-SITE DINING	•

Hilton Garden Inn Anaheim–Garden Grove ★★★½
11777 Harbor Blvd.
Garden Grove 92840
☎ 714-703-9100
hilton.com

ROOM RATING	79
COST ($=$50)	$$$+
POOL	•
ON-SITE DINING	—

Holiday Inn Burbank Media Center ★★★
150 E. Angeleno
Burbank 91502
☎ 818-841-4770
ichotelsgroup.com

ROOM RATING	69
COST ($=$50)	$$$+
POOL	•
ON-SITE DINING	•

Holiday Inn Express–Anaheim Maingate Hotel ★★★
435 W. Katella Ave.
Anaheim 92802
☎ 714-772-7755
holiday-anaheim.com

ROOM RATING	72
COST ($=$50)	$$$+
POOL	•
ON-SITE DINING	—

Holiday Inn Hotel & Suites Anaheim ★★★½
1240 S. Walnut Ave.
Anaheim 92802
☎ 714-535-0300
holiday-inn.com

ROOM RATING	82
COST ($=$50)	$$$–
POOL	•
ON-SITE DINING	•

Days Inn Anaheim West ★★½
1030 W. Ball Rd.
Anaheim 92802
☎ 714-520-0101
daysinn.com

ROOM RATING	64
COST ($=$50)	$$+
POOL	•
ON-SITE DINING	—

Days Inn & Suites Anaheim at Disneyland Park ★★½
1111 S. Harbor Blvd.
Anaheim 92805
☎ 714-533-8830
daysinn.com

ROOM RATING	56
COST ($=$50)	$$+
POOL	•
ON-SITE DINING	—

del Sol Inn Anaheim Resort ★★½
1604 S. Harbor Blvd.
Anaheim 92802
☎ 714-234-3411
delsolinn.com

ROOM RATING	61
COST ($=$50)	$$$$–
POOL	•
ON-SITE DINING	•

Disney Paradise Pier Hotel ★★★★
1717 S. Disneyland Dr.
Anaheim 92802
☎ 714-999-0990
disneyland.com

ROOM RATING	86
COST ($=$50)	$$$$$$$$$–
POOL	•
ON-SITE DINING	•

Disney's Grand Californian Hotel & Spa ★★★★½
1600 S. Disneyland Dr.
Anaheim 92802
☎ 714-635-2300
disneyland.com

ROOM RATING	90
COST ($=$50)	$$$$$$$$$$+
POOL	•
ON-SITE DINING	•

DoubleTree by Hilton Hotel Anaheim–Orange County ★★★★
100 The City Dr.
Orange 92868
☎ 714-634-4500
doubletree.com

ROOM RATING	83
COST ($=$50)	$$+
POOL	•
ON-SITE DINING	•

Extended Stay America Orange County–Anaheim Convention Center ★★★
1742 S. Clementine St.
Anaheim 92802
☎ 714-502-9988
extendedstayamerica.com

ROOM RATING	69
COST ($=$50)	$$–
POOL	•
ON-SITE DINING	—

Fairfield Inn Anaheim Disneyland Resort ★★★½
1460 S. Harbor Blvd.
Anaheim 92802
☎ 714-772-6777
marriott.com

ROOM RATING	75
COST ($=$50)	$$$+
POOL	•
ON-SITE DINING	•

Greenwood Suites Anaheim Resort ★★★½
1733 S. Anaheim Blvd.
Anaheim 92805
☎ 714-808-9000
greenwoodsuites anaheimresort.com

ROOM RATING	82
COST ($=$50)	$$$–
POOL	•
ON-SITE DINING	—

Hilton Los Angeles at Universal City ★★★★
555 Universal Hollywood Dr.
Universal City 91608
☎ 818-506-2500
hilton.com

ROOM RATING	87
COST ($=$50)	$$$$$–
POOL	•
ON-SITE DINING	•

Hilton Suites Anaheim–Orange ★★★★
400 N. State College Blvd.
Orange 92868
☎ 714-938-1111
hilton.com

ROOM RATING	86
COST ($=$50)	$$$+
POOL	•
ON-SITE DINING	•

Holiday Inn–Anaheim Resort Area ★★★½
1915 S. Manchester Ave.
Anaheim 92802
☎ 714-748-7777
holiday-inn.com

ROOM RATING	80
COST ($=$50)	$$+
POOL	•
ON-SITE DINING	•

Homewood Suites by Hilton Anaheim–Main Gate Area ★★★★
12005 Harbor Blvd.
Garden Grove 92840
☎ 714-740-1800
homewoodsuites3.hilton.com

ROOM RATING	85
COST ($=$50)	$$$$–
POOL	•
ON-SITE DINING	—

Hotel Menage ★★½
1221 S. Harbor Blvd.
Anaheim 92805
☎ 714-758-0900
hotelmenage.com

ROOM RATING	63
COST ($=$50)	$$+
POOL	•
ON-SITE DINING	•

Howard Johnson Anaheim Hotel & Water Playground ★★★½
1380 S. Harbor Blvd.
Anaheim 92802
☎ 714-776-6120
hojoanaheim.com

ROOM RATING	76
COST ($=$50)	$$$$–
POOL	•
ON-SITE DINING	—

Hotel Information Chart (continued)

Hyatt Regency Orange County ★★★★
11999 Harbor Blvd.
Garden Grove 92840
☎ **714-750-1234**
hyatt.com

ROOM RATING	89
COST ($=$50)	$$$
POOL	•
ON-SITE DINING	•

Jolly Roger Hotel Anaheim ★★★
640 W. Katella Ave.
Anaheim 92802
☎ **714-782-7500**
jollyrogerhotel.com

ROOM RATING	68
COST ($=$50)	$$$–
POOL	•
ON-SITE DINING	•

La Quinta Inn & Suites Anaheim Disneyland ★★★½
1752 S. Clementine St.
Anaheim 92802
☎ 714-635-5000
laquinta.com

ROOM RATING	76
COST ($=$50)	$$$–
POOL	—
ON-SITE DINING	—

Motel 6 Anaheim Maingate ★★½
100 W. Disney Way
Anaheim 92802
☎ 714-520-9696
motel6-anaheim.com

ROOM RATING	61
COST ($=$50)	$$–
POOL	•
ON-SITE DINING	—

Park Vue Inn ★★½
1570 S. Harbor Blvd.
Anaheim 92802
☎ 714-772-3691
parkvueinn.com

ROOM RATING	60
COST ($=$50)	$$$+
POOL	•
ON-SITE DINING	—

Peacock Suites ★★★½
1745 S. Anaheim Blvd.
Anaheim 92805
☎ 714-535-8255
shellhospitality.com

ROOM RATING	82
COST ($=$50)	$$$–
POOL	•
ON-SITE DINING	—

Ramada Limited Maingate North ★★★½
921 S. Harbor Blvd.
Anaheim 92802
☎ 714-999-0684
ramada.com

ROOM RATING	78
COST ($=$50)	$$–
POOL	•
ON-SITE DINING	—

Ramada Maingate at the Park ★★★
1650 S. Harbor Blvd.
Anaheim 92802
☎ 714-772-0440
ramadamaingate.com

ROOM RATING	67
COST ($=$50)	$$$
POOL	•
ON-SITE DINING	—

Ramada Plaza Anaheim Hotel ★★★½
515 W. Katella Ave.
Anaheim 92802
☎ 714-991-6868
ramadaanaheim.com

ROOM RATING	81
COST ($=$50)	$$$
POOL	•
ON-SITE DINING	•

Sheraton Anaheim Hotel ★★★★
900 S. Disneyland Dr.
Anaheim 92802
☎ 714-778-1700
sheraton.com

ROOM RATING	87
COST ($=$50)	$$$+
POOL	•
ON-SITE DINING	•

Sheraton Park Hotel at the Anaheim Resort ★★★★
1855 S. Harbor Blvd.
Anaheim 92802
☎ 714-750-1811
sheratonparkanaheim.com

ROOM RATING	85
COST ($=$50)	$$$+
POOL	•
ON-SITE DINING	•

Sheraton Universal Hotel ★★★★
333 Universal Hollywood Dr.
Universal City 91608
☎ 818-980-1212
starwoodhotels.com

ROOM RATING	85
COST ($=$50)	$$$$$–
POOL	•
ON-SITE DINING	•

Super 8 Motel Near Disneyland ★★½
415 W. Katella Ave.
Anaheim 92802
☎ 714-778-6900
super8.com

ROOM RATING	62
COST ($=$50)	$$
POOL	•
ON-SITE DINING	—

TownePlace Suites by Marriott Anaheim ★★★★
1730 S. State College Blvd.
Anaheim 92806
☎ 714-939-9700
tpsanaheimhotel.com

ROOM RATING	88
COST ($=$50)	$$$$
POOL	•
ON-SITE DINING	—

Travelodge Anaheim Inn & Suites on Disneyland Drive ★★★
1057 W. Ball Rd.
Anaheim 92802
☎ 714-774-7600
travelodgedisneyland.com

ROOM RATING	65
COST ($=$50)	$$+
POOL	•
ON-SITE DINING	—

Marriott Anaheim ★★★½
700 W. Convention Way
Anaheim 92802
☎ 714-750-8000
marriott.com

ROOM RATING	82
COST ($=$50)	$$$$–
POOL	•
ON-SITE DINING	•

**Marriott Los Angeles
Burbank Airport** ★★★½
2500 Hollywood Way
Burbank 91505
☎ 818-843-6000
marriottburbankairport.com

ROOM RATING	80
COST ($=$50)	$$$+
POOL	•
ON-SITE DINING	•

Marriott Suites Anaheim
★★★★
12015 Harbor Blvd.
Anaheim 92802
☎ 714-750-1000
marriott.com

ROOM RATING	85
COST ($=$50)	$$$+
POOL	•
ON-SITE DINING	•

Portofino Inn & Suites ★★★★
1831 S. Harbor Blvd.
Anaheim 92802
☎ 714-782-7600
portofinoinnanaheim.com

ROOM RATING	83
COST ($=$50)	$$$–
POOL	•
ON-SITE DINING	—

**Quality Inn & Suites Anaheim
at the Park** ★★½
1166 W. Katella Ave.
Anaheim 92802
☎ 714 774-7817
qualityinn.com

ROOM RATING	56
COST ($=$50)	$$–
POOL	•
ON-SITE DINING	—

Ramada Anaheim South ★★★
2141 S. Harbor Blvd.
Anaheim 92802
☎ 714-971-3553
ramada.com

ROOM RATING	72
COST ($=$50)	$$
POOL	•
ON-SITE DINING	•

Red Lion Hotel Anaheim
★★★★
1850 S. Harbor Blvd.
Anaheim 92802
☎ 714-750-2801
redlion.com

ROOM RATING	85
COST ($=$50)	$$$–
POOL	•
ON-SITE DINING	•

**Residence Inn Anaheim
Maingate** ★★★½
1700 S. Clementine St.
Anaheim 92802
☎ 714-533-3555
marriott.com

ROOM RATING	81
COST ($=$50)	$$$$–
POOL	•
ON-SITE DINING	•

Rodeway Inn Maingate ★★½
1211 West Pl.
Anaheim 92802
☎ 714-533-2500
rodewayinn.com

ROOM RATING	57
COST ($=$50)	$$–
POOL	—
ON-SITE DINING	—

Stanford Inn & Suites Anaheim
★★★
2171 S. Harbor Blvd.
Anaheim 92802
☎ 714-703-1220
stanfordinnanaheim.com

ROOM RATING	65
COST ($=$50)	$$+
POOL	•
ON-SITE DINING	—

**Staybridge Suites Anaheim
Resort Area** ★★★★
1855 S. Manchester Ave.
Anaheim 92802
☎ 714-748-7700
staybridge.com

ROOM RATING	84
COST ($=$50)	$$$–
POOL	•
ON-SITE DINING	—

**Super 8 Motel Anaheim–
Disneyland Drive** ★★
915 S. Disneyland Dr.
Anaheim 92802
☎ 714-778-0350
super8.com

ROOM RATING	55
COST ($=$50)	$+
POOL	•
ON-SITE DINING	—

**Travelodge Anaheim
International Inn** ★★
2060 S. Harbor Blvd.
Anaheim 92802
☎ 714-971-9393
travelodge.com

ROOM RATING	50
COST ($=$50)	$$
POOL	•
ON-SITE DINING	—

Tropicana Inn & Suites ★★★
1540 S. Harbor Blvd.
Anaheim 92802
☎ 714-635-4082
tropicanainn-anaheim.com

ROOM RATING	65
COST ($=$50)	$$$–
POOL	•
ON-SITE DINING	—

How the Hotels Compare

HOTEL	MAP NUMBER (pgs. 46–47)	OVERALL QUALITY RATING	ROOM QUALITY RATING	COST ($ = $50)	PHONE
DISNEYLAND AREA					
Disney's Grand Californian Hotel & Spa	38	★★★★½	90	$ x 10+	714-635-2300
Disneyland Hotel	36	★★★★	89	$ x 9+	714-778-6600
Hyatt Regency Orange County	56	★★★★	89	$$$	714-750-1234
TownePlace Suites by Marriott Anaheim	79	★★★★	88	$$$$	714-939-9700
Sheraton Anaheim Hotel	73	★★★★	87	$$$+	714-778-1700
Crowne Plaza Anaheim Resort	28	★★★★	86	$$$	714-867-5555
Disney Paradise Pier Hotel	37	★★★★	86	$ x 9–	714-999-0990
DoubleTree Suites by Hilton Hotel Anaheim Resort–Convention Ctr.	39	★★★★	86	$$$	714-750-3000
Hilton Suites Anaheim–Orange	49	★★★★	86	$$$+	714-938-1111
Ayres Hotel Anaheim	13	★★★★	85	$$$+	714-634-2106
Homewood Suites by Hilton Anaheim–Main Gate Area	53	★★★★	85	$$$$–	714-740-1800
Marriott Suites Anaheim	59	★★★★	85	$$$+	714-750-1000
Red Lion Hotel Anaheim	70	★★★★	85	$$$–	714-750-2801
Sheraton Park Hotel at the Anaheim Resort	74	★★★★	85	$$$+	714-750-1811
Staybridge Suites Anaheim Resort Area	76	★★★★	84	$$$–	714-748-7700
DoubleTree by Hilton Hotel Anaheim–Orange County	40	★★★★	83	$$+	714-634-4500
Embassy Suites Anaheim–South	42	★★★★	83	$$$+	714-539-3300
Portofino Inn & Suites	64	★★★★	83	$$$–	714-782-7600
Best Western Plus Stovall's Inn	20	★★★½	82	$$$–	714-778-1880
Desert Palms Hotel & Suites Anaheim Resort	35	★★★½	82	$ x 5–	714-535-1133
Greenwood Suites Anaheim Resort	45	★★★½	82	$$$–	714-808-9000
Holiday Inn Hotel & Suites Anaheim	52	★★★½	82	$$$–	714-535-0300
Marriott Anaheim	60	★★★½	82	$$$$–	714-750-8000
Peacock Suites	63	★★★½	82	$$$–	714-535-8255
Desert Inn & Suites	34	★★★½	81	$$$	714-772-5050
Hilton Anaheim	47	★★★½	81	$$$+	714-750-4321
Ramada Plaza Anaheim Hotel	69	★★★½	81	$$$	714-991-6868
Residence Inn Anaheim–Maingate	71	★★★½	81	$$$$–	714-533-3555
Anaheim Camelot Inn & Suites	7	★★★½	80	$$$	714-635-7275
Hilton Garden Inn Anaheim–Garden Grove	48	★★★½	79	$$$+	714-703-9100
Holiday Inn–Anaheim Resort Area	50	★★★½	80	$$+	714-748-7777

How the Hotels Compare (continued)

HOTEL	MAP NUMBER (pgs. 46–47)	OVERALL QUALITY RATING	ROOM QUALITY RATING	COST ($ = $50)	PHONE
Candy Cane Inn	22	★★★½	78	$$$	714-774-5284
Ramada Limited Maingate North	67	★★★½	78	$$–	714-999-0684
Howard Johnson Anaheim Hotel & Water Playground	55	★★★½	76	$$$$–	714-776-6120
La Quinta Inn & Suites Anaheim Disneyland	58	★★★½	76	$$$–	714-635-5000
Courtyard by Marriott Anaheim	29	★★★½	75	$$$+	714-740-2645
Fairfield Inn Anaheim Disneyland Resort	44	★★★½	75	$$$+	714-772-6777
Carousel Inn & Suites	23	★★★	73	$$$	714-758-0444
The Anabella	6	★★★	72	$$$+	714-905-1050
Cortona Inn & Suites	27	★★★	72	$$$	714-971-5000
Holiday Inn Express– Anaheim Maingate Hotel	51	★★★	72	$$$+	714-772-7755
Ramada Anaheim South	66	★★★	72	$$	714-971-3553
Clarion Hotel Anaheim	25	★★★	70	$$$	714-750-3131
Ayres Inn Orange	14	★★★	69	$$$	714-978-9168
Comfort Inn & Suites	26	★★★	69	$$$–	714-772-8713
Extended Stay America Orange County–Anaheim Convention Ctr.	43	★★★	69	$$–	714-502-9988
Jolly Roger Hotel Anaheim	57	★★★	68	$$$–	714-782-7500
Best Western Plus Raffles Inn & Suites	19	★★★	67	$$$–	714-750-6100
Ramada Maingate at the Park	68	★★★	67	$$$	714-772-0440
Castle Inn & Suites	24	★★★	66	$$$–	714-774-8111
Anaheim Plaza Hotel & Suites	11	★★★	65	$$$–	714-772-5900
Best Western Plus Park Place Inn & Mini Suites	17	★★★	65	$$$	714-776-4800
Stanford Inn & Suites	75	★★★	65	$$+	714-703-1220
Travelodge Anaheim Inn & Suites on Disneyland Drive	80	★★★	65	$$+	714-774-7600
Tropicana Inn & Suites	82	★★★	65	$$$–	714-635-4082
Alpine Inn	2	★★½	64	$$	714-535-2186
Days Inn Anaheim West	31	★★½	64	$$+	714-520-0101
Anaheim Carriage Inn	8	★★½	63	$$	714-740-1440
Best Western Plus Pavilions	18	★★½	63	$$$–	714-776-0140
Hotel Menage	54	★★½	63	$$+	714-758-0900
Super 8 Motel Near Disneyland	78	★★½	62	$$	714-778-6900
America's Best Value Astoria Inn & Suites	4	★★½	61	$$	714-774-3882
Best Western Plus Anaheim Inn	16	★★½	61	$$$–	714-774-1050
del Sol Inn Anaheim Resort	33	★★½	61	$$$$–	714-234-3411

How the Hotels Compare (continued)

HOTEL	MAP NUMBER (pgs. 46–47)	OVERALL QUALITY RATING	ROOM QUALITY RATING	COST ($ = $50)	PHONE
Motel 6 Anaheim Maingate	61	★★½	61	$$–	714-520-9696
Best Western Courtesy Inn	15	★★½	60	$$$–	714-772-2470
Park Vue Inn	62	★★½	60	$$$+	714-772-3691
Days Inn Anaheim Maingate	30	★★½	59	$$	714-750-5211
America's Best Inn	3	★★½	58	$$$–	714-533-2570
Anaheim Express Inn	10	★★½	57	$$+	714-971-9000
Anaheim Quality Inn & Suites	12	★★½	57	$$+	714-991-8100
Econo Lodge Maingate	41	★★½	57	$$–	714-535-7878
Rodeway Inn Maingate	72	★★½	57	$$–	714-533-2500
Days Inn & Suites Anaheim at Disneyland Park	32	★★½	56	$$+	714-533-8830
Quality Inn & Suites Anaheim at the Park	65	★★½	56	$$–	714-774-7817
Super 8 Motel Anaheim–Disneyland Drive	77	★★	55	$+	714-778-0350
Alamo Inn & Suites Anaheim	1	★★	52	$$–	714-635-8070
Budget Inn	21	★★	50	$$	714-535-5524
Travelodge Anaheim International Inn	81	★★	50	$$	714-971-9393
Hacienda Inn & Suites	46	★★	46	$+	714-750-2101
America's Best Value Fantasy Inn & Suites	5	★	38	$$–	714-776-2815
Anaheim Discovery Inn & Suites	9	★	34	$$–	714-533-4505
UNIVERSAL AREA	MAP NUMBER (pg. 48)				
Hilton Los Angeles at Universal City	4	★★★★	87	$ x 6–	818-506-2500
Sheraton Universal Hotel	7	★★★★	85	$ x 5–	818-980-1212
Chamberlain West Hollywood	2	★★★½	81	$ x 5+	310-657-7400
Marriott Los Angeles Burbank Airport	6	★★★½	80	$$$+	818-843-6000
Holiday Inn Burbank Media Center	5	★★★	69	$$$+	818-841-4770
Best Western Hollywood Plaza Inn	1	★★½	62	$ x 5	323-851-1800
Colony Inn	3	★★½	60	$$$–	818-763-2787

Continued from page 61

DIVERSIONS Exhibits, both passive and interactive. Also includes playgrounds, video arcades, and street theater.

Though not every attraction fits neatly into the above categories, the categories provide a relative comparison of attraction size and scope. Remember, however, that bigger and more elaborate does not always mean better. Peter Pan's Flight, a minor attraction, continues to be one of the park's most beloved rides. Likewise, for many small children, there is no attraction, regardless of size, that can surpass Dumbo.

2. ARRIVE EARLY! ARRIVE EARLY! ARRIVE EARLY! This is the single most important key to touring efficiently and avoiding long lines. With your admission pass in hand, be at the gate ready to go at least 30 minutes before the theme park's stated opening time. There are no lines and relatively few people first thing in the morning. The same four rides you can experience in 1 hour in the early morning will take more than 3 hours to see after 11 a.m. Have breakfast before you arrive, so you will not have to waste prime touring time sitting in a restaurant.

From a Cincinnati, Ohio, mom:

> *Arriving early made a tremendous difference. But I'll admit that at 6:15 in the morning when I was dragging our children out of bed, I thought that we'd lost our minds. But we had so much fun that morning riding rides with no waiting in line. It was worth the early arrival.*

A couple from Austin, Texas, waxed enthusiastically:

> *I am telling everyone about your book. It saved my girlfriend and me hours and hours of waiting in line (during spring break no less!). We were first in line for the parks every morning, and boy was it worth it.*

Be aware that all park guests must pass through security, set up in open tents in the Esplanade between the two parks. If you arrive before security screening begins and go straight to the turnstiles to await admittance, you will ultimately be directed to abandon your position to go through security. If this occurs, you'll find yourself behind people who arrived 20–30 minutes after you. Therefore, if you arrive before security is set up, wait in one of the open tents for the security folks to arrive.

3. AVOID BOTTLENECKS Helping you avoid bottlenecks is what this guide is all about. Bottlenecks occur as a result of crowd concentrations and/or less-than-optimal traffic engineering. Concentrations of hungry people create bottlenecks at restaurants during the lunch and dinner hours; concentrations of people moving toward the exit near closing time create bottlenecks in the gift shops en route to the gate; concentrations of visitors at new and unusually popular rides create bottlenecks and long waiting lines; rides slow to load and unload passengers create bottlenecks and long waiting lines. Avoiding bottlenecks involves being able to predict where, when, and why they occur. To this end, we provide field-tested touring plans to keep you ahead of the crowd or out of its way (see discussion following). In addition, we provide critical data on all rides and shows that helps you estimate how long you may have to wait in line, compares rides in terms of their capacity to accommodate large crowds, and rates the rides according to our opinions and the opinions of other Disneyland visitors.

TOURING PLANS

OF UTMOST IMPORTANCE: READ THIS!

IN ANALYZING READER SURVEYS we were astonished by the percentage of readers who do not use our touring plans. Scientifically tested and proven, these plans can save you 4 entire hours or more of waiting in line. Four hours! Four fewer hours of standing, 4 hours freed up to do something fun. Our groundbreaking research that created the touring plans has been the subject of front-page articles in the *Dallas Morning News* and *The New York Times* and has been cited in numerous scholarly journals. So the question is, why would you not use them?

We get a ton of mail from both our Disneyland and Walt Disney World readers—98% of it positive—commenting on our touring plans. First, from a family of four from West Chester, Pennsylvania:

> *This book and your touring plans, without a doubt, made the trip. We followed the adult one-day plans almost to the letter. Probably the longest line we stood in was 30 minutes max during one of the [busiest] times of the year. The key was getting to the parks 30 minutes or so before opening. The plans also saved arguing over what to do next. We simply followed the guide. We are believers!*

A family from Stockton, California, descended on Disneyland Park over the Easter holiday:

> *We're not much for plans and regimentation, so we winged it the first day. It was so awful that the next day we gave one of your itineraries a shot as sort of a last-ditch alternative. It worked so well that I was telling strangers about it that night like [I was] some kind of Bible thumper.*

A mom from Aurora, Colorado, offered this:

> *We went to WDW in 2007, and I didn't use the touring plans provided because, with my kids, I didn't think the extra walking would be worth it. I decided to try out the plans in Disneyland when it was just my mom and me without the kids. It was great. I was amazed that when I got to the point where it said, "Now might be a good time to grab lunch," it was 11:15 a.m. We are going to WDW in November with the kids, and I have already put together all our touring plans from your book!*

From a mom in South Jordan, Utah:

> *Your book was my Bible for our Disneyland trip. I read it three times before our trip, and my kids skimmed through it and read several parts too. I especially loved your daily itineraries and your Cars Land advice. Thanks to Fastpasses and baby switch passes, my kids were able to ride Radiator Springs twice every day for the three days we were at the parks. I appreciated your recommendation to run over for Fastpasses for Radiator Springs at Cars Land while the rest of my family was at Disneyland in the morning.*

From a Chicago mom:

I was caught off guard while flipping through the book at how many people were complaining about the rigidity of the daily touring plans. I feel strongly that you have to go into a Disney trip with a firm plan or else all you will remember of your vacation will be the squabbles and the long lines! The daily touring plans not only allowed me to see everything that I wanted but even allowed me time to revisit my favorite attractions multiple times! Those who complain that the touring plans are too rigid need a serious reality check. Yes, they are structured, but they save you mountains of time! RELAX and use the touring plans if you are going during a busy part of the year. Not only will it save you the time that you are spending complaining about the plans in the first place, but it will also save you the complaining you will be doing when you are in line for Space Mountain for 90 minutes!

A family of six from Sacramento, California:

The Unofficial Guide *was a godsend! I was not so sure how the touring plans would work, but they went over and beyond my expectations. We went to Disneyland during spring break, a very busy time, very crowded, and we hardly spent any time at all in lines for rides (as long as we stuck to the touring plans)! At one point we would get off a ride and get right on another. We did six rides within a half hour. This trip was the first time EVER that my family and I got to do everything we wanted at Disneyland!*

WHAT'S A QUEUE?

ALTHOUGH IT'S NOT COMMONLY used in the United States, queue (pronounced "cue") is the universal English word for a line, such as one in which you wait to cash a check at the bank or to board a ride at a theme park. There's a mathematical area of specialization within the field of operations research called queuing theory, which studies and models how lines work. Because the Unofficial Guide draws heavily on this discipline, we use some of its terminology. In addition to the noun, the verb *to queue* means "to get in line," and a queuing area is a waiting area that accommodates a line. When guests decline to join a queue because they perceive the wait to be too long, they are said to balk.

TOURING PLANS:
WHAT THEY ARE AND HOW THEY WORK

We followed your plans to the letter—which at times was troublesome to the dad in our party . . . somewhat akin to testing the strength of your marriage by wallpapering together!

—Unofficial Guide reader and mother of two
from Milford, Connecticut

WHEN WE INTERVIEWED DISNEYLAND VISITORS who toured the theme park(s) on slow days, they invariably waxed eloquent about the sheer delight of their experience. When we questioned visitors who toured on moderate or busy days, however, they talked at length about the jostling crowds and how much time they stood in line. What a shame, they said, that so much time and energy are spent fighting crowds in a place as special as Disneyland.

Given this complaint, our researchers descended on Disneyland to determine whether a touring plan could be devised that would liberate visitors from the traffic flow and allow them to see any theme park in one day with minimal waiting in line. On some of the busiest days of the year, our team monitored traffic into and through Disneyland Park, noting how it filled and how patrons were distributed among the attractions. We also observed which rides and attractions were most popular and where bottlenecks were most likely to occur.

After many years of collecting data, we devised preliminary touring plans, which we tested during one of the busiest weeks of the year. Each day, our researchers would tour the park using one of the preliminary plans, noting how long it took to walk from place to place and how long the wait in line was for each attraction. Combining the information gained on trial runs, we devised a master plan that we retested and fine-tuned. This plan, with very little variance from day to day, allowed us to experience all major rides and attractions and most lesser ones in one day, with an average wait in line of less than 10 minutes at each.

From this master plan, we developed alternative plans that took into account the varying tastes and personal requirements of different Disneyland patrons. Each plan operated with the same logic as the master plan but addressed the special needs and preferences of its intended users.

Finally, after all of the plans were tested by our staff, we selected (using convenience sampling) Disneyland visitors to test the plans. The only prerequisite for being chosen to test the plans was that the guests must have been visiting a Disney park for the first time. A second group of patrons was chosen for a control group. These were first-time visitors who would tour the park according to their own plans but who would make notes about what they did and how much time they spent in lines.

When the two groups were compared, the results were amazing. On days when major theme park attendance exceeded 42,000, visitors touring without our plans *averaged* 2.6 hours more waiting in line per day than the patrons touring with our plans, and they experienced 33% fewer attractions. In 2004 the application of a cutting-edge algorithm to our touring plan software increased the waiting time saved to an average of 4 hours. Our latest advancement, introduced in 2012, gives subscribers to **touringplans.com** the ability to build personalized plans online, and then use the Lines smartphone app while inside the parks to optimize their itineraries with real-time wait time data. We expect additional research to continue to improve the performance of the touring plans in future editions.

General Overview of the Touring Plans

Our touring plans are step-by-step guides for seeing as much as possible with a minimum of standing in line. They're designed to help you avoid crowds and bottlenecks on days of moderate to heavy attendance. On days of lighter attendance (see "Selecting the Time of Year for Your Visit," page 24), the plans still save time but aren't as critical to successful touring.

What You Can Realistically Expect from the Touring Plans

Though we present one-day touring plans for both of the theme parks, you should understand that Disneyland Park has more attractions than you can see in one day, even if you never wait in line. If you must cram your visit to Disneyland Park into a single day, the one-day touring plans will allow you to see as much as is humanly possible. Under certain circumstances you may not complete the plan, and you definitely won't be able to see everything. For Disneyland Park, the most comprehensive, efficient, and relaxing touring plans are the two-day plans. Although Disney California Adventure has grown recently, you should be able to see everything in one day by following our touring plans.

Variables That Will Affect the Success of the Touring Plans

How quickly you move from one ride to another; when and how many refreshment and restroom breaks you take; when, where, and how you eat meals; and your ability (or lack thereof) to find your way around will all have an impact on the success of the plans. Smaller groups almost always move faster than larger groups, and parties of adults generally can cover more ground than families with young children. Switching off (see page 119), among other things, prohibits families with little ones from moving expeditiously among attractions. Plus, some children simply cannot conform to the "early to rise" conditions of the touring plans.

A mom from Nutley, New Jersey, writes:

> [Although] the touring plans all advise getting to parks at opening, we just couldn't burn the candle at both ends. Our kids (10, 7, and 4) would not go to sleep early and couldn't be up at dawn and still stay relatively sane. It worked well for us to let them sleep a little later, go out and bring breakfast back to the room while they slept, and still get a relatively early start by not spending time on eating breakfast out. We managed to avoid long lines with an early morning, and hitting popular attractions during parades, mealtimes, and late evenings.

And a family from Centerville, Ohio, says:

> The toughest thing about your tour plans was getting the rest of the family to stay with them, at least to some degree. Getting them to pass by attractions to hit something across the park was no easy task (sometimes impossible).

A multigenerational family wonders how to know if you are on track or not, writing:

It seems like the touring plans were very time dependent, yet there were no specific times attached to the plan outside of the early morning. On more than one day, I often had to guess as to whether we were on track. Having small children and a grandparent in our group, we couldn't move at a fast pace.

There is no objective measurement for being on track. Each group's experience will differ to some degree. Regardless of whether your group is large or small, fast or slow, the sequence of attractions in the touring plans will allow you to enjoy the greatest number of attractions in the least possible time. Two quickly moving adults will probably take in more attractions in a specific time period than will a large group comprised of children, parents, and grandparents. However, given the characteristics of the respective groups, each will maximize their touring time and experience as many attractions as possible.

Finally, if you have young children in your party, be prepared for character encounters. The appearance of a Disney character is usually sufficient to stop a touring plan dead in its tracks. What's more, while some characters continue to stroll the parks, it is becoming more the rule to assemble characters in some specific venue (such as at Mickey's Toontown), where families must queue up for photos of and autographs from Mickey. Meeting characters, posing for photos, and collecting autographs can burn hours of touring time. If your kids are into character-autograph collecting, you will need to anticipate these interruptions to the touring plan and negotiate some understanding with your children about when you will follow the plan and when you will collect autographs. Our advice is to either go with the flow or alternatively set aside a certain morning or afternoon for photos and autographs. Be aware, however, that queues for autographs, especially in Fantasy Faire and Pixie Hollow at Disneyland Park, are every bit as long as the queues for major attractions. The only time-efficient way to collect autographs is to line up at the character-greeting areas first thing in the morning. Because this is also the best time to experience the more popular attractions, you may have some tough decisions to make.

While we realize that following the touring plans is not always easy, we nevertheless recommend continuous, expeditious touring until around noon. After that hour, breaks and diversions won't affect the plans significantly.

Some variables that can profoundly affect the touring plans are beyond your control. Chief among these is the manner and timing of bringing a particular ride to capacity. For example, Big Thunder Mountain Railroad, a roller coaster in Disneyland Park, has five trains. On a given morning it may begin operation with two of the five, and then add the other three if and when they are needed. If the waiting line builds rapidly before operators decide to go to full capacity, you could have a long wait, even in early morning.

Another variable relates to the time you arrive for a show. Usually your wait will be the length of time from your arrival to the end of the presentation in progress. Thus, if the *Enchanted Tiki Room* show is 15 minutes long and you arrive 1 minute after a show has begun, your wait for the next show will be 14 minutes. Conversely, if you arrive as the show is wrapping up, your wait will be only 1 or 2 minutes.

What to Do If You Lose the Thread

Anything from a blister to a broken attraction can throw off a touring plan. If unforeseen events interrupt a plan:

1. Skip one step on the plan for every 20 minutes' delay. If, for example, you lose your billfold and spend an hour finding it, skip three steps and pick up from there, or

2. Forget the plan; organize the remainder of your day using the recommended attraction visitation times included in each attraction profile.

Flexibility

The attractions included in the touring plans are the most popular attractions as determined by more than 19,000 reader surveys. Even so, your favorite attractions might be different. Fortunately, the touring plans are flexible. If the touring plan calls for an attraction that you don't wish to experience, simply skip it and move on to the next attraction on the plan. Additionally, you can substitute similar attractions in the same area of the park. If the plan calls for riding Dumbo, for example, and you're not interested but would enjoy the Mad Tea Party (which is not on the plan), then substitute the Mad Tea Party for Dumbo. As long as the substitution is a similar attraction (it won't work to substitute a show for a ride) and located pretty close to the attraction called for in the plan, you won't compromise the overall effectiveness of the touring plan.

A family of four from South Slocan, British Columbia, found that they could easily tailor the touring plans to meet their needs:

> We amended your touring plans by taking out the attractions we didn't want to do and just doing the remainder in order. It worked great, and by arriving before the parks opened, we got to see everything we wanted, with virtually no waits! The best advice by far was to get there early!

Clip-Out Pocket Outlines of Touring Plans

Select the plan appropriate for your party, and then clip the pocket version from the back of this guide and carry it with you as a quick reference at the theme park.

Will the Plans Continue to Work Once the Secret Is Out?

Yes! First, all of the plans require that a patron be there when the theme parks open. Many Disneyland patrons simply refuse to get up early while on vacation. Second, less than 1% of any day's attendance has been exposed to the plans, too little to affect results. Last, most groups tailor the plans, skipping rides or shows according to personal taste.

How Frequently Are the Touring Plans Revised?

Because Disney is always adding new attractions and changing operations, we revise the touring plans every year. Most complaints we receive about them come from readers who are using out-of-date editions of the *Unofficial Guide*. Be prepared, however, for surprises. Opening procedures and showtimes, for example, may change, and you never know when an attraction might break down.

Tour Groups from Hell

We have discovered that tour groups of up to 200 people sometimes use our plans. Unless your party is as large as that tour group, this development shouldn't alarm you. Because tour groups are big, they move slowly and have to stop periodically to collect stragglers. The tour guide also has to accommodate the unpredictability of five dozen or so bladders. In short, you should have no problem passing a group after the initial encounter.

Bouncing Around

Many readers object to crisscrossing a theme park, as our touring plans sometimes require. A woman from Decatur, Georgia, said she "got dizzy from all the bouncing around" and that the "running back and forth reminded [her] of a scavenger hunt." We empathize, but here's the rub, park by park.

In Disneyland Park, the most popular attractions are positioned across the park from one another. This is no accident. It's good planning, a method of more equally distributing guests throughout the park. If you want to experience the most popular attractions in one day without long waits, you can arrive before the park fills and see those attractions first thing (which requires crisscrossing the park), or you can enjoy the main attractions on one side of the park first thing in the morning, and then use Fastpass for the popular attractions on the other side. All other approaches will subject you to awesome waits at some attractions if you tour during busy times of the year.

The best way to minimize bouncing around at Disneyland Park is to use one of our two-day touring plans, which spread the more popular attractions over two mornings and work beautifully even when the park closes at 8 p.m. or earlier. Using Fastpass will decrease your waiting time but will increase bouncing around because you must first go to the attraction to obtain your Fastpass and then backtrack later to the same attraction to use your pass.

Disney California Adventure is configured in a way that precludes an orderly approach to touring, or to a clockwise or counterclockwise rotation. Orderly touring is further frustrated by the limited guest capacity of the midway rides in the Paradise Pier district of the park. At DCA, therefore, you're stuck with bouncing around, whether you use the touring plan or not, if you want to avoid horrendous waits.

We suggest that you follow the touring plans religiously, especially in the mornings, if you're visiting Disneyland during busy, more crowded times. The consequence of touring spontaneity in peak season is hours of otherwise avoidable standing in line. During quieter times of year, there's no need to be compulsive about following the plans.

Touring Plan Rejection

We've discovered that you can't implant a touring plan in certain personalities without vehement rejection. Some folks just do not respond well to regimentation. If you bump into this problem with someone in your party, it's best to roll with the punches, as did this couple:

The rest of the group was not receptive to the use of the touring plans. They all thought I was being a little too regimented about planning this vacation. Rather than argue, I left the touring plans behind as we ventured off for the parks. You can guess the outcome. We took our camcorder with us and when we returned home, we watched the movies. About every 5 minutes there is a shot of us all gathered around a park map trying to decide what to do next.

Finally, as a Connecticut woman alleges, the touring plans are incompatible with some readers' bladders as well as their personalities:

I want to know if next year when you write those day schedules if you could schedule bathroom breaks in there too. You expect us to be at a certain ride at a certain time and with no stops in between. In one of the letters in your book a guy writes, "You expect everyone to be theme park commandos." When I read that, I thought, there is a man who really knows what a problem the schedules are if you are a laid-back, slow-moving, careful detail noticer. What were you thinking when you made these schedules?

A Clamor for Customized Touring Plans

We're inundated by letters urging us to create additional touring plans. These include a plan for 9th- and 10th-graders, a plan for rainy days, a seniors' plan, a plan for folks who sleep late, a plan omitting rides that "bump, jerk, and clonk," a plan for gardening enthusiasts, and a plan for single women.

The touring plans in this book are intended to be flexible. Adapt them to your preferences. If you don't like rides that bump and jerk, skip them when they come up in a touring plan. If you want to sleep in and go to the park at noon, use the afternoon part of a plan. If you're a ninth-grader and want to ride Space Mountain three times in a row, do it. Will it decrease the touring plan's effectiveness? Sure, but the plan was created only to help you have fun. It's your day.

If you really want to tailor your itinerary, we highly recommend subscribing to **touringplans.com**, where you can customize your day's to-do list down to the last snack cart. Our computers will evaluate the efficiency of your chosen attraction order, and try to suggest a better path through the park. For a truly personalized experience, some of our team members (including this book's coauthor) offer professional tour-planning services; visit **touringplans.com /disneyland-resort/touring-plans/faq** for details.

WHAT TO EXPECT WHEN YOU ARRIVE AT THE PARKS

BECAUSE EACH TOURING PLAN IS BASED on being present when the theme park opens, you need to know a little about opening procedures. Disney transportation to the parks, and the respective theme park parking lots, open 1–2 hours before official opening time.

Each park has an entrance plaza just outside the turnstiles. Usually you will be held outside the turnstiles until 30 minutes before official opening time. If you are admitted before the official opening time, what happens next depends on the season of the year and the anticipated crowds for that day.

1. **MOST DAYS** You will usually be held at the turnstiles. Sometimes you might be confined in a small section of the park until the official opening time. At Disneyland Park you might be admitted to Main Street, U.S.A.; at Disney California Adventure to Buena Vista Street. If you proceed farther into a park, you will encounter a rope barrier manned by Disney cast members who will keep you from entering the remainder of the park. You will remain here until the rope drop, when the rope barrier is removed and the park and all (or most) of its attractions are opened at the official opening time.

2. **HIGH SEASON AND HOLIDAYS** Sometimes, when large crowds are expected, you will be admitted through the turnstiles 30 minutes before the official opening time. This time, however, the entire park will be up and running, and you will not encounter any rope barriers.

3. **VARIATIONS** Sometimes Disney will run a variation of the two opening procedures described above. In this situation, you will be permitted through the turnstiles and will find that one or several specific attractions are open early for your enjoyment.

A Word about the Rope Drop

In days past, Disney cast members would dive for cover when the rope was dropped as thousands of adrenaline-charged guests stampeded to the most popular attractions. This practice occasioned the legendary Space Mountain Morning Mini-Marathon and the Splash Mountain Rapid Rampage at Disneyland Park.

Well, this scenario no longer exists—at least not in the crazed versions of years past. Recently, Disney has beefed up the number of cast members supervising the rope drop in order to suppress the mayhem. A pleasantly parental prerecorded "Please walk; don't run" announcement also seems to have a somewhat subduing effect on the straining crowds. In some cases, the rope is not even dropped. Instead, it's walked back. In other words, Disney cast members lead you with the rope at a fast walk toward the attraction you're straining to reach, forcing you (and everyone else) to maintain their pace. Not until they come within close proximity of the attraction do the cast members step aside.

So, here's the scoop. If cast members persist in walking the rope back, the only way you can gain an advantage over the rest of the crowd is to arrive early enough to be one of those close to the rope. Be alert, though; sometimes the Disney folks will step out of the way after about 50 yards or so. If this happens, you can fire up the afterburners and speed the remaining distance to your destination.

FASTPASS

FASTPASS IS A SYSTEM for moderating the waiting time for popular attractions. Here's how it works.

Your handout park map, as well as signs at respective attractions, will tell you which attractions are included. Attractions that use Fastpass will have a regular line and a Fastpass line. A sign at the entrance will tell you how long the wait is in the regular line. If the wait is acceptable, hop in line. If the wait seems too long, you can insert your park admission pass into a special Fastpass machine and receive an appointment time (for a time later in the day) to come back and ride. When you return at the appointed time, you will enter the Fastpass line and proceed directly to the attraction's preshow or boarding area with minimal further wait. There is no extra charge to use Fastpass, but you can get an appointment for only one attraction per park at a time (with a few exceptions, noted below). Interestingly, this procedure was pioneered by Universal Studios Hollywood many years ago and was pretty much ignored by major theme parks at first.

Fastpass works remarkably well, primarily because Fastpass holders get amazingly preferential treatment. The effort to accommodate Fastpass holders makes anyone in the regular line feel like an illegal immigrant. As a telling indication of their status, Disney (borrowing a term from the airlines) refers to those in the regular line as standby guests. Indeed, we watched guests in the regular line stand by and stand by, shifting despondently from foot to foot while dozens and sometimes hundreds of Fastpass holders were ushered into the boarding area ahead of them. Clearly Disney is sending a message here, to wit: Fastpass is heaven; anything else is limbo at best and probably purgatory. In either event, you'll think you've been in purgatory if you get stuck in the regular line during the hot, crowded part of the day.

FASTPASS ATTRACTIONS	
DISNEYLAND PARK	DISNEY CALIFORNIA ADVENTURE
Autopia	California Screamin'
Big Thunder Mountain	Goofy's Sky School*
Haunted Mansion Holiday (operates seasonally)	Grizzly River Run
Indiana Jones Adventure	Radiator Springs Racers*
Roger Rabbit's Car Toon Spin*	Soarin' Over California*
Space Mountain*	The Twilight Zone Tower of Terror
Splash Mountain*	World of Color
Star Tours: The Adventures Continue*	

*Denotes rides that routinely issue Fastpasses for redemption 3–7 hours later.

Fastpass, however, doesn't eliminate the need to arrive at the theme park early. Because each park offers at most eight Fastpass attractions, you still need to get an early start if you want to see as much as possible in a single day. Plus, as we'll discuss later, there's only a limited supply of Fastpasses available for each attraction on a given day. So, if you don't show up until the middle of the afternoon, you might discover that all the Fastpasses have been distributed to other guests. Fastpass does, happily, make it possible to see more with less waiting than ever before, and it's a great benefit to those who like to sleep late or who enjoy an afternoon or evening at the theme parks on their arrival day. It also enables you to postpone wet rides such as the Grizzly River Run at Disney California Adventure or Splash Mountain at Disneyland Park until the warmer part of the day.

Understanding the Fastpass System

The purpose of the Fastpass system is to reduce the waiting time for designated attractions by more equally distributing the arrival of guests at those attractions over the course of the day. This is accomplished by providing a shorter wait in line for guests who are willing to postpone experiencing the attraction until sometime later in the day. The system also, in effect, imposes a penalty—that is, being relegated to standby status—to those who opt not to use it (although spreading guest arrivals more equally decreases waiting time for standby guests too).

When you insert your admission pass into a Fastpass machine, it spits out a small slip of paper about two-thirds the size of a credit card, small enough to fit in your wallet (but also small enough to lose easily). Printed on the paper will be the name of the attraction and a specific one-hour time window—for example, 1:15–2:15 p.m. You can return to enjoy the ride any time from 1:15 to 2:15 p.m. In 2013 Disneyland Resort began strictly enforcing the one-hour Fastpass windows, allowing an unofficial 15-minute grace period and exceptions for ride breakdowns. Pay close attention to the printed time when you receive your Fastpass, and plan your return accordingly. Each person in your party must have his or her own Fastpass.

When you report back to the attraction later, you'll enter a line marked FASTPASS RETURN that will route you more or less directly to the boarding area or preshow area. Each person in your party must have his or her own Fastpass and be ready to show it to the Disney cast member at the entrance of the Fastpass return line. Before you enter the boarding area, another cast member will collect your Fastpass.

You may show up at any time within the period printed on your Fastpass begins, and from our observation, no specific time is better or worse. This holds true because cast members are instructed to minimize waits for Fastpass holders. Thus, if the Fastpass return line is suddenly inundated (something that occurs more or less by chance), cast members rapidly intervene to reduce the Fastpass line. This is done by admitting as many as 25 Fastpass holders for each standby guest until the Fastpass line is down to an acceptable length. Though Fastpass will lop off as much as 80% of the wait you'd experience in the regular line, you can still expect a short wait, but usually less than 20 minutes.

You can obtain a Fastpass any time after a park officially opens (not counting early entry), though the Fastpass return lines do not begin operating until about 35–50 minutes after opening. Thus, if the attractions at Disneyland Park open at 9 a.m., the Fastpass machines will also be available at 9 a.m., and the Fastpass line will begin operating at about 9:35 a.m.

Whatever time you obtain a Fastpass, you can be assured of a period of time between when you receive your Fastpass and the beginning of your return window. The interval can be as short as 30 minutes or as long as 7 hours depending on park attendance, the popularity of the attraction, and the attraction's hourly capacity. As a general rule, the earlier in the day you secure a Fastpass, the shorter the interval between time of issue and the beginning of your return window. If on a day that the park opens at 9 a.m., you pick up a Fastpass for Splash Mountain at, say, 9:25 a.m., your recommended window for returning to ride would be something like 10–11 a.m., or perhaps 10:10–11:10 a.m. The exact time will be determined by how many other guests have obtained Fastpasses before you.

unofficial **TIP**
Use Fastpass if the wait in the regular line is more than 30 minutes.

To more effectively distribute guests over the course of a day, the Fastpass machines bump the 1-hour return period back 5 minutes for a specific number of passes issued (usually the number is equal to about 6% of the attraction's hourly capacity). When Splash Mountain opens at 9 a.m., for example, the first 125 people to obtain a

Fastpass will get a 10–11 a.m. recommended return window. The next 125 guests are issued Fastpasses that can be used between 10:05–11:05 a.m., with the next 125 assigned a 10:10–11:10 a.m. time slot. And so it goes, with the time window dropping back 5 minutes for every 125 guests. The fewer guests who obtain Fastpasses for an attraction, the shorter the interval between the receipt of your pass and the return window. Conversely, the more guests issued Fastpasses, the longer the interval. If an attraction is exceptionally popular and/or its hourly capacity is relatively small, the return window might be pushed back all the way to park closing time. When this happens, the Fastpass machines stop issuing passes. It would not be unusual, for example, for Radiator Springs Racers at Disney California Adventure to distribute an entire day's allocation of Fastpasses by 10 a.m. When this happens, the machines simply shut down and a sign is posted saying that Fastpasses are all gone for the day.

FASTPASS GUIDELINES

- Park tickets must be activated at the front turnstiles (or Downtown Disney monorail station) before being used to obtain Fastpasses, so you can't send one family member into the park while the others snooze. However, once everyone has entered, you can send one person across to the other park with everyone's tickets to retrieve Fastpasses there.

- Don't use Fastpass unless it can save you 30 minutes or more at an attraction.

- If you arrive after a park opens, obtain a Fastpass for your preferred Fastpass attraction first thing.

- Always check the Fastpass return period before obtaining your Fastpass.

- Obtain Fastpasses for Star Tours, Space Mountain, and Splash Mountain at Disneyland Park and for Soarin' Over California, Radiator Springs Racers, World of Color, and Goofy's Sky School at DCA as early in the day as practical.

- Try to obtain Fastpasses for rides not mentioned above by 1 p.m.

- Don't depend on Fastpasses being available for ride attractions after 2 p.m. during busier times of the year.

- Make sure that everyone in your party has his or her own Fastpass.

- You can obtain a second Fastpass as soon as you enter the return period for your first Fastpass or after 2 hours from issuance, whichever comes first.

- Maximize efficiency by always obtaining a new Fastpass for the next attraction before using the first Fastpass you already hold.

- Be mindful of your Fastpass return time, and plan intervening activities accordingly.

- Rides don't dispense Fastpasses during early entry, nor while they are closed for technical difficulties or special events.

Disconnected Fastpass Attractions

Some attractions' Fastpass kiosks are not hooked up to the park-wide Fastpass distribution system. Because a disconnected attraction has no way of knowing if you have a Fastpass for another attraction, it will issue you a Fastpass at any time. In Disneyland Park, Roger Rabbit's Car Toon Spin has frequently been disconnected (but was not at press time), and Radiator Springs Racers is disconnected at DCA. *World of Color*'s Fastpasses are always disconnected from the other attractions. Disney can connect and disconnect Fastpass attractions at will, so it's possible that the disconnected lineup will vary somewhat during your visit. The use of disconnected Fastpass attractions is incorporated in our touring plans. Finally, Disneyland Park's and DCA's Fastpass systems are not connected. You can obtain a Fastpass at one park and then immediately walk to the other park and obtain another Fastpass.

When to Use Fastpass

Except as discussed below, there's no reason to use Fastpass during the first 30–40 minutes a park is open. Lines for most attractions are quite manageable during this period. In addition, this is the only time of the day when the Fastpass attractions exclusively serve those in the regular line. Regardless of time of day, however, if the wait in the regular line at a Fastpass attraction is 25–30 minutes or less, we recommend joining the regular line.

Think about it. Using Fastpass requires two trips to the same attraction: one to obtain the pass and one to use it. This means that you must invest time to secure the pass (by the way, sometimes there are lines at the Fastpass machines!) and then later interrupt your touring and backtrack in order to use your Fastpass. The additional time, effort, and touring modification required, therefore, are justified only if you can save more than 30 minutes. And don't forget: Even in the Fastpass line you must endure some waiting.

Tricks of the Trade

Although Disney stipulates that you can hold a Fastpass to only one attraction at a time, it's possible to acquire a second Fastpass before using the first. Let's say you obtain a Fastpass to Star Tours at Disneyland Park with a return time slot of 10:15–11:15 a.m. Any time after your Fastpass window begins (anytime after 10:15 a.m.), you will be able to obtain another Fastpass, for Splash Mountain, for example. This is possible because the Fastpass computer system monitors only the distribution of passes, ignoring whether or when a Fastpass is used. Finally, don't forget that you can obtain a second Fastpass 2 hours after the time of issuance of the first Fastpass if that's sooner than the return time on your first Fastpass.

When obtaining Fastpasses, it's faster and more considerate of other guests if one person obtains passes for your entire party. This means entrusting one individual with both your valuable park admission passes and your Fastpasses, so choose wisely.

Fastpass Runners

If you've ever taken a walk with a dog that runs and darts all over the place while you plod along in a straight line, you'll appreciate the concept of Fastpass running. First you choose a high-energy, inexhaustible member of your party who is quick on his feet and mature and responsible enough not to lose everyone's admission passes. Second, you give him all the passes and dispatch him to the first attraction to obtain Fastpasses for the whole group. Then, about once each hour the Fastpass runner will split from the group to get the next Fastpasses. Rinse, repeat. In Disneyland Park, for example, he would speed off to Space Mountain. Because the return time is usually 1 hour or less, it won't be long until he can scoot off again to obtain Fastpasses at Splash Mountain. And so it goes. You can even send the runner across the Esplanade to get Fastpasses at the other park, provided you have Park Hopper tickets. Collecting Fastpasses this way allows the group to spend the less-crowded early-morning time visiting popular slow-loading attractions that don't offer Fastpass. A father from Petaluma, California, shares his technique:

> The trick is to always be holding Fastpasses for the next headliner ride. Sending a runner to get the Fastpasses is easy to do, as a solo adult can quickly and easily make his/her way across the park and back to rejoin the group. A time-saving maneuver I call the Fastpass Daddy Limbo works like this: the main group gets in line for a ride (the line must be at least 15–20 minutes long) while Dad takes off to get Fastpasses for another ride. Dad returns 10–15 minutes later and rejoins his group in line by going under/over/through the railing (unclasping a chain if necessary). The dad may need to wait a few minutes to rejoin his group until they are positioned at an easily accessible point. This should be possible at other accessible lines such as Star Tours and Splash Mountain, provided that the line outside is long enough.

Fastpass+

In 2013 Walt Disney World began rolling out a new iteration of Fastpass that is expected to eventually migrate west to Disneyland. Rather than retrieve timed Fastpass tickets from kiosks inside the park, guests will use their smartphones and radio-frequency-identification-enabled electronic tickets to prearrange Fastpass times days or weeks before arriving at the resort. The quantity and quality of the ride reservation you receive may depend on the type of admission ticket you buy and the hotel room you book. Details of this officially unannounced project are in flux, but rest assured that our Lines app will be ready to address any impact to your touring plans once Fastpass+ rolls out.

SAVING TIME IN LINE BY UNDERSTANDING THE RIDES

THERE ARE MANY DIFFERENT TYPES of rides in Disneyland. Some rides, such as It's a Small World, are engineered to carry several thousand people every hour. At the other extreme, rides such as Dumbo the Flying Elephant can accommodate only around 500 people in an hour. Most rides fall somewhere in between. Lots of factors figure into how long you will have to wait to experience a particular ride: the popularity of the ride, how it loads and unloads, how many people can ride at one time, how many units (cars, rockets, boats, flying elephants, or whatever) of those available are in service at a given time, and how many staff personnel are available to operate the ride. Let's take them one by one:

1. HOW POPULAR IS THE RIDE? Newer rides such as Star Tours: The Adventures Continue or Radiator Springs Racers attract a lot of people, as do longtime favorites such as the Jungle Cruise. If you know a ride is popular, you need to learn a little more about how it operates to determine when might be the best time to ride. But a ride need not be especially popular to form long lines. The lines can be the result of less-than-desirable traffic engineering; that is, it takes so long to load and unload that a line builds up. This is the situation at the Mad Tea Party and Dumbo. Only a small percentage of the visitors to Disneyland Park (mostly kids) ride Dumbo, for instance, but because it takes so long to load and unload, this ride can form long waiting lines.

2. HOW DOES THE RIDE LOAD AND UNLOAD? Some rides never stop. They are like a circular conveyor belt that goes around and around. We call these continuous loaders. The Haunted Mansion is a continuous loader. The more cars or ships or whatever on the conveyor, the more people can be moved through in an hour. The Haunted Mansion has lots of cars on the conveyor belt and consequently can move more than 2,400 people an hour.

Other rides are interval loaders. This means that cars are unloaded, loaded, and dispatched at certain set intervals (sometimes controlled manually and sometimes by a computer). Matterhorn Bobsleds is an interval loader. It has two separate tracks (in other words, the ride has been duplicated in the same facility). Each track can run up to 10 sleds, released at 23-second or greater intervals (the bigger the crowd, the shorter the interval). In another kind of interval loader, such as the Jungle Cruise, empty boats return to the starting point, where they line up waiting to be reloaded. In a third type of interval loader, one group of riders enters the vehicle while the last group of riders departs. We call these in-and-out interval loaders. Indiana Jones is a good example of an in-and-out interval loader. As a troop transport pulls up to the loading station, those who have just completed their ride exit to the left. At almost the same time, those waiting to ride enter the troop transport from the right. The troop transport is released to the dispatch point a few yards down the line where it is launched according to whatever second interval is being used. Interval loaders of all three types can be very efficient at moving people if (1) the release (launch) interval is relatively short and (2) the ride can accommodate a large number of vehicles in the system at one time.

Because many boats can be floating through Pirates of the Caribbean at a given time and the release interval is short, almost 2,300 people an hour can see this attraction.

A third group of rides are cycle rides. Another name for these same rides is stop-and-go rides; those waiting to ride exchange places with those who have just ridden. The main difference between in-and-out interval rides and cycle rides is that with a cycle ride, the whole system shuts down when loading and unloading is in progress. While one boat is loading and unloading in It's a Small World, many other boats are proceeding through the ride. But when Dumbo the Flying Elephant touches down, the whole ride is at a standstill until the next flight is launched.

In discussing a cycle ride, the amount of time the ride is in motion is called ride time. The amount of time that the ride is idle while loading and unloading is called load time. Load time plus ride time equals cycle time, or the time expended from the start of one run of the ride until the start of the succeeding run. Cycle rides are the least efficient of all the Disneyland rides in terms of traffic engineering. Disneyland Park has 6 cycle rides, while Disney California Adventure has 10, an astonishing number for a modern park.

CYCLE RIDES AT DISNEYLAND PARK		
FANTASYLAND	**MICKEY'S TOONTOWN**	**TOMORROWLAND**
Casey Jr. Circus Train	Gadget's Go Coaster	Astro Orbitor
Dumbo the Flying Elephant		
King Arthur Carrousel		
Mad Tea Party		

CYCLE RIDES AT DISNEY CALIFORNIA ADVENTURE		
A BUG'S LAND	**PARADISE PIER**	**CARS LAND**
Flik's Flyers	Golden Zephyr	Luigi's Flying Tires
Francis' Ladybug Boogie	Jumpin' Jellyfish	Mater's Junkyard Jamboree
Mickey's Fun Wheel	King Triton's Carousel	
Tuck and Roll's Drive 'Em Buggies	Silly Symphony Swings	

3. HOW MANY PEOPLE CAN RIDE AT ONE TIME? This figure is defined in terms of per-ride capacity or system capacity. Either way, the figures refer to the number of people who can ride at the same time. Our discussion above illustrates that the greater a ride's carrying capacity (all other things being equal), the more visitors it can accommodate in an hour.

4. HOW MANY UNITS ARE IN SERVICE AT A GIVEN TIME? A unit is simply a term for the vehicle you sit in during your ride. At the Mad Tea Party the unit is a teacup, and at Alice in Wonderland it's a caterpillar. On some rides (mostly cycle rides), the number of units in operation at a given time is fixed. Thus, there are always 16 elephant units operating on the

Dumbo ride, 72 horses on King Arthur Carrousel, and so on. What this fixed number of units means to you is that there is no way to increase the carrying capacity of the ride by adding more units. On a busy day, therefore, the only way to carry more people each hour on a fixed-unit cycle ride is to shorten the loading time (which, as we will see in number 5 below, is sometimes impossible) or by decreasing the riding time, the actual time the ride is in motion. The bottom line on a busy day for a cycle ride is that you will wait longer and be rewarded for your wait with a shorter ride. This is why we try to steer you clear of the cycle rides unless you are willing to ride them early in the morning or late at night.

Other rides at Disneyland can increase their carrying capacity by adding units to the system as the crowds build. The Big Thunder Mountain Railroad is a good example. If attendance is very light, Big Thunder can start the day by running one of five available mine trains. When lines start to build, more mine trains can be placed into operation. At full capacity, a total of five trains can carry about 2,400 people an hour. Sometimes a long line will disappear almost instantly when new units are brought online. On the other hand, the queue may stop altogether for a few minutes while new units are added, extending the wait for guests who were about to board. When an interval-loading ride places more units into operation, it usually shortens the dispatch interval, so more units are being dispatched more often.

5. HOW MANY CAST MEMBERS ARE AVAILABLE TO OPERATE THE RIDE? Allocation of additional staff to a given ride can allow extra units to be placed in operation, or additional loading areas or holding areas to be opened. Pirates of the Caribbean and It's a Small World can run two separate waiting lines and loading zones. The Haunted Mansion has a short preshow, which is staged in a "stretch room." On busy days a second stretch room can be activated, thus permitting a more continuous flow of visitors to the actual loading area. Additional staff make a world of difference on some cycle rides. Often, if not usually, one attendant will operate the Golden Zephyr. This single person must clear the visitors from the ride just completed, admit and seat visitors for the upcoming ride, check that all zephyrs are properly secured (which entails an inspection of each zephyr), return to the control panel, issue instructions to the riders, and finally, activate the ride (whew!). A second attendant allows for the division of these responsibilities and has the effect of cutting loading time by 25%–50%.

BEWARE OF THE DARK, WET, ROUGH, AND SCARY

 OOPS, ALMOST FORGOT: There's a member of our team you need to meet. Called a Wuffo, she's our very own character. She'll warn you when rides are too scary, too dark, or too wet. You'll bump into her throughout the book doing, well, what characters do. Pay attention to her—she knows what she's talking about.

SAVING TIME IN LINE BY
UNDERSTANDING THE SHOWS

MANY OF THE FEATURED ATTRACTIONS at Disneyland are theater presentations. While they're not as complex as rides from a traffic-engineering viewpoint, a little enlightenment concerning their operation may save some touring time.

Most Disneyland theater attractions operate in three distinct phases:

1. First, there are the visitors who are in the theater viewing the presentation.

2. Next, there are the visitors who have passed through the turnstile into a holding area or waiting lobby. These people will be admitted to the theater as soon as the current presentation is concluded. Several attractions offer a preshow in their waiting lobby to entertain the crowd until they are admitted to the main show.

3. Finally, there is the outside line. Visitors waiting here will enter the waiting lobby when there is room and then move into the theater when the audience turns over (is exchanged) between shows.

The theater capacity and popularity of the presentation, along with the level of attendance in the park, determine how long the lines will be at a given theater attraction. Except for holidays and other days of especially heavy attendance, the longest wait for a show usually does not exceed the length of one complete performance.

Because almost all Disneyland theater attractions run continually, only stopping long enough for the previous audience to leave and the waiting audience to enter, a performance will already be in progress when you arrive. If the *Enchanted Tiki Room* show lasts 15 minutes, the wait under normal circumstances should be 15 minutes if you were to arrive just after the show began.

All Disneyland theaters (except the Main Street Cinema and some amphitheater productions) are very strict when it comes to controlling access. Unlike at a regular movie theater, you can't just walk in during the middle of a performance; you will always have at least a short wait.

GUIDED TOURS AT DISNEYLAND PARK AND DCA

FOUR GUIDED TOURS ARE OFFERED. All require a valid park admission in addition to the price of the tour. All four tours can be booked up to 30 days in advance by calling ☎ 714-781-8687 for the standard tours or ☎ 714-300-7710 for the VIP treatment. All tours are subject to change without notice. During the Halloween and Christmas seasons, special tours highlighting holiday decorations may be available in addition to the following year-round offerings.

DISCOVER THE MAGIC TOUR Kids interact with Disney characters in a sort of treasure hunt to find clues to the treasure and avoid villainous characters. Designed for ages 3–9, the frenetic, fast-paced family program lasts approximately 2½ hours and includes a frozen treat and souvenir Disney pin. Prices are $59 for the first two tickets, $49 for the third and subsequent tickets.

WELCOME TO DISNEYLAND TOUR This 2½-hour tour for first-time visitors provides a warp-speed look at pretty much the entire Disneyland Resort. Guides provide background and history of the parks, attractions, and sights as you tour both theme parks, Downtown Disney, and the Disney-owned hotels. Suffice it to say, you'll do a lot of walking.

The tour includes special reserved seats for a performance at a stage show or parade (selected locations) and two Fastpasses per person for use after the tour. The tour is reasonably priced at $25.

A WALK IN WALT'S FOOTSTEPS This 3½-hour tour offers a historical perspective on both Disneyland Park and the man who created it. It provides a lot of detail as it covers Disney's vision and the challenges in bringing the groundbreaking theme park to life. The tour includes a light lunch. Highlights of the tour are an exclusive visit to the interior of Walt's original private apartment above the Main Street firehouse (sadly, no photos are allowed inside) and a glimpse of the lobby of Club 33, where Disney was to entertain his friends and dignitaries. Unfortunately, he died 5 months before the club was finished. Cost is $109 for all ages. (The tour is considered inappropriate for younger children and those who can't walk on their own.)

VIP TOURS For the well-heeled, exclusive VIP tours are available for an eye-popping $175 per hour for up to 10 guests ($295 during peak season) with a 6-hour minimum; park admission is not included. VIP guides will arrange special parade and show seating, make dining reservations, and dispense Disneyland trivia, but they won't "back door" you past the attractions queues, which limits their utility. If you want to add unlimited expedited boarding at most attractions to your VIP tour, fork over an additional $100 per hour.

CULTIVATING THE MAGIC TOUR The latest addition to Disneyland's tour lineup is a 2-hour introduction to the resort's horticultural treasures, featuring an insider's peek at the park's remarkable landscaping efforts. The tour is offered Saturday and Sunday at 9 a.m. and Monday at 10 a.m.; the cost is $49 per guest and includes "select attraction experiences" and a souvenir pin and seed packet.

PART TWO

ESSENTIALS

 The **BARE NECESSITIES**

CREDIT CARDS

AMERICAN EXPRESS, MASTERCARD, VISA, Discover, and Japan Credit Bureau credit cards are accepted for theme park admission. Disneyland shops, fast-food and counter-service restaurants, sit-down restaurants, and the Disneyland Resort hotels also accept all the cards listed above. Some vendor carts accept credit cards while others do not—ask before you order. Disney Visa cardholders can get a private character meet and greet in Disney California Adventure's (DCA's) Hollywood Land for three hours each morning, beginning 30 minutes after rope drop; the voucher you receive (one per card per day) is valid for a free 5-by-7-inch print of any PhotoPass photo with a character. Instant application kiosks can be found in Downtown Disney, with $50 gift cards often offered as an incentive to approved applicants.

RAIN

IF IT RAINS, GO ANYWAY; the bad weather will diminish the crowds. Additionally, most of the rides and attractions at the parks are under cover. Likewise, all but a few of the waiting areas are protected from inclement weather. Some outdoor attractions—such as Tom Sawyer's Island, Mad Tea Party, Alice in Wonderland, Tarzan's Treehouse, and Gadget's Go Coaster at Disneyland Park, and Radiator Springs Racers, Redwood Creek Challenge Trail, and Golden Zephyr at DCA—may close for safety reasons in inclement weather. Radiator Springs Racers may require hours of downtime after a storm before safely reopening. Roller coasters such as Big Thunder Mountain and California Screamin' can operate in a drizzle but will close down if lightning is nearby. Fireworks are rarely canceled solely due to rain but may be scuttled by strong winds, and parades may be shortened or modified for safety. A father from Petaluma, California, recommends some supplemental supplies for wet weather, writing:

Ride operators make a token effort to use a shop vac or towels, but it's good to have your own towel even on sunny days for the water ride seats. For multiday park touring in the rain, it is good to have a second pair of shoes to switch off every night at the hotel, allowing 24 hours to dry. . . . Bringing a small fan to the room also paid off, drying shoes and jackets that got wet on Splash Mountain and Grizzly River Run.

If you get caught in an unexpected downpour, raingear can be purchased at a number of shops. Whatever you do, don't flee for the parking trams during a sudden thunderstorm, or you may find yourself in an unpleasant scene like this mother of two from Los Angeles:

It was pouring rain and the park rapidly emptied out with everyone heading for the trams that take you to the parking structure. There was complete chaos by the tram loading area [with] hundreds of people pushing and shoving—desperate to get on a tram and get out of there. The trams were arriving very sporadically and tempers were rising.

Instead, wait out the storm inside a self-paced indoor attraction, such as *Great Moments with Mr. Lincoln,* Main Street Cinema, or Innoventions at Disneyland Park, and Boudin bakery tour, Blue Sky Cellar, or Disney Animation at DCA.

VISITORS WITH SPECIAL NEEDS

DISABLED VISITORS Rental wheelchairs are available just inside both parks' main gates. Daily wheelchair rentals are $12 (manual) or $50 (electric); a $20 refundable deposit is required. Note that wheelchairs and electric convenience vehicles rented inside the parks are not permitted beyond the Esplanade. A limited supply of nonelectric wheelchairs which may be taken through the Downtown Disney district are available to rent at the three Disneyland Resort hotels.

Most rides, shows, attractions, restrooms, and restaurants are engineered to accommodate the disabled. For specific inquiries call ☎ 714-781-7290. If you have an impairment that makes it difficult for you to stand in line and navigate stairs, or otherwise need special assistance, go to City Hall on Main Street in Disneyland Park or Guest Relations in the entrance plaza at DCA and ask for a Guest Assistance Card. These passes are free and available for the disabled visitor and up to five additional guests. You should not have to show a doctor's note or proof of disability, but the card does *not* entitle you to skip the lines at attractions, as a traveler from Santa Clara notes:

Keep in mind that the Guest Assistance Pass will not necessarily cut down the time that you have to wait to board a given ride, but it will provide you with a more accessible way to board.

For guests with visual or auditory impairments, digital audio and Braille guides, assistive listening devices, captioning, and sign language services are also available through City Hall and Guest

Relations. Trained service animals are welcome but must be kept on a leash at all times. Note the special symbol on park maps designating service animal relief areas in both parks.

Close-in parking is available for the disabled; inquire when you pay your parking fee. Parking trams can accommodate guests who bring their own wheelchairs, and a special transportation van is also available (ask a parking lot cast member). Curbside drop-off is only available at the Harbor Boulevard entrance, near the stops for hotel shuttles and local buses. It may be challenging for disabled guests who don't bring their own wheelchairs to walk from there into the parks. If you don't think that you can travel the necessary distance, consider renting a chair or scooter for the length of your vacation from a third-party vendor who can deliver it to your hotel.

VISITORS WITH DIETARY RESTRICTIONS Guests on special or restricted diets, including those requiring kosher meals, can arrange for assistance at City Hall at Disneyland Park or at Guest Relations at DCA. These locations can also provide information on gluten-free menu options at restaurants in the resort. For special service at Disneyland Resort restaurants, call the restaurant one day in advance for assistance.

FOREIGN-LANGUAGE ASSISTANCE Translation services are available to guests who do not speak English. Inquire by calling ☎ 714-781-7290 or visiting City Hall at Disneyland Park or at Guest Relations at DCA.

LOST ADULTS Arrange a plan for regrouping with those in your party should you become separated. Failing this, you can leave a message at City Hall or Guest Relations for your missing person. For information concerning lost children, see page 153.

MESSAGES Messages for your fellow group members can be left at City Hall in Disneyland Park or at DCA Guest Relations.

CAR TROUBLE If you elected to decrease the chance of losing your keys by locking them in your car, or decided that your car might be easier to find if you left your lights on, you may have a little problem to deal with when you return to the parking lot. Fortunately, the security patrols that continually cruise the parking lots are equipped to handle these types of situations and can quickly put you back in business.

LOST AND FOUND The lost-and-found office is located in the Guest Services building in the Esplanade to the west of the park entrances. This location services both theme parks and the Downtown Disney complex. If you do not discover your loss until you have left the parks, call ☎ 714-817-2166.

EXCUSE ME, BUT WHERE CAN I FIND . . .

SOME PLACE TO PUT ALL THESE PACKAGES? Lockers are available at both parks for $7–$15 per day, depending on size. A more convenient solution, if you plan to spend a minimum of two or more hours in the park, is to have the salesperson forward your purchases to

Package Pickup. When you leave the park, your purchases will be there waiting for you.

GROCERIES? Several convenience stores are on Harbor Boulevard near Disneyland, but no supermarkets are within easy walking distance. The closest store with a good selection is **Food-4-Less** at 1616 W. Katella Ave. about a mile west of Disneyland Resort. See **food4less.com** or call ☎ 714-539-7497. **Target** is about a 5-minute drive south of Disneyland on Harbor. The adjacent **Viva Bargain Center** dollar store is a good place for cheap snacks and supplies.

A MIXED DRINK OR BEER? If you are in Disneyland Park, you are out of luck unless you're lucky enough to have an ultraexpensive membership to the exclusive Club 33 hidden in New Orleans Square. You will have to exit the park and try one of the hotels or Downtown Disney. At DCA alcoholic beverages are readily available.

SOME RAINGEAR? At Disneyland, raingear is available at most shops but is not always displayed. You have to ask for it. Ponchos are $8.50 for adults and $7.50 for kids, and umbrellas are $10 and up.

A CURE FOR THIS HEADACHE? Aspirin and various other sundries can be purchased on Main Street at the Emporium in Disneyland Park and at Elias and Co. at the DCA entrance plaza (they keep them behind the counter, so you have to ask).

A PRESCRIPTION FILLED? Unfortunately, there is no place in Disneyland Resort to have a prescription filled. The nearest full-service pharmacy is the Walgreens on Harbor Boulevard at Chapman Avenue, about 1.5 miles south of Disneyland.

A DOCTOR? HouseCall Physicians (☎ 800-362-7911) will make house calls to your hotel room 24/7. The fee is $350 per house call plus incidentals (such as medications dispensed) payable at the time of the visit. The closest hospital to Disneyland is the **University California Irvine Medical Center,** which is about 2 miles distant at Chapman Avenue and City Drive. For dental emergencies, there is **7 Day Dental** at 637 N. Euclid St. in Anaheim, ☎ 714-793-8986 (24 hours).

SUNTAN LOTION? Suntan lotion and various other sundries can be purchased in Disneyland Park on Main Street at the Emporium and at Elias and Co. at the DCA entrance plaza (they keep them behind the counter, so you have to ask).

A SMOKE? You won't find cigarettes for sale at Disneyland parks, and you'll have a hard time finding a place to smoke any that you bring with you. Smoking is strongly discouraged throughout the parks and resorts, though there are a few designated smoking areas.

FEMININE-HYGIENE PRODUCTS? These are available in most women's restrooms at Disneyland Resort.

CASH? Basic banking services and foreign currency exchange are provided at City Hall in Disneyland Park, Guest Relations at DCA,

Travelex in Downtown Disney, and the front desks of Disneyland hotels. At Travelex you can also exchange travelers' checks or receive cash advances on MasterCard and Visa credit cards. ATMs can be found in the following places:

AT DISNEYLAND PARK

- Outside the main entrance
- On Main Street, next to the *Disneyland Story* at the Town Square end
- At the entrance to Frontierland on the left
- Near Fantasyland Theatre
- In Tomorrowland, near Starcade

AT DOWNTOWN DISNEY

- Next to Häagen-Dazs
- At the Lego Imagination Center

AT DISNEY CALIFORNIA ADVENTURE

- Outside the main entrance
- At the phone and locker complex just inside the main entrance and to the right
- Near the restrooms at Hollywood Land
- Near the restrooms on Pacific Wharf
- Near the restrooms behind Flo's V-8 Cafe in Cars Land
- Near Mickey's Fun Wheel at Paradise Pier
- Near the restrooms across from The Little Mermaid entrance

A PLACE TO LEAVE MY PET? Pets are not allowed in the parks (except for service dogs). Kennels and holding facilities are provided for the temporary care of your pets and are located at the parking garage. If you are adamant, the folks at the kennels will accept custody of just about any type of animal. Owners of pets, exotic or otherwise, must themselves place their charge in the assigned cage. Small pets (mice, hamsters, birds, snakes, turtles, alligators, and the like) must arrive in their own escape-proof quarters. Kennels cost $20 per pet per day and are located at 1313 Harbor Blvd. For more information, call ☎ 714-781-4565. There are several other details you may need to know:

- Advance reservations for animals are not accepted.
- Only cash or Disney dollars are accepted.
- Kennels open 30 minutes before and close 30 minutes after theme park operating hours.
- Pets may not be boarded overnight.
- Guests leaving exotic pets should supply food for their pet.
- On busy days, there is a one- to two-hour bottleneck at the kennel, beginning 30 minutes before the park opens. If you need to use the kennels on such a day, arrive at least one hour before the park's stated opening time.

- Pets are fed on request only (yours, not your pet's), and there is no additional charge for food.
- Proof of current rabies and distemper vaccine is required.

A PLACE TO CHARGE MY CELL PHONE? Disneyland Park now offers special cell phone charging lockers in the locker facility near Main Street's Market House. They cost $2 per hour, and you can pick one with common connectors built-in (iPhone, Android, and BlackBerry) or a standard power outlet to use with your own charger. A few free accessible power outlets can be found around the parks (our favorites are along the stage in *Great Moments with Mr. Lincoln,* inside Miss Chris's Cabin at Big Thunder Ranch, and in the balcony in the Golden Horseshoe); just be sure not to block traffic or remove any installed plugs or covers.

CAMERAS AND MEMORY CARDS? You can buy a disposable camera, with or without a flash, in both parks. You can buy film, digital memory cards, and batteries throughout the parks. If you'd rather let professionals take the pictures, Disney PhotoPass photographers are stationed at scenic spots around the parks. They'll take your snapshot with their camera (and yours, if you request) for free, and then hand you a PhotoPass identification card, which you can continue using during your vacation. Then stop by Main Street Photo Supply in Disneyland Park or Kingswell Camera Shop in DCA (go at midafternoon to avoid long lines), or log onto **disneyphotopass.com** within 30 days of your visit to preview and purchase all your pictures. You can purchase prints individually ($15 and up) along with books, mugs, and mouse pads. Or order a photo CD with all of your high-resolution pictures for about $70, and print them at your local drugstore for less. For $100 ($70 if ordered online at least 14 days in advance of your trip) PhotoPass+ combines your photo CD (including select attraction photos) with a CD of stock images and free printed photos at character restaurants. This package is a great bargain if you take full advantage of the ride and dinner photos.

PART THREE

DISNEYLAND *with* KIDS

I am very grateful for the help your book gave me. The best part was that there were no surprises that spoiled the fun. I was ready for rain, wind, cold, expensive food, small child meltdowns, and 40-minute potty stops for the grandparents (well, maybe not quite ready for the 40-minute potty stops). I did need an hour alone in the Grand Californian bar after the third day.

—Mom from Lompoc, California

The BRUTAL TRUTH *about* FAMILY VACATIONS

IT HAS BEEN SUGGESTED that the phrase *family vacation* is a bit of an oxymoron because you can never take a vacation from the responsibilities of parenting if your children are traveling with you. Though you leave work and normal routine far behind, your children require as much attention, if not more, when traveling as they do at home.

Parenting on the road requires imagination and organization. You have to do all the usual stuff (feed, dress, bathe, supervise, comfort, discipline, and so on) in an atmosphere where your children are hyperstimulated, without the familiarity of place and the resources available at home. Though not impossible—and possibly even fun— parenting on the road is not something you want to learn on the fly.

The point is that preparation, or the lack thereof, can make or break your Disneyland vacation. Believe us: You don't want to leave the success of your expensive Disney vacation to chance. Your preparation can be organized into several categories: mental, emotional, physical, organizational, and logistical. You also need a basic understanding of the two theme parks and a well-considered plan for how to go about seeing them.

MENTAL *and* EMOTIONAL PREPARATION

MENTAL PREPARATION BEGINS with realistic expectations about your Disney vacation and consideration of what each adult and child in your party most wants and needs from his or her Disneyland experience. Getting in touch with this aspect of planning requires a lot of introspection and good, open family communication.

DIVISION OF LABOR

TALK ABOUT WHAT YOU AND YOUR PARTNER need and what you expect to happen on the vacation. This discussion alone can preempt some unpleasant surprises mid-trip. If you are a two-parent family, do you have a clear understanding of how the parenting workload will be distributed? We've seen some distinctly disruptive misunderstandings in two-parent households in which one parent is (pardon the legalese) the primary caregiver. Often, the other parent expects the primary caregiver to function on vacation as she (or he) does at home. The primary caregiver, on the other hand, is ready for a break. She expects her partner to either shoulder the load equally or perhaps even assume the lion's share so she can have a real vacation. However you divide the responsibility, of course, is up to you. Just make sure that you negotiate a clear understanding before you leave home.

TOGETHERNESS

ANOTHER DIMENSION TO CONSIDER is how much togetherness seems appropriate to you. For some parents, a vacation represents a rare opportunity to really connect with their children, to talk, exchange ideas, and get reacquainted. For others, a vacation affords the time to get a little distance,

unofficial **TIP**
Try to schedule some time alone with each of your children—if not each day, then at least a couple of times during the trip.

to enjoy a round of golf while the kids are enjoying the theme park. The point here is to think about your and your children's preferences and needs concerning your time together. A typical day at a Disney theme park provides the structure of experiencing attractions together, punctuated by periods of waiting in line, eating, and so on, which facilitate conversation and sharing. Most attractions can be enjoyed together by the whole family, regardless of age ranges. This allows for more consensus and less dissent when it comes to deciding what to see and do. For many parents and children, however, the rhythms of a Disneyland day seem to consist of passive entertainment experiences alternated with endless discussions of where to go and what to do next. As a mother from Winston-Salem, North Carolina, reported:

> *Our family mostly talked about what to do next with very little sharing or discussion about what we had seen. [The conversation] was pretty task-oriented.*

Two observations: First, fighting the crowds and keeping the family moving along can easily escalate into a pressure-driven outing. Having a plan or itinerary eliminates moment-to-moment guesswork and decision making, thus creating more time for savoring and connecting. Second, external variables such as crowd size, noise, and weather, among others, can be so distracting as to preclude any meaningful togetherness. These negative impacts can be moderated, as previously discussed in Part One, by being selective concerning the time of year, day of the week, and the time of day you visit the theme parks, as well as the number of days of your visit. The bottom line is that you can achieve the degree of connection and togetherness you desire with a little advance planning and a realistic awareness of the distractions you will encounter.

LIGHTEN UP

PREPARE YOURSELF MENTALLY to be a little less compulsive on vacation about correcting small behavioral deviations and pounding home the lessons of life. Certainly, little Mildred will have to learn eventually that it's very un–Disney-like to take off her top at the pool. But there's plenty of time for that later. So what if Matt eats hamburgers for breakfast, lunch, and dinner every day? You can make him eat peas and broccoli when you get home. Roll with the little stuff, and remember when your children act out that they are wired to the max. At least some of that adrenaline is bound to spill out in undesirable ways. Coming down hard will send an already frayed little nervous system into orbit.

SOMETHING FOR EVERYONE

IF YOU TRAVEL WITH AN INFANT, toddler, or any child who requires a lot of special attention, make sure that you have some energy and time remaining for the rest of your brood. In the course of your planning, invite each child to name something special to do or see at Disneyland with Mom or Dad alone. Work these special activities into your trip itinerary. Whatever else, if you commit, write it down so that you don't forget. Remember that a casually expressed willingness to do this or that may be perceived as a promise.

WHOSE IDEA *WAS* THIS, ANYWAY?

THE DISCORD THAT MANY VACATIONING families experience arises from the kids being on a completely different wavelength from Mom and Dad. Parents and grandparents are often worse than children when it comes to conjuring fantasy scenarios of what a Disneyland vacation will be like. It can be many things, but believe us when we tell you that there's a lot more to it than just riding Dumbo and seeing Mickey.

In our experience, most parents and nearly all grandparents expect children to enter a state of rapture at Disneyland, bouncing from attraction to attraction in wide-eyed wonder, appreciative beyond words to their adult benefactors. What they get, more often than not, is not even in the same ballpark. Preschoolers will, without a doubt, be wide-eyed, often with delight but also with a general sense of being overwhelmed by noise, crowds, and Disney characters as big as tool-sheds. We've substantiated through thousands of interviews and surveys that the best part of a Disney vacation for a preschooler is the hotel swimming pool. With some grade-schoolers and pre-driving-age teens, you get near-manic hyperactivity coupled with periods of studied nonchalance. This last phenomenon, which relates to the importance of being cool at all costs, translates into a maddening display of boredom and a "been there, done that" attitude. Older teens are frequently the exponential version of the younger teens and grade-schoolers, except without the manic behavior.

As a function of probability, you may escape many—but most likely not all—of the above behaviors. Even in the event that they are all visited on you, however, take heart; there are antidotes.

For preschoolers, you can keep things light and happy by limiting the time you spend in the theme parks. The most critical point is that the overstimulation of the parks must be balanced by adequate rest and more-mellow activities. For grade-schoolers and early teens, you can moderate the hyperactivity and false ennui by enlisting their help in planning the vacation, especially by allowing them to take a leading role in determining the itinerary for days at the theme parks. Putting them in charge of specific responsibilities that focus on the happiness of other family members also works well. For example, one reader turned a 12-year-old liability into an asset by asking him to help guard against attractions that might frighten his 5-year-old sister. Knowledge enhances anticipation and at the same time affords a level of comfort and control that helps kids understand the big picture. The more they feel in control, the less they will act out of control.

 unofficial **TIP**
The more information your kids have before arriving at Disneyland, the less likely they'll be to act out.

BASIC CONSIDERATIONS:
Is Disneyland for You?

ALMOST ALL VISITORS ENJOY Disneyland on some level and find things to see and do that they like. In fact, for many, the theme park attractions are just the tip of the iceberg. The more salient question, then (since this is a family vacation), is whether the members of your family basically like the same things. If you do, fine. If not, how will you handle the differing agendas?

A mother from Toronto wrote a couple of years ago describing her husband's aversion to Disney's (in his terms) "phony, plastic, and idealized version of life." Touring the theme parks, he was a real cynic and managed to diminish the experience for the rest of the family. As it happened, however, Dad's pejorative point of view didn't extend to the area golf courses. So Mom packed him up and sent him golfing while the family enjoyed the theme parks.

If you have someone in your family who doesn't like theme parks or, for whatever reason, doesn't care for Disney's brand of entertainment, it helps to get the attitude out in the open. We recommend dealing with the person up front. Glossing over or ignoring the contrary opinion and hoping that "Tom will like it once he gets there" is naive and unrealistic. Either leave Tom at home or help him discover and plan activities that he will enjoy, resigning yourself in the process to the fact that the family won't be together at all times.

DIFFERENT FOLKS, DIFFERENT STROKES

IT'S NO SECRET THAT we at the Unofficial Guides believe that thorough planning is an essential key to a successful Disneyland vacation. It's also no secret that our emphasis on planning rubs some folks the wrong way. Bob's sister and her husband, for example, are spontaneous people and do not appreciate the concept of detailed planning or, more particularly, following one of our touring plans when they visit the theme parks. To them the most important thing is to relax, take things as they come, and enjoy the moment. Sometimes they arrive at 10:30 in the morning (impossibly late for us Unofficial Guide types), walk around enjoying the landscaping and architecture, and then sit with a cup of espresso, watching other guests race around the park like maniacs. They would be the first to admit that they don't see many attractions, but experiencing attractions is not what lights their sparklers.

Not coincidentally, most of our readers are big on planning. When they go to the theme park, they want to experience the attractions, and the shorter the lines, the better. In a word, they are willing to sacrifice some spontaneity for touring efficiency.

We want you to have the best possible time, whatever that means to you, so plan (or not) according to your preference. The point here is that most families are not entirely in agreement on this planning versus spontaneity issue. If you are a serious planner and your oldest daughter and husband are free spirits, you've got the makings of a problem. In practice, the way this and similar scenarios shake out is that the planner (usually the more assertive or type-A person) just takes over. Sometimes daughter and husband go along and everything works out, but just as often they feel resentful. There are as many ways of developing a win-win compromise as there are well-intentioned people on different sides of this situation. How you settle it is up to you. We're simply suggesting that you examine the problem and work out the solution before you go on vacation.

THE NATURE OF THE BEAST

THOUGH MANY PARENTS DON'T REALIZE IT, there is no law that says you must take your kids to Disneyland or Walt Disney World. Likewise, there's no law that says you will enjoy Disneyland. And although we will help you make the most of any visit, we can't change the basic nature of the beast—er, mouse. A Disneyland vacation is an active and physically demanding undertaking. Regimentation, getting up early, lots of walking, waiting in lines, fighting crowds, and (often) enduring the hot California sun are as intrinsic to a Disneyland vacation as stripes are to a zebra. Especially if you're traveling with children, you'll need a sense of humor, more than a modicum of patience, and the ability to roll with the punches.

KNOW THYSELF AND NOTHING TO EXCESS

THIS GOOD ADVICE WAS MADE AVAILABLE to ancient Greeks courtesy of the oracle of Apollo at Delphi. First, concerning the "know thyself" part, do some serious thinking about what you want in a vacation. Entertain the notion that having fun and deriving pleasure from your vacation may be very different indeed from doing and seeing as much as possible.

Because Disneyland Resort is expensive, many families confuse seeing everything to get your money's worth with having a great time. Sometimes the two are compatible, but more often they're not. So if sleeping in, relaxing with the paper over coffee, sunbathing by the pool, or taking a nap rank high on your vacation hit parade, you need to accord them due emphasis on your Disney visit (are you listening?), even if it means that you see less of the theme parks.

unofficial **TIP**
You can have a perfectly wonderful time at Disneyland if you're realistic, organized, and prepared.

Which brings us to the "nothing to excess" part. At the Disneyland parks, especially if you're touring with children, less is definitely more. Trust us: It's tough to go full tilt from dawn to dusk in the theme parks. First you'll get tired, then you'll get cranky, and then you'll adopt a production mentality ("we've got three more rides and then we can go back to the hotel"). Finally, you'll hit the wall because you just can't maintain the pace.

unofficial **TIP**
Get a grip on your needs and preferences before you leave home, and develop an itinerary that incorporates all the things that make you happiest.

This mom had a great vacation, but not exactly the vacation she had been expecting:

> Unfortunately, I was unprepared for traveling with a 2-year-old. All the indoor rides were deemed too dark and scary, and all she wanted to do was see the characters (which I thought she'd be petrified of!). We had a great trip once I threw all my maps and plans out the window and just went with the flow! . . . We all would have appreciated more pool time. I would definitely warn people to think twice before bringing a 2-year-old. It is one exhausting trip!

Plan on seeing the Disneyland parks in bite-size chunks with plenty of swimming, napping, and relaxing in between. Most Disneyland vacations are short. Even if you have to stay an extra day to build in some relaxation, you'll be happier while you're there and more rested when you get home. Ask yourself over and over in both the planning stage and while you are at Disneyland: What will contribute the greatest contentedness, satisfaction, and harmony? Trust your instincts. If stopping for ice cream or returning to the hotel for a dip feels like more fun than seeing another attraction, do it—even if it means wasting the remaining hours of an expensive admissions pass.

The AGE THING

THERE'S A LOT OF SERIOUS COGITATION among parents and grandparents in regard to how old a child should be before embarking on a trip to Disneyland. The answer, not always obvious, stems from the personalities and maturity of the children, and the personalities and parenting style of the adults.

Disneyland for Infants and Toddlers

We believe that traveling with infants and toddlers is a great idea. Developmentally, travel is a stimulating learning experience for even the youngest of children. Infants, of course, won't know Mickey Mouse from a draft horse but will respond to sun and shade, music, bright colors, and the extra attention they receive from you. From first steps to full mobility, toddlers respond to the excitement and spectacle of the Disneyland parks, though of course in a much different way than you do. Your toddler will prefer splashing in fountains and clambering over curbs and benches to experiencing most attractions, but no matter: He or she will still have a great time.

An Iowa City, Iowa, mother of three says, "Get over it!":

> *Get over it! In my opinion, people think too much about the age thing. If taking your 3-year-old would make you happy, that's all that counts. End of story. It doesn't matter if the trip is really for you or your child—it's all good. You shouldn't have to jump through a bunch of hoops to give yourself permission to go.*

Somewhere between 4 and 6 years of age, your child will experience the first vacation that he or she will remember as an adult. Though more likely to remember the coziness of the hotel room than the theme parks, the child will be able to experience and comprehend many attractions. Even so, his or her favorite activity is likely to be swimming in the hotel pool.

As concerns infants and toddlers, there are good reasons and bad reasons for vacationing at Disneyland. A good reason for taking your little one to Disneyland Resort is that you want to go and there's no one available to care for your child during your absence. Philosophically, we are very much against putting your life (including your vacation) on hold until your children are older.

Especially if you have children of varying ages (or plan to, for that matter), it's better to take the show on the road than to wait until the

unofficial **TIP**
Traveling with infants and toddlers sharpens parenting skills and makes the entire family more mobile and flexible, resulting in a richer, fuller life for all.

youngest reaches the perceived ideal age. If your family includes a tod-dler or infant, you will find everything from private facilities for breast-feeding to changing tables in both men's and women's rest-rooms to facilitate baby's care.

An illogical reason, however, for taking an infant or toddler to Disneyland Resort is that you think Disneyland is the perfect vacation des-tination for babies. It's not, so think again if you are contemplating Disneyland Resort primarily for your child's enjoyment. For starters, attrac-tions are geared more toward older children and adults. Even designer play areas such as the Pirate's Lair on Tom Sawyer Island in Disneyland Park are developed with older children in mind.

unofficial **TIP**
Baby supplies—including disposable diapers, formula, and baby food—are for sale, and rockers and special chairs are available for nursing mothers.

By way of example, Bob has a friend who bought a video camera when his first child was born. He delighted in documenting his son's reaction to various new experiences on video. One memorable night when the baby was about 18 months old, he recorded the baby eating a variety of foods (from whipped cream to dill pickles) that the baby had never tried before. While some of the taste sensations elicited wild expressions and animated responses from the baby, the exercise was clearly intended for the amusement of Dad, not junior.

Along similar lines, remember when you were little and you got that nifty electric train for Christmas, the one with which Dad wouldn't let you play? Did you ever wonder for whom that train was really? Ask yourself the same question about your vacation to Disneyland Resort. Whose dream are you trying to make come true: yours or your child's?

That said, let us stress that for the well prepared, taking a toddler to Disneyland Resort can be a totally glorious experience. There's truly nothing like watching your child respond to the color, the sound, the festivity, and, most of all, the characters. You'll return home with scrapbooks of photos that you will treasure forever. Your little one won't remember much, but never mind. Your memories will be unforgettable.

If you elect to take your infant or toddler to Disneyland Resort, rest assured that their needs have been anticipated. The theme parks have centralized facilities for infant and toddler care. Every-thing necessary for changing diapers, preparing formula, and warm-ing bottles and food is available. At the Disneyland Park, the Baby Center is next to the Plaza Inn at the end of Main Street and to the right. At DCA the Baby Center is tucked out of the way next to the Ghirardelli Chocolate Factory in the Pacific Wharf area of the park. Dads in charge of little ones are welcome at the centers and can use most services offered. In addition, men's rooms in the parks have changing tables.

Infants and toddlers are allowed to experience any attraction that doesn't have minimum height or age restrictions. A mother of three from Utah wrote to us, saying:

We traveled with my 9-month-old, so we did the switching-off option a lot. However, I would appreciate it if you listed in the guide a complete list of all the rides that babies can be carried on. I was there alone with all three kids while my husband had to work for part of the time, and it would've been really nice to just look at a list of all the rides that we could've gone on with a baby.

It's actually far easier to list the attractions that you *can't* take a baby on at Disneyland. Unless a minimum height or age requirement is explicitly posted, children of any size—even handheld infants—are welcome on any ride. That includes all the family dark rides, kiddie carnival attractions, and slow-moving boats. Opposite is a table of all the rides that do impose a height restriction; if a ride isn't listed, you can bring the young 'uns along. But as a Minneapolis mother reports, some attractions are better for babies than others:

Theater and boat rides are easier for babies (ours was almost 1 year old, not yet walking). Rides where there's a bar that comes down are doable but harder. Peter Pan was our first encounter with this type, and we had barely gotten situated when I realized that he might fall out of my grasp. The [3-D] films are too intense; the noise level is deafening, and the images inescapable. You don't have a rating system for babies, and I don't expect to see one, but I thought you might want to know what a baby thought (based on his reactions).

At the Park: Jungle Cruise—didn't get into it. Pirates—slept through it. Riverboat—the horn made him cry. Small World— wide-eyed, took it all in. Peter Pan—couldn't really sit on the seat. A bit dangerous. He didn't get into it. Railroad—liked the motion and scenery. Tiki Room—loved it. Danced, clapped, sang along.

The same mom also advises:

We used a baby sling on our trip and thought it was great when standing in the lines—much better than a stroller, which you have to park before getting in line and navigate through crowds. My baby was still nursing when we went. It is impractical to go to the baby station every time, so a nursing mom should be comfortable nursing in public situations.

unofficial **TIP**
In addition to providing an alternative to carrying your child, a stroller serves as a handy cart for diaper bags, water bottles, and other necessary items.

The rental strollers at the parks are designed for toddlers and children up to 4 and 5 years old but definitely not for infants. Still, if you bring pillows and padding, the strollers can be made to work. You can alternatively bring your own stroller, but unless it's collapsible, you will not be able to take it on Disney parking lot trams.

Even if you opt for a stroller (your own or a rental), we nevertheless recommend that you also bring a baby sling or baby/child backpack. Simply put, there will be many times in the theme parks when you will have to park the stroller and carry your child. As an aside, if you

Attraction Minimum Height Requirements

DISNEYLAND PARK

AUTOPIA 32" minimum height (54" to drive unassisted)

BIG THUNDER MOUNTAIN RAILROAD 40" minimum height

GADGET'S GO COASTER 35" minimum height

INDIANA JONES ADVENTURE 46" minimum height

MATTERHORN BOBSLEDS 42" minimum height

SPACE MOUNTAIN 40" minimum height

SPLASH MOUNTAIN 40" minimum height

STAR TOURS: THE ADVENTURES CONTINUE 40" minimum height

DISNEY CALIFORNIA ADVENTURE

CALIFORNIA SCREAMIN' 48" minimum height

GOOFY'S SKY SCHOOL 42" minimum height

GRIZZLY RIVER RUN 42" minimum height

JUMPIN' JELLYFISH 40" minimum height

LUIGI'S FLYING TIRES 32" minimum height

MATER'S JUNKYARD JAMBOREE 32" minimum height

RADIATOR SPRINGS RACERS 40" minimum height

REDWOOD CREEK CHALLENGE TRAIL (rock wall and zip line only) 42" minimum height

SILLY SYMPHONY SPRINGS 40" minimum height (tandem swing)   48" minimum height (single swing)

SOARIN' OVER CALIFORNIA 40" minimum height

TUCK AND ROLL'S DRIVE 'EM BUGGIES 36" minimum height

THE TWILIGHT ZONE TOWER OF TERROR 40" minimum height

haven't checked out baby slings and packs lately, you'll be amazed by some of the technological advances made in these products.

One point that needs addressing is the previous reader's perception that there are not many good places in the theme parks for breast-feeding. Many nursing moms recommend breast-feeding during a dark Disney theater presentation. This only works, however, if the presentation is long enough for the baby to finish nursing. Shows at the Hyperion Theater at DCA are long enough at about 45 minutes, but the theater is not as dark as those that show films. *Captain EO* at Disneyland Park is way too loud, as is *Muppet-Vision 3-D* at DCA.

Many Disney shows run back-to-back with only 1 or 2 minutes in between to change the audience. If you want to breast-feed and require more time than the length of the show, tell the cast

unofficial **TIP**
Infants are easy travelers. As long as they are fed and comfortable, there is really no limit to what you can do when on the road with little ones. Food plus adequate rest is the perfect formula for happy babies.

member on entering that you want to breast-feed and ask if you can remain in the theater while your baby finishes.

If you can adjust to nursing in more public places with your breast and the baby's head covered with a shawl or some such, nursing will not be a problem at all. Even on the most crowded days, you can always find a back corner of a restaurant or a comparatively secluded park bench or garden spot to nurse.

Disneyland for 4-, 5-, and 6-year-olds

Kids in this age group vary immensely in their capacity to comprehend and enjoy Disneyland Resort. With this age group, the go/no-go decision is a judgment call. If your child is sturdy, easygoing, and fairly adventuresome, and demonstrates a high degree of independence, the trip will probably work. On the other hand, if your child tires easily, is temperamental, or is a bit timid or reticent in embracing new experiences, you're much better off waiting a few years. Whereas the travel and sensory-overload problems of infants and toddlers can be addressed and (usually) remedied on the go, discontented 4- to 6-year-olds have the ability to stop a family dead in its tracks, as this mother of three from Cape May, New Jersey, attests:

> My 5-year-old was scared pretty badly on Snow White's Scary Adventures our first day. From then on for the rest of the trip, we had to coax and reassure her before each and every ride before she would go.

If you have a retiring, clinging, and/or difficult 4- to 6-year-old who, for whatever circumstances, will be part of your group, you can sidestep or diminish potential problems with a bit of preparation. Even if your preschooler is plucky and game, the same prep measures (described later in this section) will enhance his or her experience and make life easier for the rest of the family.

Parents who understand that a visit with 4- to 6-year-old children is going to be more about the cumulative experience than about seeing it all will have wonderful memories of their children's amazement.

The Ideal Age

Though our readers report successful trips as well as disasters with children of all ages, the consensus is that children's ages ideal for family compatibility and togetherness at Disneyland are 8–12 years. This age group is old enough, tall enough, and sufficiently stalwart to experience, understand, and appreciate practically all Disney attractions. Moreover, they are developed to the extent that they can get around the parks on their own steam without being carried or collapsing. Best of all, they are still young enough to enjoy being with Mom and Dad. From our experience, ages 10–12 are better than 8–9, though what you gain in maturity is at the cost of that irrepressible, wide-eyed wonder so prevalent in the 8- and 9-year-olds.

Disneyland for Teens

Teens love Disneyland, and for parents of teens, Disneyland Resort is a nearly perfect, albeit expensive, vacation choice. Although your teens might not be as wide-eyed and impressionable as their younger sibs, they are at an age where they can sample, understand, and enjoy practically everything Disneyland Resort has to offer.

For parents Disneyland Resort is a vacation destination where you can permit your teens an extraordinary amount of freedom. The entertainment is wholesome, the venues are safe, and the entire complex of hotels, theme parks, restaurants, and shopping is easily accessible on foot. Because most adolescents relish freedom, you may have difficulty keeping your teens with the rest of the family. Thus, if one of your objectives is to spend time with your teenage children during your Disneyland vacation, you will need to establish some clear-cut guidelines regarding togetherness and separateness before you leave home. Make your teens part of the discussion and try to meet them halfway in crafting a decision with which everyone can live. For your teens, touring on their own at Disneyland is tantamount to being independent in an exotic city. It's intoxicating, to say the least, and can be an excellent learning experience, if not a rite of passage. In any event, we're not suggesting that you just turn them loose. Rather, we are just attempting to sensitize you to the fact that for your teens, some transcendent issues are involved. (Children must be at least 14 years old to enter a Disneyland Resort park without an accompanying parent or guardian.)

Most teens crave the company of other teens. If you have a solitary teen in your family, do not be surprised if he or she wants to invite a friend on your vacation. If you are invested in sharing intimate, quality time with your solitary teen, the presence of a friend will make this more difficult, if not impossible. However, if you turn down the request to bring a friend, be prepared to go the extra mile to be a companion to your teen at Disneyland. If you're a teen, it's not much fun to ride Space Mountain by yourself.

One specific issue that absolutely should be addressed before you leave home is what assistance (if any) you expect from your teen in regard to helping with younger children in the family. Once again, try to carve out a win-win compromise. Consider the case of the mother from Indiana who had a teenage daughter from an earlier marriage and two children under age 10 from a second marriage. After a couple of vacations where she thrust the unwilling teen into the position of being a surrogate parent to her half sisters, the teen declined henceforth to participate in family vacations.

Some parents have written the Unofficial Guide asking if there are unsafe places at Disneyland Resort or places where teens simply should not be allowed to go. Although the answer depends more on your family values and the relative maturity of your teens than on Disneyland Resort, the basic answer is no. Though it's true that teens (or adults, for that matter) who are looking for trouble can find it anywhere, there is absolutely nothing at Disneyland Resort that could be construed as a precipitant or a catalyst. Be advised, however, that adults consume alcohol at most Disneyland Resort restaurants outside of Disneyland Park. Also, be aware that some of the movies available at the cinemas at Downtown Disney demand the same discretion you exercise when allowing your kids to see movies at home.

About **INVITING** *Your* **CHILDREN'S FRIENDS**

IF YOUR CHILDREN WANT TO INVITE FRIENDS on your Disneyland vacation, give your decision careful thought. First, consider the logistics of numbers. Is there room in the car? Will you have to leave something at home that you had planned on taking to make room in the trunk for the friend's luggage? Will additional hotel rooms or a larger suite be required? Will the increased number of people in your group make it hard to get a table at a restaurant?

If you determine that you can logistically accommodate one or more friends, the next step is to consider how the inclusion of the friend will affect your group's dynamics. Generally speaking, the presence of a friend will make it harder to really connect with your own children. So if one of your vacation goals is an intimate bonding experience with your children, the addition of friends will possibly frustrate your attempts to realize that objective.

If family relationship building is not necessarily a primary objective of your vacation, it's quite possible that the inclusion of a friend will make life easier for you. This is especially true in the case of only children, who may otherwise depend exclusively on you to keep them happy and occupied. Having a friend along can take the pressure off and give you some much-needed breathing room.

If you decide to allow a friend to accompany you, limit the selection to children you know really well and whose parents you also know. Your Disneyland vacation is not the time to include "my friend Eddie from school" whom you've never met. Your children's friends who have spent time in your home will have a sense of your parenting style, and you will have a sense of their personality, behavior, and compatibility with your family. Assess the prospective child's potential to fit in well on a long trip. Is he or she polite, personable, fun to be with, and reasonably mature? Does he or she relate well to you and to the other members of your family?

Because a Disneyland vacation is not, for most of us, a spur-of-the-moment thing, you should have adequate time to evaluate potential candidate friends. A trip to the mall including a meal in a sit-down restaurant will tell you volumes about the friend. Likewise, inviting the friend to share dinner with the family and then spend the night will provide a lot of relevant information. Ideally this type of evaluation should take place early on in the normal course of family events, before you discuss the possibility of a friend joining you on your vacation. This will allow you to size things up without your child (or the friend) realizing that an evaluation is taking place.

By seizing the initiative, you can guide the outcome. Ann, a Redding, California, mom, for example, anticipated that her 12-year-old son would ask to take a friend on their vacation. As she pondered the various friends her son might propose, she came up with four names. One, an otherwise sweet child, had a medical condition that Ann felt unqualified to monitor or treat. A second friend was overly aggressive with younger children and was often socially inappropriate for his age. Two other friends, Chuck and Marty, with whom she had had a generally positive experience, were good candidates for the trip. After orchestrating some opportunities to spend time with each of the boys, she made her decision and asked her son,

 unofficial **TIP**
We suggest that you arrange for the friend's parents to reimburse you after the trip for things such as restaurant meals and admissions. This is much easier than trying to balance the books after every expenditure.

"Would you like to take Marty with us to Disneyland?" Her son was delighted, and Ann had diplomatically preempted having to turn down friends her son might have proposed.

We recommend that you do the inviting, instead of your child, and that the invitation be extended parent to parent (to avoid disappointment, you might want to sound out the friend's parent before broaching the issue with your child). Observing this recommendation will allow you to query the friend's parents concerning food preferences, any medical conditions, how discipline is administered in the friend's family, how the friend's parents feel about the way you administer discipline, and the parents' expectation regarding religious observations while their child is in your care.

Before you extend the invitation, give some serious thought to who pays for what. Make a specific proposal for financing the trip a part of your invitation, for example: "There's room for Marty in the hotel room, and transportation's no problem because we're driving. So we'll just need you to pick up Marty's meals, theme park admissions, and spending money."

A **FEW WORDS** *for* **SINGLE PARENTS**

BECAUSE SINGLE PARENTS ARE GENERALLY also working parents, planning a special getaway with your children can be the best way to spend some quality time together. But remember, the vacation is not just for your child—it's for you too. You might invite a grandparent or a favorite aunt or uncle along; the other adult provides nice company for you, and your child will benefit from the time with family members. You might likewise consider inviting an adult friend.

Though bringing along another adult is the best option, the reality is that many single parents don't have friends, grandparents, or favorite aunts or uncles who can make the trip. And while spending time with your child is wonderful, it is very difficult to match the energy level of your child if you are the sole focus of his or her world.

One alternative: Try to meet other single parents at Disneyland. It may seem odd, but most of them are in the same boat as you; besides, all you have to do is ask. Another option, albeit expensive, is to take along a trustworthy babysitter (18 or up) to travel with you.

The easiest way to meet other single parents is to hang out at the hotel pool. Make your way there on the day you arrive, after traveling by car or plane and without enough time to blow a full admission ticket at a theme park. In any event, a couple of hours spent poolside is a relaxing way to start your vacation.

If you visit Disneyland Resort with another single parent, get adjoining rooms; take turns watching all the kids; and, on at least one night, get a sitter and enjoy an evening out.

Throughout this book we mention the importance of good planning and touring. For a single parent, this is an absolute must. In addition, make sure that every day you set aside downtime back at the hotel.

Finally, don't try to spend every moment with your children on vacation. Instead, plan some activities for your children with other children. Then take advantage of your free time to do what you want to do: Read a book, have a massage, take a long walk, or enjoy a catnap.

"He Who Hesitates Is Launched!"
TIPS and WARNINGS for GRANDPARENTS

SENIORS OFTEN GET INTO PREDICAMENTS caused by touring with grandchildren. Run ragged and pressured to endure a blistering pace, many seniors just concentrate on surviving Disneyland rather than enjoying it. The theme parks have as much to offer older visitors as they do children, and seniors must either set the pace or dispatch the young folks to tour on their own.

An older reader writes:

Being a senior is not for wussies. At Disney [parks] particularly, it requires courage and pluck. Things that used to be easy take a lot of effort, and sometimes your brain has to wait for your body to catch up. Half the time, your grandchildren treat you like a crumbling ruin, amd then turn around and trick you into getting on a roller coaster in the dark. Seniors have to be alert and not trust anyone. Not their children or even the Disney people, and especially not their grandchildren. When your grandchildren want you to go on a ride, don't follow along blindly like a lamb to the slaughter. Make sure

*you know what the ride is all about. Stand your ground and do not
waffle. He who hesitates is launched!*

If you don't get to see much of your grandchildren, you might
think that Disneyland is the perfect place for a little bonding and
togetherness. Wrong! Disneyland can potentially send children into
system overload and precipitates behaviors that pose a challenge
even to adoring parents, never mind grandparents. You don't take
your grandchildren straight to Disneyland for the same reason you
don't buy your 16-year-old son a Ferrari: Handling it safely and well
requires some experience.

Begin by spending time with your grandchildren in an environment
that you can control. Have them over one at a time for dinner and to
spend the night. Check out how they respond to your oversight and discipline. Most of all, zero in on whether you are compatible, enjoy each
other's company, and have fun together. Determine that you can set
limits and that they will accept those limits. When you reach this stage,
you can contemplate some outings to the zoo, the mall, or the state fair.
Gauge how demanding your grandchildren are when you are out of the
house. Eat a meal or two in a full-service restaurant to get a sense of
their social skills and their ability to behave appropriately. Don't expect
perfection, and be prepared to modify your behavior a little too. As a
senior friend of mine told her husband (none too decorously), "You
can't see Disneyland sitting on a stick."

If you have a good relationship with your grandchildren and have
had a positive one-on-one experience taking care of them, you might
consider a trip to Disneyland. If you do, we have two recommendations. Visit Disneyland without them to get an idea of what you're
getting into. A scouting trip will also provide you an opportunity to
enjoy some of the attractions that won't be on the itinerary when you
return with the grandkids.

Tips for Grandparents

1. It's best to take one grandchild at a time, two at the most. Cousins can be better than siblings because they don't fight as much. To preclude sibling jealousy,
   try connecting the trip to a child's milestone, such as finishing the sixth grade.

2. Let your grandchildren help plan the vacation, and keep the first one short. Be
   flexible, and don't overplan.

3. Discuss mealtimes and bedtime. Fortunately, many grandparents are on an
   early dinner schedule, which works nicely with younger children.

4. Gear plans to your grandchildren's age levels, because if they're not happy,
   you won't be happy.

5. Create an itinerary that offers some supervised activities for children in case
   you need a rest.

6. If you're traveling by car, this is the one time we highly recommend earphones
   or earbuds. Kids' musical tastes are vastly different from most grandparents'.
   It's simply more enjoyable when everyone can listen to his or her own
   preferred style of music, at least for some portion of the trip.

7. Take along a night-light.

8. Carry a notarized statement from parents for permission for medical care in case of an emergency. Also be sure that you have insurance information and copies of any prescriptions for medicines the kids may take. Ditto for eyeglass prescriptions.

9. Tell your grandchildren about any medical problems you may have, so they can be prepared if there's an emergency.

10. Many attractions and hotels offer discounts for seniors, so be sure to check ahead of time for bargains.

11. Plan your evening meal early to avoid long waits. And make reservations if you're dining in a popular spot, even if it's early. Take some crayons and paper to keep kids occupied. If planning a family-friendly trip seems overwhelming, try a tour operator–travel agent aimed at kids and their grandparents.

HOW *to* CHILDPROOF *a* HOTEL ROOM

TODDLERS AND SMALL CHILDREN up to 3 years of age (and sometimes older) can wreak mayhem if not outright disaster in a hotel room. They're mobile, curious, and amazingly fast, and they have a penchant for turning the most seemingly innocuous furnishing or decoration into a lethal weapon. Here's what to look for.

Always begin by checking the room for hazards that you cannot neutralize, such as balconies, chipping paint, cracked walls, sharp surfaces, shag carpeting, and windows that can't be secured shut. If you encounter anything that you don't like or is too much of a hassle to fix, ask for another room.

If you use a crib supplied by the hotel, make sure the mattress is firm and covers the entire bottom of the crib. If there is a mattress cover, it should fit tightly. Slats should be 2⅜ inches (about the width of a soda can) or less apart. Test the drop sides to ensure that they work properly and that your child cannot release them accidentally. Examine the crib from all angles (including from underneath) to make sure that it has been assembled correctly and that there are no sharp edges. Check for chipping paint and other potentially toxic substances that your child might ingest. Wipe down surfaces that your child might touch to diminish the potential of infection transmitted from a previous occupant. Finally, position the crib away from drape cords, heaters, wall sockets, and air conditioners.

If your infant can turn over, we recommend changing him or her on a pad on the floor. Likewise, if you have a child seat of any sort, place it where it cannot be knocked over, and always strap your child in.

If your child can roll, crawl, or walk, you should bring about eight electrical outlet covers and some cord to tie cabinets shut and to bind drape cords and the like out of reach. Check for appliances, lamps, ashtrays, ice buckets, and anything else that your child might pull down on him- or herself. Have the hotel remove coffee tables with sharp edges and both real and artificial plants that are within your child's reach. Round up items from tables and countertops such as matchbooks, courtesy toiletries, and drinking glasses and store them out of reach.

If the bathroom door can be accidentally locked, cover the locking mechanism with duct tape or a doorknob cover. Use the security chain or upper latch on the room's entrance door to ensure that your child doesn't open it without your knowledge.

Inspect the floor and remove pins, coins, and other foreign objects that your child might find. Don't forget to check under beds and furniture. One of the best tips we've heard came from a Fort Lauderdale, Florida, mother who crawls around the room on her hands and knees in order to see possible hazards from her child's perspective.

If you rent a suite, you'll have more territory to childproof and will have to deal with the possible presence of cleaning supplies, a stove, a refrigerator, cooking utensils, and low cabinet doors, among other things. Sometimes the best option is to seal off the kitchen with a folding safety gate.

PHYSICAL PREPARATION

YOU'LL FIND THAT SOME PHYSICAL CONDITIONING, coupled with a realistic sense of the toll that Disneyland takes on your body, will preclude falling apart in the middle of your vacation. As one of our readers put it, "If you pay attention to eat, heat, feet, and sleep, you'll be OK."

As you contemplate the stamina of your family, it's important to understand that somebody is going to run out of steam first, and when they do, the whole family will be affected. Sometimes a cold drink or a snack will revive the flagging member. Sometimes, however, no amount of cajoling or treats will work. In this situation it's crucial that you recognize that the child, grandparent, or spouse is at the end of his or her rope. The correct decision is to get them back to the hotel. Pushing the exhausted beyond their capacity will spoil the day for them—and you. Accept that stamina and energy levels vary, and be prepared to administer to members of your family who poop out. One more thing: No guilt trips. "We've driven 300 miles to take you to Disneyland and now you're going to ruin everything!" is not an appropriate response.

unofficial **TIP**
If your children (or you, for that matter) think that wearing socks isn't cool, get over it! Bare feet, whether encased in Nikes, Weejuns, Docksides, or Crocs, will turn into lumps of throbbing red meat if you tackle a Disney park without socks.

THE AGONY OF THE FEET

IF YOU SPEND A DAY AT DISNEYLAND PARK, you will walk 3–6 miles! If you walk to the park from your hotel, you can add 1–2 miles, and tack on another couple of miles if you park-hop to DCA. The walking, however, will be nothing like a 5-mile hike in the woods. At Disneyland Park and DCA, you will be in direct sunlight most of the time, navigate through huge jostling crowds, walk on hot pavement, and endure waits in line between bursts of walking. The bottom line, if you haven't figured it out, is that Disney theme parks (especially in the summer) are not for wimps!

Though most children are active, their normal play usually doesn't condition them for the exertion of touring a Disney theme park. We recommend starting a program of family walks six weeks or more before your trip. A Pennsylvania mom who did just that offers the following:

> We had our 6-year-old begin walking with us a bit every day one month before leaving—when we arrived, her little legs could carry her and she had a lot of stamina.

A father of two had this to say:

> My wife walked with my son to school every day when it was nice. His stamina was outstanding.

A Riverside, Utah, dad forgot to train this year:

> I think you really need to stress the importance of starting a walking regimen before going to Disneyland. Last year we had a six-day hopper, and I started walking a month ahead and ran around that place like a champ. This year I didn't walk much at all and was worn out the first day, and we only had a five-day hopper!

The first thing you need to do, immediately after making your hotel reservation, is to get thee to a footery. Take the whole family to a shoe store and buy each member the best pair of walking, hiking, or running shoes you can afford. When trying on the shoes, wear exactly the kind of socks that you will wear when using them to hike. Do not under any circumstances attempt to tour Disneyland shod in plastic sandals, cheap flip-flops, loafers, or any kind of high heel or platform shoe (though one of our authors swears by high-quality leather sandals or river-rafting footwear, especially for water rides).

Good socks are as important as good shoes. When you walk, your feet sweat like a mule in a peat bog, and moisture increases friction. To minimize friction, wear a pair of SmartWool or CoolMax hiking socks, available at most outdoor retail (camping equipment) stores, as well as Target and online retailers. To further combat moisture, dust your feet with some antifungal talcum powder.

unofficial **TIP**
Be sure to give your kids adequate recovery time between training walks (48 hours will usually be enough), however, or you'll make the problem worse.

Now that you have some good shoes and socks, the next thing to do is to break the shoes in. You can accomplish this painlessly by wearing the shoes in the course of normal activities for about three weeks.

Once the shoes are broken in, it's time to start walking. The whole family will need to toughen up their feet and build endurance. As you begin, remember that little people have little strides, and though your 6-year-old may create the appearance of running circles around you, consider that (1) he won't have the stamina to go at that pace very long, and (2) more to the point, he probably has to take two strides or so to every one of yours to keep up.

Start by taking short walks around the neighborhood, walking on pavement, and increasing the distance about 0.25 mile on each outing. Older children will shape up quickly. Younger children should build endurance more slowly and incrementally. Increase distance until you can manage a 6- or 7-mile hike without requiring CPR. And remember, you're not training to be able to walk 6–7 miles just once; at Disneyland you will be hiking 5–7 miles or more almost every day of your visit. So unless you plan to crash after the first day, you need to prepare your feet to walk long distances for three to five consecutive days.

unofficial TIP
If your child is age 8 or younger, we recommend regular foot inspections whether he or she understands the hot spot idea or not. Even the brightest child will fail to sound off when distracted.

Not all feet are created equal. Some folks are blessed with really tough feet, whereas the feet of others sprout blisters if you look at them sideways. Assuming that there's nothing wrong with either shoes or socks, a few brisk walks will clue you in to what kind of feet your family members have. If you have a tenderfooted family member, walks of incrementally increased distances will usually toughen up his or her feet to some extent. For those whose feet refuse to toughen, your only alternative is preventive care. After several walks, you will know where your tenderfoot tends to develop blisters. If you can anticipate where blisters will develop, you can cover sensitive spots in advance with moleskin, a friction-resistant adhesive dressing.

When you initiate your walking program, teach your children to tell you if they feel a hot spot on their feet. This is the warning that a blister is developing. If your kids are too young, oblivious, or preoccupied, or don't understand the concept, your best bet is to make regular foot checks. Have your children remove their shoes and socks and present their feet for inspection. Look for red spots and blisters, and ask if they have any places on their feet that hurt.

unofficial TIP
If you have a child who will physically fit in a stroller, rent one, no matter how well conditioned your family is.

During your conditioning, and also at Disneyland, carry a foot emergency kit in your day pack or hip pack. The kit should contain gauze, Betadine antibiotic ointment, an assortment of Band-Aid Blister Bandages, a sewing needle or some such to drain blisters, as well as matches to sterilize the needle. An extra pair of dry socks and talc are optional.

If you discover a hot spot, dry the foot and cover the spot immediately with a blister bandage. If a blister has fully or partially developed, first air out and dry the foot. Next, using a sterile needle, drain the fluid but do not remove the top skin. Clean the area with Betadine, and place a Band-Aid Blister Bandage over the blister. If you do not have Band-Aid Blister Bandages, do not try to cover the hot spot or blister with regular Band-Aids. Regular Band-Aids slip and wad up.

A stroller will provide the child the option of walking or riding, and, if he poops out, you won't have to carry him. Even if your child hardly uses the stroller, it serves as a convenient place for water bottles and other stuff you may not feel like carrying. Strollers at Disneyland are covered in detail on pages 135–138.

SLEEP, REST, AND RELAXATION

OK, WE KNOW THAT THIS DISCUSSION is about physical preparation before you go, but this concept is so absolutely critical that we need to tattoo it on your brain right now.

Physical conditioning is important but is not a substitute for rest. Even marathon runners need recovery time. If you push too hard and try to do too much, you'll either crash or, at a minimum, turn what should be fun into an ordeal. Rest means plenty of sleep at night and, if possible, naps during the afternoon and planned breaks in your vacation itinerary. And don't forget that the brain needs rest and relaxation as well as the body. The stimulation inherent in touring a Disney theme park is enough to put many children and some adults into system overload. It is imperative that you remove your family from this unremitting assault on the senses and do something relaxing and quiet such as swimming or reading.

unofficial **TIP**
If your kids are little and don't mind a hairdo change, consider getting them a short haircut before you leave home. Not only will they be cooler and more comfortable, but— especially with your girls—you'll save them (and yourselves) the hassle of tangles and about 20 minutes of foo-fooing a day.

The theme parks are pretty big, so don't try to see everything in one day. Even during the off-season, when the crowds are smaller and the temperatures more pleasant, the size of the theme parks will exhaust most children under age 8 by lunchtime. A Texas family underscores the importance of naps and rest:

> Despite not following any of your tours, we did follow the theme of visiting a specific park in the morning, leaving midafternoon for either a nap back at the room or a trip to the pool, and then returning to one of the parks in the evening. On the few occasions when we skipped your advice, I was muttering to myself by dinner. I can't tell you what I was muttering.

When it comes to naps, this mom does not mince words:

> One last thing for parents of small kids—take the book's advice and get out of the park and take the nap, take the nap, TAKE THE NAP! Never in my life have I seen so many parents screaming at, ridiculing, or slapping their kids. (What a vacation!) Disney [parks are] overwhelming for kids and adults.

A mom from Rochester, New York, was equally adamant:

> [You] absolutely must rest during the day. Kids went from 8 a.m. to

9 p.m. in the park. Kids did great that day, but we were all completely worthless the next day. Definitely must pace yourself.

If you plan to return to your hotel at midday and would like your room made up, let housekeeping know.

Routines That Travel

If when at home you observe certain routines—for example, reading a book before bed or having a bath first thing in the morning—try to incorporate these familiar activities into your vacation schedule. They will provide your children with a sense of security and normalcy.

Maintaining a normal routine is especially important with toddlers, as a mother of two from Lawrenceville, Georgia, relates:

The first day, we tried an early start, so we woke the children (ages 2 and 4) and hurried them to get going. BAD IDEA with toddlers. This put them off schedule for naps and meals the rest of the day. It is best to let young ones stay on their regular schedule and see Disney at their own pace, and you'll have much more fun.

DEVELOPING *a* GOOD PLAN

ALLOW YOUR CHILDREN to participate in the planning of your time at Disneyland. Guide them diplomatically through the options, establishing advance decisions about what to do each day. Begin with your trip to Disneyland, deciding what time to depart, who sits by the window, whether to stop for meals or eat in the car, and so on. For the Disneyland part of your vacation, build consensus for wake-up call, bedtime, and building naps into the itinerary, and establish ground rules for eating, buying refreshments, and shopping. Determine the order for visiting the two theme parks and make a list of must-see attractions. To help you fill in the blanks of your days, and especially to prevent you from spending most of your time standing in line, we offer a number of field-tested touring plans. The plans are designed to minimize your

---

THE GREAT DISNEYLAND EXPEDITION

COCAPTAINS Mary and Jack Shelton

TEAM MEMBERS Lynn and Jimmy Shelton

EXPEDITION FUNDING The main Expedition Fund will cover everything except personal purchases. Each team member will receive $40 for souvenirs and personal purchases. Anything above $40 will be paid for by team members with their own money.

EXPEDITION GEAR Each team member will wear an official expedition T-shirt and carry a hip pack.

PRE-DEPARTURE Jack makes dining reservations at Disneyland restaurants. Mary, Lynn, and Jimmy make up trail mix and other snacks for the hip packs.

SHELTON FAMILY ITINERARY

DAY 1: FRIDAY

6:30 p.m.	Dinner
After dinner	Pack car
10 p.m.	Lights out

DAY 2: SATURDAY

7 a.m.	Wake up!
7:15 a.m.	Breakfast
8 a.m.	Depart Portland for Hampton Inn Oakland–Hayward; Confirmation #DE56432; Lynn rides shotgun
About noon	Stop for lunch; Jimmy picks restaurant
7 p.m.	Dinner
9:30 p.m.	Lights out

DAY 3: SUNDAY

7 a.m.	Wake up!
7:30 a.m.	Breakfast
8:15 a.m.	Depart Oakland for Disneyland, Disneyland Hotel; Confirmation #L124532; Jimmy rides shotgun
About noon	Stop for lunch; Lynn picks restaurant
5 p.m.	Check in, buy park admissions, and unpack
6–7 p.m.	Mary and Jimmy shop for breakfast food for cooler
7:15 p.m.	Dinner at Rainforest Cafe at Downtown Disney
After dinner	Explore Downtown Disney
10 p.m.	Lights out

DAY 4: MONDAY

7 a.m.	Wake up! Cold breakfast from cooler in room
8 a.m.	Depart room for Disneyland Park
Noon	Lunch at park
1 p.m.	Return to hotel for swimming and a nap
5 p.m.	Return to park for touring, dinner, and *Fantasmic!*
9:30 p.m.	Return to hotel
10:30 p.m.	Lights out

DAY 5: TUESDAY

7 a.m.	Wake up! Cold breakfast from cooler in room
7:45 a.m.	Depart room for DCA
Noon	Lunch at park
2:30 p.m.	Return to hotel for swimming and a nap
6 p.m.	Drive to dinner at Outback Steakhouse
7:30 p.m.	Return to DCA for touring
10 p.m.	Return to hotel
11 p.m.	Lights out

DAY 6: WEDNESDAY	
ZZZZZZ!	Lazy morning—sleep in!
10:30 a.m.	Late-morning swim
Noon	Check out of Disneyland Hotel
1 p.m.	Fast-food lunch
1:45 p.m.	Depart Anaheim for Hollywood; Sheraton Universal Hotel; Confirmation #3542986X; Lynn rides shotgun
7:30 p.m.	Dinner at Universal CityWalk
9:15 p.m.	Return to hotel
10:30 p.m.	Lights out
DAY 7: THURSDAY	
7 a.m.	Wake up! Cold breakfast from cooler in room
7:45 a.m.	Depart for Universal Studios
11:30 a.m.	Lunch at park
4:45 p.m.	Return to hotel for downtime
7:30 p.m.	Dinner at Asakuma Rice, 848 N. La Cienga Blvd., West Hollywood
10 p.m.	Return to hotel
11:45 p.m.	Lights out
DAY 8: FRIDAY	
7:30 a.m.	Wake up!
8:30 a.m.	After fast-food breakfast, depart for Vagabond Inn Executive, Old Town Sacramento; Confirmation #SD234; Jimmy rides shotgun
About noon	Stop for lunch; Lynn picks restaurant
7 p.m.	Dinner
10 p.m.	Lights out
DAY 9: SATURDAY	
7 a.m.	Wake up!
7:45 a.m.	Depart for home after fast-food breakfast; Lynn rides shotgun
About noon	Stop for lunch; Jimmy picks restaurant
5:30 p.m.	Home, sweet home!

waiting time at each park by providing step-by-step itineraries that route you counter to the flow of traffic. The plans are explained in greater detail starting on page 72.

Generally, it's better to just sketch in the broad strokes on the master plan. The detail of what to do when you actually arrive at the park can be decided the night before you go, or with the help of one of our touring plans once you get there. Above all, be flexible. One important caveat: Make sure that you keep any promises or agreements that you make when planning. They may not seem important to you, but they will to your children, who will remember for a long, long time if you let them down.

The more you can agree to and nail down in advance, the less potential you'll have for disagreement and confrontation once you arrive.

unofficial **TIP**

To keep your thinking fresh and to adequately cover all bases, develop your plan in two or three family meetings no longer than 40 minutes each. You'll discover that all members of the family will devote a lot of thought to the plan both in and between meetings. Don't try to anticipate every conceivable contingency, or you'll end up with something as detailed and unworkable as the tax code.

Because children are more comfortable with the tangible than the conceptual, and also because they sometimes have short memories, we recommend typing up all of your decisions and agreements and providing a copy to each child. Create a fun document, not a legalistic one. You'll find that your children will review it in anticipation of all the things they will see and do, will consult it often, and will even read it to their younger siblings.

By now you're probably wondering what one of these documents looks like, so we've provided a sample on pages 122–123. Incidentally, this itinerary reflects the preferences of its creators, the Shelton family, and is not meant to be offered as an example of an ideal itinerary. It does, however, incorporate many of our most basic and strongly held recommendations, such as setting limits and guidelines in advance, getting enough rest, getting to the theme parks early, and saving time and money by having a cooler full of food for breakfast. As you will see, the Sheltons go pretty much full tilt without much unstructured time and will probably be exhausted by the time they get home, but that's their choice. One more thing—the Sheltons visited Disneyland in late June, when all of the theme parks stay open late.

Notice that the Sheltons' itinerary on pages 122–123 provides minimum structure and maximum flexibility. It specifies which park the family will tour each day without attempting to nail down exactly what the family will do there. No matter how detailed your itinerary is, be prepared for surprises at Disneyland, both good and bad. If an unforeseen event renders part of the plan useless or impractical, just roll with it. And always remember that it's your itinerary; you created it, and you can change it. Just try to make any changes the result of family discussion and be especially careful not to scrap an element of the plan that your children perceive as something you promised them.

■ LOGISTIC PREPARATION

WHEN WE RECENTLY LAUNCHED into our spiel about good logistic preparation for a Disneyland vacation, a friend from Phoenix said, "Wait, what's the big deal? You pack clothes, a few games for the car, and then go!" So OK, we confess, that will work, but life can be sweeter and the vacation smoother (as well as less expensive) with the right gear.

CLOTHING

LET'S START WITH CLOTHES. We recommend springing for vacation uniforms. Buy for each child several sets of jeans (or shorts) and

T-shirts, all matching, and all the same. For a one-week trip, for example, get each child three pairs of khaki shorts, three light-yellow T-shirts, and three pairs of SmartWool or CoolMax hiking socks. What's the point? First, you don't have to play fashion designer, coordinating a week's worth of stylish combos. Each morning

the kids put on their uniform. It's simple, it saves time, and there are no decisions to make or arguments about what to wear. Second, uniforms make your children easier to spot and keep together in the theme parks. Third, the uniforms give your family, as well as the vacation itself, some added identity. If you're like the Shelton family who created the sample itinerary in the previous section, you might go so far as to create a logo for the trip to be printed on the shirts.

When it comes to buying your uniforms, we have a few suggestions. Purchase well-made, durable shorts or jeans that will serve your children well beyond the vacation. Active children can never have too many pairs of shorts or jeans. As far as the T-shirts go, buy short-sleeve shirts in light colors for warm weather, or long-sleeve, darker-colored T-shirts for cooler weather. We suggest that you purchase your colored shirts from a local T-shirt printing company. These firms will be happy to sell you either printed T-shirts or unprinted T-shirts (called blanks)

with long or short sleeves. You can select from a wide choice of colors not generally available in retail clothing stores and will not have to worry about finding the sizes you need. Plus, the shirts will cost a fraction of what a clothing retailer would charge. Most shirts come in the more durable 100% cotton or in the more wrinkle-resistant 50% cotton and 50% polyester (50–50s). The cotton shirts are a little cooler and more comfortable in hot, humid weather. The 50–50s dry a bit faster if they get wet.

LABELS A great idea, especially for younger children, is to attach labels with your family name, hometown, the name of your hotel, the dates of your stay, and your cell phone number inside the shirt—for example:

**HODDER FAMILY OF DENVER, CO.;
CAMELOT INN; MAY 5–12; 303-555-2108**

Instruct your smaller children to show the label to an adult if they get separated from you. Elimination of the child's first name (which most children of talking age can articulate in any event) allows you to order labels that are all the same, that can be used by anyone in the family, and that can also be affixed to such easily lost items as caps, hats, jackets, hip packs, ponchos, and umbrellas. If fooling with labels sounds like too much of a hassle, check out "Lost Children" (see page 153) for some alternatives.

DRESSING FOR COOLER WEATHER Southern California experiences temperatures all over the scale November–March, so it could be a bit chilly if you visit during those months. Our suggestion is to layer: for example, a breathable, waterproof or water-resistant Windbreaker over a light, long-sleeve polypro shirt over a long-sleeve T-shirt. As with the baffles of a sleeping bag or down coat, it is the air trapped between the layers that keeps you warm. If all the layers are thin, you won't be left with something bulky to cart around if you want to pull off one or more. Later in this section, we'll advocate wearing a hip pack. Each layer should be sufficiently compactible to fit easily in that hip pack along with whatever else is in it.

ACCESSORIES

I (BOB) WANTED TO CALL THIS PART "Belts and Stuff," but our editor (who obviously spends a lot of time at Macy's) thought "Accessories" put a finer point on it. In any event, we recommend pants for your children with reinforced elastic waistbands that eliminate the need to wear a belt (one less thing to find when you're trying to leave). If your children like belts or want to carry an item suspended from their belts, buy them military-style 1½-inch-wide web belts at any Army–Navy surplus or camping-equipment store. The belts weigh less than half as much as leather, are cooler, and are washable.

SUNGLASSES Smog notwithstanding, the California sun is so bright and the glare so blinding that we recommend sunglasses for each family member. For children and adults of all ages, a good accessory item is a polypro eyeglass strap for spectacles or sunglasses. The best models have a little device for adjusting the amount of slack in the strap. This allows your child to comfortably hang sunglasses from his or her neck when indoors or, alternately, to secure them fast to his or her head while experiencing a fast ride outdoors.

HIP PACKS AND WALLETS Unless you are touring with an infant or toddler, the largest thing anyone in your family should carry is a hip pack or fanny pack. Each person should have one. The pack should be large enough to carry at least a half-day's worth of snacks and other items deemed necessary (lip balm, bandanna, antibacterial hand gel, and so on) and still have enough room left to stash a hat, poncho, or light Windbreaker. We recommend buying full-size hip packs at outdoor retailers as opposed to small, child-size hip packs. The packs are light; can be made to fit any child large enough to tote a hip pack; have slip-resistant, comfortable, wide belting; and will last for years.

Do not carry billfolds or wallets, car keys, Disney Resort IDs, or room keys in your hip packs. We usually give this advice because hip packs are vulnerable to thieves (who snip them off and run), but pickpocketing and theft are not all that common at Disneyland. In this instance, the advice stems from a tendency of children to inadvertently drop their wallet in the process of rummaging around in their hip packs for snacks and other items.

You should weed through your billfold and remove to a safe place anything that you will not need on your vacation (photos, library card, department store credit cards, business cards, and so on). In addition to having a lighter wallet to lug around, you will decrease your exposure in the event that your wallet is lost or stolen. When we are working at Disneyland, we carry a small profile billfold with a driver's license, a credit card, our room key, and a small amount of cash. You don't need anything else.

DAY PACKS We see a lot of folks at Disneyland carrying day packs (that is, small, frameless backpacks) and/or water bottle belts that strap around your waist. Day packs might be a good choice if you plan to carry a lot of camera equipment or if you need to carry baby supplies on your person. Otherwise, try to travel as light as possible. Packs are hot, cumbersome, not very secure, and must be removed every time you get on a ride or sit down for a show. Hip packs, by way of contrast, can simply be rotated around the waist from your back to your abdomen if you need to sit down. Additionally, our observation has been that the contents of one day pack can usually be redistributed to two or so hip packs (except in the case of camera equipment).

> *un*official **TIP**
> About two weeks before arriving, ship a box to your hotel containing food, plastic cutlery, and toiletries, plus pretty much any other consumables that might come in handy during your stay. If you fly, this helps avoid overweight fees and problems with liquid restrictions for carry-on luggage.

CAPS Kids pull caps on and off as they enter and exit attractions, restrooms, and restaurants, and—big surprise—they lose them. In fact, they lose them by the thousands.

If your children are partial to caps, a device sold at ski and camping supply stores might increase the likelihood of the cap returning home with the child. Essentially, it's a short, light cord with little alligator clips on both ends. Hook one clip to the shirt collar and the other to the hat. It's a great little invention. Bob uses one when he skis in case his cap blows off.

RAINGEAR Rain is a fact of life, though persistent rain day after day is unusual. Check out the Weather Channel or weather forecasts on the Internet for three or so days before you leave home to see if there are any major storm systems heading for Southern California. Weather predictions concerning systems and fronts four to seven days out are pretty reliable. If it appears that you might see some rough weather during your visit, you're better off bringing raingear from home. If, however, nothing big is on the horizon weather wise, you can take your chances.

We at the Unofficial Guides usually do not bring raingear. Ponchos sell for about $8.50 adults, $7.50 child, and are available in seemingly every retail shop; they're even cheaper at local discount stores (such as Target). Moreover, in the theme parks, a surprising number of attractions and queuing areas are under cover. Finally, we prefer to travel light.

Respect for the Sun

Health and science writer Avery Hurt sheds some light on the often confusing products and methods for avoiding sunburn.

No matter what time of year you make your trip, don't underestimate the Southern California sun. Even in winter, it can be a problem.

The most obvious precaution is to slather on sunscreen. Choose a sunscreen that is convenient for you to use. Some prefer sprays, others lotions. The form of the sunscreen doesn't matter as much as the technique of applying it. Apply sunscreen 30 minutes before going out, and be sure to get enough on you. One ounce per application is recommended—that means a full shot glass worth each time you apply. The 1-ounce amount was calculated for average adults in swimsuits; larger adults will need proportionately more. For a 1-year-old child wearing a bathing suit, figure about one-third of an ounce (10 cc) per application. An average 7-year-old will probably take two-thirds of an ounce (20 cc). It's a good idea to measure that ounce in your hands (at home, when an ounce measure—shot glass or whatever—is handy), so that you will be familiar with what an ounce looks like in your palms. It really is far more sunscreen than you tend to think.

Don't miss any spots. Even the most dedicated sunscreen users usually do an abysmal job of applying it. Don't forget areas such as the ears and the tops of feet. Get a generous covering on all exposed skin. Then reapply (another full shot glass) every two hours or after swimming or sweating. No matter what it says on the label, water resistance is limited. And none lasts all day.

MAKING SENSE OF SPF

SPF stands for "sun protection factor" and is a measure of how long the protection will last. Geniuses in lab coats come up with this number by calculating how long it will take a person to burn without sunscreen and comparing that to how long the same person takes to burn with sunscreen. Theoretically, a sunscreen with an SPF of 15 will protect you 15 times longer than if you wore no sunscreen at all.

This might make it sound like the higher the SPF the better, but studies have not borne that out. The effect diminishes as the number gets higher, and the initial estimate doesn't take into account the fact that during the day your sunscreen rubs off, washes off, and sweats off. In fact, it is much safer to choose a lower (and typically less expensive) SPF (as long as it is at least 15) and apply it more often. The American Academy of Dermatology recommends an SPF of at least 30. And be sure to choose a product that has broad-spectrum coverage, meaning that it filters out both UVA and UVB rays.

CHILDREN AND THE SUN

It is best to keep babies under 6 months covered and out of the sun. However, the American Academy of Pediatrics condones a small amount of sunscreen on

If you do find yourself in a big storm, however, you'll want to have both a poncho and an umbrella. As one Unofficial reader puts it, "Umbrellas make the rain much more bearable. When rain isn't beating down on your ponchoed head, it's easier to ignore."

And consider this tip from a Memphis, Tennessee, mom:

Scotchgard your shoes. The difference is unbelievable.

MISCELLANEOUS ITEMS

MEDICATION Some parents of hyperactive children on medication discontinue or decrease the child's normal dosage at the end of the school vulnerable areas, such as the nose and chin, when you have your baby out. Be very careful to monitor your baby even if he or she is wearing a hat and sitting under an umbrella. The sun moves. A spot that was shady when you ordered your funnel cake might be baking by the time you've finished eating it. If your child develops a rash while using sunscreen, get the baby out of the sun, stop using the sunscreen, and call your doctor.

With older children, slather liberally and often. Don't make the mistake of thinking that because you've coated your children in a bazillion-SPF-water-resistant-all-day-protection-top-of-the-line sunscreen that you don't have to worry until dinnertime. Reapply and check for redness often. Sunburn can be sneaky. Children aren't likely to notice the mild discomfort of impending sunburn, especially when they are having fun. Check them often and get them out of the sun as soon as you see even slight redness. You don't have to pay extra for special formulas made for children. As long as the SPF is at least 30 and offers broad-spectrum protection, one brand can serve the whole family.

NOT JUST SKIN DEEP

It is just as important to protect the eyes and lips as the skin. Using a lip gloss with an SPF of 15 is pretty easy to do but also easy to forget. Keep several tubes in your bag or pocket and reapply often to your own lips and those of your kids. Again, the brand is less important than choosing something that you will use—and remembering to use it.

Sunglasses are also a must. Too much sun exposure can contribute to age-related macular degeneration (among other things). This may not seem much of an issue when you are young and healthy, but when you get old and go blind, you'll wish that you had remembered to put on some shades. Not all sunglasses filter out damaging rays. Be sure to choose shades (for adults and kids) that have 99% UV protection. Large lenses and wraparound styles might not look as cool, but they offer much better protection. You may have to spend a little more to be sure that you are getting adequate protection, but you don't want to skimp on this. Much of the damage to the eyes from too much sun is irreversible, and, like sun damage to the skin, it starts accumulating in childhood.

If you do slip up and get a burn, cool baths, aloe gels, and ibuprofen (or for adults, aspirin) usually help ease the suffering. Occasionally sunburns can be as dangerous in the short term as they are in the long term. If you or your child experience nausea, vomiting, high fever, severe pain, confusion, or fainting, seek medical care immediately.

All of the above is important—and sunscreen is a must if you are headed to Disneyland after a nice, cushy winter indoors in less-sun-drenched climes—but don't let that little bottle with its inscrutable numbers get you off your guard. You still need to wear a hat and stay well-hydrated.

year. If you have such a child, be aware that the Disneyland parks might overly stimulate him or her. Consult your physician before altering your child's medication regimen. Also, if your child has attention-deficit disorder, remember that especially loud sounds can drive him or her right up the wall. Unfortunately, some Disney theater attractions are almost unbearably loud.

SUNSCREEN Overheating and sunburn are among the most common problems of younger children at Disneyland. Carry and use sunscreen of SPF 15 or higher. Be sure to put some on kids in strollers, even if the stroller has a canopy. Some of the worst cases of sunburn we've seen were on the exposed foreheads and feet of toddlers and infants in strollers. Protect skin from overexposure. To avoid overheating, rest regularly in the shade or in an air-conditioned restaurant or show.

WATER BOTTLES Don't count on keeping young children hydrated with soft drinks and water fountains. Long lines may impede buying refreshments, and fountains may not be handy. Furthermore, excited children may not realize or tell you that they're thirsty or hot. We recommend renting a stroller for children age 6 and younger and carrying bottles of water and sports drinks. Bottled water runs about $3 in all major parks, or bring your own water bottle and strap from home.

COOLERS AND MINI-FRIDGES If you drive to Disneyland, bring two coolers: a small one for drinks in the car and a large one for the hotel room. If you fly and rent a car, stop and purchase a large Styrofoam cooler, which can be discarded at the end of the trip. If you will be without a car, book a hotel with mini-fridges in each room. All on-site Disneyland hotels provide free mini-fridges and coffeemakers. If mini-fridges aren't provided, rent one from the hotel.

Coolers and mini-fridges allow you to have breakfast in your hotel room, store snacks and lunch supplies to take to the theme parks, and supplant expensive vending machines for snacks and beverages at the hotel. To keep the contents of your cooler cold, freeze a 2-gallon milk jug full of water before you head out. In a good cooler, it will take the jug five or more days to thaw. If you buy a Styrofoam cooler, you can use bagged ice and ice from the ice machine at your hotel. Even if you have to rent a mini-fridge, you will save a bundle of cash as well as significant time by reducing dependence on restaurant meals and expensive snacks and drinks purchased from vendors.

FOOD-PREP KIT If you plan to make sandwiches, bring along condiments and seasonings from home. A typical travel kit will include mayonnaise, ketchup, mustard, salt and pepper, and packets of sugar or artificial sweetener. Also throw in some plastic knives and spoons, napkins, plastic cups, and zip-top plastic bags. For breakfast you will need some plastic bowls for cereal. Of course, you can buy this stuff in Anaheim, but you probably won't consume it all, so why waste the money? If you drink bottled beer or wine, bring a bottle opener and corkscrew.

ENERGY BOOSTERS Kids get cranky when they're hungry, and when that happens, your entire group has a problem. Like many parents you might, for nutritional reasons, keep a tight rein on snacks available to your children at home. At Disneyland, however, maintaining energy and equanimity trumps between-meal snack discipline. For maximum zip and contentedness, give your kids snacks containing complex carbohydrates (fruits, crackers, nonfat energy bars, and the like) before they get hungry or show signs of exhaustion. You should avoid snacks that are high in fats and proteins because these foods take a long time to digest and will tend to unsettle your stomach if it's a hot day.

An experienced and wise grandma underscores the point:

Children who get cranky during a visit often do so from all that time and energy expended without food. Feed them! A snack at any price goes a long way to keeping the little kids happy and enjoying the parks, and keeping parents sane. Oh, and the security people are very nice about you taking snacks or drinks in, but DO NOT bring glass containers! That is apparently what they are really looking for.

ELECTRONICS   Regardless of your children's ages, always bring a nightlight. Flashlights are also handy for finding stuff in a dark hotel room after the kids are asleep.

MP3 players and iPods with earphones, as well as some electronic games, are often controversial gear for a family outing. We recommend compromise. Earbuds allow kids to create their own space even when they're with others, and that can be a safety valve. That said, try to agree before the trip on some earphone parameters, so you don't begin to feel as if they're being used to keep other family members and the trip itself at a distance. If you're traveling by car, take turns choosing the radio station or CD for part of the trip.

Likewise, mobile phones are a mixed blessing. On the one hand, they can be invaluable in an emergency or if your party wants to split up, and if you have a smartphone, you can use our Lines app to see current wait times in the parks. Unfortunately, they also lead to guests missing out on what's around them and bumping into each other because they're glued to a tiny screen. If you bring yours, consider disabling high-speed data, Wi-Fi, and Bluetooth to save on batteries.

DON'T FORGET THE TENT   This is not a joke and has nothing to do with camping. When Bob's daughter was preschool age, he almost went crazy trying to get her to sleep in a shared hotel room. She was accustomed to having her own room at home and was hyperstimulated whenever she traveled. Bob tried makeshift curtains and room dividers and even rearranged the furniture in a few hotel rooms to create the illusion of a more private, separate space for her. It was all for naught. It wasn't until she was around 4 years old and Bob took her camping that he seized on an idea that had some promise. She liked the cozy, secure, womblike feel of a backpacking tent and quieted down much more readily than she ever had in hotel rooms. So the next time the family stayed in a hotel, he pitched his backpacking tent in the corner of the room. In she went, nested for a bit, and fell asleep.

Since the time of Bob's daughter's childhood, there has been an astounding evolution in tent design. Tent manufacturers have developed a broad range of tents with self-supporting frames that can be erected virtually anywhere without ropes or stakes. Affordable and sturdy, many are as simple to put up as opening an umbrella. So if your child is too young for a room of his or her own or you can't afford a second hotel room, try pitching a small tent. Modern tents are self-contained with floors and an entrance that can be zipped up for privacy but cannot be locked. Kids appreciate having their own space and enjoy the adventure of being in a tent, even one set up in the corner of a hotel room. Sizes range from children's play tents with a 2- to 3-foot base to models large enough to sleep two or three husky teens. Light and compact when stored, a two-adult-size tent in its own storage bag (called a stuff sack) will take up about one-tenth or less of a standard overhead bin on a commercial airliner. Another option for infants and toddlers is to drape a sheet over a portable crib or playpen to make a tent.

THE BOX Bob here: On one memorable Disneyland excursion when my children were younger, we began each morning with an immensely annoying, involuntary scavenger hunt. Invariably, seconds before our scheduled departure to the theme park, we discovered that some combination of shoes, billfolds, sunglasses, hip packs, or other necessities were unaccountably missing. For the next 15 minutes we would root through the room like pigs hunting truffles in an attempt to locate the absent items. When my kids lost something, they always searched where it was easiest to look, as opposed to where the lost article was most likely to be. I would be jammed under a bed feeling around while my children stood in the middle of the room intently inspecting the ceiling. As my friends will tell you, I'm as open to a novel theory as the next guy, but we never did find any shoes on the ceiling. Anyway, here's what I finally did: I swung by a local store and mooched a big empty box. From then on, every time we returned to the room, I had the kids deposit shoes, hip packs, and other potentially wayward items in the box. After that the box was off-limits until the next morning, when I doled out the contents.

> **unofficial TIP**
> Often little ones fall asleep in their strollers (hallelujah!). Bring a large lightweight cloth to drape over the stroller to cover your child from the sun. A few clothespins will keep it in place.

PLASTIC GARBAGE BAGS At the Grizzly River Run raft ride at DCA and Splash Mountain in Disneyland Park, you are certain to get wet and possibly soaked. If it's really hot and you don't care, then fine. But if it's cool or you're just not up for a soaking, bring a large plastic trash bag or a cheap poncho to the park. By cutting holes in the top and on the sides, you can fashion a sack poncho that will keep your clothes from getting wet. On the raft ride, you will also get your feet wet. If you're not up for walking around in squishing, soaked shoes, bring a second, smaller plastic bag to wear over your feet while riding.

SUPPLIES FOR INFANTS AND TODDLERS

BASED ON RECOMMENDATIONS from hundreds of Unofficial Guide readers, here's what we suggest that you carry with you when touring with infants and toddlers:

- A disposable diaper for every hour you plan to be away from your hotel
- A cloth diaper or kitchen towel to put over your shoulder for burping
- Two receiving blankets: one to wrap the baby, one to lay the baby on or to drape over you when you nurse

- Ointment for diaper rash
- A package of wipes
- Prepared formula in bottles if you are not breast-feeding
- A washable bib, baby spoon, and baby food if your infant is eating solids
- For toddlers, a small toy for comfort and to keep them occupied during attractions

Baby-care centers at the theme parks will sell you just about anything that you forget or run out of. Like all things Disney, prices will be higher than elsewhere, but at least you won't need to detour to a drugstore in the middle of your touring day.

REMEMBERING *Your* TRIP

1. Purchase a notebook for each child and spend time each evening recording the day's events. If your children have trouble getting motivated or don't know what to write about, start a discussion; otherwise, let them write or draw whatever they want to remember from the day.

2. Collect mementos along the way and create a treasure box in a small tin or cigar box. Months or years later, it's fun to look at postcards, pins, seashells, or ticket stubs to jump-start a memory.

3. Add inexpensive postcards to your photographs to create an album; then write a few words on each page to accompany the images.

4. Give each child a disposable camera to record his or her version of the trip. One 5-year-old snapped an entire series of photos that never showed anyone above the waist—his view of Disneyland (and the photos were priceless).

5. Nowadays, many families travel with a video camera, digital camera, or camera phone, though we recommend using one sparingly—parents end up viewing the trip through the lens rather than being in the moment. If you must, take it along, but only record a few moments of major sights (too much is boring anyway). And let the kids record and narrate. On the topic of narration, speak loudly so as to be heard over the not insignificant background noise of the parks. Make use of lockers at all of the parks when the camera becomes a burden or when you're going to experience an attraction that might damage it or get it wet. Unless you have a camera designed for underwater shots or a waterproof carrying case, leave it behind on Splash Mountain, the Grizzly River Run, and any other ride where water is involved. Don't forget extra batteries.

6. Another inexpensive way to record memories is a palm-size tape recorder. Let all family members describe their experiences. Hearing a small child's voice years later is so endearing, and those recorded descriptions will trigger an album's worth of memories, far more focused than what many novices capture with a camcorder.

7. Consider using Disney's PhotoPass service for some professional-quality pictures; it's free to use and you only pay for the images you want to keep (see page 99 for details).

Finally, when it comes to taking photos and collecting mementos, don't let the tail wag the dog. You are not going to Disneyland to build the biggest scrapbook in history. Or as this Houston mom put it:

Tell your readers to get a grip on the photography thing. We were so busy shooting pictures that we kind of lost the thread. We had to get our pictures developed when we got home to see what all we did [while on vacation].

▌ TRIAL RUN

IF YOU GIVE THOUGHTFUL CONSIDERATION to all areas of mental, physical, organizational, and logistical preparation discussed in this chapter, what remains is to familiarize yourself with the Disneyland parks and, of course, to conduct your field test. Yep, that's right, we want you to take the whole platoon on the road for a day to see if you are combat ready. No joke—this is important. You'll learn who tuckers out first, who's prone to developing blisters, who has to pee every 11 seconds, who keeps losing her cap, and, given the proper forum, how compatible your family is in terms of what you like to see and do.

For the most informative trial run, choose a local venue that requires lots of walking, dealing with crowds, and making decisions on how to spend your time. Regional theme parks and state fairs are your best bets, followed by large zoos and museums. Devote the whole day. Kick off the morning with an early start, just like you will at Disneyland, paying attention to who's organized and ready to go and who's dragging his or her butt and holding up the group. If you have to drive one or two hours to get to your test venue, no big deal. You may have to do some commuting at Disneyland too. Spend the whole day, eat a couple of meals, and stay late.

Don't bias the sample (that is, mess with the outcome) by telling everyone that you are practicing for Disneyland. Everyone behaves differently when they know that they are being tested or evaluated. Your objective is not to run a perfect drill but to find out as much as you can about how the individuals in your family, as well as the family as a group, respond to and deal with everything they experience during the day. Pay attention to who moves quickly and who is slow; who is adventuresome and who is reticent; who keeps going and who needs frequent rest breaks; who sets the agenda and who is content to follow; who is easily agitated and who stays cool; who tends to dawdle or wander off; who is curious and who is bored; who is demanding and who is accepting. You get the idea.

Discuss the findings of the test run with your spouse the next day. Don't be discouraged if your test day wasn't perfect; few (if any) are. Distinguish between problems that are remediable and problems that are intrinsic to your family's emotional or physical makeup (no amount of hiking, for example, will toughen up some people's feet).

Establish a plan for addressing remediable problems (further conditioning, setting limits before you go, trying harder to achieve family consensus) and develop strategies for minimizing or working around problems that are a fact of life (waking sleepyheads 15 minutes early, placing moleskin on likely blister sites before setting out, or packing familiar food for the toddler who balks at restaurant fare). If you are an attentive observer, a fair diagnostician, and a creative problem solver, you'll be able to work out many of the problems you're likely to encounter at Disneyland before you leave home.

ABOUT THE UNOFFICIAL GUIDE TOURING PLANS Parents who embark on one of our touring plans are often frustrated by the various interruptions and delays occasioned by their small children. In case you haven't given the subject much thought, here is what to expect:

1. Many small children will stop dead in their tracks whenever they see a Disney character. Our advice: Live with it. An attempt to haul your children away before they have satisfied their curiosity is likely to precipitate anything from whining to a full-scale revolt.

2. The touring plans call for visiting attractions in a specified sequence, often skipping certain attractions along the way. Children do not like skipping anything! If they see something that attracts them, they want to experience it now. Some children can be persuaded to skip attractions if parents explain things in advance. Other kids severely flip out at the threat of skipping something, particularly something in Fantasyland. A mom from Charleston, South Carolina, had this to say:

   Following the touring plans turned out to be a train wreck. The main problem with the plan is that it starts in Fantasyland. When we were on Dumbo, my 5-year-old saw eight dozen other things in Fantasyland she wanted to see. The long and the short is that after Dumbo, there was no getting her out of there.

3. Children seem to have a genetic instinct when it comes to finding restrooms. We have seen perfectly functional adults equipped with all manner of maps search interminably for a restroom. Small children, on the other hand, including those who cannot read, will head for the nearest restroom with the certainty of a homing pigeon. While you may skip certain attractions, you can be sure that your children will ferret out (and want to use) every restroom in the theme park.

∎ STROLLERS

STROLLERS ARE AVAILABLE for about $15 per day for a single, $25 per day for two; the rental covers the entire day and is good at both parks. If you rent a stroller and later decide to go back to your hotel for lunch, a swim, or a nap, turn in your stroller but hang on to your rental receipt. When you return to either park later in the day, present your receipt. You will be issued another stroller with no additional charge. The rental procedure is fast and efficient, and a central stroller rental facility is in the Main Entrance Plaza between Disneyland and

DCA. Likewise, returning the stroller is a breeze. Even in the evening, when several hundred strollers are turned in following the fireworks or water show, there is no wait or hassle. Note: Rented strollers are not permitted in Downtown Disney.

The strollers come with sun canopies and small cargo compartments under the seat. For infants and toddlers, strollers are a must, and we recommend a small pillow or blanket to help make them more comfortable for your child during what may be long periods in the seat. We have also observed many sharp parents renting strollers for somewhat older children. Strollers prevent parents from having to carry children when they run out of steam and provide an easy, convenient way to carry water, snacks, diaper bags, and the like.

unofficial **TIP**
Strollers are also great for older kids who tire easily.

When you enter a show or board a ride, you will have to park your stroller, usually in an open, unprotected area. If it rains before you return, you'll need a cloth, towel, or spare diaper to dry off the stroller.

Bringing Your Own Stroller

You are allowed to bring your own stroller to the theme parks. However, only collapsible strollers are allowed on the monorail and parking-lot trams. Your stroller is unlikely to be stolen, but mark it with your name. We strongly recommend bringing your own stroller. In addition to the parks there is the walk from and to your hotel, the parking-lot tram, or the bus/hotel-shuttle boarding area, not to mention many other occasions at your hotel or during shopping when you will be happy to have a stroller handy.

unofficial **TIP**
Beware of stroller stealers. With so many identical strollers, it's easy to grab the wrong one. Mark yours with a bandanna or some other easily identifiable flag.

If you do not want to bring your own stroller, you may consider buying one of the umbrella-style collapsible strollers. You may even consider ordering online at places such as **walmart.com, toysrus.com,** or **sears.com** and shipping it right to your hotel. Make sure you leave enough time between your order and arrival dates.

Having her own stroller was indispensable to this mother of two toddlers:

> How I was going to manage to get the kids from the parking [garage] to the park was a big worry for me before I made the trip. I didn't read anywhere that it was possible to walk to the entrance of the parks instead of taking the tram, so I wasn't sure I could do it.
>
> I found that for me personally, since I have two kids ages 1 and 2, it was easier to walk to the entrance of the park from the parking [garage] with the kids in [my own] stroller than to take the kids out of the stroller, fold the stroller (while trying to control the two kids and associated gear), load the stroller and the kids onto the tram, etc. . . . No matter where I was parked, I could always just walk to the entrance. . . . It sometimes took a while, but it was easier for me.

An Oklahoma mom, however, reports a bad experience with bringing her own stroller:

The first time we took our kids we had a large stroller (big mistake). It is so much easier to rent one in the park. The large [personally owned] strollers are nearly impossible to get on [airport shuttle] buses and are a hassle at the airport. I remember feeling dread when a bus pulled up that was even semi-full of people. People look at you like you have a cage full of live chickens when you drag heavy strollers onto the bus.

Stroller Wars

Sometimes strollers disappear while you are enjoying a ride or a show. Do not be alarmed. You won't have to buy the missing stroller, and you will be issued a new stroller for your continued use. Lost strollers can be replaced at the main rental facility near the respective park entrances.

While replacing a ripped-off stroller is not a big deal, it is an inconvenience. One family complained that their stroller had been taken six times in one day. Even with free replacements, larceny on this scale represents a lot of wasted time. Through our own experiments and suggestions from readers, we have developed several techniques for hanging on to your rented stroller:

1. Write your name in permanent marker on a 6-by-9-inch card, put the card in a transparent freezer bag, and secure the bag to the handle of the stroller with masking or duct tape.

2. Affix something personal (but expendable) to the handle of the stroller. Evidently most strollers are pirated by mistake (since they all look the same) or because it's easier to swipe someone else's stroller (when yours disappears) than to troop off to the replacement center. Since most stroller theft is a function of confusion, laziness, or revenge, the average pram-pincher will balk at hauling off a stroller bearing another person's property. After trying several items, we concluded that a bright, inexpensive scarf or bandanna tied to the handle works well, and a sock partially stuffed with rags or paper works even better (the weirder and more personal the object, the greater the deterrent). Best of all is a dead mackerel dangling from the handle, though in truth, the kids who ride in the stroller prefer the other methods.

A multigenerational family tried this:

[We] took the suggestion from one of your readers and "decorated" our stroller with electrical tape to make it stand out. We also zip tied an unused, small, insulated diaper bag to the handle to make carrying things easier. One of your readers mentioned using a bike chain or cable lock to insure their stroller was not stolen but said the Disney cast members were a little disturbed. So I took an extra firearm lock (looks like a mini-bike lock) to lock a wheel to the frame while parked. My son added a small cow bell to make it clang if moved. The stroller could then be moved easily for short distances by lifting the back, but trying to go farther would be uncomfortable and noisy.

We receive quite a few letters from readers debating the pros and cons of bringing your own stroller versus renting one of Disney's. A mother with two small children opted for her own pram:

> *I took my own stroller because the rented strollers aren't appropriate for infants (we had a 5-year-old and a 5-month-old). No one said anything about me using a bike lock to secure our brand-new Aprica stroller. However, an attendant came over and told us not to lock it anywhere because it's a fire hazard! (Outside?) When I politely asked the attendant if she wanted to be responsible for my $300 stroller, she told me to go ahead and lock it but not tell anyone! I observed the attendants constantly moving the strollers. This seems very confusing—no wonder people think their strollers are getting ripped off!*

As the reader mentioned, Disney cast members often rearrange strollers parked outside an attraction. Sometimes this is done simply to tidy up. At other times the strollers are moved to make additional room along a walkway. In any event, do not assume that your stroller is stolen because it is missing from the exact place you left it. Check around. Chances are it will be neatly arranged just a few feet away.

▮ BABYSITTING

CHILD-CARE SERVICES ARE UNAVAILABLE in the Disney parks. The services of Pinocchio's Workshop, a child-care facility at the Grand Californian Hotel, are available only to guests of the three Disneyland Resort hotels. Children ages 5–12 can be left for up to 4 hours at a cost of $13 per hour, per child. Pinocchio's Workshop requires a minimum of 2 hours, and its hours are 5 p.m.–midnight. Dinner is available for an additional fee.

Fullerton Child Care Agency, an independent organization, provides in-room sitting for infants and children. If you pay the tab, Fullerton sitters will even take your kids to Disneyland. All sitters are experienced and licensed to drive, and the Fullerton Child Care Agency is fully insured. The basic rate for in-room sitting for one or two children is $48 for the first 4 hours, with a 4-hour minimum, and $10 each hour thereafter. The charge for each additional child varies with the sitter. There is no transportation fee, but the client is expected to pay for parking when applicable. All fees and charges must be paid in cash at the end of the assignment. To reserve a sitter, one or two days' advance notice is requested. They fill up quickly, so a couple of weeks' notice is ideal. You can reach the Fullerton Child Care Agency by calling ☎ 714-528-1640.

DISNEY, KIDS, *and* SCARY STUFF

DISNEYLAND PARK and Disney California Adventure are family theme parks. Yet some of the Disney adventure rides can be intimidating to small children. On certain rides, such as Splash Mountain and the roller coasters (California Screamin', Space Mountain, Matterhorn Bobsleds, and Big Thunder Mountain Railroad), the ride itself may be frightening. On other rides, such as The Haunted Mansion and Snow White's Scary Adventures, it is the special effects. We recommend a little parent-child dialogue coupled with a "testing the water" approach. A child who is frightened by Pinocchio's Daring Journey should not have to sit through The Haunted Mansion. Likewise, if Big Thunder Mountain Railroad is too much, don't try Space Mountain or California Screamin'.

Disney rides and shows are adventures. They focus on the substance and themes of all adventure, and indeed of life itself: good and evil, beauty and the grotesque, fellowship and enmity, quest, and death. Though the endings are all happy, the impact of the adventures, with Disney's gift for special effects, is often intimidating and occasionally frightening to small children.

There are rides with menacing witches, rides with burning towns, and rides with ghouls popping out of their graves, all done tongue-in-cheek and with a sense of humor, provided you are old enough to understand the joke. And there are bones, lots of bones—human bones, cattle bones, and whole skeletons are everywhere you look. There have to be more bones at Disneyland Park than at the Smithsonian and the UCLA Medical School combined. A stack of skulls is at the headhunter's camp on the Jungle Cruise; a veritable platoon of skeletons sail ghost ships in Pirates of the Caribbean; a macabre assemblage of skulls and skeletons are in The Haunted Mansion; and more skulls, skeletons, and bones punctuate Snow White's Scary Adventures, Peter Pan's Flight, and Big Thunder Mountain Railroad.

One reader wrote us after taking his preschoolers on Star Tours:

We took a 4-year-old and a 5-year-old and they had the *#%^! scared out of them at Star Tours. We did this first thing in the morning, and it took hours of Tom Sawyer Island and It's a Small World to get back to normal.

Our kids were the youngest by far in Star Tours. I assume that either other adults had more sense or were not such avid readers of your book. Preschoolers should start with Dumbo and work up

to the Jungle Cruise in the late morning, after being revved up and
before getting hungry, thirsty, or tired. Pirates of the Caribbean is out
for preschoolers. You get the idea.

The reaction of young children to the inevitable system overload of Disney parks should be anticipated. Be sensitive, alert, and prepared for almost anything, even behavior that is out of character for your child at home. Most small children take Disney's variety of macabre trappings in stride, and others are quickly comforted by an arm around the shoulder or a little squeeze of the hand. For parents who have observed a tendency in their kids to become upset, we recommend taking it slowly and easily by sampling more benign adventures such as the Jungle Cruise, gauging reactions, and discussing with children how they felt about the things they saw. A mother of two reported this:

The one thing I regret is taking my 4-year-old on the Tower of
Terror—the drops and jolts didn't bother him, but the holographic
"ghosts" sure did!

Sometimes, small children will rise above their anxiety in an effort to please their parents or siblings. This behavior, however, does not necessarily indicate a mastery of fear, much less enjoyment. If children come off a ride in ostensibly good shape, we recommend asking if they would like to go on the ride again (not necessarily right now, but sometime). The response to this question will usually give you a clue as to how much they actually enjoyed the experience. There is a lot of difference between having a good time and mustering the courage to get through something.

Evaluating a child's capacity to handle the visual and tactile effects of the Disney parks requires patience, understanding, and experimentation. Each of us, after all, has his own demons. If a child balks at or is frightened by a ride, respond constructively. Let your children know that lots of people, adults as well as children, are scared by what they see and feel. Help them understand that it is OK if they get frightened and that their fear does not lessen your love or respect. Take pains not to compound the discomfort by making a child feel inadequate; try not to undermine self-esteem, impugn courage, or subject a child to ridicule. Most of all, do not induce guilt, as if your child's trepidation is ruining the family's fun. When older siblings are present, it is sometimes necessary to restrain their taunting and teasing.

A visit to a Disney park is more than an outing or an adventure for a small child. It is a testing experience, a sort of controlled rite of passage. If you help your little one work through the challenges, the time can be immeasurably rewarding and a bonding experience for both of you.

The Fright Factor

While each youngster is different, there are essentially seven attraction elements that alone or combined can push a child's buttons:

1. THE NAME OF THE ATTRACTION Small children will naturally be apprehensive about something called The Haunted Mansion or Snow White's Scary Adventures.

2. THE VISUAL IMPACT OF THE ATTRACTION FROM OUTSIDE Splash Mountain, The Twilight Zone Tower of Terror, and Big Thunder Mountain Railroad look scary enough to give even adults second thoughts. To many small kids, the rides are visually terrifying.

3. THE VISUAL IMPACT OF THE INDOOR QUEUING AREA Pirates of the Caribbean with its dark bayou scene and The Haunted Mansion, with its "stretch rooms" are capable of frightening small children before they even board the ride.

4. THE INTENSITY OF THE ATTRACTION Some attractions are so intense as to be overwhelming; they inundate the senses with sights, sounds, movement, and even smell. *Captain EO, Muppet-Vision 3-D,* and *It's Tough to Be a Bug!,* for instance, combine loud music, tactile effects, lights, and 3-D cinematography to create a total sensory experience. For some preschoolers, this is two or three senses too many.

5. THE VISUAL IMPACT OF THE ATTRACTION ITSELF As previously discussed, the sights in various attractions range from falling boulders to lurking buzzards, from underwater volcanoes to attacking hippos. What one child calmly absorbs may scare the owl poop out of another child the same age.

6. DARK Many Disneyland attractions are dark rides—that is, they operate indoors in a dark environment. For some children, this fact alone is sufficient to trigger significant apprehension. A child who is frightened on one dark ride, for example Snow White's Scary Adventures, may be unwilling to try other indoor rides.

7. THE RIDE ITSELF: THE TACTILE EXPERIENCE Some Disney rides are downright wild—wild enough to induce motion sickness, wrench backs, and generally discombobulate patrons of any age.

A Bit of Preparation

We receive many tips from parents relating how they prepared their children for the Disneyland experience. A common strategy is to acquaint kids with the characters and the stories behind the attractions by reading Disney books and watching Disney DVDs at home.

Thanks to half the population of California walking around the parks with video cameras, you can view a clip of every attraction and show on **youtube.com.** Videos of dark rides aren't stellar but are good enough to get a sense of what you're in for. The mother of a 7-year-old found YouTube quite effective:

> We watched every ride and show on YouTube before going so my timid 7-year-old daughter would be prepared, and we cut out all the

Continued on page 144

Small-Child Fright-Potential Chart

As a quick reference, we provide this chart to warn you which attractions to be wary of and why. The chart represents a generalization and all kids are different. The chart relates specifically to kids 3–7 years of age. On average, as you would expect, children at the younger end of the age range are more likely to be frightened than children in their 6th or 7th year.

DISNEYLAND PARK

MAIN STREET, U.S.A.

DISNEYLAND RAILROAD Tunnel with dinosaur display frightens some small children.

THE DISNEYLAND STORY, PRESENTING *GREAT MOMENTS WITH*
  MR. LINCOLN Brief battle sound effects may surprise small children.

ADVENTURELAND

ENCHANTED TIKI ROOM A small thunderstorm momentarily surprises very young children.

INDIANA JONES ADVENTURE Visually intimidating, with intense effects and a jerky ride. Switching-off option (see page 149).

JUNGLE CRUISE Moderately intense, with some macabre sights; a good test attraction for little ones.

TARZAN'S TREEHOUSE Not frightening in any respect.

NEW ORLEANS SQUARE

HAUNTED MANSION Name of attraction raises anxiety, as do sights and sounds of waiting area. An intense attraction with humorously presented macabre sights. The ride itself is gentle.

PIRATES OF THE CARIBBEAN Slightly intimidating queuing area; an intense boat ride with gruesome (though humorously presented) sights and two short, unexpected slides down flumes.

CRITTER COUNTRY

DAVY CROCKETT'S EXPLORER CANOES Not frightening in any respect.

THE MANY ADVENTURES OF WINNIE THE POOH Not frightening in any respect.

SPLASH MOUNTAIN Visually intimidating from the outside. Moderately intense visual effects. The ride itself is somewhat hair-raising for all ages, culminating in a 52-foot plunge down a steep chute. Switching-off option (see page 149).

FRONTIERLAND

BIG THUNDER MOUNTAIN RAILROAD Visually intimidating from the outside; moderately intense visual effects. The roller coaster may frighten many adults, particularly seniors. Switching-off option (see page 149).

FRONTIERLAND SHOOTIN' EXPOSITION Not frightening in any respect.

GOLDEN HORSESHOE STAGE Not frightening in any respect.

MARK TWAIN RIVERBOAT Not frightening in any respect.

PIRATE'S LAIR ON TOM SAWYER ISLAND Some very small children are intimidated by dark walk-through tunnels that can be easily avoided.

SAILING SHIP COLUMBIA Not frightening in any respect.

FANTASYLAND

ALICE IN WONDERLAND Pretty benign but frightens a small percentage of preschoolers.

CASEY JR. CIRCUS TRAIN Not frightening in any respect.

DUMBO THE FLYING ELEPHANT A tame midway ride; a great favorite of most small children.

IT'S A SMALL WORLD Not frightening in any respect.

KING ARTHUR CARROUSEL Not frightening in any respect.

MAD TEA PARTY Midway-type ride can induce motion sickness in all ages.

MATTERHORN BOBSLEDS The ride itself is wilder than Big Thunder Mountain Railroad but not as wild as Space Mountain. Switching-off option (see page 149).

MR. TOAD'S WILD RIDE Name of ride intimidates some. Moderately intense spook-house-genre attraction with jerky ride. Frightens only a small percentage of preschoolers.

PETER PAN'S FLIGHT Not frightening in any respect.

PINOCCHIO'S DARING JOURNEY Less frightening than Alice in Wonderland but scares a few very young preschoolers.

SNOW WHITE'S SCARY ADVENTURES Moderately intense spook-house-genre attraction with some grim characters. Absolutely terrifying to many preschoolers.

STORYBOOK LAND CANAL BOATS Not frightening in any respect.

MICKEY'S TOONTOWN

CHIP 'N DALE TREEHOUSE Not frightening in any respect.

GADGET'S GO COASTER Tame as far as coasters go; frightens some small children.

GOOFY'S PLAYHOUSE Not frightening in any respect.

MICKEY'S HOUSE Not frightening in any respect.

MINNIE'S HOUSE Not frightening in any respect.

MISS DAISY, DONALD DUCK'S BOAT Not frightening in any respect.

ROGER RABBIT'S CAR TOON SPIN Intense special effects, coupled with a dark environment and wild ride; frightens many preschoolers.

TOMORROWLAND

ASTRO ORBITOR Waiting area is visually intimidating to preschoolers. The ride is a lot higher, but just a bit wilder, than Dumbo.

AUTOPIA The noise in the waiting area slightly intimidates preschoolers; otherwise, not frightening.

Small-Child Fright-Potential Chart (cont'd)

DISNEYLAND PARK (continued)

TOMORROWLAND (continued)

BUZZ LIGHTYEAR ASTRO BLASTERS Intense special effects plus a dark environment frighten some preschoolers.

CAPTAIN EO Extremely intense visual effects and the loud volume scare many preschoolers.

DISNEYLAND MONORAIL Not frightening in any respect.

FINDING NEMO SUBMARINE VOYAGE Being enclosed, as well as certain ride effects, may frighten preschoolers.

SPACE MOUNTAIN Very intense roller coaster in the dark; Disneyland's wildest ride and a scary roller coaster by anyone's standards. Switching-off option (see page 149).

STAR TOURS: THE ADVENTURES CONTINUE Extremely intense visually for all ages; the ride is one of the wildest in Disney's repertoire. Switching-off option (see page 149).

DISNEY CALIFORNIA ADVENTURE

A BUG'S LAND

FLIK'S FUN FAIR Not frightening in any respect.

IT'S TOUGH TO BE A BUG! Loud and extremely intense with special effects that will terrify children under 8 years or anyone with a fear of insects.

CONDOR FLATS

SOARIN' OVER CALIFORNIA Frightens some children 7 years and under. Really a very sweet ride.

GRIZZLY PEAK

GRIZZLY RIVER RUN Frightening to guests of all ages. Wet too!

REDWOOD CREEK CHALLENGE Trail is a bit overwhelming to preschoolers but not frightening.

HOLLYWOOD LAND

DISNEY ANIMATION Not frightening in any respect.

Continued from page 141

ones that looked too scary to her. She still did not like, and cried at, It's Tough to Be a Bug.

A mother from Gloucester, Massachusetts, handled her son's preparation a bit more extemporaneously:

The 3½-year-old liked It's a Small World [but] was afraid of The Haunted Mansion. We just pulled his hat over his face and quietly talked to him while we enjoyed [the ride].

DISNEY JUNIOR Not frightening in any respect.

HOLLYWOOD BACKLOT STAGE Not frightening in any respect.

HYPERION THEATER Some productions are both very intense and loud.

MONSTERS, INC. MIKE AND SULLEY TO THE RESCUE May frighten children under 7 years of age.

MUPPET-VISION 3-D Intense and loud with a lot of special effects. Frightens some preschoolers.

THE TWILIGHT ZONE TOWER OF TERROR Frightening to guests of all ages.

PACIFIC WHARF

BOUDIN BAKERY Not frightening in any respect.

PARADISE PIER

CALIFORNIA SCREAMIN' Frightening to guests of all ages.

GOLDEN ZEPHYR Frightening to a small percentage of preschoolers.

GOOFY'S SKY SCHOOL Frightening to the under-8 crowd.

JUMPIN' JELLYFISH The ride's appearance frightens some younger children. The ride itself is exceedingly tame.

KING TRITON'S CAROUSEL Not frightening in any respect.

THE LITTLE MERMAID: ARIEL'S UNDERSEA ADVENTURE Moderately intense effects; Ursula may frighten children under 7 years of age.

MICKEY'S FUN WHEEL The ride in the stationary cars is exceedingly tame. The ride in the swinging cars is frightening to guests of all ages.

SILLY SYMPHONY SWINGS Height requirement keeps preschoolers from riding. Moderately intimidating to younger grade-schoolers.

TOY STORY MIDWAY MANIA! Loud and intense but not frightening.

CARS LAND

LUIGI'S FLYING TIRES Not frightening in any respect.

MATER'S JUNKYARD JAMBOREE Midway-type ride can induce motion sickness in all ages.

RADIATOR SPRINGS RACERS Moderately intense effects, with high-speed sections that may frighten younger children. Switching-off option (see page 149).

A Word about Height Requirements

A number of attractions require children to meet minimum height and age requirements, usually 40 inches tall to ride with an adult, or at least 40 inches and 7 years of age or older to ride alone. If you have children too short or too young to ride, you have several options, including switching off (described on page 149). Although the alternatives may resolve some practical and logistical issues, be forewarned that your smaller children might nonetheless be resentful of their older (or taller) siblings who qualify to ride. A mom from Virginia bumped into just such a situation, writing:

You mention height requirements for rides but not the intense sibling jealousy this can generate. Frontierland was a real problem in that respect. Our very petite 5-year-old, to her outrage, was stuck hanging around while our 8-year-old went on Splash Mountain and [Big] Thunder Mountain with Grandma and Granddad, and the nearby alternatives weren't helpful [too long a line for rafts to Tom Sawyer Island, and so on]. If we had thought ahead, we would have left the younger kid back in Mickey's Toontown with one of the grown-ups for another roller-coaster ride or two and then met up later at a designated point. The best areas had a playground or other quick attractions for short people near the rides with height requirements.

The reader makes a valid point, though splitting the group and then meeting later can be more complicated in practical terms than she might imagine. If you choose to split up, ask the Disney greeter at the entrance to the height-restricted attraction(s) how long the wait is. If you tack 5 minutes for riding onto the anticipated wait, and then add 5 or so minutes to exit and reach the meeting point, you'll have an approximate sense of how long the younger kids (and their supervising adult) will have to do other stuff. Our guess is that even with a long line for the rafts, the reader would have had more than sufficient time to take her daughter to Tom Sawyer Island while the sibs rode Splash Mountain and Big Thunder Mountain with the grandparents. For sure she had time to tour Tarzan's Treehouse in adjacent Adventureland.

Additionally, children under age 7 must be accompanied on all attractions by another guest age 14 or older, who must sit in the same ride vehicle in the same row or an adjacent one. While this shouldn't pose a problem on most attractions, some with small vehicles (such as Gadget's Go Coaster) may require use of a baby swap (see page 149) if your party has an uneven ratio of little members to big ones; ask a cast member at the ride entrance for assistance if you have questions.

Attractions that Eat Adults

You may spend so much energy worrying about Junior's welfare that you forget to take care of yourself. If the ride component of the attraction (that is, the actual motion and movement of the conveyance itself) is potentially disturbing, persons of any age may be adversely affected. Several attractions likely to cause motion sickness or other problems for older children and adults are listed in the chart on page 148. Fast, jerky rides are also noted with icons in the attraction profiles.

WAITING-LINE STRATEGIES *for* ADULTS *with* SMALL CHILDREN

CHILDREN HOLD UP BETTER through the day if you minimize the time they have to spend in lines. Arriving early and using the touring plans in this guide will reduce waiting time immensely. There are, however, additional measures you can employ to reduce stress on little ones.

1. LINE GAMES It is a smart parent who anticipates how restless children get waiting in line and how a little structured activity can relieve the stress and boredom. In the morning, kids handle the inactivity of waiting in line by discussing what they want to see and do during the course of the day. Later, however, as events wear on, they need a little help. Watching for, and counting, Disney characters is a good diversion. Simple guessing games such as 20 Questions also work well. Lines for

POTENTIALLY PROBLEMATIC ATTRACTIONS FOR ADULTS
DISNEYLAND PARK
ADVENTURELAND Indiana Jones Adventure
CRITTER COUNTRY Splash Mountain
FANTASYLAND Mad Tea Party | Matterhorn Bobsleds
FRONTIERLAND Big Thunder Mountain Railroad
TOMORROWLAND Space Mountain | Star Tours: The Adventures Continue
DISNEY CALIFORNIA ADVENTURE
CARS LAND Mater's Junkyard Jamboree | Radiator Springs Racers
GRIZZLY PEAK Grizzly River Run
HOLLYWOOD LAND The Twilight Zone Tower of Terror
PARADISE PIER California Screamin' | Goofy's Sky School Mickey's Fun Wheel (swinging)

rides move so continuously that games requiring pen and paper are cumbersome and impractical. Waiting in the holding area of a theater attraction, however, is a different story. Here, tic-tac-toe, hangman, drawing, and coloring can really make the time go by.

2. LAST-MINUTE ENTRY If a ride or show can accommodate an unusually large number of people at one time, it is often unnecessary to stand in line. The *Mark Twain* riverboat in Frontierland is a good example. The boat holds about 450 people, usually more than are waiting in line to ride. Instead of standing uncomfortably in a crowd with dozens of other guests, grab a snack and sit in the shade until the boat arrives and loading is well under way. After the line has all but disappeared, go ahead and board.

In large-capacity theaters, such as the one showing *Captain EO* in Tomorrowland, ask the entrance greeter how long it will be until guests are admitted to the theater for the next show. If the answer is 15 minutes or more, use the time for a restroom break or to get a snack; you can return to the attraction just a few minutes before the show starts. You will not be permitted to carry any food or drink into the attraction, so make sure you have time to finish your snack before entering.

To help you determine which attractions to target for last-minute entry, we provide the chart below.

ATTRACTIONS YOU CAN USUALLY ENTER AT THE LAST MINUTE
DISNEYLAND PARK
FRONTIERLAND *Mark Twain* Riverboat | Sailing Ship *Columbia*
MAIN STREET, U.S.A. *Disneyland Story,* presenting *Great Moments with Mr. Lincoln*
TOMORROWLAND *Captain EO*
DISNEY CALIFORNIA ADVENTURE
HOLLYWOOD LAND Disney Animation | *Muppet-Vision 3-D*

3. THE HAIL MARY PASS Certain waiting lines are configured in such a way that you and your smaller children can pass under the rail to join your partner just before boarding or entry. This technique allows the kids and one adult to rest, snack, cool off, or tinkle, while another adult or older sibling does the waiting. Other guests are understanding when it comes to using this strategy to keep small children content. You are likely to meet hostile opposition, however, if you try to pass older children or more than one adult under the rail. Attractions where it is usually possible to complete a Hail Mary pass are listed on the chart below.

ATTRACTIONS WHERE YOU CAN USUALLY COMPLETE A HAIL MARY PASS
DISNEYLAND PARK
FANTASYLAND Casey Jr. Circus Train | Dumbo the Flying Elephant King Arthur Carrousel | Mad Tea Party | Mr. Toad's Wild Ride | Peter Pan's Flight Snow White's Scary Adventures | Storybook Land Canal Boats
TOMORROWLAND Autopia
DISNEY CALIFORNIA ADVENTURE
PARADISE PIER Golden Zephyr | Jumpin' Jellyfish | King Triton's Carousel
CARS LAND Luigi's Flying Tires | Mater's Junkyard Jamboree

4. SWITCHING OFF (ALSO KNOWN AS THE BABY SWAP) Several attractions have minimum height and/or age requirements; children usually 40 inches tall or under must ride with an adult, or be at least 7 years of age *and* 40 inches tall to ride alone. Some couples with children too small or too young forgo these attractions, while others split up and take turns riding separately. Missing out on some of Disney's best rides is an unnecessary sacrifice, and waiting in line twice for the same ride is a tremendous waste of time.

A better way to approach the problem is to take advantage of an option known as switching off or the baby swap. Switching off requires at least two adults. Everybody waits in line together, both adults and children. When you reach a Disney attendant (known as a greeter), say you want to switch off. The greeter will allow everyone, including the small children, to enter the attraction. When you reach the loading area, one adult will ride while the other stays with the kids. The riding adult then disembarks and takes responsibility for the children while the other adult rides. A third adult in the party can ride twice, once with each of the switching-off adults, so they do not have to experience the attraction alone. The 12 attractions where switching off is routinely practiced are listed on the chart on page 150.

Disney has been experimenting with a new switching-off procedure for certain Fastpass attractions. Here the cast member gives two Fastpasses to the parent who will be waiting with the child. That parent and the child then leave the queue and are free to do other things while the riding parent is waiting in line and experiencing the attraction. When the family regroups, the nonriding parent can use

ATTRACTIONS WHERE SWITCHING OFF IS COMMON
DISNEYLAND PARK
ADVENTURELAND   Indiana Jones Adventure
CRITTER COUNTRY   Splash Mountain
FANTASYLAND   Matterhorn Bobsleds
FRONTIERLAND   Big Thunder Mountain Railroad
TOMORROWLAND   Space Mountain | Star Tours: The Adventures Continue
DISNEY CALIFORNIA ADVENTURE
CARS LAND   Radiator Springs Racers
GRIZZLY PEAK   Grizzly River Run
CONDOR FLATS   Soarin' Over California
HOLLYWOOD LAND   The Twilight Zone Tower of Terror
PARADISE PIER   California Screamin' | Goofy's Sky School

her Fastpasses to ride, taking another member of the family with her if she desires.

An Ada, Michigan, mother discovered that the procedure for switching off varies from attraction to attraction and offered this suggestion:

> *Parents need to tell the very first attendant they come to that they would like to switch off. Each attraction has a different procedure for this. Tell every other attendant too because they forget quickly.*

Finally, you don't have to be a baby to utilize the baby swap; it works just as well for older children and adults who are unable or unwilling to ride an attraction but still want to experience the queue with their party.

5. HOW TO RIDE TWICE IN A ROW WITHOUT WAITING Many small children like to ride a favorite attraction two or more times in succession. Riding the second time often gives the child a feeling of mastery and accomplishment. Unfortunately, repeat rides can be time-consuming, even in the early morning. If you ride Dumbo as soon as Disneyland Park opens, for instance, you will only have a 1- or 2-minute wait for your first ride. When you come back for your second ride, your wait will be about 12 minutes. If you want to ride a third time, count on a 20-minute or longer wait.

The best way for getting your child on the ride twice (or more) without blowing your whole morning is by using the Chuck-Bubba Relay (named in honor of a reader from Kentucky):

1. Mom and little Bubba enter the waiting line.

2. Dad lets a certain number of people go in front of him (32 in the case of Dumbo) and then gets in line.

3. As soon as the ride stops, Mom exits with little Bubba and passes him to Dad to ride the second time.

4. If everybody is really getting into this, Mom can hop in line again, no less than 32 people behind Dad.

The Chuck-Bubba Relay will not work on every ride because of differences in the way the waiting areas are configured (that is, it is impossible in some cases to exit the ride and make the pass). The rides where the Chuck-Bubba Relay does work appear on the chart along with the number of people to count off.

ATTRACTIONS WHERE THE CHUCK-BUBBA RELAY USUALLY WORKS	
DISNEYLAND PARK	**Number of people between adults**
ALICE IN WONDERLAND (tough, but possible)	38 people
CASEY JR. CIRCUS TRAIN	34 people, if 2 trains are operating
DAVY CROCKETT'S EXPLORER CANOES	94 people, if 6 canoes are operating
DUMBO THE FLYING ELEPHANT	32 people
KING ARTHUR CARROUSEL	70 people
MAD TEA PARTY	53 people
MR. TOAD'S WILD RIDE	32 people
PETER PAN'S FLIGHT	25 people
SNOW WHITE'S SCARY ADVENTURES	30 people
DISNEY CALIFORNIA ADVENTURE	**Number of people between adults**
GOLDEN ZEPHYR	64 people
JUMPIN' JELLYFISH	16 people
KING TRITON'S CARROUSEL	64 people

When practicing the Chuck-Bubba Relay, if you are the second adult in line, you will reach a point in the waiting area that is obviously the easiest place to make the handoff. Sometimes this point is where those exiting the ride pass closest to those waiting to board. In any event, you will know it when you see it. Once there, if the first parent has not arrived with little Bubba, just let those behind you slip past until Bubba shows up.

6. LAST-MINUTE COLD FEET If your small child gets cold feet at the last minute after waiting for a ride (where there is no age or height requirement), you can usually arrange with the loading attendant for a switch-off; see the chart on page 150. This situation arises frequently at Pirates of the Caribbean—small children lose their courage en route to the loading area.

There is no law that says you have to ride. If you get to the boarding area and someone is unhappy, just tell a Disney attendant that you have changed your mind, and one will show you the way out.

7. THROW YOURSELF ON THE GRENADE, MILDRED! For by-the-book, do-the-right-thing parents determined to sacrifice themselves on behalf of their children, we provide a One-Day Touring Plan for Disneyland Park called the Dumbo-or-Die-in-a-Day Touring Plan for Parents with Small Children. This touring plan, detailed on page 367, will ensure that you run yourself ragged. Designed to help you forfeit everything of personal interest for the sake of your children's pleasure, the plan is guaranteed to send you home battered and exhausted with extraordinary stories of devotion and heroic perseverance. By the way, the plan really works. Anyone under 8 years old will love it.

8. DISNEY CALIFORNIA ADVENTURE This is not a great park for little ones. With the exception of Flik's Fun Fair, The Little Mermaid, three play areas, and a carousel, the remaining attractions will be either boring or too frightening for most preschoolers. Elementary school–age children will fare better but will probably be captivated by the low-capacity/long-line rides at the Paradise Pier district of the park. Although designed to be appealing to the eye, these attractions are simply gussied-up versions of midway rides your kids can enjoy less expensively and with a fraction of the wait at a local amusement park or state fair.

9. AUTOPIA Though the Autopia at Disneyland Park is a great treat for small children, they are required to be 54 inches tall in order to drive unassisted. To work around the height requirement issues, go on the ride with your small child. After getting into the car, shift your child over behind the steering wheel. From your position you will still be able to control the foot pedals. To your child, it will feel like driving. Because the car travels on a self-guiding track, there is no way your child can make a mistake while steering.

LOST CHILDREN

unofficial **TIP**
We suggest that children younger than 8 years be color coded by dressing them in purple T-shirts or equally distinctive clothes.

LOST CHILDREN NORMALLY do not present much of a problem at Disneyland Resort. All Disney employees are schooled in handling such situations. If you lose a child while touring, report the situation to a Disney employee; then check in at City Hall (Disneyland Park) or Guest Relations (DCA) where lost-children logs are maintained. In an emergency, an alert can be issued throughout the park through internal communications. If a Disney cast member encounters a lost child, the cast member will escort the child to the Baby Care Center located at the central-hub end of Main Street in Disneyland Park and at the entrance plaza in DCA. Guests age 11 or under are taken to the Baby Care Center in the Pacific Wharf area at DCA. Guests age 12 and older may leave a written message at City Hall or the Guest Relations lobby or wait there.

It is amazingly easy to lose a child (or two) at a Disney park. It is a good idea to sew a label into each child's shirt that states his or her name, your name, and the name of your hotel. The same task can be accomplished by writing the information on a strip of masking tape; hotel security professionals suggest that the information be printed in small letters, and that the tape be affixed to the outside of the child's shirt 5 inches or so below the armpit.

HOW KIDS GET LOST

CHILDREN GET SEPARATED FROM PARENTS EVERY DAY at the Disney parks under circumstances that are remarkably similar (and predictable).

1. PREOCCUPIED SOLO PARENT In this scenario the only adult in the party is preoccupied with something such as buying refreshments,

TIPS FOR KEEPING TRACK OF YOUR BROOD

• Same-colored T-shirts for the whole family will help you gather your troops in an easy and fun way. Opt for just a uniform color or have the T-shirts printed with a logo such as "The Brown Family's Assault on the Mouse." You might also include the date or the year of your visit. Light-colored T-shirts can even be autographed by the Disney characters.

• Clothing labels are great, of course. If you don't sew, buy labels that you can iron on the garment. If you own a cell phone, be sure to include the number on the label. If you do not own a cell phone, put in the phone number of the hotel where you'll be staying.

• An easier option is a temporary tattoo with your child's name and your phone number. Unlike other methods, the tattoos cannot fall off or be lost. Temporary tattoos last about two weeks, won't wash or sweat off, and are not irritating to the skin. They can be purchased online at **safetytat.com** or **tattooswithapurpose.com.** Special tattoos are available for children with food allergies or cognitive impairment such as autism.

• In pet stores you can have name tags printed for a very reasonable price. These are great to add to necklaces and bracelets, or attach to your child's shoelaces or a belt loop.

• When you check into the hotel, take a business card of the hotel for each member in your party, especially those old enough to carry wallets and purses.

• Always agree on a meeting point before you see a parade, fireworks, and nighttime spectacles. Make sure the meeting place is in the park (as opposed to the car or some place outside the front gate).

• If you have a digital camera or camera phone, you may elect to take a picture of your kids every morning. If they get lost, the picture will show what they look like and what they are wearing.

• If all members of your party have cell phones, it's easy to locate each other. However, the noise in the parks is so loud that you probably won't hear your cell phone ring. Carry your phone in a front pants pocket and program the phone to vibrate. Or communicate via text message. If any of your younger kids carry cell phones, secure the phones with a strap.

• Save key tags and luggage tags for use on items you bring to the parks, including your stroller, diaper bag, and backpack or hip pack.

• Don't underestimate the power of the permanent marker, such as a Sharpie. They are great for labeling pretty much anything. Mini-Sharpies are great for collecting character autographs.

loading the camera, or using the restroom. Junior is there one moment and gone the next.

2. THE HIDDEN EXIT Sometimes parents wait on the sidelines while allowing two or more young children to experience a ride together. As it usually happens, the parents expect the kids to exit the attraction in one place, and, lo and behold, the young ones pop out somewhere else. The exits of some Disney attractions are considerably distant from the entrances. Make sure that you know exactly where your children will emerge before letting them ride by themselves.

3. AFTER THE SHOW At the completion of many shows and rides, a Disney staffer will announce, "Check for personal belongings and take small children by the hand." When dozens, if not hundreds, of people leave an attraction at the same time, it is easy for parents to temporarily lose contact with their children unless they have them directly in tow.

4. RESTROOM PROBLEMS Mom tells 6-year-old Tommy, "I'll be sitting on this bench when you come out of the restroom." Three situations: One, Tommy exits through a different door and becomes disoriented (Mom may not know there is another door). Two, Mom decides belatedly that she will also use the restroom, and Tommy emerges to find her absent. Three, Mom pokes around in a shop while keeping an eye on the bench but misses Tommy when he comes out. A restroom adjacent to the Rancho del Zocalo Restuarante in Frontierland accounts for many lost children. Because it's located in a passageway connecting Frontierland and Fantasy Faire, children can wander into a totally different area of the park from where they came by simply making a wrong turn out of the restroom.

If you can't be with your child in the restroom, make sure that there is only one exit. Designate a meeting spot more distinctive than a bench, and be specific in your instructions: "I'll meet you by this flagpole. If you get out first, stay right here." Have your child repeat the directions back to you.

5. PARADES There are many special parades and shows at the theme park during which the audience stands. Children, because they are small, tend to jockey around for a better view. By moving a little this way and a little that way, it is amazing how much distance kids can put between themselves and you before anyone notices.

6. MASS MOVEMENTS Another situation to guard against is when huge crowds disperse after shows, fireworks, parades, or at park closing. With 5,000–12,000 people suddenly moving at once, it is very easy to get separated from a small child or others in your party. Extra caution is recommended following the evening parades, fireworks, and *Fantasmic!* Families should develop specific plans for what to do and where to meet in the event they are separated.

7. CHARACTER GREETINGS A fair amount of activity and confusion is commonplace when the Disney characters are on the scene. See the next section on meeting the Disney characters.

The DISNEY CHARACTERS

FOR YEARS THE COSTUMED, walking versions of Mickey, Minnie, Donald, Goofy, and others have been a colorful supporting cast at Disneyland and Walt Disney World. Known unpretentiously as the Disney characters, these large and friendly figures help provide a link between Disney animated films and the Disney theme parks.

Audiences, it has been observed, cry during the sad parts of Disney animated films and cheer when the villain is vanquished. To the emotionally invested, the characters in these features are as real as next-door neighbors; never mind that they are simply drawings on plastic. In recent years, the theme park personifications of Disney characters have likewise become real to us. For thousands of visitors, it is not just some person in a mouse costume they see—it is really Mickey. Similarly, running into Goofy or Snow White in Fantasyland is a memory to be treasured, an encounter with a real celebrity.

About 250 of the Disney animated-film characters have been brought to life in costume. Of these, a relatively small number (about 50) are greeters (the Disney term for characters who mix with the patrons). The remaining characters are relegated exclusively to performing in shows or participating in parades. Some appear only once or twice a year, usually in Christmas parades or Disney anniversary celebrations.

CHARACTER ENCOUNTERS

CHARACTER WATCHING has developed into a pastime. Where families were once content to stumble across a character occasionally, they now pursue them armed with autograph books and cameras. For those who pay attention, some characters are more frequently encountered than others. Mickey, Minnie, and Goofy, for example, are seemingly everywhere, while Thumper rarely appears. Other characters are seen regularly but limit themselves to a specific location.

The fact that some characters are seldom seen has turned character watching into character collecting. Mickey Mouse may be the best-known and most-loved character, but from a collector's perspective he is also the most common. To get an autograph from Mickey is no big deal, but Daisy Duck's signature is a real coup. Commercially tapping into the character-collecting movement, Disney sells autograph books throughout the parks.

One Unofficial Guide reader offers this suggestion regarding character autographs:

> Young children learn very quickly! If they see another child get an autograph, then they will want an autograph book as well. I recommend buying an autograph book right away. My 4-year-old daughter saw a child get Goofy's autograph, and right away she wanted to join the fun.

PREPARING YOUR CHILDREN TO MEET THE CHARACTERS Because most small children are not expecting Minnie Mouse to be the size of a forklift, it's best to discuss the characters with your kids before you go. Almost all of the characters are quite large, and several, such as Br'er Bear, are huge! All of them can be extremely intimidating to a preschooler.

On first encounter, it is important not to thrust your child upon the character. Allow the little one to come to terms with this big thing from whatever distance the child feels safe. If two adults are present, one should stay close to the youngster while the other approaches the character and demonstrates that the character is safe and friendly. Some kids warm to the characters immediately, while some never do. Most take a little time, and often require several different encounters.

There are two kinds of characters: those whose costume includes a face-covering headpiece (animal characters plus some human characters such as Captain Hook), and face characters, or actors who resemble the cartoon characters to such an extent that no mask or headpiece is necessary. Face characters include Mary Poppins, Ariel, Jasmine, Aladdin, Cinderella, Mulan, Tarzan, Jane, Belle, Snow White, and Prince Charming, to name a few.

unofficial **TIP**
Don't underestimate your child's excitement at meeting the Disney characters—but also be aware that very small kids may find the large, costumed characters a little frightening.

Only the face characters are allowed to speak. Headpiece characters, called furs in Disney-speak, do not talk or make noises of any kind. Because the cast members could not possibly imitate the distinctive voice of the characters, the Disney folks have determined that it is more effective to keep them silent. Lack of speech notwithstanding, the headpiece characters are extremely warm and responsive, and they communicate very effectively with gestures. As with the characters' size, children need to be forewarned that the characters do not talk. The only exceptions are the costumed stars of some newer shows and parades, who boast articulated facial features that blink and flap in sync with the soundtracks.

Parents need to understand that some of the character costumes are very cumbersome and that cast members often suffer from very poor visibility. You have to look closely, but the eye holes are frequently in the mouth of the costume or even down on the neck. What this means in practical terms is that the characters are sort of clumsy and have a limited field of vision. Children who approach the character from the back or the side may not be noticed, even if the child is touching the character. It is perfectly possible in this situation for the character to accidentally step on the child or knock him or her down. The best way for a child to approach a character is from the front, and occasionally not even this works. For example, the various duck characters (Donald, Daisy, Uncle Scrooge, and so on) have to peer around their bills. If it appears that the character is ignoring your child, pick your child up and hold her in front of the character until the character responds.

It is OK to touch, pat, or hug the character if your child is so inclined. Understanding the unpredictability of children, the characters will keep their feet very still, particularly refraining from moving backward or to the side. Most of the characters will sign autographs or pose for pictures. Once again, be sure to approach from the front so that the character will understand your intentions. If your child collects autographs, it is a good idea to carry a big, fat pen about the size of a Magic Marker. The costumes make it exceedingly difficult for the characters to wield a smaller pen, so the bigger the better.

unofficial **TIP**
Explain to your children that the headpiece characters do not talk. Keep in mind, too, that the characters are clumsy and have a limited field of vision.

THE BIG HURT Many children expect to bump into Mickey the minute they enter a park and are disappointed when he is not around. If your children are unable to settle down and enjoy things until they see Mickey, simply ask a Disney cast member where to find him. If the cast member does not know Mickey's whereabouts, he or she can find out for you in short order.

"THEN SOME CONFUSION HAPPENED" Be forewarned that character encounters give rise to a situation during which small children sometimes get lost. There is usually a lot of activity around a character, with both adults and children touching the character or posing for pictures. In the most common scenario, the parents stay in the crowd while their child marches up to get acquainted. With the excitement of the encounter, all the milling people, and the character moving around, a child may get turned around and head off in the wrong direction. In the words of a Salt Lake City mom:

> Milo was shaking hands with Dopey one moment, then some confusion happened and he [Milo] was gone.

Families with several small children, and parents who are busy fooling around with cameras, can lose track of a youngster in a heartbeat. Our recommendation for parents of preschoolers is to stay with the kids when they meet the characters, stepping back only long enough to take a picture, if necessary.

MEETING CHARACTERS You can *see* the Disney characters in live shows and in parades. For times, consult your *Times Guide*. If you have the time and money, you can share a meal with the characters (more about this later). But if you want to *meet* the characters, get autographs, and take photos, it's helpful to know where the characters hang out.

Responding to guest requests, Disneyland Resort has added a lot of information about characters to its handout park maps and entertainment *Times Guide*. A listing specifies where and when certain characters will be available and also provides information on character dining. On the maps of the parks themselves, Mickey's gloved hand is used to denote locations where characters can be found.

At DCA, look for characters in Hollywood Land near the Animation Building, in parades, and in shows at the Hyperion Theater. Elsewhere around the park, characters will be less in evidence than at Disneyland Park, but they will make periodic appearances at Flik's Fun Fair and Buena Vista Street (the central hub).

The last few years have seen a number of Disney initiatives aimed at satisfying guests' inexhaustible desire to meet the characters. At Disneyland Park, Disney relegated four (Mickey, Minnie, Pluto, and Donald) of the "fab five" to all-day tours of duty in Mickey's Toontown. The fifth "fab," Goofy, works a similar schedule most days in Frontierland but also spends plenty of time in Toontown. Likewise, Pooh and Tigger can usually be found in Critter Country, Princess Tiana in New Orleans Square's Court of Angels, Merida from *Brave* in Fantasyland near Pinocchio's ride, and Aladdin and Jasmine in Adventureland. The new Fantasy Faire plaza adjacent to Sleeping Beauty Castle is the prime place to meet Aurora, Ariel, Cinderella, Belle, and Rapunzel. Tinker Bell and her fairy friends draw long lines at their Pixie Hollow area off the central hub between Tomorrowland and the Matterhorn. Characters less in demand roam the "lands" consistent with their image (Br'er Bear and Br'er Fox in Critter Country, for example).

While making the characters routinely available has taken the guesswork out of finding them, it has likewise robbed character encounters of much of their surprise and spontaneity. Instead of chancing on a character as you turn a corner, it is much more common now to wait in a queue to meet the character. Be aware that lines for face characters move much more slowly than do lines

unofficial **TIP**
Characters make appearances in all the "lands" but are especially thick in Fantasyland, Mickey's Toontown, and Town Square on Main Street.

for nonspeaking characters, as you might surmise. Because face characters are allowed to talk, they do, often engaging children in lengthy conversations, much to the consternation of the families stuck in the queue.

If you believe that Disneyland Park already has quite enough lines, and, furthermore, if you prefer to bump into your characters on the run, here's a quick rundown of where the bears and chipmunks roam. There will almost always be a character in Town Square on Main Street and often at the central hub. Snow White hangs out near her wishing well in the courtyard of the castle; the aforementioned Br'ers cruise Critter Country; and Alice and her *Wonderland* friends wander around Fantasyland. Any characters whom we haven't specifically mentioned generally continue to turn up randomly throughout the park. Character selection can vary seasonally, with some (such as Jack Skellington) appearing only around Halloween or Christmas.

Characters are also featured in the afternoon and evening parades, Frontierland waterfront shows, *Fantasmic!*, and Disney Princess Fantasy Faire. Performance times for all of the shows and parades are listed in the Disneyland Park's daily *Times Guide* entertainment listings. After the shows, characters will sometimes stick around to greet the audience.

Mickey Mouse is available to meet guests and pose for photos all day long in his dressing room at Mickey's Movie Barn in Mickey's Toontown. To reach the Movie Barn, proceed through the front door of Mickey's House and follow the crowd. If the line extends back to the entrance of Mickey's House, it will take you about 25–30 minutes to actually reach Mickey. When you finally get to his dressing room, one or two families at a time are admitted for a short personal audience with Mickey.

Many children are so excited about meeting Mickey that they cannot relax to enjoy the other attractions. If Mickey looms large in your child's day, board the Disneyland Railroad at the Main Street Station as soon as you arrive at the park, and proceed directly to Mickey's Toontown (half a circuit). If you visit Mickey before 10 a.m., your wait will be short.

Minnie receives guests at her house in Toontown most of the day as well, and Donald and Pluto are frequently available for photographs and autographs in the gazebo in front of the Toontown Town Hall. There is, of course, a separate line for each character. Also, be aware that the characters bug out for parades and certain other special performances. Check the daily *Times Guide* entertainment listings for performance times and plan your visit to Toontown accordingly.

CHARACTER DINING

FRATERNIZING WITH DISNEY CHARACTERS has become so popular that Disney offers character breakfasts, brunches, and dinners where families can dine in the presence of Minnie, Goofy, and other costumed versions of animated celebrities. Character meals provide a familiar, controlled setting in which young children can warm gradually to the characters. All meals are attended by several characters. Adult prices apply to persons age 10 or older, children's prices to ages 3–9. Little ones under age 3 eat free. Because character dining is very popular, we recommend that you arrange reservations as far in advance (up to 60 days) as possible.

unofficial **TIP**
Arrange dining reservations as far in advance as possible. Your wait for a table will usually be less than 15 minutes.

CHARACTER DINING: WHAT TO EXPECT Character meals are bustling affairs, held in hotels' or theme parks' largest table-service or "buffeteria" restaurants. Character breakfasts (there are five) offer a fixed menu served family-style or as a buffet. The typical family-style breakfast includes scrambled eggs; bacon, sausage, and ham; hash browns; waffles, pancakes, or French toast; biscuits, rolls, or pastries; and fruit. The meal is

"Casting! This is George at the character breakfast. There's been a mistake. We were supposed to get the Assorted Character Package with one Mickey, one Goofy, one Donald, one Pluto. . . ."

served in large skillets or platters at your table. If you run out of something, you can order seconds (or thirds) at no additional charge. Buffets offer much the same fare, but you have to fetch it yourself.

Whatever the meal, characters circulate around the room while you eat. During your meal, each of the three to five characters present will visit your table, arriving one at a time to cuddle the kids (and sometimes the adults), pose for photos, and sign autographs. Keep autograph books (with pens) and loaded cameras handy. For the best photos, adults should sit across the table from their children. Always seat the children where characters can reach them most easily. If a table is against a wall, for example, adults should sit with their backs to the wall and children should sit nearest the aisle.

You will not be rushed to leave after you've eaten. Remember, however, lots of eager children and adults might be waiting not so patiently to be admitted.

You can dine with Disney characters at the Plaza Inn in Disneyland Park, at Goofy's Kitchen at the Disneyland Hotel, at Ariel's Grotto at DCA, at the Storytellers Café at the Grand Californian Hotel, and at Disney's PCH Grill at the Paradise Pier Hotel. For information about character meals and to make dining reservations up to 60 days in advance, call ☎ 714-781-DINE (3463).

ARIEL'S DISNEY PRINCESS CELEBRATION Overlooking Paradise Bay, Ariel's Grotto hosts breakfast and lunch with Ariel and friends daily until

3:55 p.m. Breakfast costs $33 for adults and $18 for kids, and lunch is $37 for adults and $20 for kids. Fixed-price dinners include *World of Color* reservations, but Ariel et al end their appearances midafternoon.

DISNEY'S PCH (PACIFIC COAST HIGHWAY) GRILL PCH Grill at the Paradise Pier Hotel serves a Surf's Up! Breakfast with Mickey & Friends buffet 7–11 a.m. that features traditional Mexican breakfast items such as *chilaquiles* in addition to the usual American fare. Prices are $32 for adults and $17 for kids. Mickey (wearing beach togs) entertains you, along with Stitch, Minnie, and Pluto. This is usually the least crowded of the hotel character meals.

GOOFY'S KITCHEN Located at the Disneyland Hotel, Goofy's Kitchen serves a character breakfast buffet 7 a.m.–noon (2 p.m. weekends) and a character dinner buffet 5–9 p.m. Breakfast is $33 for adults and $17 for kids. Dinners run $36 and $16, respectively. Goofy, of course, is the head character, but he's usually joined by Minnie, Pluto, and others.

PLAZA INN Located at the end of Main Street and to the right, the Plaza Inn character buffet is usually packed because it hosts character breakfasts that are included in vacation packages sold by the Disney Resort Travel Sales Center. Served from opening until 11 a.m., the buffet costs $32 for adults and $17 for children. Characters present usually include Minnie, Goofy, Pluto, and Chip 'n' Dale.

STORYTELLERS CAFÉ Storytellers Café, located at the Grand Californian Hotel, is the most attractive of the character-meal venues. A breakfast buffet, as well as à la carte items, is served 7–11 a.m. The buffet costs $26 for adults and $14 for children; à la carte entrées are $7.50–$23. Chip 'n Dale, the featured characters, are usually assisted by critters from *Tarzan, Brother Bear,* and *Pocahontas.*

PART FOUR

DINING *and* SHOPPING *in and around* DISNEYLAND

DINING *in* DISNEYLAND RESORT

IN THIS SECTION, we aim to help you find good food without going broke or tripping over one of Disneyland Resort's many culinary land mines. More than 50 restaurants operate in Disneyland Resort, including about 25 full-service restaurants, several of which are inside the theme parks. Collectively, Disney restaurants offer reasonable variety, serving everything from Louisiana Creole to Texas barbecue, but sadly, international cuisines other than Mexican, Asian, Mediterranean, and Italian are not represented.

On the upside, we've never seen as dramatic an improvement in Disneyland restaurant quality as we have in the last few years. And this year is no exception. Ingredients are fresher, preparation is more careful, and even steam tables and buffets are under almost constant supervision. As a whole, the culinary team has definitely stepped up their game, and we are the winners. Many establishments have undergone complete menu makeovers, with terrific results. Unlike other attractions and shops inside the resort, the food and beverage operation remains in constant flux. Venues open and close, add and delete menu items, and change decor throughout the year. We strive to provide you with the most accurate information possible; however, we do eventually have to go to press with the most current information we have at the time. Keep this in mind when using the guide.

You can expect to pay heavy prices for food within Disneyland Resort. Every meal, snack, and drink is anywhere from 100% to 400% more inside the parks than outside (not counting Downtown Disney).

With fine dining offered at California Adventure, you can enjoy a glass of wine, a mug of beer, or even a cocktail inside the resorts without having to exit the park. Downtown Disney offers a wide variety of dining options, from mediocre to awesome, from intimate and adult to wild and kid-friendly. The Grand Californian Hotel is home to **Napa Rose,** one of the finest dining spots in all of Southern California, and even character meals at eateries such as **Ariel's Grotto** and **Disney's PCH Grill** offer better, healthier food than ever before.

Note: Disneyland dining reservations are the Disney-restaurant equivalent of Fastpass. This feature is available where noted and gives you the option of picking a time and cutting to the head of the line. You may still have to wait, but it's from the front of the line instead of the back.

GETTING IT RIGHT

ALTHOUGH WE WORK HARD to be objective and accurate, many readers think that we're too critical of the restaurants at Disneyland. One Charleston, West Virginia, woman came out swinging:

> *Get a life! It's crazy and unrealistic to be so snobbish about restaurants at a theme park. Considering the number of people Disney feeds each day, I think they do a darn good job. Also, you act so surprised that the food is expensive. Have you ever eaten at an airport? HELLO IN THERE? . . . Surprise, you're a captive! It's a theme park!*

And a mom from Erie, Pennsylvania, struck a practical note:

> *Most of the food is OK. In our experience, more of it is good than bad. If you pay attention to what other visitors say and what's in the guidebooks, you can avoid the yucky places. You pay more than you should, but it's more convenient [to eat Disney food] than to try to find cheaper restaurants somewhere else.*

As you might infer from the reader comments above, getting our dining coverage right is a bit of a challenge. While researching and reviewing restaurants may appear to be a straightforward endeavor, we can assure you that it is fraught with peril. We've read dining reviews by writers who turn up their noses at anything except four-star French restaurants (of which there are a whole lot fewer than people think). Likewise, we've seen reviewers who totally avoid Thai and Indian restaurants (among others) because they don't understand those cuisines, and we've read critiques absolutely devoid of criticism, written by "experts" unwilling to risk offending the sources of their free meals. Finally, we've seen reviews that are wholly based on surveys submitted by diners whose credentials for evaluating fine dining are mysterious at best and questionable at least.

unofficial **TIP**
It's necessary, we believe, to present both an expert and a popular opinion of each restaurant.

How, then, do we go about presenting the best possible dining coverage? What is the best way to get it right? We at the Unofficial Guides have elected to begin with highly qualified culinary experts and then balance their opinions with those of our readers.

The expert opinion is essential because it's important to be able to differentiate what the restaurant really serves from what it purports to serve. Many years ago in Lexington, Kentucky, by way of example, there was only one Chinese restaurant. It was wildly successful even though it was Chinese in name only. Still, its specialty dishes, essentially American vegetable casseroles smothered in cornstarch, were happily consumed by patrons who had never been exposed to real Chinese cooking. The food wasn't bad, mind you, but it wasn't Chinese either. Visitors from out of town, inquiring about a good local Chinese restaurant, were often directed to this place. As you would expect, they were routinely horrified by the fare.

In this guide, we think that you deserve to know whether or not you're getting the real thing. If we recommend, say, the *pommes frites* with Cajun rémoulade (seasoned french fries served with cheese and a mayonnaise-based sauce with chopped onion, Creole mustard, and paprika) at Café Orléans, it's pretty essential that our dining critics know what rémoulade is, how it should be prepared, how it should be served, and how it should taste. In our opinion, it's almost impossible to publish a creditable restaurant review without the help of a knowledgeable, professional dining critic.

The ultimate test of success for a restaurant, however, is not the authenticity of its dishes but the satisfaction of its patrons. If diners have a bad experience and don't come back, the restaurant will fail. Thus, we regard our experts' opinions and our readers' feedback as two halves of a whole: both are necessary to inform your dining decisions.

Our experts are knowledgeable, seasoned professionals who have studied culinary arts around the world and who have written cookbooks or columns. They are well versed in ethnic dishes and have no prejudice about high or low cuisine. Our experts also conduct their reviews anonymously and always pay full menu prices for their meals. Additionally, many of our experts spent years working in the industry; they empathize with the operators and recognize how difficult it is to prove themselves worthy with every plate many times over every day.

We encourage you to fill out the dining survey on **touringplans .com**. If you want to share your dining experience in depth, write to us at the address listed on page 8, or send us an e-mail at **unofficial guides@menasharidge.com**.

DISNEY DINING 101

DISNEYLAND RESORT RESTAURANT RESERVATIONS: WHAT'S IN A NAME

DISNEY TINKERS CEASELESSLY with its restaurant-reservations policy. Disneyland dining reservations (previously known as Priority Seating) issues reservations that aren't exactly reservations. When you call Disney Dining at ☎ 714-781-3463, option 4, your name and essential information are taken, well, as if you were making a reservation. The Disney representative then tells you that you have dining reservations for the restaurant on the date and time you requested, usually explaining that you will be seated ahead of walk-ins—that is, those guests without reservations. In case you can't figure out how to place a voice call with your fancy smartphone, you can also book tables by e-mailing your name, phone number, party size, restaurant, and preferred seating time to **dine@disneyland.com.**

Travelers who have experienced Walt Disney World's Advanced Dining Reservations system will be relieved to discover that Disneyland's dining reservation scheme is far simpler to navigate. Unlike in Orlando, there is no need to hit the phones at 7 a.m. on the 180th day before your Anaheim vacation; except on the busiest days, most restaurants in the parks and hotels offer same-day availability. If you do want to schedule a seating, the process is much less complex in California; there is no interactive website for Disneyland dining reservations yet, and phone and e-mail bookings don't even generate confirmation numbers.

BEHIND THE SCENES AT DISNEYLAND RESORT DINING

DISNEY RESTAURANTS OPERATE on what they call a template system. Instead of scheduling reservations for actual tables, reservationists fill time slots. The number of slots available is based on the average observed length of time that guests occupy a table at a particular restaurant, adjusted for seasonality.

Here's a rough example of how it works: let's say that the Blue Bayou Restaurant at Disneyland Park has 38 tables for four and 10 tables for six, and that the average length of time for a family to be seated, order, eat, pay, and depart is 40 minutes. Add 5 minutes to bus the table and set it up for the next guests, and the tables are turning every 45 minutes. The restaurant provides Disneyland Resort Dining (DRD) with a computer template of its capacity, along with the average time the table is occupied. Thus, when DRD makes reservations for four people at 6:15 p.m., the system removes one table for four from overall capacity for 45 minutes. The template on the reservationist's computer indicates that the table will not be available for reassignment until 7 p.m. (45 minutes later). And so it goes for all the tables in the restaurant, each being subtracted from overall capacity for 45 minutes, then listed as available again, then assigned to other guests and subtracted again, and so on, throughout the meal period. DRD tries to fill every time slot for every seat in the restaurant, or come as close to filling every slot as possible. No seats—repeat, none—are *reserved* for walk-ins, though all restaurants accommodate such customers on a space-available basis.

unofficial **TIP**
Dining reservations are available to all Disneyland visitors—not just guests of the resort hotels. In the theme parks, you can make reservations for later in the day at the door of the restaurant.

Templates are filled differently depending on the season. During slower times of year, when dining reservations are easier to get, DRD will overbook a restaurant for each time slot, assuming that there will be a lot of no-shows. During busy times of year, when reservations are harder to come by, there are very few no-shows, so the restaurant is booked according to its actual capacity.

With dining reservations, your waiting time will almost always be less than 20 minutes during peak hours, and often less than 10 minutes. If you just walk in, especially during busier seasons, expect to wait 40–75 minutes.

GETTING YOUR ACT TOGETHER

IF YOU WANT TO PATRONIZE any of the Disneyland Resort full-service restaurants, especially buffets or character-dining eateries, you should consider dining reservations (call ☎ 714-781-3463, option 4, up to 60 days in advance). DRD handles reservations for both Disney-owned and independent restaurants at the theme parks, Disney hotels, and Downtown Disney. The sole exception is the **Rainforest Cafe** at Downtown Disney, which makes its own reservations at ☎ 714-772-0413.

If you fail to make dining reservations before you leave home, or if you want to make your dining decisions spontaneously, your chances of getting a table at the restaurant of your choice are good. Blue Bayou at Disneyland Park, Napa Rose at the Grand Californian Hotel, and the various character-meal venues are the most likely to sell out. If, however, you visit Disneyland during a very busy time of year, it's to your advantage to make dining reservations.

In 2013 Disneyland announced a new policy (adopted from Walt Disney World) of collecting a credit card number with every dining reservation. If you poop out in the theme park and are a no-show for your meal, you will be charged $10 per person. Your reservation will be voided 15 minutes after the scheduled time, and the penalty will apply unless you call DRD at least 24 hours before your seating. This same cancellation policy also applies to makeover appointments at Studio Disney 365 and Bibbidi Bobbidi Boutique, as well as cabanas at the hotel pools. At press time, implementation of this policy had been indefinitely suspended; if it is reinstated, you will be informed at the time that you make your reservations. If you've lined up many seatings, it's a good idea to phone DRD a few days before you arrive to make sure that everything is in order. If you stay at a Disney resort, Guest Services can print out a summary of all your dining reservations. If you have a seating for a theme park restaurant at a time before park opening, as is sometimes the case for a character breakfast, simply proceed to the turnstiles and inform a cast member, who will admit you to the park.

DRESS

DRESS IS INFORMAL at all theme park restaurants, but dressy casual is appropriate for resort restaurants such as Napa Rose. That means dress slacks (or dress shorts) with a collared shirt for men and slacks, skirts, or dress shorts with a blouse or sweater (or a dress) for women. You may be surprised how comfortable you feel when you're dressed appropriately.

FOOD ALLERGIES AND SPECIAL REQUESTS

IF YOU HAVE FOOD ALLERGIES or follow a specific type of diet (such as kosher or gluten-free), make your needs known when you arrange your dining reservation. Does it work? Well, a Phillipsburg, New Jersey, mom reports her family's experience:

> My 6-year-old has many food allergies, and we often have to bring food with us to restaurants when we go out to eat. I was able to make reservations at the Disney restaurants in advance and indicate these allergies to the reservation clerk. When we arrived at the restaurants, the staff was already aware of my child's allergies and assigned our table a chef who double-checked the list of allergies with us. Each member of the waitstaff was also informed of the allergies. The chefs were very nice and made my son feel very special (to the point where my other family members felt a little jealous).

A FEW CAVEATS

BEFORE YOU BEGIN eating your way through Disneyland, take our advice:

1. However creative and enticing the menu descriptions, avoid fancy food at full-service restaurants in the theme parks. Order dishes that the kitchen is unlikely to botch. Stick with what's familiar in most cases and you won't be disappointed.

2. Don't order baked, broiled, poached, or grilled seafood unless the restaurant specializes in seafood or rates at least ★★★½ in our dining profiles.

3. Theme park restaurants rush their customers to make room for the next group of diners. Eating at high speed may appeal to a family with young, restless children, but for people wanting to relax, it's more like dining in a pressure chamber.

    If you want to linger over your expensive meal, don't order your entire dinner at once. Order drinks, study the menu while you sip, and then order appetizers. Tell the waiter you need more time to decide among entrées. Order your main course only after appetizers have been served. Dawdle over coffee and dessert. The exceptions to this rule may be the Wine Country Trattoria and Carthay Circle Restaurant inside DCA, upscale venues that encourage a respite over a glass or bottle of premium wine. But, sadly, you may feel pressure even there in peak season.

4. If you're dining in a theme park and cost is an issue, make lunch your main meal. Entrées are similar to those on the dinner menu, but prices may be slightly lower.

DISNEYLAND RESORT RESTAURANT CATEGORIES

IN GENERAL, food and beverage offerings at Disneyland Resort are defined by service, price, and convenience:

FULL-SERVICE RESTAURANTS   Full-service restaurants are in all Disneyland Resort hotels, both parks, and Downtown Disney. Disney operates most of the restaurants in the theme parks and its hotels; contractors or franchisees operate those at Downtown Disney. The restaurants accept Visa, MasterCard, American Express, Discover, and Diners Club.

BUFFETS AND FIXED-PRICE MEALS With set-price character meals such as Ariel's Grotto at DCA, you can choose one item each from a limited selection of appetizers, salads, main courses, and desserts. Character buffets such as the one at Goofy's Kitchen in the Disneyland Hotel have a separate children's menu featuring kid favorites such as hot dogs, burgers, chicken nuggets, pizza, macaroni and cheese, and spaghetti and meatballs, as well as healthier options such as sliced fruit, yogurt, and whole-grain baked goods. Dining reservations are highly recommended for all character meals.

COUNTER SERVICE Counter-service fast food is available at both theme parks and Downtown Disney. The food compares in quality with McDonald's, Captain D's, Pizza Hut, or Taco Bell but is more expensive, though it's often served in larger portions.

HARD CHOICES

DINING DECISIONS will definitely affect your Disneyland Resort experience. If you're short on time and you want to see the theme parks, avoid full service. Ditto if you're short on funds. If you want to try a Disney full-service restaurant, arrange dining reservations—this won't reserve you a table, but it will minimize your wait.

Integrating Meals into the Unofficial Guide Touring Plans

Arrive before the park of your choice opens. Tour expeditiously, using your chosen plan (taking as few breaks as possible), until about 11–11:30 a.m. Once the park becomes crowded around midday, meals and other breaks won't affect the plan's efficiency. If you intend to stay in the park for evening parades, fireworks, or other events, eat dinner early enough to be finished in time for the festivities.

Character Dining

A number of restaurants, primarily those that serve all-you-can-eat buffets and family-style meals, offer character dining. At character meals, you pay a fixed price and dine in the presence of one to five Disney characters who circulate throughout the restaurant, hugging children, posing for photos, and signing autographs. Character breakfasts, lunches, and dinners are served at restaurants in and out of the theme parks. For an extensive discussion of character dining, see page 160.

> *unofficial* **TIP**
> Bottom line: Young children are the rule, not the exception, at Disney restaurants.

FULL-SERVICE DINING FOR FAMILIES WITH YOUNG CHILDREN

NO MATTER HOW FORMAL a restaurant appears, the staff is accustomed to wiggling, impatient, and often boisterous children. In Disneyland Resort's finest dining rooms, it's not unusual to find at least two dozen young diners attired in basic black . . . mouse ears.

Almost all Disney restaurants offer children's menus, and all have booster seats and high chairs. Waiters will supply little ones with crackers and rolls and serve your dinner much faster than in comparable restaurants elsewhere. In fact, letters from readers suggest that being served too quickly is much more common than having a long wait.

QUIET, ROMANTIC PLACES TO EAT

RESTAURANTS WITH GOOD FOOD *and* a couple-friendly ambience are rare in the theme parks. **Blue Bayou** at Disneyland Park satisfies both requirements. In Disney California Adventure, the **Wine Country Trattoria** offers one of the quietest and more relaxed environments, along with a California wine country–inspired menu, while the elegant **Carthay Circle Restaurant** ranks as one of the best restaurants in any theme park. Among the hotels at the resort, **Napa Rose** at the Grand Californian Hotel & Spa is the leading candidate for a romantic adult dining experience. At Downtown Disney, try **Ralph Brennan's Jazz Kitchen**; ask for a quiet table, though, if you're not interested in the jazz music. **Catal** in Downtown Disney also offers a quiet ambience and an ambitious gourmet menu geared mostly to adults.

Eating later in the evening and choosing a restaurant we've mentioned will improve your chances for intimate dining; nevertheless, know that children, well behaved or otherwise, are everywhere at Disneyland, and you can't escape them.

FAST FOOD IN THE THEME PARKS

BECAUSE MOST MEALS during a Disneyland vacation are consumed on the run while touring, we'll tackle counter-service and vendor foods first. Plentiful at all theme parks are hot dogs, hamburgers, chicken sandwiches, salads, and pizza. They're augmented by special items that relate to the park's theme or the part of the park you're touring. In the alpine village setting of Fantasyland, for example, counter-service bratwurst and apple strudel are sold; in New Orleans Square, Cajun and Creole dishes are available. Counter-service prices are fairly consistent from park to park. Expect to pay the same amount for your coffee or hot dog at DCA that you would at Disneyland Park.

Getting your act together in regard to counter service is more a matter of courtesy than necessity. Rude guests rank fifth among reader complaints. A mother from Fort Wayne, Indiana, points out that indecision can be as maddening as outright discourtesy, especially when you're hungry:

> *Every fast-food restaurant has menu signs the size of billboards, but do you think that anybody reads them? People waiting in line spend enough time in front of these signs to memorize them and still don't have a clue what they want when they finally get to the order taker. Tell your readers to PULEEEZ get their orders together ahead of time!*

Another reader offers a tip about counter-service food lines:

> *[Many] counter-service registers serve two queues each, one to the left and one to the right of each register. People are not used to this and will instinctively line up in one queue per register. We had register*

operators wave us up to the front several times to start a left queue
instead of waiting behind others on the right.

Healthful Food at Disneyland Resort

One of the most commendable developments in food service at Disneyland has been the introduction of healthier foods and snacks. Diabetics, vegetarians, weight watchers, those requiring kosher meals, and guests on restricted diets should have no trouble finding something to eat. The same goes for anyone seeking wholesome, nutritious food. Health-conscious choices are available at most fast-food counters and even from vendors. A simple request is likely to get you what you need even if it doesn't necessarily appear on the menu.

Cutting Your Dining Time at the Theme Parks

Even if you confine your meals to vendor and counter service fast food, you lose a lot of time getting sustenance in the theme parks. At Disneyland Park and DCA, everything begins with a line and ends with a cash register. When it comes to fast food, *fast* may apply to the time you spend eating it, not the time invested in obtaining it.

Here are suggestions for minimizing the time you spend hunting and gathering food:

1. Don't waste touring time on breakfast at the parks. Restaurants outside Disneyland offer some outstanding breakfast specials. Many hotels furnish small refrigerators in their guest rooms, or you can rent one. If you can get by on cold cereal, rolls, fruit, and juice, having a fridge in your room will save a ton of time. If you can't get a fridge, bring a cooler.

2. After a good breakfast, buy snacks from vendors in the parks as you tour, or stuff some snacks in a hip pack. This is very important if you're on a tight schedule and can't spend a lot of time waiting in line for food.

3. All theme park restaurants are busiest between 11:30 a.m.–2:15 p.m. for lunch and 6–9 p.m. for dinner. For shorter lines and faster service, don't eat during these hours, especially 12:30–1:30 p.m.

4. Many counter-service restaurants sell cold sandwiches. Buy a cold lunch (except for drinks) before 11:30 a.m., and carry it until you're ready to eat. Ditto for dinner. Bring small plastic bags in which to pack the food; purchase drinks at the appropriate time from any convenient vendor.

5. Most fast-food eateries have more than one service window. Regardless of the time of day, check the lines at all windows before queuing. Sometimes a window that's staffed but out of the way will have a much shorter line or none at all. Note, however, that some windows may offer only certain items.

6. If you're short on time and the park closes early, stay until closing and eat dinner outside Disneyland before returning to your hotel. If the park stays open late, eat dinner about 4 or 4:30 p.m. at the restaurant of your choice. You should miss the last wave of lunchers and sneak in just ahead of the dinner crowd. Be warned, however, that most eateries at Downtown Disney and the Disneyland Resort hotels stop serving at 10 p.m., even when the parks are open until midnight.

7. Crowds also pack nearby eateries before, during, and immediately after special events, parades, and shows such as the wildly popular *World of Color* in DCA. Conversely, dining venues far from the action are almost empty during their run times, and you can typically walk right up to the counter without any wait at all.

Beyond Counter Service: Tips for Saving Money on Food

Though buying food from counter-service restaurants and vendors will save you time and money compared with full-service dining, additional strategies can bolster your budget and maintain your waistline. Over the years, our readers have offered the following suggestions:

1. Go to Disneyland during a period of fasting and abstinence. You can save a fortune *and* save your soul!

2. Wear clothes that are slightly too small and make you feel like dieting. (No spandex allowed!)

3. Whenever you're feeling hungry, ride the Mad Tea Party, California Screamin', or other attractions that can induce motion sickness.

4. Leave your cash and credit cards at your hotel. Buy food only with money your children fish out of fountains and wishing wells.

Cost-conscious readers also have volunteered ideas for stretching food dollars. A Missouri mom writes:

> We shopped and arrived with our cooler well stocked with milk and sandwich fixings. I froze a block of ice in a milk bottle, and we replenished it daily from the resort ice machine. I also froze small packages of deli meats for later in the week. We ate cereal, milk, and fruit each morning, with boxed juices. I also had a hot pot to boil water for instant coffee, oatmeal, and soup.
>
> Each child had a belt bag of his own, which he filled from a special box of goodies each day. I made a great mystery of filling that box in the weeks before the trip. Some things were actual food, [such as] packages of crackers and cheese [and] packets of peanuts and raisins. Some were worthless junk, [such as] candy and gum. They grazed from their bags at will throughout the day, with no interference from Mom and Dad. Each also had a small, rectangular plastic water bottle that could hang on the belt. We filled these at water fountains before getting into lines and were the envy of many.
>
> We left the park before noon; ate sandwiches, chips, and soda in the room; and napped. We purchased our evening meal in the park at a counter-service eatery. We budgeted for morning and evening snacks from a vendor but often did not need them. It made the occasional treat all the more special. Our cooler had been pretty much emptied by the end of the week, but the block of ice was still there.

*un*official **TIP**
Restaurants with a Mickey Check logo on their menu boards (showing Mickey's head with a check mark) offer special meals for kids ages 3–9. Menu items (including meat loaf, roast turkey, and mac and cheese) are designed to meet balanced nutritional guidelines with zero saturated and trans fats, less sugar, and reduced sodium.

A mom from Whiteland, Indiana, who purchases drinks in the parks, offers this suggestion:

One must-take item if you're traveling with younger kids is a supply of small cups to split drinks, which are both huge and expensive.

We interviewed one woman who brought a huge picnic for her family of five packed in a large diaper–baby paraphernalia bag. She stowed the bag in a locker on Main Street and retrieved it when the family was hungry.

Note: Disney has a rule against bringing your own food and drink into the parks. Although since 9/11 all packs, purses, diaper bags, and such have been searched, security usually does not enforce the ban except for prohibiting glass containers and alcoholic beverages.

THEME PARK COUNTER-SERVICE RESTAURANT
Mini-Profiles

TO HELP YOU FIND palatable fast-service foods that suit your taste, we have developed mini-profiles of Disneyland Park and DCA counter-service restaurants. The restaurants are listed alphabetically by park. Detailed profiles of all Disneyland full-service restaurants follow this section, beginning on page 182.

Disney Dining's response to the recession is to whittle down portions while maintaining or raising prices. Disney claims that it was accommodating the desires of health-conscious guests. Give us a break. Especially hard hit are salads and pasta dishes with chicken, where the chicken is largely AWOL.

The restaurants profiled in the following pages are rated for quality and portion size as well as value. The value rating ranges from A to F as follows:

A	*Exceptional value; a real bargain*
B	*Good value*
C	*Fair value; you get exactly what you pay for*
D	*Somewhat overpriced*
F	*Extremely overpriced*

Note: Because of special or unusual offerings, the following counter-service restaurants are profiled in full and are listed with the full-service restaurants:

The French Market *Disneyland Park*

River Belle Terrace *Disneyland Park*

Rancho del Zocalo Restaurante *Disneyland Park*

Best Eats at Disneyland Resort

We share our snacking insights on keeping your tummy happy at The Happiest Place on Earth. Call ☎ 714-781-0112 for a recorded message that reveals what candy will be made that week.

DISNEYLAND PARK

- Frozen lemonade *(vending cart)* • Barbecue pork shank *(Edelweiss Snacks)*
- Caramel apple pie *(Plaza Inn)* • Peanut brittle *(Main Street, Candy Palace)*
- Honey-pot krispie *(Pooh's Hunny Spot)* • Turkey legs *(vending cart)*
- DL Tigger tails *(Pooh's Hunny Spot)* • Pommes frites *(Café Orléans)*
- Pickles *(fruit cart near Hungry Bear)* • English toffee *(Candy Palace)*
- Fritter trio *(New Orleans Square)* • Snickerdoodles *(Pooh's Hunny Spot)*
- Apple pie apple *(Pooh's Hunny Spot)* • Pumpkin fudge *(Candy Palace)*
- Chicken on a stick *(Bengal Barbecue)* • Taffy *(Candy Palace)*
- Mint juleps *(nonalcoholic; Mint Julep Bar)*
- Chocolate-dipped Oreos *(Pooh's Hunny Spot)*
- Bacon-wrapped asparagus *(Bengal Barbecue)*
- Mickey-shaped waffles *(breakfast at Carnation Café)*
- Mickey-shaped pancakes *(breakfast at River Belle Terrace)*
- Chili-lime corn on the cob *(Edelweiss Snacks)*
- Coconut macaroons shaped like the Matterhorn *(Jolly Holiday Bakery)*
- Ice cream in a freshly made, chocolate-dipped waffle cone *(Gibson Girl)*
- Pretzels stuffed with jalapeño cheese *(Refreshment Corner, Bengal Barbecue)*
- Pineapple—Dole whips, Dole whip floats, pineapple spears *(Tiki Juice Bar near Tiki Room)*

DISNEY CALIFORNIA ADVENTURE

- Red's apple freeze *(Cozy Cone Motel)*
- Orange sorbet *(Wine Country Trattoria)*
- Hand-dipped ice cream bars *(Clarabelle's)*
- *Cars*-inspired candy apples *(Trolley Treats)*
- Funky flavored popcorn *(Cozy Cone Motel)*
- Ugly crust apple-Cheddar pie *(Flo's V8 Café)*
- Edamame with *sriracha* *(Lucky Fortune Cookery)*
- Chocolate-covered pineapple skewer *(Trolley Treats)*

DOWNTOWN DISNEY

- Chunky strawberry *(Jamba Juice)*
- Candy unique to Disneyland *(Marceline's)*
- Coconut ice cream with hot fudge *(Häagen-Dazs)*
- Fried shrimp po'boy *(Ralph Brennan's Jazz Kitchen Express)*

RESORT RESTAURANTS

- Panko-crusted long beans *(Trader Sam's at Disneyland Hotel)*
- Bananas Foster French toast *(breakfast character meal at Storytellers Café at Grand Californian)*

DISNEYLAND PARK

Bengal Barbecue

QUALITY Good–Excellent   **VALUE** B   **PORTION** Small   **LOCATION** Adventureland

Selections Beef, chicken, or vegetable skewers; jalapeño cheese–stuffed pretzels.

Comments Skewers are small, but nothing costs more than $10. The bacon-wrapped asparagus and hot-and-spicy Banyan beef skewers are best, proving the old adage that everything tastes better on a stick. This is a great fast-food alternative to the dine-in options inside the park.

Daisy's Diner

QUALITY Good   **VALUE** C   **PORTION** Medium   **LOCATION** Mickey's Toontown

Selections Pepperoni and cheese pizzas.

Comments Fine for eating on the run—no convenient place to sit.

Golden Horseshoe

QUALITY Fair   **VALUE** C   **PORTION** Medium   **LOCATION** Frontierland

Selections Chicken nuggets, fish-and-chips, crispy chicken salad, chili, and ice cream sundaes.

Comments The Golden Horseshoe hosts the best live entertainment in the park. Meaty chili is a tribute to Walt and available in an unadvertised side portion perfect for a snack, if you don't want it on a pile of fries or in a bread bowl. Service can be slow; the leftmost open register usually has the shortest line. Gazebo-style seating next to the stage is best.

Harbour Galley

QUALITY Good   **VALUE** A–   **PORTION** Medium–Large   **LOCATION** Critter Country

Selections Broccoli and Cheddar cheese soup, steak gumbo, clam chowder, or vegetarian chili, all served in a sourdough bread bowl; also steak salad or grilled salmon salad; stuffed baked potatoes. Kids' meal includes string cheese, yogurt, and fruit.

Comments The broccoli and cheese soup is really good on cool days. Limited seating, but other seats are available along the dock around the back of the restaurant. The popular overstuffed baked potatoes (with broccoli, bacon, or barbecue chicken) formerly found at Troubadour Tavern are now served here.

Hungry Bear Restaurant

QUALITY Fair–Good   **VALUE** B+   **PORTION** Medium–Large   **LOCATION** Critter Country

Selections A huge, one-third-pound chili cheeseburger topped with a fried onion ring (skip the chili; it's pasty and bland), a fried green tomato sandwich with a side of jicama coleslaw (some of the best greens in the park), and a fried chicken sandwich with honey mustard. Healthier choices include a turkey and provolone sandwich on a multigrain roll and Big Al's smoked chicken salad with lettuce, watermelon, candied pecans, dried cherries, and pickled red onions with a sweet-tart honey-lime vinaigrette. Kids can feast on healthier meals with string cheese, nonfat yogurt, sliced apples, and whole-grain fish crackers.

Comments The sweet potato fries are really tasty. Popular and crowded during busier times of the year. During slower times, grab a snack and sit on the deck overlooking the Rivers of America. We highly recommend the heirloom tomato sandwich (with Havarti and rémoulade on hearty whole grain) to lacto-ovo vegetarians and carnivores alike. The lemon cupcakes and seasonal berry pie desserts are also really good.

Jolly Holiday Bakery

QUALITY Good   **VALUE** B–   **PORTION** Medium   **LOCATION** Main Street, U.S.A.

Selections Broccoli-cheese quiche; house salad with pecans and Feta; toasted cheese sandwich with tomato soup; turkey, roast beef, tuna, or Caprese sandwich; grilled vegetable salad; assorted pastries.

Comments The former annual pass processing center (originally Stouffer's Plaza Pavilion restaurant) is once again an eatery. Themed to *Mary Poppins,* with stained glass penguin waiter windows, this is a good spot for a light breakfast or lunch, though lines can grow long at peak mealtimes. Seating is outdoors only, and soup and quiche portions are small, but the salads and sandwiches are substantial and savory. Don't miss the massive Matterhorn coconut macaroons.

Market House

QUALITY Good   **VALUE** B–   **PORTION** Medium   **LOCATION** Main Street, U.S.A.

Selections Starbucks coffee drinks, pastries, and snacks.

Comments Disneyland ended the Market House's long tradition of house-blended brews and free same-day refills when it invited Starbucks to take over this location in 2013. The expanded coffee shop encompasses what was once the Disneyana shop, whose goods were merged with the Disney Gallery. Look for a potbellied stove, checkerboard, and antique telephones, all holdovers from the former decor.

Pluto's Dog House

QUALITY Good   **VALUE** C   **PORTION** Medium   **LOCATION** Mickey's Toontown

Selections Hot dog basket, kids' turkey dog, and mac and cheese.

Comments Food's not bad, but there's really no place to sit and eat it.

Redd Rockett's Pizza Port

QUALITY Good   **VALUE** C   **PORTION** Medium–Large   **LOCATION** Tomorrowland

Selections Redd Rockett's is set up cafeteria-style, typically with two or three kinds of pasta available, as well as pizzas and salads. All hot items sit under heat lamps until someone grabs them, but servers will be happy to mix up a fresh bowl of pasta or a pizza on request (a much better choice). Try the Asian chicken salad if it's available—slightly spicy with good flavor. Free drink refills are available.

Comments The cafeteria-style setup usually means less waiting. The A/C system is on steroids, making it a really cool place on a hot day. Even on the busiest days, there's ample room to sit on the outdoor patio.

Refreshment Corner

QUALITY Good   **VALUE** C   **PORTION** Medium   **LOCATION** Main Street, U.S.A.

Selections Hot dogs, chili-cheese dogs, and chili in a bread bowl.

Comments Not much of a selection, but dogs are good. Limited seating.

Royal Street Veranda

QUALITY Good   **VALUE** B   **PORTION** Medium   **LOCATION** New Orleans Square

Selections Steak gumbo, vegetarian gumbo, and clam chowder, all served in a sourdough bread bowl; coffee, espresso, cappuccino, and fritters (fried dough balls) for dessert.

Comments Usually not crowded. Veggie gumbo and clam chowder are the best, though all are seasoned well. You have to look hard to find any steak in the steak gumbo. Don't miss the fritters with fruit dipping sauce.

Stage Door Café

QUALITY Good   **VALUE** C   **PORTION** Medium   **LOCATION** Frontierland

Selections Chicken nuggets, fish-and-chips, funnel cakes, and corn dogs.

Comments The stand on Main Street has better corn dogs, but the fish-and-chips are decent. Try the funnel cakes if you like those (who doesn't?).

Tomorrowland Terrace

QUALITY Fair   **VALUE** C+   **PORTION** Large   **LOCATION** Tomorrowland

Selections Turkey, roast beef, grilled veggie, and grilled chicken sandwiches; burgers; fresh salads; baked fish sandwich.

Comments The food isn't anything special, although the bread is fresh. The grilled veggie sandwich or any of the salads may be your best choice. Seating is available outdoors overlooking the Tomorrowland Terrace stage, which hosts live music and the popular *Jedi Training Academy*.

Troubadour Tavern

QUALITY Good–Fair   **VALUE** C+   **PORTION** Medium   **LOCATION** Fantasyland

Selections Bratwurst with sauerkraut, sweet corn on the cob, pretzel bites with cheese sauce, cinnamon-apple pastry twists, and apple slices with caramel sauce.

Comments Built as a concession stand for Fantasyland Theatre, it is overwhelmed during shows but overlooked the rest of the day. The only quick-service sausage vendor serving spicy brown mustard. For a quick snack, try Maurice's Treats, close to Fantasy Faire; it serves sweet (if overpriced) strawberry or chocolate pastry twists, as well as a boysenberry apple freeze. Its Cheddar garlic bagel twist is tough and tasteless.

Vendor Treats

LOCATIONS Throughout the park

Selections Popcorn, french fries, smoked turkey legs, ice cream, churros, chimichangas, and more.

Comments We love the smoked turkey legs—big enough for a whole meal. Plus, there's something delightfully Neanderthal and exhibitionist about tucking into a huge, meaty bone as you stroll the park.

Village Haus

QUALITY Good   **VALUE** B–   **PORTION** Medium   **LOCATION** Fantasyland

Selections Premium cheeseburger, chicken sausage sandwich, veggie burger, pepperoni and cheese pizzas, apple Cheddar salad, and mac and cheese kids' meals. Black Forest cupcake or apple strudel for dessert.

Comments The flatbread pizzas and heart-stopping pastrami cheeseburger

are actually pretty good. Kids love the Pinnochio-themed seating area.
Try the salad with fruit and cheese in a tangy yogurt-honey dressing.

DISNEY CALIFORNIA ADVENTURE
Award Wieners

QUALITY Fair–Good **VALUE** B **PORTION** Medium **LOCATION** Hollywood Land

Selections Chili-cheese dogs, grilled sausages, and hot dogs; grilled mushroom, onion, and pepper sandwich.

Comments The grilled sausages are moderately spicy and good.

Boardwalk Pizza & Pasta

QUALITY Good **VALUE** A **PORTION** Medium **LOCATION** Paradise Pier

Selections Flatbread pizzas run the gamut from a traditional cheese or pepperoni to a portobello mushroom and spinach. Pasta offerings include spaghetti and meatballs, chicken pasta in a sun-dried tomato cream sauce, or pesto ravioli. Freshly tossed salads include a chicken Caesar and a Mediterranean chef salad with provolone, salami, fresh mozzarella, ham, roasted peppers, and olives in a red-wine vinaigrette.

Comments Formerly known as Pizza Oom Mow Mow, it has been rethemed as part of Paradise Garden, a Victorian-era outdoor dining courtyard. Freestanding beer and corn dog stands sit outside the plaza. Salads are large enough to split three ways; say "hold the olives" (or another ingredient) for a fresh-mixed serving.

Cocina Cucamonga Mexican Grill

QUALITY Good **VALUE** B– **PORTION** Large **LOCATION** Pacific Wharf

Selections Tacos, burritos, tamales, grilled chicken, fajita salad, and chicken Caesar salad. Kids' choices include arroz con pollo (chicken with rice), bean and cheese burrito, and chicken tacos.

Comments Salads are a safe choice. The chicken is marinated with cumin, garlic, cilantro, and citrus, and it comes with flour tortillas. Very tasty. The carne asada has improved but still lacks the full flavor and texture that you would expect. The burritos include a lot of beans.

Cozy Cone Motel

QUALITY Good **VALUE** B– **PORTION** Small–Medium **LOCATION** Cars Land

Selections Chili, ice cream, churros, and pretzel bites. For breakfast, cone #3 sells scrambled eggs in a bread cone. Cone #5 coats popcorn in unusual favors such as dill pickle and bacon Cheddar, with two rotating varieties offered daily. Signature beverages include a syrupy pomegranate limeade and Red's Apple Freeze, a curiously addictive blend of tart frozen apple juice and sweet toasted marshmallow.

Comments Each conical commissary in this food court, based on Sally's construction-cone motel from the film, serves different snacks and drinks with punny names such as "chili cone queso" and "route beer floats." Check the selections before you line up because each of the five cones vends a different menu. The bacon breakfast cone could use more bacon, but the cheese sauce is delightfully savory.

Fiddler, Fifer & Practical Café

QUALITY Good–Excellent   **VALUE** B   **PORTION** Medium   **LOCATION** Buena Vista St.

Selections Starbucks coffee, hot breakfast sandwiches, cinnamon rolls with cream cheese icing, sandwiches (including roast beef and Cheddar, turkey Reuben, and paneer and roasted vegetable), and soups (such as cream spinach, chicken tortilla, or meat stew).

Comments This new quick-service eatery, named after both the Three Little Pigs and an imaginary songstress trio whose manufactured mementos hang inside, boasts a large open dining area in the Arts & Crafts style. The turkey Reuben and cheesy enchilada soup make a super combo. Expect long waits here at opening, as guests line up for their morning caffeine fix. Starbucks loyalty cards are not valid here for free refills or other discounts.

Flo's V8 Café

QUALITY Good–Excellent   **VALUE** B+   **PORTION** Medium–Large   **LOCATION** Cars Land

Selections French toast, chicken tamales, pork loin with cola barbecue sauce, New York strip loin, vegetarian shepherd's pie, and fruit pies. Try the pork loin with a side of chili-style baked beans. The veggie bake's bulgur-cheese blend is tasty enough to attract meat eaters.

Comments The portions are huge but similarly priced to other counter service. The kids' meal comes in a Lightning McQueen car. Sit on the back patio for a spectacular view of Radiator Springs Racers' high-speed finale.

Lucky Fortune Cookery

QUALITY Fair–Good   **VALUE** C–   **PORTION** Medium   **LOCATION** Pacific Wharf

Selections Steamed rice bowls with vegetables and your choice of chicken, beef, or tofu, all with your choice from a variety of pan-Asian sauces, including a popular teriyaki and a sweet, tangy Korean sauce; edamame; mango slices; teriyaki chicken and rice for kids.

Comments The tofu bowl is good, the chicken and beef are average, and the coconut curry sauce is bland. Edamame makes a nice side to share, especially dipped in spicy *sriracha* sauce.

Pacific Wharf Café

QUALITY Good   **VALUE** A   **PORTION** Medium   **LOCATION** Pacific Wharf

Selections Fresh soups and salads served in hollowed-out sourdough loaves from San Francisco's famous Boudin bakery for grown-ups, and turkey wraps and string cheese for the kids. The Carmel roast beef sandwich and the Sonoma chicken and apple salad are good, as is the broccoli and cheese soup. The clam chowder is actually quite good, with heaps of clams in a creamy, slightly salty base.

Comments Food and ambience that adults will appreciate as well as a very kid-friendly menu (nonfat yogurt, sliced apples, and whole-grain fish crackers). For dessert, try the candy, hot cocoa, ice cream sundae, or milk shake at Ghirardelli Soda Fountain & Chocolate Shop nearby.

Paradise Garden Grill

QUALITY Good   **VALUE** A   **PORTION** Medium   **LOCATION** Paradise Pier

Selections Variety of skewers (beef, chicken, and tofu) served with rice

Disneyland Resort Restaurants by Cuisine

CUISINE	LOCATION	OVERALL RATING	COST	QUALITY RATING	VALUE RATING
AMERICAN					
Big Thunder Ranch Barbecue	Disneyland Park	★★★½	Exp	★★★½	★★★★
The River Belle Terrace*	Disneyland Park	★★★½	Mod	★★★½	★★★½
Tangaroa Terrace*	Disneyland Hotel	★★★½	Mod	★★★½	★★★½
Ariel's Grotto*	DCA	★★★	Exp	★★★	★★★½
Carnation Café*	Disneyland Park	★★★	Mod	★★★	★★★
ESPN Zone	Downtown Disney	★★½	Mod	★★★	★★★
Rainforest Cafe*	Downtown Disney	★★½	Mod	★★★	★★½
Disney's PCH Grill*	Paradise Pier Hotel	★★½	Mod	★★½	★★½
Goofy's Kitchen*	Disneyland Hotel	★★	Exp	★★	★★★
Plaza Inn*	Disneyland Park	★½	Mod	★★½	★★½
CALIFORNIA/FUSION					
Napa Rose	Grand Californian	★★★★½	V. Exp	★★★★★	★★★½
Carthay Circle Restaurant	DCA	★★★★½	Exp	★★★★½	★★★½
Wine Country Trattoria	DCA	★★★★	Mod	★★★★	★★★½
Storytellers Café*	Grand Californian	★★★★	Exp	★★★★	★★★
CAJUN/CREOLE					
Ralph Brennan's Jazz Kitchen*	Downtown Disney	★★★★	Mod	★★★½	★★★
Café Orléans	Disneyland Park	★★★½	Mod	★★★½	★★★
Blue Bayou	Disneyland Park	★★★½	Exp	★★★½	★★★
The French Market	Disneyland Park	★★★	Mod	★★★★	★★★
Crossroads at House of Blues	Downtown Disney	★★★	Mod	★★★½	★★½
CHARACTER DINING					
Storytellers Café*	Grand Californian	★★★★	Exp	★★★★	★★★★
Ariel's Grotto*	DCA	★★★	Exp	★★★	★★★½
Disney's PCH Grill*	Paradise Pier Hotel	★★½	Mod	★★½	★★½
Goofy's Kitchen*	Disneyland Hotel	★★	Exp	★★	★★★
Plaza Inn*	Disneyland Park	★½	Mod	★★½	★★½

Serves breakfast.

Disneyland Resort Restaurants by Cuisine

CUISINE	LOCATION	OVERALL RATING	COST	QUALITY RATING	VALUE RATING
DELI/BAKERY					
La Brea Bakery Café*	Downtown Disney	★★★	Inexp	★★½	★★★
Napolini	Downtown Disney	★★½	Inexp	★★★	★★½
ITALIAN					
Napolini	Downtown Disney	★★½	Inexp	★★★	★★½
Naples Ristorante Pizzeria	Downtown Disney	★★½	Mod	★★½	★★½
MEDITERRANEAN					
Catal Restaurant & Uva Bar*	Downtown Disney	★★★	Mod/ Exp	★★★½	★★★
MEXICAN					
Tortilla Jo's	Downtown Disney	★★★	Mod/Exp	★★½	★★½
Rancho del Zocalo Restaurante	Disneyland Park	★★	Mod	★★	★★½
POLYNESIAN					
Tangaroa Terrace*	Disneyland Hotel	★★★½	Mod	★★★½	★★★½
STEAK HOUSE					
Steakhouse 55*	Disneyland Hotel	★★★★	V. Exp	★★★★	★★★

Serves breakfast.

pilaf and a pita, and fresh salads, including a classic Greek. For kids, there's a grilled chicken or beef skewer, served with choice of sauce.

Comments This open-air dining venue, themed to a Victorian beer garden, shares seating with Boardwalk Pizza. The backstory is about an immigrant family whose humble roadside grill grew into a dining empire. A selection of sauces are offered with the skewers, and you can request more than one; the *kefta* with tandoori yogurt or tzatziki is especially flavorful.

Taste Pilots' Grill

QUALITY Good   **VALUE** B–   **PORTION** Medium–Large   **LOCATION** Condor Flats

Selections Choose from American comfort food such as burgers, chicken sandwiches, and grilled chicken salad.

Comments The burgers come with a variety of toppings and sauces, and a separate toppings bar is available in case you need to stack on more. The onion rings are decent, and this is the only place in DCA that you can get them.

DISNEYLAND RESORT
RESTAURANTS: *Rated and Ranked*

TO HELP YOU MAKE YOUR DINING CHOICES, we've developed profiles of full-service restaurants at Disneyland Resort. Each profile lets you quickly check the restaurant's cuisine, location, star rating, cost range, quality rating, and value rating. Profiles are listed alphabetically by restaurant. In addition to all full-service restaurants, we also list and profile a couple of delis and self-serve restaurants in the theme parks that transcend basic burgers, hot dogs, and pizza.

STAR RATING The star rating represents the entire dining experience: style, service, and ambience, in addition to taste, presentation, and food quality. Five stars, the highest rating, indicates that the restaurant offers the best of everything. Four-star restaurants are above average, and three-star restaurants offer good, though not necessarily memorable, meals. Two-star restaurants serve mediocre fare, and one-star restaurants are below average. Our star ratings don't correspond to ratings awarded by AAA, Mobil, Zagat, or other restaurant reviewers.

COST RANGE The next rating tells how much a complete meal will cost: a main dish with vegetable or side dish and a choice of soup or salad. Appetizers, desserts, drinks, and tips aren't included. We've rated the cost as inexpensive, moderate, or expensive.

INEXPENSIVE	$15 or less per person
MODERATE	$15–$28 per person
EXPENSIVE	More than $28 per person

QUALITY RATING The food quality is rated on a scale of one to five stars, five being the best. The quality rating is based on the taste, freshness of ingredients, preparation, presentation, and creativity of food. There is no consideration of price. If you want the best food available and cost is no issue, look no further than the quality ratings.

VALUE RATING If, on the other hand, you are looking for both quality and value, check the value rating, also expressed as stars.

★★★★★	Exceptional value; a real bargain
★★★★	Good value
★★★	Fair value; you get exactly what you pay for
★★	Somewhat overpriced
★	Significantly overpriced

PAYMENT All Disney restaurants accept American Express, MasterCard, Visa, Diners Club, Discover, and Japanese Credit Bureau.

New Treats at DCA

Several new eateries have opened at Disney California Adventure.

At Buena Vista Street, **Clarabelle's Hand-Scooped Ice Cream** serves hand-dipped ice cream bars coated in sprinkles, chocolate, nuts, and Pop Rocks, as well as chocolate-dipped waffle cones. This ice cream parlor adjoining the **Fiddler, Fifer & Practical Café** (see page 179) offers hand-scooped Dreyer's desserts from an old-fashioned soda fountain counter. For a few extra bucks, your sundae can be served in a souvenir trolley-shaped dish. Go ahead and splurge on a second scoop; it's only 50¢ more.

Trolley Treats, also located at Buena Vista Street, is a classic candy shop with an exposed kitchen, where you can watch taffy, marshmallows, fudge, and other sweets being made. Candied apples shaped like *Cars* characters are especially cute. Check out the Big Rock Candy Mountain model in the window, inspired by plans for a never-built Disneyland attraction.

Mortimer's Market is the closest place to the park entrance to get a snack. This grab-and-go location is named after Walt's original appellation for his animated mouse; Walt's wife urged him to make it Mickey instead. Cold drinks and fresh fruit are available here.

At Cars Land, counter-service dining includes **Fillmore's Taste-In, Cozy Cone Motel** (see page 178), and **Flo's V8 Café** (see page 179). Fillmore's Taste-In offers fruit juices, bottled water, and other healthy snacks. Located inside a geodesic dome near the Cars Land entrance, this grab-and-go snack bar is themed after the groovy VW microbus character voiced by the late George Carlin.

Ariel's Grotto ★★★

CHARACTER DINING/AMERICAN EXPENSIVE QUALITY ★★★ VALUE ★★★½

Disney California Adventure; ☎ 714-781-DINE

Reservations Recommended. **When to go** Anytime. **Entrée range** Fixed-price meals, $19–$50. **Service** ★★★★. **Friendliness** ★★★★★. **Bar** The Cove bar is upstairs. **Dress** Casual. **Disabled access** Yes. **Hours** Daily, 9 a.m.–10 p.m.

SETTING AND ATMOSPHERE You're "under the sea" with bright 3-D ocean-themed murals, jellyfish lanterns, and seashell tables, all with views of the wharf, Paradise Bay, and Paradise Pier. The overstuffed semicircular booths along the back wall are the best seats in the house and well worth waiting for.

HOUSE SPECIALTIES At breakfast, fruit, pastries, eggs, potatoes, and waffles. At lunch and dinner, slow-roasted tri-tip steak, a cioppino that's more like a seafood soup, herb-crusted chicken, and rich pasta dishes. Each table starts with a tower of antipasto and finishes with a dessert platter featuring lava cake and s'mores.

OTHER RECOMMENDATIONS Herb-crusted chicken and a kids' menu featuring chicken skewered on sugarcane and spaghetti.

SUMMARY AND COMMENTS Ariel's Grotto is *fun* but very pricey and is also one of the most popular dining spots in DCA. Kids will love the fact that Ariel and two to four other Disney princesses—Snow White, Cinderella, Aurora, or Belle—are on hand for pictures and autographs at breakfast and lunch. One set price buys adults an antipasto starter and salad, main course, and dessert, or a kids' appetizer of celery and carrot sticks with ranch dressing, a main course, and dessert (slices of Granny Smith apples and caramel dipping sauce or fruit parfait). Even toddlers will enjoy the bright surroundings and nonthreatening character visits. Evening diners don't get to meet princesses, but they do receive reserved viewing passes for *World of Color*. Demand is high here for obvious reasons, so book your reservations early. Adults can escape upstairs to The Cove alfresco bar for a cocktail, glass of wine, or bottle of beer. The Cove also serves a small selection of appetizers, including enormous lobster nachos. This is a good spot for catching *World of Color* without a Fastpass; views of the fountains from here are great, but the oblique angle to the projection screens isn't ideal.

Big Thunder Ranch Barbecue ★★★½

AMERICAN	EXPENSIVE	QUALITY ★★★½	VALUE ★★★★

Disneyland Park; ☎ 714-781-DINE

Reservations Available. **When to go** Lunch or dinner. **Entrée range** $15–$25. **Service** ★★★★. **Friendliness** ★★★★. **Dress** Casual. **Disabled access** Yes. **Hours** Daily, 11 a.m.–10 p.m.

SETTING AND ATMOSPHERE Outdoor, family-style seating on long wooden tables and benches with lots of Western Americana touches such as hurricane lamps and checkered tablecloths.

HOUSE SPECIALTIES Family-style, all-you-can-eat barbecue featuring buckets of pork ribs and chicken in a sweet but nicely balanced barbecue sauce, a tangy citrus coleslaw, warm corn bread with sweet butter, and smoked sausages. The skillet chocolate-chip cookie with vanilla ice cream and hot fudge will definitely put you over the edge.

OTHER RECOMMENDATIONS Vegetarians can request a barbecue skewer with potatoes, squash, bell peppers, mushrooms, and tofu.

SUMMARY AND COMMENTS Prices may surprise you, but if the family is ready to pound some serious grub, this never-ending, all-you-can-eat palace to excess is just the spot. Drinks (served in Mason jars) and dessert are à la carte. The dinner menu is the same as lunch, plus smoked sausage and corn cob wheels. A charming couple of singing cowpokes in Dale Evans and Roy Rogers costumes, accompanied by a honky-tonk piano player, perform kid-friendly comedic skits while you eat, improvising special occasion telegrams and leading sing-alongs of "Rocky Top" and "The Ballad of Davy Crockett." You can often get a seat here (especially for lunch) without advance reservations, even on busy days.

Blue Bayou ★★★½

CAJUN/CREOLE	EXPENSIVE	QUALITY ★★★½	VALUE ★★★

Disneyland Park; ☎ 714-781-DINE

Reservations Required. **When to go** Early or late lunch, early evening. **Entrée range** $30–$46. **Service** ★★★. **Friendliness** ★★★. **Dress** Casual. **Disabled access** Yes. **Hours** Daily, 11 a.m.–4 p.m. and 5:30–10 p.m.

SETTING AND ATMOSPHERE The Blue Bayou overlooks Pirates of the Caribbean and maintains an appropriately dark, moist ambience. The best tables ring the perimeter and afford a view of the faux bayou, replete with fireflies flickering among the weeping willows and mangroves, dilapidated houseboats, and soft lantern lights. If you're not lucky enough to get a table bayou-side, there's still enough wrought iron, uneven lighting, and twilight allure to soften the most hardened soul.

HOUSE SPECIALTIES Pan-seared crab cakes, New York strip steak, and Le Special de Monte Cristo sandwich.

OTHER RECOMMENDATIONS Jambalaya, Tesoro Island chicken, or fork-tender short ribs. Spring for the saffron-infused bouillabaisse if offered as a seasonal special. Entrées include a cup of mild gumbo or a superb side salad with candied pecans and Craisins.

SUMMARY AND COMMENTS Easily the best restaurant in Disneyland Park, Blue Bayou is as close to fine dining as you'll get here. The restaurant fills quickly and stays busy, so make reservations before you leave home (up to 60 days in advance) or obtain a same-day reservation at the restaurant door as soon as you get to the park. Although there's a children's menu, this isn't the place to bring wound-up or tired kids for a leisurely meal; they'll be bored. Tables are tightly packed, and nothing disrupts the busy servers more than wild kids up and out of their seats. Blue Bayou is more of a place where adults can escape the noise and happy chaos in the rest of the park without having to exit the gates. For lunch, we love the Monte Cristo sandwich, a deep-fried turkey, ham, and cheese creation that you don't find on many menus these days. Side dishes—including the Blue Bayou potatoes, a house gratin, and fresh vegetables—are quite good as well. The crème brûlée is also a crowd-pleaser. Servers are Disney-pleasant, if a tad harried, but they're more than happy to accommodate the random request. And the dinner rolls are great! If seated at an unromantically over-lit table near the kitchen, don't be shy about requesting a relocation.

La Brea Bakery Café ★★★

BAKERY/DELI	INEXPENSIVE	QUALITY ★★½	VALUE ★★★

Downtown Disney; ☎ 714-490-0233 or 714-781-DINE; labreabakery.com

Reservations Available. When to go Breakfast. Entrée range $6–$28. Service ★★. Friendliness ★★. Bar Limited. Dress Casual. Disabled access Yes. Hours Sunday–Friday, 8 a.m.–10 p.m., Saturday, 8 a.m.–11 p.m. Open 1 hour later in summer.

SETTING AND ATMOSPHERE This indoor-outdoor space is rich with the yeasty aromas of breads and cakes, plus whiffs of herbs and spices. Hardwood floors and large glass display counters distinguish the dining room. A pleasant patio with colorful umbrellas fronting the café is the perfect perch for a quick cappuccino and pastry while you people-watch.

HOUSE SPECIALTIES For breakfast, nothing beats a large fruit muffin and your coffee drink of choice. The panini at lunch and dinner are better than the ones at Napolini.

OTHER RECOMMENDATIONS Take home one or more loaves of the artisanal breads. Or try this sandwich on for size: thick sourdough layered with Gruyère cheese, smoked ham, and marinated onions.

SUMMARY AND COMMENTS It's all about the bread . . . and the muffins, pastries, desserts, and anything else containing baked flour and yeast. Breakfast is the obvious time to enjoy La Brea, and if you must supplement your carbohydrate fix, add some quiche or vegetable egg pie. At lunch and dinner, the salads and sandwiches take over. Service has improved markedly in recent years; servers are more attentive and pleasant. Get there early—it's the first eatery at the east end of the resort entrance, and a popular starting (and ending) place for tourists and locals alike. You can get Starbucks-branded coffee here, usually with a shorter queue than you'll find inside the parks.

Café Orléans ★★★½

CAJUN/CREOLE	MODERATE	QUALITY ★★★½	VALUE ★★★

Disneyland Park; ☎ 714-781-DINE

Reservations Recommended. **When to go** Early or late lunch, early evening. **Entrée range** $6–$20. **Service** ★★★★. **Friendliness** ★★★★. **Dress** Casual. **Disabled access** Yes. **Hours** Daily, 11 a.m.–park closing.

SETTING AND ATMOSPHERE Across the alley from Blue Bayou, Café Orléans overlooks the Rivers of America. There's a small patio and limited inside seating, but the table-side service offers a nice break from the serve-yourself and buffet options in the same price range. After a day of traipsing around the park, it's nice to kick back amid the wrought iron and scrolled-wood accents.

HOUSE SPECIALTIES The chef's *pommes frites* have to be among the best sides in the park: traditional thick-cut french fries tossed with Parmesan cheese, garlic, and parsley and served with a mildly spicy Cajun rémoulade sauce. If they aren't served piping hot, send them back. Mickey-shaped beignets are also a treat for dessert.

OTHER RECOMMENDATIONS A decent French onion soup with melted Gruyère cheese; an artery-clogging Monte Cristo sandwich in two versions, traditional and three-cheese; and a nice selection of sweet and savory crêpes.

SUMMARY AND COMMENTS The *pommes frites* are worth the price of admission. If you don't eat anything else in the park your entire visit, try these. We like to hit Café Orléans for a midafternoon break, kick our feet up for a soda or sweet tea, and pick through a plate of the fries while we people-watch. The small menu makes ordering easy, provided you bring a big appetite and aren't afraid of a little cholesterol and trans fat. The Monte Cristo sandwiches are as good as Blue Bayou's and a few bucks cheaper. Kids will love the three-cheese version: Swiss, mozzarella, and double-cream Brie between thick slices of deep-fried egg-battered bread. The gumbo is passable, if a little bland, while the salads, including a blackened-chicken Caesar and the Crescent City salad (a mix of baby spinach, field greens, caramelized pecans, roasted corn, grapes, orange slices, and pan-seared salmon in an orange-cilantro vinaigrette), are very good. For something different, try the crêpes—paper-thin pancakes stuffed with a variety of fillings, including chicken gumbo or seafood. A Dixieland jazz band periodically provides lively entertainment.

Carnation Café ★★★

AMERICAN	MODERATE	QUALITY ★★★	VALUE ★★★

Disneyland Park; ☎ 714-781-DINE

Reservations Recommended. When to go Breakfast or late lunch. Entrée range $6–$15. Service ★★★★. Friendliness ★★★★. Dress Casual. Disabled access Yes. Hours Daily, 8 a.m.–park closing.

SETTING AND ATMOSPHERE A Main Street staple since the park opened in 1955, the Carnation Café serves up an American menu heavy with traditional favorites—hamburgers and meat loaf, pancakes and Mickey-shaped waffles, and fried chicken—in a parlor circa 1890. For those in the know, Oscar Martinez, Disneyland's longest-tenured employee (55 years at the park), is the café's ambassador. The café was expanded in 2012, adding indoor seating and revamping the menu.

HOUSE SPECIALTIES The loaded baked potato soup (a hot, creamy concoction with Cheddar cheese, chives, and large chunks of baked potato) is a favorite. New specialties include huevos rancheros at breakfast and a green chile cheeseburger (topped with Manchego cheese, roasted poblanos, and a fried egg) for lunch. Oscar recommends the catch of the day, pan-seared with edamame succotash.

OTHER RECOMMENDATIONS For starters, try the deep-fried dill pickle spears, dipped in a rémoulade-style sauce. The updated menu features a beef-and-pork meat loaf, smoked turkey sandwich on a pretzel roll, and warm spinach salad topped with grilled chicken and shiitake mushrooms.

SUMMARY AND COMMENTS The Carnation Café is still a place where the adults can find a decent plate, the kids can choose from their favorites, and it's easy on the wallet. Because of its location along Main Street, close to bathrooms and across from the locker facility, it gets busy—expect to see waiting lines stretching down the street. Service is friendly and unusually patient; someone's briefed these young cast members on how an hour's wait and low blood sugar can quickly erode a diner's mood. Once you're seated, the order comes quickly and with a smile.

Carthay Circle Restaurant ★★★★½

CALIFORNIA	EXPENSIVE	QUALITY ★★★★½	VALUE ★★★½

Disney California Adventure; ☎ 714-781-DINE

Reservations Recommended. When to go Lunch or dinner. Entrée range About $48. Service ★★★½. Friendliness ★★★★. Bar Beer and wine. Dress Dressy casual. Disabled access Yes. Hours Daily, 11 a.m.–10 p.m.

SETTING AND ATMOSPHERE Intimate booths, wood paneling, and candle sconces evoke the setting of the opening night in 1937 of *Snow White and the Seven Dwarfs*.

HOUSE SPECIALTIES Crispy firecracker duck wings with chili sauce, Colorado rack of lamb, tiger prawns, and fried biscuits with Cheddar, bacon, and jalapeño.

OTHER RECOMMENDATIONS For lunch try the udon noodle bowl or Kobe beef cheek sliders with horseradish whip; for dinner, try the fish ceviche in avocado cream, grilled quail, or *cavatelli* with tender shreds of braised lamb. Salmon is served mid-rare with a delicate beurre blanc. The signature biscuits (more like cheese-filled fritters) are heavy but have built a fanatical cult following, as have the surprisingly meaty *sriracha*-laced duck wings. For dessert, order the fried banana split Monte Cristo sundae or warm country pie. The kids' menu offers a sloppy joe with slaw, mini crispy tacos, or pasta.

SUMMARY AND COMMENTS The chefs of Napa Rose developed the Southern Californian menu. A downstairs lounge serves appetizers and quick meals, while the larger upstairs restaurant takes reservations. Complimentary center-stage seats for *World of Color* are available if an entrée and appetizer or dessert are purchased. A three-course fixed-price *World of Color* menu is also offered ($59 adults, $29 kids). Terrace seating is available. Though service is sometimes unexpectedly inattentive, this is among the finest restaurants found inside the gates of any American theme park (including the vaunted Club 33) and one of the best dining experiences at Disneyland Resort outside of its sibling at the Grand Californian, at a slightly less astronomical price point.

Catal Restaurant & Uva Bar ★★★

MEDITERRANEAN　　MODERATE–EXPENSIVE　　QUALITY ★★★½　　VALUE ★★★

Downtown Disney; ☎ 714-774-4442; patinagroup.com/catal

Reservations Recommended. **When to go** Anytime. **Entrée range** $6–$41. **Service** ★★★. **Friendliness** ★★★. **Bar** Full bar and extensive wine list. **Dress** Dressy casual. **Disabled access** Yes. **Hours** *Catal:* Daily, 8 a.m.–3 p.m. and 5–10 p.m. *Uva Bar:* Daily, 11 a.m.–3 p.m. and 5–10 p.m.

SETTING AND ATMOSPHERE Uva Bar, a circular open-air lounge, sits immediately outside the restaurant and is a good place for a quick bite (sans line) or a leisurely cocktail while you watch the crowds go by. The outside bistro has undergone both a face-lift and a menu revamp, adding more tables and focusing the menu on Cal-Mediterranean gastropub cuisine. Inside is an elegant Art Deco–inspired restaurant with hardwood floors, spacious dining areas, and fine accoutrements. There are two fireplaces and a large central bar; a narrow balcony with tables wraps around the entire top floor.

HOUSE SPECIALTIES Smoked salmon hash or shrimp and grits for breakfast, house-made charcuterie, suckling pig with tart apples and quinoa, lamb shank in braising jus, and Skuna Bay salmon with beets and *farro*. Sample the *a la plancha* entrées, such as the lamb burger with *piquillo* peppers, Feta, arugula, lemon-dill aioli, and pickled red onion; or the market fish with Brussels sprouts, preserved lemon purée, and applewood bacon at Uva.

OTHER RECOMMENDATIONS Try a huge and very tasty plate of paella with chicken, chorizo Bilbao, saffron rice, and lemon-garlic aioli; the classic Uva street fries with chorizo Bilbao, spicy *crema,* pickled garlic, and melted cheese; or the enormous Prince Edward Island mussels steamed in a delicious white wine sauce.

SUMMARY AND COMMENTS Catal & Uva Bar are a Patina Group pairing, one in a chain of eateries operated by celebrity chef Joachim Splichal. Despite overblown descriptions, the menu is pretty straightforward. The small plates—mainly appetizers, salads, and a few pasta dishes—

are better than the rest of the menu and a real value for the money. When the weather cooperates, Uva is the better of the two venues. Be cautious when ordering some of the more complex or unusual offerings; they can be very inconsistent. Side dishes shine though. Price notwithstanding, this is a very adult experience.

Crossroads at House of Blues ★★★

CAJUN/CREOLE	MODERATE	QUALITY ★★★½	VALUE ★★½

Downtown Disney; ☎ 714-778-BLUE; hob.com/venues/clubvenues/anaheim

Reservations Recommended. **When to go** Dinner. **Entrée range** $11–$29. **Service** ★★★. **Friendliness** ★★★. **Bar** Wine list and full bar. **Dress** Casual. **Disabled access** Yes. **Hours** Daily, 11 a.m.–1:30 a.m.

SETTING AND ATMOSPHERE Think rustic-but-trendy blues club somewhere along the Mississippi River, maybe St. Louis. It's dark except for outside patios and a second-story terrace, with hardwood floors, small intimate tables, and indirect lighting. The walls feature a fantastic collection of American folk artists, some of whom (such as Missionary Mary Proctor) have works that hang in prestigious museums.

HOUSE SPECIALTIES Jambalaya, St. Louis–style ribs, pulled pork sandwich, and build-your-own burgers.

OTHER RECOMMENDATIONS Jamaican jerk chicken wings and steak "street" tacos with tomatillo salsa.

SUMMARY AND COMMENTS House of Blues is first and foremost a major concert site, with marquee names, up-and-comers, and strong local talent taking the stage every night. Unless stated otherwise, the separately ticketed concert hall is strictly an adult venue (18 and older), though children are always welcome in the restaurant. In 2012 House of Blues (which has rebranded its restaurants as Crossroads at House of Blues) enlisted Food Network celebrity chef Aaron Sanchez to overhaul the menu. The resulting fare bursts with fresher, bolder flavors befitting a blend of Southern soul food with Sanchez's Latino background. Happy hour (Monday–Friday, 2–5 p.m., and daily, 10 p.m.–close) offers discounted drinks and cut-price appetizers. Tables are small and scrunched close together for maximum capacity.

Disney's PCH Grill ★★½

CHARACTER DINING/AMERICAN	MODERATE	QUALITY ★★½	VALUE ★★½

Disneyland Paradise Pier Hotel; ☎ 714-781-DINE

Reservations Available. **When to go** Breakfast and dinner. **Entrée range** $11–$30. **Service** ★★★★. **Friendliness** ★★★★. **Bar** Wine and beer. **Dress** Casual. **Disabled access** Yes. **Hours** Daily, 6:30–10:30 a.m. and 5–11 p.m.

SETTING AND ATMOSPHERE A taste of Southern California beach life: bright primary colors, potted palms, and decorative elements such as surfboards, oversize kites, and beach chairs.

HOUSE SPECIALTIES Banana caramel French toast and Mickey-shaped waffles at breakfast. Wood-fired flatbread pizzas and burgers.

OTHER RECOMMENDATIONS The steaks and salads are actually quite good, if a little pricey. Breakfasts are your best bet with an omelet station for the grown-ups and a kids' buffet. What kid doesn't like choosing his or her own dining destiny?

SUMMARY AND COMMENTS If you can take one more character breakfast, this time with Mickey and friends, get the kids up early and hit the "beach." Since reopening in 2010 with a revamped menu, the food has improved.

ESPN Zone ★★½

AMERICAN	MODERATE	QUALITY ★★★	VALUE ★★★

Downtown Disney; ☎ 714-781-DINE; espnzone.com

Reservations Recommended. **When to go** Lunch or dinner. **Entrée range** $11–$28. **Service** ★★★. **Friendliness** ★★★. **Bar** Full bar. **Dress** Casual. **Disabled access** Yes. **Hours** Sunday–Thursday, 11 a.m.–11 p.m.; Friday–Saturday, 11 a.m.–midnight.

SETTING AND ATMOSPHERE Maybe the most entertaining place outside the park walls, with a little something for everyone except the very youngest, the ESPN Zone is a massive, two-story sports enthusiast's dream. Huge flat-panel TVs are everywhere, and there's not a bad seat in the house. There's also a TV and radio broadcast facility inside (from which you can catch live broadcasts, especially when the local teams are playing) as well as a massive game and interactive sports arcade.

HOUSE SPECIALTIES A variety of sliders (three little sandwiches such as cheeseburgers and barbecued pork) and the barbecued baby back ribs. A variety of salads are fresher and livelier than they have been in the past.

OTHER RECOMMENDATIONS Most of what comes off the grill or as a sandwich or appetizer is a safe bet. The more complicated the dish, the more likely it won't measure up to expectations. Wings, burgers, sliders, and a surprisingly good mahimahi tostada rank as your best options.

SUMMARY AND COMMENTS The ESPN Zone is a three-ring circus—food and beverages oozing from every corner, more televised sports feeds than you can count, and an interactive game zone. Kids will love the manic pace and endless ways to spend more of your money, as well as the kid-friendly fare. Even teens will have a reason to smile here (hoops, a batting cage, and a climbing wall). And adults won't feel guilty over letting the youngsters run amok while they soak up quite possibly the largest televised sports feed on the planet. The food's improved, the service is steady (patient if not a little distracted at times), and you may find yourself in the studio audience for one of the many taped and live sports broadcasts produced right in front of you. When local teams (Lakers, Dodgers, Kings, Angels, Clippers, or Galaxy) are being televised, waits for tables can be excruciatingly long, even with reservations.

The French Market ★★★

CAJUN/CREOLE	MODERATE	QUALITY ★★★★	VALUE ★★★

Disneyland Park; ☎ 714-781-DINE

Reservations Not accepted. **When to go** Lunch and dinner. **Entrée range** $11–$14. **Service** ★★★. **Friendliness** ★★★. **Dress** Casual. **Disabled access** Yes. **Hours** Daily, 11 a.m.–10 p.m.

SETTING AND ATMOSPHERE In the heart of New Orleans Square, The French Market suggests a laid-back Southern vibe with lots of wrought iron under the shade of large, mature ficus trees. There's a small indoor dining area, but the best seating is outdoors on a large patio, covered with umbrellas and shadowed further by the trees.

HOUSE SPECIALTIES The menu features roasted chicken breast with citrus and Cajun spices, panko-crusted red snapper, and roast beef with Cognac. The jambalaya is a hearty, savory alternative that hits the spot on cooler winter days. Most meals come with a side of rice or mashed potatoes and corn bread.

OTHER RECOMMENDATIONS Hearty soups; a few fresh and flavorful salads (including a yam and apple salad).

SUMMARY AND COMMENTS The French Market features comfort food with a Cajun-Creole flair and periodic entertainment from one or more of the roving park musicians or groups.

Goofy's Kitchen ★★

CHARACTER DINING/AMERICAN   EXPENSIVE   QUALITY ★★   VALUE ★★★

Disneyland Hotel; ☎ 714-781-DINE

Reservations Available. **When to go** Breakfast. **Entrée range** $16–$36. **Service** ★★★★. **Friendliness** ★★★★. **Bar** Wine, beer, and cocktails. **Dress** Casual. **Disabled access** Yes. **Hours** Daily, 7 a.m.–noon and 5–9 p.m.

SETTING AND ATMOSPHERE Goofy's was recently redone as part of the Disneyland Hotel renovation, but aside from fresh paint, new furniture, and your typical Disney artistic touches, it feels much like the old Goofy's.

HOUSE SPECIALTIES It's a buffet and your chef is Goofy . . . which should tell you everything that you need to know. Breakfast features Mickey-shaped waffles, sausages, pancakes, bacon, scrambled eggs, and other traditional breakfast items. Dinner offers everything from prime rib to premium salads.

OTHER RECOMMENDATIONS The kids love Goofy's peanut butter pizza.

SUMMARY AND COMMENTS You come for two reasons: 1) It's easy and convenient, especially if you're staying at the resort, and 2) the youngsters haven't yet had their fill of dining with a rotating cast of Disney characters. Goofy and all his friends always put a smile to kids' faces. Breakfast is your best option for both food and wait times. Goofy's Kitchen has many fans, including this Alpine, Utah, grandmother:

Goofy's Kitchen, even at the staggering price, was well worth it. The food was really good, a lot of the menu is designed for children, and the character visits are worth the price. What a thrill to see my grandchildren's delight at being visited by Minnie, Pluto, Chip, and Snow White (with whom my 2-year-old grandson flirted brazenly!).

Napa Rose ★★★★½

CALIFORNIA/FUSION   VERY EXPENSIVE   QUALITY ★★★★★   VALUE ★★★½

Grand Californian Hotel; ☎ 714-781-DINE

Reservations Recommended. **When to go** Dinner. **Entrée range** $39–$45; $90 for four courses. **Service** ★★★★★. **Friendliness** ★★★★. **Bar** Impressive wine list. **Dress** Dressy casual. **Disabled access** Yes. **Hours** Daily, 5–10 p.m.

SETTING AND ATMOSPHERE Napa Rose is Disneyland Resort's flagship fine-dining experience. The Grand Californian's Craftsman theme is carried into this premier room with sweeping views of Disney California Adventure from virtually every table. A large, open demonstration kitchen lets you watch the magic happen, and wine, in all of its glory, is displayed at every turn. Fine linens and china are the norm. This is an absolutely gorgeous room with food and service to match.

HOUSE SPECIALTIES The menu, rotated seasonally, focuses on the cuisine of California's wine region, ranchlands, farm belts, and coastline. Wine finds its way onto most of the menu in sauces, reductions, infusions, and dressings. Dishes include sautéed portobello mushroom bisque "cappuccino," cedar-roasted duck breast, grilled wild monkfish, and braised Angus beef short rib, as well as warm butterscotch bread pudding for dessert.

OTHER RECOMMENDATIONS Game meat, ranch and free-range beef and poultry, and the chef's prix fixe Vintner's Table are constantly changing and always exciting. It's the equivalent of hopping on a new ride inside the park that you've never experienced.

SUMMARY AND COMMENTS Napa Rose may be the best restaurant in Orange County and has been at the top of most critics' lists since its debut. Top talent in the kitchen (award-winning chef Andrew Sutton leads the charge) and in the dining room—a beautiful space with panoramic views and a wine cellar second to none—make this an incomparable gustatory experience. Every server has earned sommelier status, a designation that takes years of study and practical experience with wine and winemaking, easing the chore of choosing a wine from its cellar of more than 16,000 bottles. The waitstaff brings the whole experience, from wine rookies to experts, to match your level of knowledge and tastes. Look for unusual ingredients (Tahitian vanilla, smoked sturgeon, truffled quail eggs, lemongrass, almond oil) married to top-notch staples (Colorado lamb, Berkshire pork, pheasant breast, sustainable fresh fish), all deftly handled by a world-class kitchen crew. And although staff are very accommodating in the usual Disney manner, this is definitely not an adventure for the kids. Napa Rose should be on every adult's Disney bucket list, a must-do at least once. If the full menu is too rich for your blood, sit in the cozy lounge and order appetizers. An Albuquerque woman tried both Napa Rose and Steakhouse 55 (in the Disneyland Hotel) and offers this comparison:

Prices were quite high, but we had a very good time. Napa Rose was the highlight of the trip, and our waiter was very good. Steakhouse 55 was the biggest letdown. We were expecting to repeat our experience at Napa Rose, but the staff and food didn't come close.

Naples Ristorante e Pizzeria ★★½

ITALIAN	MODERATE	QUALITY ★★½	VALUE ★★½

Downtown Disney; ☎ 714-776-6200 or 714-781-DINE; patinagroup.com/naples

Reservations Recommended. **When to go** Late lunch or early dinner. **Entrée range** $14–$25. **Service** ★★. **Friendliness** ★★★. **Bar** Extensive wine list and full bar. **Dress** Casual. **Disabled access** Yes. **Hours** Sunday–Thursday, 11 a.m.–10 p.m.; Friday–Saturday, 11 a.m.–11 p.m.

SETTING AND ATMOSPHERE Food aside, this is a really fun restaurant: modern, colorful, and spacious, with tile floors, an open demonstration kitchen, and whimsical design touches that mirror nearby Disneyland. It's also noisy and crowded, typically filled with families. During peak hours, it's difficult to hear yourself think, let alone carry on a meaningful conversation. Nonetheless, it's a great gathering place, and there's something to appeal to everyone from small children to adults.

HOUSE SPECIALTIES Wood-fired Neapolitan-style pizzas: thin, crispy crusts with a hearty, almost spicy red sauce; handmade mozzarella cheese; and fresh toppings of choice.

OTHER RECOMMENDATIONS Some of the nonpasta entrées—pan-seared salmon with roasted tomatoes and green beans and a citrus-and-herb-rubbed chicken, for example—are the real highlights.

SUMMARY AND COMMENTS Another Patina–Joachim Splichal venture where most of the effort went into the design. While the menu seems sophisticated, the recipes are rather bland and uninspired with a few exceptions. The kids will enjoy the colorful decor and activities; adults can get a good glass of wine or a cocktail and feed the entire crew for less than $100.

Napolini ★★½

ITALIAN/DELI	INEXPENSIVE	QUALITY ★★★	VALUE ★★½

Downtown Disney; ☎ 714-781-DINE

Reservations Not accepted. **When to go** Lunch or a quick dinner. **Entrée range** $4–$13. **Service** ★★★. **Friendliness** ★★★. **Bar** Wine and beer only. **Dress** Casual. **Disabled access** Yes. **Hours** Sunday–Thursday, 11 a.m.–10 p.m.; Friday–Saturday, 11 a.m.–midnight.

SETTING AND ATMOSPHERE This is next-door Naples's cousin—a quick-in, quick-out deli with most of what you'd expect, from swinging salamis to large jars of peppers. Counter and table service continue to improve, but expect a lapse in attitude once in awhile. They want to get it right, but when frustrated, servers lose patience.

HOUSE SPECIALTIES Wood-fired Neapolitan-style pizzas, panini, salads.

OTHER RECOMMENDATIONS Best bets are the panini—grilled sandwiches on thick Italian bread, loaded to order with salami, veggies, peppers, onions, and such.

SUMMARY AND COMMENTS Don't set your expectations too high and you won't be disappointed here. Servers get flustered easily, and order mistakes are common (our guess is that Napolini serves as a training ground for Naples). Noise spills over from Naples on busy nights, as do impatient diners who don't want to wait for a table next door, making for a volatile mix that can have you feeling very uncomfortable in a hurry. But maybe that's the plan: to get you in with the sweet, spicy aromas of Italian cooking and then out quickly.

Plaza Inn ★½

CHARACTER DINING/AMERICAN	MODERATE	QUALITY ★★½	VALUE ★★½

Disneyland Park; ☎ 714-781-DINE

Reservations Recommended. **When to go** When you need a compromise, the kids insist, or you arrive right at the meal switch. **Entrée range** $11–$22. **Service**

★★★. **Friendliness** ★★★. **Dress** Casual. **Disabled access** Yes. **Hours** Daily, 8 a.m.–midnight.

SETTING AND ATMOSPHERE Probably the high point of your meal at the Plaza Inn is the gorgeous Victorian B&B ambience—comfortable, widely spaced tables in a spacious dining room with lots of brocade and brass. A pleasant patio with huge umbrellas rings the east end of the circle at the top of Main Street.

HOUSE SPECIALTIES The menu has been revamped (and continues to be tweaked) with new items, but it's still a "buffeteria" that can be hit or miss; see if you can catch something being freshly delivered. Timing is everything. Best bets are the pot roast or the roasted chicken, two items that rarely suffer from sitting on the steam table.

OTHER RECOMMENDATIONS The little ones will love the character breakfast hosted by Minnie Mouse and two to four other characters. Adults will suffer through rubbery pancakes and soggy bacon.

SUMMARY AND COMMENTS Don't expect fine dining when you eat at the Plaza Inn, but some strides have been made in the quality of the food and the steam table's maintenance. Hit this place right when everything comes fresh, during the transitions from breakfast to lunch and from lunch to dinner, but it's still your basic been-in-the-steam-table-too-long scenario. Kosher meals are also available; call in advance to make arrangements. But the large spacious patio commands a great view of Main Street, where parades, strolling musicians, and the massive variety of visitors endlessly entertain us.

Rainforest Cafe ★★½

AMERICAN	MODERATE	QUALITY ★★★	VALUE ★★½

Downtown Disney; ☎ 714-772-0413; rainforestcafe.com

Reservations Available. **When to go** Lunch or dinner. **Entrée range** $13–$27. **Service** ★★. **Friendliness** ★★★. **Bar** Full bar. **Dress** Casual. **Disabled access** Yes. **Hours** Sunday–Thursday, 8 a.m.–10:30 p.m.; Friday–Saturday, 8 a.m.–midnight.

SETTING AND ATMOSPHERE Couldn't get enough of the Jungle Cruise next door *and* you're starving? Exit the park and head to the Rainforest Cafe, a lush tropical experience that attracts a few thousand of your fellow diners on a daily basis. Take a safari through the winding sections of greenery, faux wildlife, and piped-in jungle sounds, and wade through a menu as large as the Orinoco Basin.

HOUSE SPECIALTIES Stick to the basics: burgers, simple sandwiches, and salads. The Volcanic Cobb Salad—a huge mix of romaine and iceberg greens, olives, crumbled blue cheese, chopped egg, bacon, and grilled chicken in a balsamic vinaigrette—is arguably the best one on the menu.

OTHER RECOMMENDATIONS The Mojo Bones (barbecued baby back ribs) are passable; the Volcano chocolate dessert (complete with sparkler top) is gargantuan and irresistible, so invite your posse because you'll never find the bottom of the bowl alone. The sandwich wraps are also a good alternative with some tasty meat and sauce mixes.

SUMMARY AND COMMENTS If the Adventureland experience just doesn't satisfy your lust for all things green, lush, and wildlike, this is the place for you. The menu is massive (maybe a little too large) and mostly palatable, but none of it is truly great. They do make up in quantity for any lack of quality; plates are enough for two in most circumstances. Children love the rain forest theme, and you can count on any number of the chain's signature animal characters to show up during the meal for photo ops and a little interaction with the kiddies. All in all, a bit distracting—but maybe that's the point.

Ralph Brennan's Jazz Kitchen ★★★★

CAJUN/CREOLE	MODERATE	QUALITY ★★★½	VALUE ★★★

Downtown Disney; ☎ 714-776-5200; rbjazzkitchen.com

Reservations Available. **When to go** Lunch or dinner. **Entrée range** $7–$33. **Service** ★★★. **Friendliness** ★★½. **Bar** Full bar. **Dress** Casual. **Disabled access** Yes. **Hours** Sunday Thursday, 8 a.m.–4 p.m. and 4:30–10 p.m., Friday–Saturday, 8 a.m. 4 p.m. and 4:30 p m –11 p m ; Sunday *(zydeco jazz brunch),* 10 a.m.–3 p.m.

SETTING AND ATMOSPHERE Take a step back in time and space to the 19th-century French Quarter of New Orleans. Almost half the seating area is an open-air courtyard surrounded by wrought iron, hanging ferns, and milled hardwood. Above a small stage where live jazz plays daily, there's a pounded-copper ceiling; to stage left is a beautiful enamel-finished grand piano. You can people-watch from a balcony dining area, but no matter where you sit, you're going to enjoy the ambience and music.

HOUSE SPECIALTIES Gumbo Ya-Ya, blackened fish, and New York steak with Tchoupitoulas sauce.

OTHER RECOMMENDATIONS Barbecue shrimp and grits, grilled filet mignon medallions, and pasta jambalaya are all good. A $30 three-course special is a good value.

SUMMARY AND COMMENTS This used to be one of our favorite restaurants in or immediately around the resort, but it seems to have suffered a little through the recession. The Brennan family is still intimately involved with every aspect of the menu, but both quality and presentation suffer between visits from the New Orleans crew. Servers, including actual Southerners and even a smattering of Louisiana natives, exude a laid-back (sometimes too laid-back), gracious attitude most of the time but have been known to get a little testy and impatient during the restaurant's busy times. This is a dining experience best suited to adults. Add live jazz to the mix (the zydeco brunch is especially fun), and, all things considered, you have one of Disneyland's better dining experiences. For a quick early breakfast, the sugar-dusted beignets and chicory coffee from the adjoining quick-service counter can't be beat. The N'awlins Brunch Fest menu (featuring chicken and waffles and Cajun omelets) is offered every Sunday morning 10 a.m.–3 p.m., accompanied by a made-to-order Bloody Mary bar and table-side card tricks.

Rancho del Zocalo Restaurante ★★

MEXICAN	MODERATE	QUALITY ★★	VALUE ★★½

Disneyland Park; ☎ 714-781-DINE

Reservations Not accepted. **When to go** Early lunch or early dinner. **Entrée range** $10–$15. **Service** ★★★. **Friendliness** ★★★. **Dress** Casual. **Disabled access** Yes. **Hours** Daily, 11 a.m.–10 p.m.

SETTING AND ATMOSPHERE Welcome to the hacienda! Faux adobe, wooden beams, and Mexican tile ring a dark interior and covered outdoor patio. Tucked away from the throngs in the northeast area of Frontierland, this can be a nice, quiet place for a meal.

HOUSE SPECIALTIES The enchiladas are your best bet, probably because they lend themselves to the buffet-style dining here.

OTHER RECOMMENDATIONS Hit or miss: If you can catch a tray of soft tacos, burritos, or grilled chicken fresh from the commissary, you score.

SUMMARY AND COMMENTS Three words sum up the Zocalo: Mexican, cafeteria style. On the bright side, most of the cuisine holds up well under the heat lamps and over the steam tables, the enchiladas and grilled chicken in particular. The rest of the menu—the typical tacos, burritos, Mexican rice, and refried beans—is resolutely average, except at opening or right before the dinner rush, when the food is fresh and uncorrupted. The tortillas, both corn and flour, are consistently good. Anybody not intimately familiar with really good Mexican cuisine may rate this place higher. Zocalo is also a great choice when you've brought the kids along and you can't possibly choke down another hot dog, burger, or pizza slice. And because it's off the beaten path, it tends to be quiet and restful.

The River Belle Terrace ★★★½

AMERICAN	MODERATE	QUALITY ★★★½	VALUE ★★★½

Disneyland Park; ☎ 714-781-DINE

Reservations Not accepted. **When to go** Breakfast and lunch. **Entrée range** $12–$15. **Service** ★★★. **Friendliness** ★★★. **Dress** Casual. **Disabled access** Yes. **Hours** Daily, 9 a.m.–10 p.m.

SETTING AND ATMOSPHERE Situated between New Orleans Square and Frontierland, The River Belle Terrace has an Old South–style exterior replete with wrought iron and wood siding. Large shuttered windows belie a small indoor-dining area; most of the seating is outdoors on a large patio covered with colorful umbrellas.

HOUSE SPECIALTIES Mickey-shaped pancakes, country potatoes, and bacon are breakfast diner favorites. Little kids love the Mickey-shaped peanut-butter-and-jelly sandwiches.

OTHER RECOMMENDATIONS The turkey, barbecued-pork, and vegetable sandwiches are very good, served on fresh baguettes with a choice of tasty sides; a fixin's bar includes sautéed mushrooms and onions, red onions, sauces, tomatoes, and pickles.

SUMMARY AND COMMENTS This 1955 Disneyland original seems to survive by keeping the menu fresh and flexible. Disney lore places Walt here every morning for breakfast for Mickey pancakes, scrambled eggs, bacon, sausage, and large, buttery cinnamon rolls dripping with buttercream frosting (a staff favorite). We like this place for light lunches or dinners when you don't want to take a lot of time for a formal sit-down meal. Grab a hot sandwich, a PB&J or turkey sandwich for the kids, and a tall lemonade, and people-watch or just take in the view of Rivers of America from the patio.

Steakhouse 55 ★★★★

STEAK HOUSE	VERY EXPENSIVE	QUALITY ★★★★	VALUE ★★★

Disneyland Hotel; ☎ 714-781-DINE

Reservations Recommended. **When to go** Breakfast or dinner. **Entrée range** $11–$65. **Service** ★★★★. **Friendliness** ★★★★. **Bar** Wine list and full bar. **Dress** Business casual. **Disabled access** Yes. **Hours** Daily, 7–11 a.m. and 5:30–10 p.m.

SETTING AND ATMOSPHERE In 2011 Steakhouse 55 received new decor (as part of the Disneyland Hotel's entire renovation) with an update on classic American steak house. The big, overstuffed red leather booths are gone and in their place are stylishly Art Deco–inspired hardwood tables, sleek leather chairs, and smaller banquettes. The indirect lighting casts a warm glow over everything, including an impressive collection of black-and-white photographs from Disney's storied past.

HOUSE SPECIALTIES Breakfast features eggs Benedict and New York steak and eggs. At dinner it's all about the meat—grilled certified Angus beef seasoned with the restaurant's signature rub—but you can also order one of the fresh seafood choices or delectable lamb, pork, or chicken. Choose a bottle of wine from an impressive wine cellar, or simply engage one of the numerous sommeliers to choose a wine to complement your meal.

OTHER RECOMMENDATIONS The lobster and steak combination is actually very good, but the price can catch you by surprise; always ask up front before ordering unless you have very deep pockets.

SUMMARY AND COMMENTS This underrated eatery has been a well-kept secret for years and matches many of the more well-known steak houses in the area (Morton's and Ruth's Chris) steak for steak. The recent renovation has only made the place more alluring and comfortable, a perfect place to spend a grown-up evening over a leisurely meal matched to premium wines. Longtime chef Jason Martin has had years to refine his menu and has been consistently recognized by local and visiting critics as a bona fide culinary talent. Best to leave the kids behind for this experience; they'll bore easily and may disrupt what could be one of the best adult nights you're likely to have during your stay.

Storytellers Café ★★★★

CHARACTER DINING/CALIFORNIA	EXPENSIVE	QUALITY ★★★★	VALUE ★★★

Grand Californian Hotel; ☎ 714-781-DINE

Reservations Recommended. **When to go** Breakfast or dinner. **Entrée range** $12–$31. **Service** ★★★★★. **Friendliness** ★★★★. **Bar** Extensive wine list and full bar. **Dress** Casual. **Disabled access** Yes. **Hours** Daily, 7 a.m.–10 p.m.

SETTING AND ATMOSPHERE The Storytellers Café carries the Grand Californian's Arts and Crafts theme throughout with large, open beams; natural wood and wood carvings; milled stone; and stained glass. The walls are adorned with impressive murals depicting the state's rich literary history, from Mark Twain's "The Celebrated Jumping Frog of Calaveras County" to Scott O'Dell's *Island of the Blue Dolphins*.

HOUSE SPECIALTIES Children under age 10 will love the character breakfast. Hosted by Chip 'n Dale, the meal features a complement of woodland friends who visit the tables, sing songs, and pose for photos between bites of omelets, waffles, and hotcakes. The Sonoma Valley braised chicken and lemon prawns are dinner favorites.

OTHER RECOMMENDATIONS Health-conscious diners will love the café's salads, such as the Lobster Cobb Salad (with avocado, bacon, tomato, and blue cheese topped by a low-fat citrus-chive vinaigrette). The grilled chicken sandwich, with caramelized onion, tomato, and cheese, is great.

SUMMARY AND COMMENTS You may experience a little sticker shock at first, but there's real value here. It's not quite on par with Napa Rose across the way, but the same dedication to quality and originality is evident from the menu to the service. Kids will find lots to like about the menu, along with enough distractions between the colorful menus, murals, and character visits to let the adults enjoy a wide range of California wine country–inspired menu options (from pastas to steaks to fresh fish) and a leisurely cocktail or glass of wine. Dinner gives diners the option to order from the menu or visit the buffet. You'll want to save some room for dessert too—who could pass up warm seasonal-fruit cobbler heaped with vanilla ice cream or a warm chocolate brownie?

Tangaroa Terrace ★★★½

AMERICAN/POLYNESIAN	MODERATE	QUALITY ★★★½	VALUE ★★★½

Disneyland Hotel; ☎ 714-781-DINE

Reservations Not accepted. **When to go** Anytime. **Entrée range** $6–$15.

Service ★★★★. **Friendliness** ★★★★. **Bar** Beer, wine, and cocktails. **Dress** Casual. **Disabled access** Yes. **Hours** Daily, 7 a.m.–10 p.m.

SETTING AND ATMOSPHERE This is Disneyland Hotel's poolside tropical retreat. Tiki torches and South Seas music are a dead giveaway that they want to evoke that island feeling.

HOUSE SPECIALTIES Breakfast starts with French toast with bacon and banana-caramel sauce or grilled cinnamon-spiced oatmeal cakes. Lunch and dinner feature a one-third-pound Hawaiian cheeseburger with teri-yaki sauce, bacon, and grilled pineapple on a multigrain bun, or try the Asian chicken salad with red and yellow bell peppers, cashews, and rice noodles in sesame vinaigrette.

OTHER RECOMMENDATIONS Dinner gets a little more involved with different Island Plate Dinners, such as miso-crusted salmon, tamarind-glazed pork shanks, or katsu-style panko-crusted chicken. Caution: The sweet potato fries may be habit forming.

SUMMARY AND COMMENTS Recently remodeled along with the rest of the Disneyland Hotel, this poolside eatery has something for everyone, as long as everyone enjoys food with an Asian/Polynesian flare. Adults can enjoy a cocktail (maybe something a little exotic with fruit garnish and little pink umbrellas) while kids frolic in the nearby pool in between bites. The adjoining Trader Sam's Enchanted Tiki Bar serves exotic cocktails and Asian-inspired appetizers in an intimate and elaborately decorated environment reminiscent of Walt Disney World's extinct Adventurers Club. Order an Uh Oa, Krakatoa Punch, or Shipwreck on the Rocks to see some explosive special effects. The hotel's best bet for late-night snacks are Sam's panko-crusted long beans or sweet and spicy Asian wings. If the interior is at capacity (a frequent occurrence on weekends), try the patio, which has live music and a cozy fireplace.

Tortilla Jo's ★★★

MEXICAN	MODERATE–EXPENSIVE	QUALITY ★★½	VALUE ★★½

Downtown Disney; ☎ 714-535-5000; patinagroup.com/tortillajos

Reservations Available. **When to go** Lunch or dinner. **Entrée range** $15–$24. **Service** ★★★. **Friendliness** ★★★. **Bar** Full bar. **Dress** Casual. **Disabled access** Yes. **Hours** Sunday–Thursday, 11 a.m.–10 p.m., Friday–Saturday, 11 a.m.–11 p.m.; *taqueria:* Sunday–Thursday, 11 a.m.–11:30 p.m., Friday–Saturday, 11 a.m.–1 a.m.

SETTING AND ATMOSPHERE Old-world Mexico meets California modern. Mexican touchstones such as glazed tiles; thick, crude glass; and wrought iron accent an open dining room with modern, eclectic touches. You can grab a quick bite at the taqueria, and the bartender pours from a huge selection of more than 100 premium and super-premium tequilas at an outdoor cantina. The place goes crazy on the weekends, so gird yourself for a raucous, booze-shooting, beer-chasing good time.

HOUSE SPECIALTIES Start with Tableside Guacamole, which they make fresh at your table. For an entrée, any one of the gigantic burritos are good, especially the signature Fajitas Burrito.

OTHER RECOMMENDATIONS Try the gorditas or the mahimahi taco.

SUMMARY AND COMMENTS Another Patina Group eatery from überchef Joachim Splichal, Tortilla Jo's is upscale Mexican with a culinary twist.

You can customize any taco or burrito. The eclectic, hybrid menu (and the loosey-goosey crowd) may be too much for the kids, but adults will appreciate a shot of Sauza Silver tequila and a tall glass of ice-cold Corona beer, complete with a lime wedge. Strolling mariachi musicians fill the dining room and bar with foot-stomping traditional Mexican music.

Wine Country Trattoria ★★★★

CALIFORNIA NOUVELLE	MODERATE	QUALITY ★★★★	VALUE ★★★½

Disney California Adventure; ☎ 714-781-DINE

Reservations Recommended. **When to go** Lunch or dinner. **Entrée range** $13–$36. **Service** ★★. **Friendliness** ★★. **Bar** Wine and beer. **Dress** Casual. **Disabled access** Yes. **Hours** Daily, 11 a.m.–9:30 p.m.

SETTING AND ATMOSPHERE Arguably one of the best dining options at either park, the trattoria is a leisurely place to park yourself and family away from the frenetic crowds. Whether you choose one of three themed patios outside or the "patio" inside, this spacious bistro captures the California-casual mood. The park recently redesigned both interior and exterior patios with plenty of tile, wood, and trellised greenery, whisking you away from downtown Anaheim and positing you in the middle of California wine country.

HOUSE SPECIALTIES Try the pasta your way: your choice of pasta styles including spaghetti, *campanelle*, or tagliatelle with a choice of both cream-based white sauces and tomato-based red sauces.

OTHER RECOMMENDATIONS Wine Country shrimp on polenta with a lemon-caper butter sauce and the herb-roasted chicken breast.

SUMMARY AND COMMENTS With a revamped menu, the redesigned trattoria is a popular spot for a Mediterranean-style or California-inspired meal, paired with a glass of wine from its extensive cellar. Braised lamb shank and sustainable fish with citrus pesto is delicious. The Wine Country shrimp and fritto misto qualify as full-blown entrées. And to finish: Authentic tiramisu with sweetened Italian mascarpone is an exotic treat for adults among the more kid-friendly sweets that dominate in the rest of the resort. Wine Country Trattoria appeals more to adults without children, though an improved kids' menu and World of Color fixed-price dining packages has made this a more attractive option for families. Note that World of Color lunch and dinner patrons each receive a Preferred Viewing ticket. Also note that the fixed-price World of Color menu is separate from the posted à la carte selections. The soup or salad and dessert sampler included in the viewing package are all excellent, but some of the entrées are disappointing; avoid the filet if you like your beef rare. For a refreshing late-afternoon break, order a glass of wine and plate of fritto misto at the patio bar. From a Richfield, Ohio, mom:

One place we all agreed on was the Wine Country Trattoria at DCA. The service was a bit on the slow side, but the food from start to finish was delicious and fresh. We arrived around 1:30 and enjoyed lunch and the parade, which passed by at 2. Delicious meal and a parade too!

DINING *outside*
DISNEYLAND RESORT

UNOFFICIAL GUIDE RESEARCHERS LOVE GOOD FOOD and invest a fair amount of time scouting new places to eat. And because food at Disneyland Resort (all of the Disney complex including the theme parks, hotels, and Downtown Disney) is so expensive, we (like you) have an economic incentive for finding palatable meals off campus. Redevelopment of the surrounding real estate has attracted a whole new glut of fine-dining and fast-casual options. Choices abound from the familiar (**Cheesecake Factory, Roy's Hawaiian Fusion Cuisine, Ruth's Chris Steak House**) to local favorites (**Yard House, Umami Burger, The Catch**). Unique dining experiences abound. While the average Disneyland visitor only stays for two to four nights, there are more than enough fine-dining and fast-casual venues outside Disneyland Resort to keep you happy, if not confused, for that amount of time. Good ethnic dining, however, is woefully underrepresented. Especially hard to find are high-quality Thai, Chinese, Mexican, Japanese, Korean, and Greek restaurants. We've confined our coverage to restaurants that you can reach by car or cab in 15 minutes or less. If you're willing to range farther afield, your choices increase exponentially.

Among specialty restaurants in and out of Disneyland Resort, location and price will determine your choice. There is, for example, a decent Italian restaurant in Downtown Disney and several independent Italian eateries within 5 miles of the Disney complex. Which one you select depends on how much you want to spend and how convenient the place is.

Better restaurants outside Disneyland Resort cater primarily to adults and aren't as well equipped to deal with children. This is a plus, however, if you're looking to escape children and eat in peace and quiet.

The GardenWalk retail and entertainment complex is east of the park. Popular chains such as **The Cheesecake Factory, Roy's Hawaiian Fusion Cuisine, California Pizza Kitchen,** and **Bubba Gump Shrimp Co.** are doing brisk business. The best of the lot is probably **McCormick & Schmick's Grille,** which serves well-prepared fresh seafood at outrageous prices.

BUFFETS AND MEAL DEALS
OUTSIDE DISNEYLAND RESORT

BUFFETS, RESTAURANT SPECIALS, AND DISCOUNT DINING abound in the area surrounding Disneyland Resort, especially on Harbor Boulevard and Katella Avenue. The local visitor magazines, which are distributed free at non-Disney hotels, among other places, are packed with advertisements and discount coupons for seafood feasts, buffets (Chinese, Indian, and the like), and a host of combination specials for everything from lobster to barbecue. For a family trying to economize on meals, some of the come-ons are mighty attractive. But are these places any good? Is the food fresh, tasty, and appealing? Are the restaurants clean and inviting? Armed with little more than a roll of Tums, the Unofficial research team tried all the eateries that advertise heavily in the tourist publications. Here's what we discovered.

Chinese Super Buffets

Whoa! Talk about an oxymoron. If you've ever tried preparing Chinese food, especially a stir-fry, you know that split-second timing is required to avoid overcooking. So it should come as no big surprise that Chinese dishes languishing on a buffet lose their freshness, texture, and flavor in a hurry. On the bright side, however, the super buffets are so cheap that you really can't go wrong. So what if it's not the best Chinese food you've ever had if you can scarf down all you want for $10? All the Chinese buffets serve chicken prepared a dozen different ways but also offer such goodies as peel-and-eat shrimp, various fish and shellfish, the occasional carved meat, salads, soups, and sometimes sushi. Desserts are usually lackluster, but most folks are too stuffed to eat them anyway. The best Chinese buffet within a 15-minute drive of Disneyland Resort is as follows:

HARBOR SEAFOOD BUFFET 12761 Harbor Blvd., Ste. I1, Garden Grove; ☎ 714-636-3338; **theharborseafoodbuffet.net.** Dinner: $14.99 adults, Monday–Thursday; $15.99 adults, Friday–Sunday; $1.30 per year old for children ages 2–10, free for children under age 2. Seniors and military receive 10% off. Discount coupons available. Features Japanese food, sushi, and Mongolian barbecue in addition to Chinese dishes.

Indian Buffets

Indian food survives the ravages of heat lamps and steam tables much better on a buffet than Chinese food does. The mainstays of Indian buffets are curries. *Curry,* you may be surprised to know, is essentially the Indian word for "stew." Curry powder, as sold in the United States, is nothing more than a prepackaged blend of spices to flavor a stew. In India each curry is prepared with a different combination of spices (dominated by cumin), and no self-respecting cook would dream of using an off-the-shelf mix. The salient point about Indian buffets is that curries, unlike stir-fries, actually improve with a little aging. If you've ever reheated a leftover stew at home and noticed that it tasted better the second time around, it's because the flavors and ingredients continued to marry during the storage period, making the stew richer and tastier.

In the Disneyland Resort area, most Indian restaurants offer buffets at lunch only—not too convenient if you plan on spending your day at the theme parks. If you're out shopping or taking a day off, here is one Indian buffet worth trying:

GANDHI PALACE Ramada Plaza Hotel, 515 W. Katella Ave., Anaheim; ☎ 714-808-6777; **gandhipalace.com.** Lunch buffet: Monday–Saturday, $9. Discount coupons available.

Anaheim-Area Restaurants by Cuisine

CUISINE/LOCATION	OVERALL RATING	COST	QUALITY RATING	VALUE RATING
AMERICAN				
Clancy's Bar & Grill S. Harbor Blvd.	★★★	Mod	★★★	★★★
CHINESE/NORTHERN				
Mas' Chinese Islamic Restaurant E. Orangethorpe Ave.	★★★½	Mod	★★★	★★★½
ETHIOPIAN				
Abyssinia Ethiopian Cuisine W. Lincoln Ave.	★★★½	Inexp	★★★★	★★★★½
GASTROPUB				
Haven Gastropub S. Glassell St.	★★★	Mod	★★★★	★★★½
GERMAN				
The Phoenix Club S. Sanderson Ave.	★★★½	Mod	★★★½	★★★★
Jagerhaus E. Ball Rd.	★★★	Inexp	★★★½	★★★
ITALIAN				
Anaheim White House S. Anaheim Blvd.	★★★★½	Exp	★★★★½	★★★★
Luigi's D'Italia S. State College Blvd.	★★★½	Inexp/ Mod	★★★½	★★★★
Carolina's Italian Restaurant Chapman Ave.	★★★	Inexp	★★★	★★★½
MEXICAN				
Gabbi's Mexican Kitchen S. Glassell St.	★★★	Mod	★★★★	★★★½
SEAFOOD				
The Catch E. Katella Ave	★★★½	Exp	★★★★	★★★½
McCormick & Schmick's Grille W. Katella Ave.	★★★	Mod	★★★	★★★
STEAK				
Park Ave Steaks & Chops Beach Blvd.	★★★★½	Exp	★★★★	★★★★
JW's Steakhouse Marriott Anaheim	★★★★	Exp	★★★★	★★★★
Morton's S. Harbor Blvd.	★★★★	Exp	★★★½	★★★½
The Catch E. Katella Ave.	★★★½	Exp	★★★★	★★★½
Prime Cut Café & Wine Bar W. Katella Ave.	★★★	Mod	★★★	★★★½

Salad Buffets

The most popular of these in the Disneyland Resort area is **Souplantation** (5939 W. Chapman Ave., Garden Grove; ☎ 714-895-1314; **souplantation.com**). The buffet features prepared salads and an extensive array of ingredients to build your own. In addition to the rabbit food, Souplantation offers a variety of soups, a modest pasta bar, a baked-potato bar, an assortment of fresh fruit, and ice cream sundaes. Dinner runs $10.69 for adults, $5.29 for children ages 6–12, and $2.99 for children ages 3–5. Lunch is $8.99 for adults during the week and $9.19 on weekends; kids eat for the same price as at dinner.

ANAHEIM-AREA FULL-SERVICE RESTAURANTS

SOUTHERN CALIFORNIA IS A MOTHER LODE of wonderful dining, and if we directed you to Newport Beach, La Jolla, or LA, we could guarantee you a fantastic eating experience every night. In that you've chosen Disneyland as your destination, however, we've elected to profile only solid restaurants that you can reach by car or cab in 15 minutes or less. That said, here are our picks.

Abyssinia Ethiopian Cuisine ★★★½

ETHIOPIAN	INEXPENSIVE	QUALITY ★★★★	VALUE ★★★★½

2751 W. Lincoln Ave., Anaheim; ☎ 714-826-5656; abyssiniaethiocuisine.com

Reservations Recommended on weekends. **When to go** Dinner. **Entrée range** $8–$15. **Service** ★★★★. **Friendliness** ★★★★. **Bar** None. **Dress** Casual. **Disabled access** Yes. **Hours** Tuesday–Sunday, 11:30 a.m.–9 p.m.

SETTING AND ATMOSPHERE Intimate restaurant located in a four-store retail strip. The dining area, with mostly four-tops and two-tops, is casual with earth-toned carpet and drapes and plexiglass table covers. The room is generally subdued but becomes noisy when most tables are occupied. Service is extremely friendly and knowledgeable.

HOUSE SPECIALTIES Ethiopian dishes are eaten without utensils by scooping up food with small pieces of injera, a spongy flatbread that serves as napkin, platter, spoon, and starch all in one. Though the main ingredients of Ethiopian cuisine are fairly straightforward, they are enhanced by intense and addictive seasonings that recall Ethiopia's years as the crossroads of the spice routes. Dishes, primarily stews, are distant forebears of soul food. *Wats* (or *wots*) and *alechas* (sometimes *alichas*) are the major types of stews, the first always spicy and the second either mild or hot. The three primary sauces—berbere, *awaze,* and *mitmita*—are all hot, but berbere is the hottest.

OTHER RECOMMENDATIONS Unless you're experienced with Ethiopian cuisine, we recommend the Abyssinia Veggie Combination or, for meat lovers, the Abyssinia Special. Both provide a generous and varied selection of dishes. One of each for the table will feed two or three adults.

Great Eats in and around Anaheim

BEST BURGER

In-N-Out Burger 600 S. Brookhurst St., Anaheim; ☎ 800-786-1000; in-n-out.com. This small family-owned chain is the gold standard for burgers. Hamburgers, cheeseburgers, fries, and shakes are all it offers—and nobody does them better. Ask for the Double-Double (double meat, double cheese), "animal" style (heavy on all the condiments).

BEST CHINESE

Grand China Restaurant 575 W. Chapman Ave., Anaheim; ☎ 714-740-1888. Really outstanding service differentiates this spot from its nearby competitors. The menu's pretty standard, but what it does, it does well—and with a big smile. The broccoli with beef and sweet-and-sour chicken are first-rate.

BEST FAMILY/ICE CREAM

Tiffy's Family Restaurant 1060 W. Katella Ave., Anaheim; ☎ 714-635-1801. Tiffy's has been serving up solid breakfasts, lunches, and dinners since Disneyland was built. Great Belgian waffles and homemade ice cream are its hallmarks. Quality and service can be sketchy at times, but Tiffy's has an entrenched and fiercely loyal following.

BEST INDIAN

Punjabi Tandoor 327 S. Anaheim Blvd., Ste. A, Anaheim; ☎ 714-635-3155; punjabitandoor.com. The fresh tandoori in the evening is exceptional. Offers original dishes and excellent naan.

BEST JAPANESE

Koisan Japanese Cuisine 1132 E. Katella Ave., Orange; ☎ 714-639-2330; koisanjapanesecuisine.com. Cozy and intimate, it's perfect for theme park decompression, and the menu is pretty extensive.

BEST MEDITERRANEAN

Zankou Chicken 2424 W. Ball Rd., Anaheim; ☎ 714-229-2060; zankouchicken.com. Forget that this place is a chain, disregard the cheesy ambience, and go for the spit-roasted chicken, hummus, and shawarma beef. Inexpensive and delicious.

BEST MEXICAN

La Casa Garcia 531 W. Chapman Ave., Anaheim; ☎ 714-740-1108; lacasagarcia.com. An Anaheim institution with an authentic Tex-Mex twist on traditional Mexican food. Carnitas, *barbacoa* (beef slow-cooked in a red-chile sauce), and three-flavor chimichangas are not to be missed.

Los Sanchez 11906 Garden Grove Blvd., Garden Grove; ☎ 714-590-9300; lossanchez.com. This locals-only gem serves authentic Sonoran cuisine at ridiculously reasonable prices. Fish ceviche, *lengua* (tongue) tacos, seafood soup, and the best chicken mole you've ever had, served in an authentically unpretentious environment, with all the fresh radishes and cilantro you can eat.

Ingredients for all dishes are explained on the menu. If you're a coffee drinker, try the Ethiopian coffee, served in a clay *jebena* (percolator).

SUMMARY AND COMMENTS The communal platter style of service makes Ethiopian dining a truly sociable experience. There are no alcoholic beverages on the menu, but there is a package store in the same retail complex. There's no corkage fee, and the restaurant will supply glasses.

Anaheim White House ★★★★½

ITALIAN	EXPENSIVE	QUALITY ★★★★½	VALUE ★★★★

887 S. Anaheim Blvd., Anaheim; ☎ 714-772-1381; anaheimwhitehouse.com

Reservations Recommended. When to go Dinner. Entrée range $15–$33. Service ★★★★★. Friendliness ★★★★. Bar Full bar; plentiful wine list. Dress Business casual. Disabled access Yes. Hours Monday–Friday, 11:30 a.m.–2 p.m. and 5–10 p.m.; Saturday, 5–10 p.m.; Sunday, 11 a.m.–3 p.m. and 5–10 p.m.

SETTING AND ATMOSPHERE A local institution, the Anaheim White House sits in a restored Victorian originally built in 1909. It has nine different dining rooms, all with thick gold-and-white drapes and bright-gold accents against a bright-white background. Tables are set with fine bone china and the best flatware. Service is extremely gracious and knowledgeable.

HOUSE SPECIALTIES Italian seafood recipes from northern Italy highlight an extensive menu. Braised boneless beef short ribs, steamed salmon (served with a Belgian white chocolate mashed potato purée), and lobster-and-basil ravioli in a ginger-citrus sauce are its signature dishes.

OTHER RECOMMENDATIONS Chicken stuffed with ham and mozzarella cheese in a light mushroom sauce.

SUMMARY AND COMMENTS The White House only seems to get better. The menu of northern Italian recipes is kept fresh and timely, and service is spot-on. This is an elegant restaurant—leave the kids with a sitter.

Carolina's Italian Restaurant ★★★

SOUTHERN ITALIAN	INEXPENSIVE	QUALITY ★★★	VALUE ★★★½

12045 Chapman Ave., Garden Grove; ☎ 714-971-5551; carolinasitalianrestaurant.com

Reservations Recommended. When to go Dinner. Entrée range $9–$23. Service ★★½. Friendliness ★★★½. Bar Extensive beer and wine lists. Dress Casual. Disabled access Yes. Hours Sunday–Thursday, 11 a.m.–10 p.m.; Friday–Saturday, 11 a.m.–midnight.

SETTING AND ATMOSPHERE A classic Italian family restaurant replete with wall murals of the motherland, comfortable seating, and the overwhelming aroma of garlic and olive oil. It's like walking through a time warp.

HOUSE SPECIALTIES You can't go wrong with any one of more than three dozen hearty pasta dishes, from a very traditional meat sauce to an outstanding lasagna. The kitchen's showcase is a slab of fresh Atlantic salmon in a butter-garlic-mustard sauce.

OTHER RECOMMENDATIONS The Taste of Italy features the colors of Italy's flag with a combination of chicken penne pesto, shrimp fettuccine Alfredo, and spaghetti with meatballs. The house-made tiramisu, if you can manage more food after the large plates, is a treat.

SUMMARY AND COMMENTS Family owned and operated for three gener-
ations, Carolina's also features more than 200 beers from around the
globe and a rather well-selected wine list for such a place. Portions
tend toward the gigantic, so bring your appetite.

The Catch ★★★½

SEAFOOD/STEAK	EXPENSIVE	QUALITY ★★★★	VALUE ★★★½

2100 E. Katella Ave., Ste. 104, Anaheim; ☎ 714-935-0101;
catchanaheim.com

Reservations Recommended. When to go Lunch or dinner. Entrée range $11–
$60. Service ★★★. Friendliness ★★★½. Bar Full bar. Dress Business casual. Dis-
abled access Yes. Hours Monday–Friday, 11:30 a.m.–10 p.m.; Saturday,
11:30 a.m.–4 p.m. and 5–10 p.m.; Sunday, 11:30 a.m.–4 p.m. and 5–9 p.m.

SETTING AND ATMOSPHERE Clean, contemporary take on a steak house
classic, The Catch exudes urban chic with a comfortable blend of hardwood, glass, and tile. Expect to see dozens of young urban professionals;
old, diehard loyalists; and even a smattering of professional athletes
who play for the local Angels baseball and Anaheim Ducks hockey teams
dallying at the bar and/or enjoying dinner with friends and family.

HOUSE SPECIALTIES Grilled fresh fish, premium meats, and chops dominate the menu. The Drunken Mahimahi, a lightly blackened fresh fillet
splashed with tequila, is as good as it is simple. And for steak lovers, the
top sirloin may be the best cut you're likely to sample anywhere.

OTHER RECOMMENDATIONS The lunch menu features butcher-block
sandwiches: piles of thinly sliced meats or fish piled high on fresh slabs
of bread, accompanied by all the usual condiments and some not-so-
common spreads such as lemon aioli. For dinner, try the terrific bone-in
rib eye.

SUMMARY AND COMMENTS The Catch reopened in 2010 under new lead-
ership and in a brand-new location. Yes, the place is very expensive, but
you're not likely to find a more beautiful yet comfortable room, attentive service, or high-quality food prepared with love and care anywhere close by. It has a vibrant bar scene favored by local luminaries, a
beautiful dining room, and even a nicely appointed patio.

Clancy's Bar & Grill ★★★

AMERICAN	MODERATE	QUALITY ★★★	VALUE ★★★

2191 S. Harbor Blvd., Anaheim; ☎ 714-750-7500; clancysbarandgrill.com

Reservations Available. When to go Lunch or dinner. Entrée range $8–$30.
Service ★★. Friendliness ★★★. Bar Full bar. Dress Casual. Disabled access
Yes. Hours Daily, 4–11 p.m.

SETTING AND ATMOSPHERE Pure sports bar with full, high-definition flat-
panel TVs in every direction, a few booths, and several rooms of tables,
all with a view of the televised action.

HOUSE SPECIALTIES Wings marinated, baked, fried, and broiled to perfection with all the usual sauces, as well as a very different mango habañero. The pulled pork sandwich swims in a signature barbecue sauce.

OTHER RECOMMENDATIONS The steaks, including a baseball-cut top sirloin (a ball of meat with all the flavor of a sirloin and the tenderness of a filet mignon), are surprisingly good for a sports bar.

SUMMARY AND COMMENTS Clancy's is a great alternative to the crammed insanity of the ESPN Zone in Downtown Disney. The menu is expansive and has sports bar staples such as chicken wings and a decent cut of beef. Lots of locals and a friendly vibe; service can be sporadic.

Gabbi's Mexican Kitchen ★★★

GOURMET MEXICAN	MODERATE	QUALITY ★★★★	VALUE ★★★½

141 S. Glassell St., Orange; ☎ 714-633-3038; gabbipatrick.com

Reservations Recommended. **When to go** Lunch or dinner. **Entrée range** $9–$24. **Service** ★★★. **Friendliness** ★★★. **Bar** Full bar. **Dress** Casual. **Disabled access** Yes. **Hours** Daily, 11 a.m.–11 p.m.

SETTING AND ATMOSPHERE Locals flock to Gabbi's vintage storefront that has no sign (look for the *poquito* patio next door to the Army surplus store). Just steps south of Orange's beloved plaza in charming Old Town, Gabbi's adds style to the narrow space with tall ceilings, exposed brick, and giant, colorful Mexican urns.

HOUSE SPECIALTIES Puerco Poc-Chuc (a Mayan recipe of grilled pork, onions, and habañero salsa), quesadillas with cuitlacoche and a poblano cream sauce, and squash blossom chiles rellenos.

OTHER RECOMMENDATIONS Chicken enchiladas and signature margaritas made from a tequila collection that would make a desperado blush.

SUMMARY AND COMMENTS In this county teeming with taco stands and burrito counters, chef-owner Gabbi Patrick stands apart with her more refined, regional takes on Mexican food that reflect both her Napa training and her Latino family's roots in the restaurant business.

Haven Gastropub ★★★

GASTROPUB	MODERATE	QUALITY ★★★★	VALUE ★★★½

190 S. Glassell St., Orange; ☎ 714-221-0680; havengastropub.com

Reservations Recommended. **When to go** Lunch or dinner. **Entrée range** $8–$34. **Service** ★★★. **Friendliness** ★★★½. **Bar** Beer and wine. **Dress** Casual. **Disabled access** Yes. **Hours** Daily, 11 a.m.–2 a.m.

SETTING AND ATMOSPHERE The restaurant is in Old Town Orange, a historic area of preserved homes and businesses including this little gem. Like its neighbor, Gabbi's, Haven is housed in a restored brick building. Inside, you'll find a large open dining room packed with tables and booths, framed by a massive bar on one side and an open kitchen on the other.

HOUSE SPECIALTIES House-made potato chips are first soaked in beer, fried, and served with a sprinkling of herbs and a side of garlic aioli. Try the lamb burger with onion jam, tzatziki, and onion sprouts on a squishy brioche bun.

OTHER RECOMMENDATIONS Crisp braised pork belly (thick bacon) with clams, coconut velouté, and pickled chili peppers; a whole roasted suckling pig served family style for parties of eight or more (reserve one week in advance).

SUMMARY AND COMMENTS Think beer, anything made with beer, and all the food that goes with beer, and you have a grasp of what executive chef Greg Daniels has put together here. More than 200 craft beers on tap and in a bottle—and a service crew who knows every one of them intimately—together with an adventurous menu of faux familiar and exotic foods, and you have Haven. The place is a favorite for the local college students and fills quickly on weekends but stays open late every night until 2 a.m.

Jägerhaus ★★★

GERMAN	INEXPENSIVE	QUALITY ★★★½	VALUE ★★★

2525 E. Ball Rd., Anaheim; ☎ 714-520-9500; jagerhaus.net

Reservations Recommended only for large parties. **When to go** Breakfast. **Entrée range** $5–$20. **Service** ★★½. **Friendliness** ★★★★. **Bar** Wine list and extensive imported draft beer offerings. **Dress** Casual. **Disabled access** Yes. **Hours** Monday–Friday, 7 a.m.–9 p.m.; Saturday–Sunday, 8 a.m.–9 p.m.

SETTING AND ATMOSPHERE We don't think that anything has changed since this restaurant opened decades ago. Wood paneling dominates. Pictures of alpine meadows and picturesque old-world villages hang beneath shelves of kitschy accoutrements from delicate porcelain teapots to hearty beer steins—but it's clean and neat.

HOUSE SPECIALTIES The German pancakes, dense, doughy, platter-size egg cakes flavored with everything from lemon and powdered sugar to fruit jams and even fresh fruit; fat, juicy bratwursts.

OTHER RECOMMENDATIONS Omelets, corned beef hash, and house-made sausage patties.

SUMMARY AND COMMENTS Everyone from recent German émigrés and tourists to descendants of the original German settlers gather here to eat fat, fluffy German pancakes and sausage and gossip over coffee. The huge menu offers something for everyone, from burgers to bratwurst and bagels to Wiener schnitzel.

JW's Steakhouse ★★★★

STEAK HOUSE	EXPENSIVE	QUALITY ★★★★	VALUE ★★★★

Marriott Anaheim, 700 W. Convention Way, Anaheim; ☎ 714-750-8000; marriottanaheimhotel.com

Reservations Recommended. **When to go** Dinner. **Entrée range** $19–$56. **Service** ★★★★. **Friendliness** ★★★★. **Bar** Wine list and full bar. **Dress** Dressy casual. **Disabled access** Yes. **Hours** Daily, generally 5–10 p.m. (hours vary according to hotel occupancy; there's no set schedule)

SETTING AND ATMOSPHERE The restaurant is, in a word, gorgeous. Minimalist modern with an Asian touch.

HOUSE SPECIALTIES Steak . . . almost any of the featured cuts are outstanding. Try the Kobe flatiron, rubbed with spices and pepper, grilled to order, and served as cutlets. It's an underrated cut that's as lean as most filets and more flavorful than a sirloin.

OTHER RECOMMENDATIONS Wedge salad: one quarter head of iceberg lettuce with Gorgonzola-cheese dressing and maple bacon.

SUMMARY AND COMMENTS Right around the corner and down the street from Morton's, JW's actually serves a better steak in a nicer room with better service. The room is absolutely stunning (ask for the cozy, private nook behind the fireplace), the meat nearly flawless, and the service sharp and warm. The trick is to catch the restaurant open: the hotel closes it when occupancy falls, so operating hours can be erratic.

Luigi's D'Italia ★★★½

ITALIAN	INEXPENSIVE–MODERATE	QUALITY ★★★½	VALUE ★★★★

801 S. State College Blvd., Anaheim; ☎ 714-490-0990; italianoc.com

Reservations Recommended. **When to go** Lunch or dinner. **Entrée range** $7–$26. **Service** ★★★. **Friendliness** ★★★. **Bar** Wine and beer. **Dress** Casual. **Disabled access** Yes. **Hours** Monday–Friday, 11 a.m.–10 p.m.; Saturday–Sunday, noon–10 p.m.

SETTING AND ATMOSPHERE Classic tacky Italian, reminiscent of just about every neighborhood mom-and-pop pizzeria in America (think faux grapevines, funky murals, and Chianti-bottle candleholders). But there is something homey and comforting in this (you probably have a place just like this in your hometown), and the service is generally warm and friendly.

HOUSE SPECIALTIES Better-than-average hand-tossed pizzas with all the familiar toppings (pepperoni, mushroom, sausage, and such); a very tasty (and hearty) eggplant Sorrentino.

OTHER RECOMMENDATIONS The pastas, including a superb spaghetti Bolognese, are commendable.

SUMMARY AND COMMENTS When the pocketbook can't take another huge hit no matter how good the menu looks, head to Luigi's. Old-fashioned Italian fare, a welcoming (if kitschy) ambience, and friendly smiles await. The pizzas and pastas, Italian staples, are all familiar, hearty, and tasty, if not overly generous in their portions. The kids will love watching the pizzas get tossed, and your credit card will breathe a sigh of relief.

Mas' Chinese Islamic Restaurant ★★★½

NORTHERN CHINESE	MODERATE	QUALITY ★★★	VALUE ★★★½

601 E. Orangethorpe Ave., Anaheim; ☎ 714-446-9553

Reservations Recommended. **When to go** Lunch or dinner. **Entrée range** $7–$26. **Service** ★★★. **Friendliness** ★★★½. **Bar** None. **Dress** Casual but modest (no shorts). **Disabled access** Yes. **Hours** Monday and Wednesday–Thursday, 11 a.m.–3 p.m. and 5–9:30 p.m.; Friday–Sunday, 11 a.m.–3 p.m. and 5–10 p.m.

SETTING AND ATMOSPHERE One of a small chain of Islamic Chinese restaurants, this is the real deal. Mas' Islamic's dining room is spacious, with comfortable booths and large tables. The decor blends Middle Eastern and Chinese motifs with lots of tile, repetitive patterned mosaics, and lofty arches.

HOUSE SPECIALTIES Get the thick sesame bread with green onions as a starter. Any lamb dish is a sure bet, especially the one served with *sa cha*, a spicy brown sauce.

OTHER RECOMMENDATIONS The warm pots—northern-Chinese stews—
are great, as is the beef with green onions.

SUMMARY AND COMMENTS This is a veritable institution among local
Muslims (Arabs and East and Southeast Asians), so expect to see women
in veils and burkas and men dressed very conservatively; also, note that
no alcohol is served. Service is gracious, if a bit English-challenged. Stick
to the northern-Chinese specialties—the more familiar Chinese side of
the menu is less exciting.

McCormick & Schmick's Grille ★★★

SEAFOOD	MODERATE	QUALITY ★★★	VALUE ★★★

321 W. Katella Ave., Anaheim; ☎ 714-535-9000;
mccormickandschmicks.com

Reservations Recommended. When to go Lunch or dinner. Entrée range $15–
$50. Service ★★★. Friendliness ★★★★. Bar Full bar and extensive wine list.
Dress Business casual. Disabled access Yes. Hours Monday–Wednesday and
Sunday, 11:30 a.m.–10 p.m.; Thursday–Saturday, 11:30 a.m.–11 p.m.

SETTING AND ATMOSPHERE This large chain of seafood eateries designs
each of its units differently to match its local surroundings. In addition
to lots of dark hardwoods and spacious booths, the decor here takes its
cues from the rich agricultural history of the area.

HOUSE SPECIALTIES Fish—fresh and infinitely variable. Each chef is free
to choose from among 80 different preparations, and there's an abun-
dance of fresh selections. You can't miss with king crab, lobster, fresh
salmon, or killer fresh swordfish.

SUMMARY AND COMMENTS This is a very popular spot with local business
types, and waits without reservations can be long. The menu can be
overwhelming; on the other hand, there's something for everyone,
even folks who don't eat fish. Happy hour specials (daily, 3–6 p.m.)
somewhat soften the sting of expensive entrées; the $5 steamed
mussels are an especially good deal.

Morton's ★★★★

STEAK HOUSE	EXPENSIVE	QUALITY ★★★½	VALUE ★★★½

1895 S. Harbor Blvd., Anaheim; ☎ 714-621-0101; mortons.com

Reservations Recommended. When to go Dinner. Entrée range $23–$85.
Service ★★★★. Friendliness ★★★★. Bar Extensive wine list and full bar. Dress
Dressy casual. Disabled access Yes. Hours Monday–Saturday, 5:30–11 p.m.;
Sunday, 5–10 p.m.

SETTING AND ATMOSPHERE Classic steak house with overstuffed booths,
soft lighting, and dark hardwoods.

HOUSE SPECIALTIES Try the center-cut filet mignon Oscar-style (with lump
crab, asparagus, and béarnaise sauce).

OTHER RECOMMENDATIONS The bone-in rib eye is a Chicago staple and
beef-eater's dream: 22 ounces of prime steak, grilled to order.

SUMMARY AND COMMENTS Morton's is a carnivore's delight—beef,
lamb, and chicken dominate the menu. Of course, there's a smattering
of fish options, including shrimp in several different iterations, but this
place is really about the beef.

Park Ave Steaks & Chops ★★★★½

STEAK HOUSE	EXPENSIVE	QUALITY ★★★★	VALUE ★★★★

11200 Beach Blvd., Stanton; ☎ 714-901-4400; parkavedining.com

Reservations Recommended. **When to go** Dinner. **Entrée range** $13–$45. **Service** ★★★. **Friendliness** ★★★½. **Bar** Full bar. **Dress** Dressy casual/business. **Disabled access** Yes. **Hours** Tuesday–Friday, 11 a.m.–midnight; Saturday–Sunday, 4 p.m.–midnight.

SETTING AND ATMOSPHERE From the flagstone walls and Sputnik-like lighting to red leather booths, this place exudes 1950s modern chic. There's also an expansive terrace and meticulously maintained grounds, where the chef grows his own herbs, vegetables, and fruit.

HOUSE SPECIALTIES Bone-in rib eye and the five-spiced baked salmon drizzled with honey.

OTHER RECOMMENDATIONS The chef does a marvelous job with a salad featuring marinated skirt steak, dripping with a ginger, molasses, and soy sauce.

SUMMARY AND COMMENTS Park Ave is a throwback to all things mid-20th century—except the menu. The proprietors have managed to avoid the kitsch and concentrate on those things that evoke a simpler, less complicated era—down to a friendly bar shaking up some of the meanest martinis in Orange County. The food is exceptionally good (award winning), but service gets a little sloppy, especially on slower nights. They've also opened a more casual garden restaurant on the same grounds, offering a compact menu of Italian classics.

The Phoenix Club ★★★½

GERMAN	MODERATE	QUALITY ★★★½	VALUE ★★★★

1340 S. Sanderson Ave., behind Honda Center, Anaheim; ☎ 714-563-4166; thephoenixclub.com

Reservations Recommended. **When to go** Lunch or dinner. **Entrée range** $9–$20. **Service** ★★★. **Friendliness** ★★★★. **Bar** Wine list, extensive draft beer offerings, and full bar. **Dress** Casual. **Disabled access** Yes. **Hours** Tuesday–Thursday and Sunday, 11 a.m.–9 p.m.; Friday–Saturday, 11 a.m.–10 p.m.

SETTING AND ATMOSPHERE Once a private club reserved for family members of the original German settlers of Anaheim and more recent émigrés, this famous landmark is now open to the public (members are still welcome and enjoy a few extra privileges). Choose from the formal, elegantly appointed Loreley dining room or the boisterous Bierstube, with more than a half dozen German beers on tap. The Bierstube's menu is more limited than the Loreley's, trending toward less-fancy preparations, but it's these basic dishes that keep folks coming back. Where the Loreley is quiet and peaceful, the Bierstube is conducive to raucous eating, drinking, and carousing. Live music seems omnipresent, from local and guest polka bands to renowned accordion artists.

HOUSE SPECIALTIES Wursts, kraut, pork roast, mixed platters, and sauerbraten are the best in a 100-mile radius.

OTHER RECOMMENDATIONS Pork in a creamy mushroom truffle sauce.

SUMMARY AND COMMENTS The bastion of Anaheim's founding families and subsequent waves of German immigrants, The Phoenix Club offers a little taste of the *mutterland* far from home. The food is good, occasionally great; the beer is always cold; and the help is always ready to show you a good time, German or not. During Oktoberfest, the place rocks. The kids will love the early reminders of a rough and rural Anaheim and the oompah bands, Mom and Dad will love the German beers, and everyone will love the sweet-and-sour flavors of German cuisine.

Prime Cut Café & Wine Bar ★★★

STEAK HOUSE	MODERATE	QUALITY ★★★	VALUE ★★★½

1547 W. Katella Ave. (Stadium Promenade Center), Ste. 101, Orange; ☎ 714-532-4300; primecutcafe.com

Reservations Recommended. **When to go** Lunch or dinner. **Entrée range** $11–$33. **Service** ★★★. **Friendliness** ★★★. **Bar** Wine and cocktails. **Dress** Casual. **Disabled access** Yes. **Hours** Sunday–Thursday, 11 a.m.–9:30 p.m.; Friday–Saturday, 11 a.m.–10:30 p.m.

SETTING AND ATMOSPHERE Polished but laid-back, this dapper newcomer is a welcome independent in a sea of chain operations. A massive granite bar anchors the attractive space that also offers a roomy patio overlooking the center's water fountain.

HOUSE SPECIALTIES Slow-roasted prime rib is offered in three sizes, all partnered with good Yorkshire pudding and rich creamed spinach. A huge pork chop is another winner, paired with green beans, roasted potatoes, and golden beets. For starters, don't miss the terrific house-smoked salmon with horseradish.

OTHER RECOMMENDATIONS Prime rib may hog the spotlight, but steaks, burgers, and entrée salads often outshine the showy star of the menu. Sides such as potato gratin or mascarpone polenta are scene-stealers, as are from-scratch desserts.

SUMMARY AND COMMENTS Prime Cut Café does a good job of making first-rate dining affordable and approachable. Eighty-plus wines sold by the glass, taste, or bottle is an attraction for wine lovers, though wine snobs might find the list a bit lowbrow. The menu offers lots of appetizers and snacks that pair well with wine, making this a great option for a quick bite or grown-up get-together. The central location means that crowds swell or recede according to events at nearby Anaheim Stadium, Honda Pond, or even what's hot at the adjacent multiplex cinema.

▮ SHOPPING *at* DISNEYLAND

SHOPS ADD REALISM AND ATMOSPHERE to the various theme settings and offer souvenirs, clothing, novelties, jewelry, decorator items, and more. Much of the merchandise displayed (with the exception of Disney trademark souvenir items), though, is available back home and elsewhere, so we recommend bypassing the shops on a one-day visit. If you have two or more days to spend at Disneyland Resort, browse in the early afternoon, when many attractions are crowded.

Downtown Disney

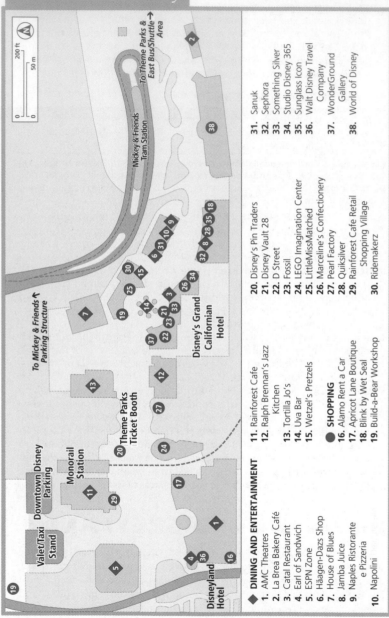

◆ DINING AND ENTERTAINMENT

1. AMC Theatres
2. La Brea Bakery Café
3. Catal Restaurant
4. Earl of Sandwich
5. ESPN Zone
6. Häagen-Dazs Shop
7. House of Blues
8. Jamba Juice
9. Naples Ristorante
   e Pizzeria
10. Napolini
11. Rainforest Cafe
12. Ralph Brennan's Jazz
    Kitchen
13. Tortilla Jo's
14. Uva Bar
15. Wetzel's Pretzels

● SHOPPING

16. Alamo Rent a Car
17. Apricot Lane Boutique
18. Blink by Wet Seal
19. Build-a-Bear Workshop

20. Disney's Pin Traders
21. Disney Vault 28
22. D Street
23. Fossil
24. LEGO Imagination Center
25. LittleMissMatched
26. Marceline's Confectionery
27. Pearl Factory
28. Quiksilver
29. Rainforest Cafe Retail
    Shopping Village
30. Ridemakerz

31. Sanuk
32. Sephora
33. Something Silver
34. Studio Disney 365
35. Sunglass Icon
36. Walt Disney Travel
    Company
37. WonderGround
    Gallery
38. World of Disney

Our recommendations notwithstanding, we realize that for many guests, Disney souvenirs and memorabilia are irresistible. One of our readers writes:

People have a compelling need to buy Disney stuff at Disneyland. When you get home, you wonder why you ever got a cashmere sweater with Mickey Mouse embroidered on the breast, or a tie with tiny Goofys all over it. Maybe they put something in the food?

If you don't want to lug your packages around, you can leave them at the information stand just inside the front gate and pick them up as you exit the park. Retrieving your purchases might take a while if you depart after a parade or fireworks show or at closing, when guests exit en masse. If you're staying at a Disneyland Resort hotel, your loot will be delivered directly to your resort's bellhop desk (by 7 a.m. the following day) on request. If you have a problem with your purchases or need to make a return, call Disneyland Exclusive Merchandise at ☎ 800-760-3566, Monday–Friday, 8 a.m.–5 p.m. PST. If you return home and realize that you forgot to buy those Rastafarian mouse ears or some similarly essential tchotchke, a large selection of park-exclusive merchandise is now available to order at **disneyparks.com/store.**

DOWNTOWN DISNEY

DOWNTOWN DISNEY, verdant and landscaped by day, pops alive with neon and glitter at night. The complex offers more than 300,000 square feet of specialty shopping, clubs, restaurants, and movie theaters. Many of the restaurants offer entertainment in addition to dining, including **Crossroads at House of Blues** and **Ralph Brennan's Jazz Kitchen.** The **ESPN Zone** is a sports bar and restaurant with dozens of giant TV screens. Other restaurant options include the **Naples Ristorante e Pizzeria, Tortilla Jo's** Mexican restaurant, **Earl of Sandwich,** and jungle-themed dining at the **Rainforest Cafe.**

If you're not hungry, there's always shopping and a 12-theater **AMC Movieplex** with IMAX 3-D to keep you occupied. A 40,000-square-foot **World of Disney** store, the second largest on the planet, anchors the shopping scene. Other retailers include **Sanuk,** a shoe store; **Little-MissMatched,** selling socks that don't match (for more than you'd pay for socks that do); **Apricot Lane,** for fashion apparel, jewelry, handbags, and accessories; **Studio Disney 365,** offering hairstyling and braiding for girls who are a little too old for a princess makeover at Bibbidi Bobbidi Boutique in Disneyland Park; cosmetics at **Sephora;** and **Something Silver,** specializing in jewelry. The recently renovated **LEGO Imagination Center** features interactive play tables with LEGO bricks and life-size statues of Disney characters made entirely of LEGOs. At **Build-A-Bear Workshop,** you can customize a teddy bear, starting from scratch with the bearskin, stuffing it, and then accessorizing it.

Our map of Downtown Disney, listing storefronts and restaurants, appears on page 214.

ANAHEIM GARDENWALK

ANAHEIM GARDENWALK is a shopping, dining, and entertainment venue that stretches from West Katella Avenue to Disney Way. Built on three levels and nicely landscaped, the GardenWalk effectively doubles the restaurant, lounge, and shopping choices for Disneyland Resort visitors and attendees of conventions at nearby Anaheim Convention Center. Restaurants include **Bar Louie, Bubba Gump Shrimp Co., California Pizza Kitchen, The Cheesecake Factory, Fire + Ice, McCormick & Schmick's Grille, P.F. Chang's Chinese Bistro,** and **Roy's Hawaiian Fusion Cuisine.**

For entertainment, there's an UltraLuxe 14-screen movie theater with D-Box motion seats and in-seat beverage service, a 41-lane bowling complex and nightspot combo, a 24-hour fitness center, and an ultra lounge. The complex also hosts film festivals and a haunted house at Halloween. Among the retailers are **Harley-Davidson, Fresh Produce, LUSH Cosmetics,** and **White House/Black Market.** In late 2012 the complex was purchased by new investors who are seeking to attract new dining and entertainment offerings. Until then, expect the mix of tenants to be in flux. For additional information, see **anaheimgarden walk.com** or call ☎ 714-635-7410.

PART FIVE

DISNEYLAND PARK

ARRIVING *and* GETTING ORIENTED

IF YOU DRIVE, you will probably be directed to the massive Mickey and Friends parking garage on West Street near Ball Road. Parking costs $16 for cars, $21 for RVs, and $26 for buses. Be sure to make a note of your section, row, and space. A tram will transport you to a loading/unloading area connected to the entrance by a pedestrian corridor. Many locals prefer to park in the Toy Story surface lot on Harbor Boulevard south of Katella Avenue, which offers shuttle service to the east side of the resort entrance Esplanade. Most pedestrians enter the resort from Harbor Boulevard to the east, passing though the bus drop-off area on their way to the ticket booths; on-site hotel guests approach from the west through Downtown Disney. Because security screening is conducted just before passing through the turnstiles, the lines to enter the park are often quite lengthy. Two entrance gates, 14 and 19, are blocked by trees situated in the entrance plaza about 10 feet from the security checkpoint. The trees sometimes inhibit the formation of a line in front of both of the obstructed gates. These gates (14 and 19) are staffed nonetheless and draw guests from adjacent lines 13 or 15 and 18 or 20. When this happens, it significantly speeds up the entry process for guests waiting in lines 13 and 20. Our advice on arriving, therefore, is to inspect the lines leading to gates 14 and 19 and join whichever looks to be shortest. Later in the day, the outside gates (1 and 32) tend to be fastest for reentry. Stroller and wheelchair rentals are available in the Main Entrance Plaza between Disneyland and DCA. As you enter Main Street, City Hall is to your left, serving as the center for general information, lost and found, and entertainment information.

To combat rampant resales of unexpired tickets, Disneyland Resort has implemented a policy of photographing all multiday pass holders upon their first park entry. Have your ticket ready for scanning by a

Disneyland Park

Main Street, U.S.A.

Adventureland

New Orleans Square

Disneyland Park
1. Alice in Wonderland
2. Astro Orbitor
3. Autopia
4. Big Thunder Mountain Railroad
5. Buzz Lightyear Astro Blasters
6. Captain Eo
7. Casey Jr. Circus Train
8. Chip 'n Dale Treehouse
9. Davy Crockett's Explorer Canoes
10. Disneyland Monorail
11. Disneyland Railroad
12. *The Disneyland Story,*
    presenting Great Moments
    with Mr. Lincoln
13. Dumbo the Flying Elephant
14. *Enchanted Tiki Room*
15. Fantasy Faire
16. Fantasyland Theatre
17. Finding Nemo Submarine Voyage
18. Frontierland Shootin' Exposition
19. Gadget's Go Coaster
20. The Golden Horseshoe
21. Goofy's Playhouse
22. The Haunted Mansion
23. Indiana Jones Adventure
24. Innoventions

25. It's a Small World
26. *Jedi Training Academy*
27. Jungle Cruise
28. King Arthur Carrousel
29. Mad Tea Party
30. Main Street Cinema
31. The Many Adventures
    of Winnie the Pooh
32. *Mark Twain Riverboat*
33. Matterhorn Bobsleds
34. Mickey's House and Meet Mickey
35. Minnie's House
36. *Miss Daisy,* Donald's Boat
37. Mr. Toad's Wild Ride
38. Peter Pan's Flight
39. Pinocchio's Daring Journey

40. Pirate's Lair on Tom Sawyer Island
41. Pirates of the Caribbean
42. Raft to Tom Sawyer Island
43. Roger Rabbit's Car Toon Spin
44. Sailing Ship *Columbia*
45. Sleeping Beauty Castle
46. Snow White's Scary Adventures
47. Space Mountain
48. Splash Mountain
49. Starcade
50. Star Tours: The Adventures Continue
51. Storybook Land Canal Boats
52. Tarzan's Treehouse

NOT TO BE MISSED AT DISNEYLAND PARK
ADVENTURELAND Indiana Jones Adventure
CRITTER COUNTRY Splash Mountain
FRONTIERLAND Big Thunder Mountain Railroad | Golden Horseshoe
NEW ORLEANS SQUARE The Haunted Mansion | Pirates of the Caribbean
TOMORROWLAND Space Mountain | Star Tours: The Adventures Continue
LIVE ENTERTAINMENT *Fantasmic!*

cast member just before you enter the turnstiles; if your mug isn't yet in Mickey's mainframe, you'll be asked to pose before proceeding. These added steps significantly slow the line at the start of the day, and there's no express lane for single-day guests or Annual Pass holders. As long as this inefficient plan is imposed, we suggest that you arrive 5–10 minutes earlier than you otherwise would have, and bring extra patience.

Be sure to pick up a park map as you pass through the turnstiles. Maps are also available in the passages connecting the park entrance to Main Street, U.S.A.; at City Hall; and at a number of shops throughout the park. Also, pick up a *Times Guide*. This pamphlet contains the daily entertainment schedule for live shows, parades, fireworks, and other events and tells you where you can find the characters. If a *Times Guide* is not available for the day you visit (a very rare occurrence), the daily entertainment schedule will be included in the park map. The park map lists all the attractions, shops, and eateries and provides helpful information about first aid, baby care, assistance for the disabled, and more.

Notice on your map that Main Street ends at a central hub from which branch the entrances to four other sections of Disneyland: **Adventureland, Frontierland, Fantasyland,** and **Tomorrowland.** Two other "lands," **New Orleans Square** and **Critter Country,** can be reached through Adventureland and Frontierland. **Mickey's Toontown** is located on the far side of the railroad tracks from It's a Small World in Fantasyland. **Sleeping Beauty Castle,** the entrance to Fantasyland, is a focal landmark and the visual center of the park. The castle is a great place to meet if your group decides to split up for any reason during the day, and it can serve as an emergency meeting place if you are accidentally separated. Keep in mind, however, that the castle covers a lot of territory, so be specific about *where* to meet at the castle. Also be forewarned that parades and live shows sometimes make it difficult to access the entrance of the castle fronting the central hub. Another good meeting spot is the *Partners* statue of Mickey and Walt in the central hub.

STARTING THE TOUR

EVERYONE WILL SOON FIND his or her own favorite and not-so-favorite attractions in Disneyland Park. Be open-minded and adventuresome. Don't dismiss a particular ride or show as not being for you until *after* you have tried it. Our personal experience as well as our research indicates that each visitor is different in terms of which Disney offerings he or she most enjoys. So don't miss seeing an attraction because a friend from home didn't like it; that attraction may turn out to be your favorite.

We do recommend that you take advantage of what Disney does best—the fantasy adventures such as Indiana Jones Adventure and The Haunted Mansion and the Audio-Animatronics (talking robots, that is) attractions such as Pirates of the Caribbean. Unless you have almost unlimited time, don't burn a lot of daylight browsing through the shops. Except for some special Disney souvenirs, you can find much of the same merchandise elsewhere. Try to minimize the time you spend on midway-type rides, as you probably have an amusement park, carnival, or state fair close to your hometown. Don't, however, mistake rides such as Splash Mountain and the Big Thunder Mountain Railroad for amusement park rides. They may be of the flume ride or the roller coaster genre, but they represent pure Disney genius. Similarly, do not devote a lot of time to waiting in line for meals. Eat a good early breakfast before you come, snack on vendor-sold foods during the touring day, or follow the suggestions for meals incorporated into the various touring plans presented.

SINGLE-RIDER LINES

YOU CAN OFTEN SAVE TIME WAITING IN LINE by taking advantage of single-rider lines, a separate line for people who are alone or don't mind riding alone or with a stranger. The objective of single-rider lines is to fill odd spaces left by groups who don't quite fill the entire ride vehicle. Because there aren't many singles and most groups aren't willing to split up, single-rider lines are usually much shorter than the regular line. In Disneyland Park, Indiana Jones Adventure, the Matterhorn Bobsleds, and Splash Mountain have single-rider lines. Ask an attraction employee how to enter the single-rider queue; you'll usually be given a paper pass and directed up the exit.

MAIN STREET, U.S.A.

THIS SECTION OF DISNEYLAND PARK is where you'll begin and end your visit. We have already mentioned that assistance and information are available at City Hall. The Disneyland Railroad stops at the Main Street Station, and you can board here for a grand circle tour of the park, or you can get off the train in New Orleans Square, Mickey's Toontown/Fantasyland, or Tomorrowland.

Main Street is an idealized version of a turn-of-the-20th-century American small-town street. Many visitors are surprised to discover that all the buildings are real, not elaborate props. Attention to detail is exceptional—interiors, furnishings, and fixtures conform to the

Main Street Services

Most of the park's service facilities are centered in the Main Street section, including the following:

Baby Care Center At the central-hub end of Main Street

Banking Services/Currency Exchange At City Hall at the railroad station end of Main Street

Disneyland and Local Attraction Information At City Hall

First Aid First Aid Center two doors from Plaza Inn at the central-hub end of Main Street

Live Entertainment and Parade Information At City Hall, at the railroad station end of Main Street

Lost Adults and Messages At City Hall

Lost and Found Lost and Found for the entire resort is located west of the entrance to Disneyland Park

Lost Children At the central-hub end of Main Street

Storage Lockers Down Main Street one block (as you walk toward the castle) and to the right

period. As with any real Main Street, the Disney version is essentially a collection of shops and eating places, with a city hall, a fire station, and an old-time cinema. A mixed-media attraction combines static exhibits recalling the life of Walt Disney with a patriotic remembrance of Abraham Lincoln. Horse-drawn trolleys, fire engines, and horseless carriages give rides along Main Street and transport visitors to the central hub.

Disneyland Railroad ★★★

APPEAL BY AGE	PRESCHOOL ★★★★	GRADE SCHOOL ★★★★	TEENS ★★★½
YOUNG ADULTS ★★★½		OVER 30 ★★★★	SENIORS ★★★★

What it is Scenic railroad ride around the park's perimeter; also transportation to New Orleans Square, Mickey's Toontown, Fantasyland, and Tomorrowland. **Scope and scale** Major attraction. **When to go** After 11 a.m. or when you need transportation. **Special comments** The Main Street and Tomorrowland Stations are usually the least-congested boarding points. **Duration of ride** About 22 minutes for a complete circuit. **Average wait in line per 100 people ahead of you** 8 minutes. **Assumes** 3 trains operating. **Loading speed** Fast.

Thumbs Up for the Whole Family

DESCRIPTION AND COMMENTS A transportation ride that blends an eclectic variety of sights and experiences with an energy-saving way of getting around the park. In addition to providing a glimpse of all the lands except Adventureland, the train passes through the Grand Canyon Diorama (between Tomorrowland and Main Street), a three-dimensional replication of the canyon, complete with wildlife, as it appears from the southern rim. Another sight on the train circuit is Primeval World, a depiction of a prehistoric peat bog and rain forest populated by audio-animatronic (robotic) dinosaurs. Opened in 1966 Primeval World uses animatronics recycled from the Disney-designed Ford's Magic Sky-way pavilion for the 1964 World's Fair, and was a precursor to a similar presentation at Epcot's Universe of Energy.

TOURING TIPS Save the train ride until after you have seen the featured attractions, or use it when you need transportation. It can also be a helpful way to relax during the peak times of the day when the crowds are swelling. You can get a good estimate of how long you'll wait for the next train by using the posted wait time sign outside each station. It will either list 5 minutes (three trains operating), 10 minutes (two trains), or 20 minutes (only one train). If you have small children who are hell-bent to see Mickey first thing in the morning, you might con-sider taking the train to Mickey's Toontown (a half circuit) and visiting Mickey in his dressing room as soon as you enter the park. Many fami-lies find that this tactic puts the kids in a more receptive frame of mind for the other attractions. On busy days, lines form at the New Orleans Square and Mickey's Toontown/Fantasyland Stations but rarely at the Main Street or Tomorrowland Stations.

The Disneyland Story, presenting *Great Moments with Mr. Lincoln* ★ ★ ★ ½

APPEAL BY AGE	PRESCHOOL ★ ★	GRADE SCHOOL ★ ★ ★ ½	TEENS ★ ★ ★
YOUNG ADULTS ★ ★ ★ ★	OVER 30 ★ ★ ★ ★		SENIORS ★ ★ ★ ★ ½

What it is Nostalgic exhibits documenting the Disney success story followed by an Audio-Animatronics patriotic presentation. **Scope and scale** Minor attraction. **When to go** During the hot, crowded period of the day. **Duration of show** 15 minutes includ-ing preshow. **Preshow** Disney exhibits. **Probable waiting time** Usually no wait.

Thumbs Up for the Whole Family

DESCRIPTION AND COMMENTS A warm and well-presented remembrance of the man who started it all. Well worth seeing; especially touching for those old enough to remember Walt Disney him-self. The attraction consists of a museum of Disney memorabilia. Especially interesting are rotating Disney Gallery displays of concept artwork and historical artifacts, most recently honoring the *Enchanted Tiki Room*'s 50th anniversary. A short film starring comedian (and former Disneyland cast member) Steve Martin and Donald Duck, originally created to celebrate the park's 50th anniversary in 2005, screens in the lobby as a preshow. Beyond the Disney memorabilia, guests are admitted to a large theater where *Great Moments with Mr. Lin-coln* is presented. A patriotic performance, *Great Moments* stars an extremely lifelike and sophisticated Audio-Animatronics Abe Lincoln delivering an amalgamation of his notable speeches (though the over-familiar "Gettysburg Address" is not recited in full) as originally recorded by Royal Dano for the 1964 World's Fair. Lincoln's recently upgraded head is stunningly emotive, capable of wrinkling his brow and pursing his lips with unrivaled realism. New surround sound effects and songs borrowed from Epcot's *American Adven-ture* add to this brief but inspiring biography of America's 16th president.

TOURING TIPS You usually do not have to wait long for this show, so see it during the busy times of day when lines are long elsewhere or as you are leaving the park. Sit up close to best see the detail on the Lincoln figure, or sit a few rows back for a more comfortable view of the screen.

Main Street Cinema ★★

APPEAL BY AGE	PRESCHOOL ★★½	GRADE SCHOOL ★★	TEENS ★★
YOUNG ADULTS ★½	OVER 30 ★★		SENIORS ★★

What it is Vintage Disney cartoons. **Scope and scale** Diversion. **When to go** Whenever you want. **Special comments** Wonderful selection of old-time flicks. **Duration of show** Runs continuously. **Preshow** None. **Probable waiting time** No waiting.

DESCRIPTION AND COMMENTS An opening-day attraction, this small theater shows six classic Disney cartoons simultaneously. Early black-and-white Mickey Mouse shorts such as "Steamboat Willie" and "Plane Crazy" are screened, along with the celebrity caricature–stocked oddity "Mickey's Polo Team." The films are played at a low enough volume that the theater remains a quiet respite from the rest of the park.

TOURING TIPS Good place to get out of the sun or rain or to kill time while others in your group shop on Main Street. Fun, but not something you can't afford to miss. No seats; viewers stand.

Transportation Rides

DESCRIPTION AND COMMENTS Trolleys, buses, and the like add color to Main Street. One-way only.

TOURING TIPS The rides will save you a walk to the central hub. Not worth waiting in line. If you catch the first trolley of the morning, you may be serenaded onboard by the Dapper Dans.

DISNEY DISH WITH JIM HILL

GUESTS SHOULD GET QUITE A CHARGE OUT OF ANNIVERSARY CELEBRATION Disneyland Park will celebrate its 60th anniversary in 2015. If the rumors prove to be true, an old favorite may be returning with a bold new look to commemorate this milestone. The current plan calls for an all-new version of the Main Street Electrical Parade (which premiered at Disneyland in June 1972 and then, after running at DCA for nine years, ended its run at the Disneyland Resort in April 2010). The parade would feature one introductory float plus six units, each representing a different decade that Disneyland has been in business, followed by a finale—with each of these units also paying tribute to a particularly memorable character or design element from the original Main Street Electrical Parade.

ADVENTURELAND

ADVENTURELAND IS THE FIRST "LAND" to the left of Main Street and somehow manages to seamlessly combine South Pacific island, Middle Eastern bazaar, and African safari themes. Transitions from one part of Adventureland to another feel quite natural, and the identity crisis inherent in the mixed-theme cocktail never registers in the minds of most guests. Space is tight in Adventureland, however, making for some of the worst pedestrian congestion in any of the Disney theme parks. If you're just passing through Adventureland, say on your way to Splash Mountain, you can avoid the congestion by transiting Frontierland instead.

Enchanted Tiki Room ★ ★ ★ ½

| APPEAL BY AGE | PRESCHOOL ★ ★ ★ ★ ½ | GRADE SCHOOL ★ ★ ★ ★ | TEENS ★ ★ ★ |
| YOUNG ADULTS ★ ★ ★ ½ | OVER 30 ★ ★ ★ ★ | | SENIORS ★ ★ ★ ★ |

What it is Audio-Animatronics Pacific island musical show. **Scope and scale** Minor attraction. **When to go** Anytime. **Special comments** Very, very unusual. **Duration of show** 14½ minutes. **Preshow** Talking totem poles. **Probable waiting time** 11 minutes.

Dark Loud

DESCRIPTION AND COMMENTS An unusual sit-down theater performance in which more than 200 birds, flowers, and tiki-god statues sing and whistle through a Polynesian-style musical program. One of Walt's first large-scale uses of Audio-Animatronics, *Tiki Room* might be more impressive for the technology it took to get the show (ahem) flying in 1963. Beloved by Disneyland fans for its detail and immersive setting, the current version of the show is only slightly altered from the original.

TOURING TIPS One of the most bizarre (yet endearing) of the Disneyland Park entertainments and rarely very crowded. We like it in the late afternoon, when we can especially appreciate sitting for a bit in an air-conditioned theater. Back row seats provide the broadest view with the least neck strain.

The Tiki Juice Bar that straddles the *Tiki Room* entrance dispenses Dole Whip, a delectable blend of pineapple slush and vanilla soft-serve ice cream that is one of the park's most popular snacks. Dole sponsors the attraction, so you can enjoy your Tiki Juice Bar treats while watching the show. There are service windows both inside and outside of the attraction's waiting area. The line outside may look longer, but it often moves much faster.

Indiana Jones Adventure *(Fastpass)* ★ ★ ★ ★ ★

| APPEAL BY AGE | PRESCHOOL ★ ★ | GRADE SCHOOL ★ ★ ★ ★ | TEENS ★ ★ ★ ★ ★ |
| YOUNG ADULTS ★ ★ ★ ★ ★ | OVER 30 ★ ★ ★ ★ ½ | | SENIORS ★ ★ ★ ½ |

What it is Motion-simulator dark ride. **Scope and scale** Super-headliner. **When to go** Before 9:30 a.m. or use Fastpass. **Special comments** Not to be missed; must be 46" tall to ride; switching-off option provided (see page 149). **Duration of ride** 3½ minutes. **Average wait in line per 100 people ahead of you** 3 minutes. **Assumes** Full-capacity operation with 18-second dispatch interval. **Loading speed** Fast.

Dark Loud Scary Queasy Rough Muss Your 'Do

DESCRIPTION AND COMMENTS This is a combination track ride and motion simulator. You ride a military troop–transport vehicle; in addition to moving along its path, the vehicle bucks and pitches (the simulator part) in sync with the visuals and special effects. Though the plot is complicated and not altogether clear, the bottom line is that if you look into the Forbidden Eye, you're in big trouble. The Forbidden Eye, of course, stands out like Rush Limbaugh in a diaper, and *everybody* stares at it. The rest of the ride consists of a mad race to escape the temple as it collapses around you. In the process, you encounter snakes, spiders, lava pits, rats, swinging bridges, and the house-size granite bowling ball that everyone remembers from *Raiders of the Lost Ark.*

The Indiana Jones ride is a Disney masterpiece—nonstop action from beginning to end with brilliant visual effects. Elaborate even by Disney standards, the attraction provides a level of detail and variety of action that make use of the entire Imagineering arsenal of high-tech gimmickry. Combining a setting as rich as Pirates of the Caribbean with a ride that rivals Star Tours, Indiana Jones is a powerhouse. Recently, the ride received a long overdue top-to-bottom refurbishment, which improved the dramatic lighting and restored some disabled effects (though the long-lost "crumbling ceiling" remains missing in action).

Sophisticated in its electronic and computer applications, Indiana Jones purports to offer a different experience on each ride. According to the designers, there are veritable menus of special effects that the computer can mix and match. In practice, however, we could not see much difference from ride to ride. There are, no doubt, subtle variations, but the ride is so wild and frenetic that it's hard to apprehend subtlety. Between explosions and falling rocks, your poor fried brain simply does not register nuance.

The adventure begins in the queue, which sometimes extends out the entrance of the attraction and over the bridge leading to Adventureland! When you ultimately work your way into the attraction area, you find yourself at the site of an archaeology expedition with the Temple of the Forbidden Eye entrance beckoning only 50 feet away. After crossing a wooden bridge, you finally step into the temple. The good news is that you are out of the California sun. The bad news is that you have just entered Indiana Jones's indoor queuing area, a system of tunnels and passageways extending to within 50 yards of the Santa Monica Pier.

Fortunately, the queuing area is interesting. You wind through caves, down the interior corridors of the temple, and into subterranean rotundas where the archaeologists have been hard at work. Along the way there are various surprises (be sure to disregard any DO NOT TOUCH signs you see on supporting poles or safety ropes), as well as a succession of homilies etched in an "ancient" language on the temple walls. You will eventually stumble into a chamber where a short movie will explain the plot. From there it's back into the maze and finally on to the loading area. The ride itself is memorable.

TOURING TIPS Indiana Jones stays fairly mobbed all day. Try to ride during the first hour the park is open or use Fastpass. Another alternative, if you don't mind riding alone, is to take advantage of the single-rider line. Guests from the single-rider lines are tapped, one at a time, to fill any odd seats remaining in the ride vehicles before they are dispatched. Generally the wait for guests in the single-rider line is about one-third that of guests in the regular queue. Be forewarned that the single-rider line at Indiana Jones is a bit of a maze, requiring you to negotiate your way up the exit ramp, up one elevator, across a walkway over the track, and then down another elevator to the loading area.

During the first hour or so the park is open, Indiana Jones cast members often employ a line management technique known as stacking. Simply stated, they allow the line for Indiana Jones to form outside of the attraction, leaving the cavernous inside queuing area virtually empty. Guests, of course, assume that the attraction is packed to the gills and that the outside line is overflow. Naturally, this discourages guests from getting in line. The reality is that the wait is not nearly as bad as it looks, and that it is probably as short as it will be all day. If you arrive in the park early and the Indiana Jones line appears huge, have the rest of your party get in line while you enter Indiana Jones *through the attraction exit* and check out the inside queue. If it is empty or sparsely populated, stacking is being practiced. Join your party in line and enjoy the attraction; your wait will be comparatively short. If the inside queue is bumper to bumper, try Indiana Jones later or use Fastpass or the single-rider line. Stacking is also sometimes practiced during the hour just before the park closes.

There is one other thing you should know. Indiana Jones, because it is high-tech, breaks down a lot. The Disney people will announce that the ride is broken but usually will not estimate how long repairs will take. From our experience, most glitches are resolved in approximately 15–30 minutes, and probably the best advice is to stick it out.

If you miss Indiana Jones in the early morning and the Fastpasses are all gone, use the single-rider line or try again during a parade or *Fantasmic!*, or during the hour before the park closes. Regarding the latter, the Disney folks will usually admit to the attraction anyone in line at closing time. During a recent visit to Indiana Jones, Disneyland Park closed at 8 p.m. We hopped in the line for Indiana Jones at 7:45 p.m. and actually got on the ride at 8:30 p.m.

Though the Indiana Jones ride is wild and jerky, the motion has been somewhat toned down since its debut, and it is primarily distinguished by its visual impact and realistic special effects. Thus, we encourage the over-50 crowd to give it a chance: we think you'll like it. As for children, most find the ride extremely intense and action-packed but not particularly frightening. We encountered very few children who met the 46-inch minimum-height requirement who were in any way intimidated.

Jungle Cruise ★★★

APPEAL BY AGE	PRESCHOOL ★★★★	GRADE SCHOOL ★★★★	TEENS ★★★½
YOUNG ADULTS ★★★★	OVER 30 ★★★★		SENIORS ★★★★

What it is A Disney outdoor-adventure boat ride. **Scope and scale** Major attraction. **When to go** Before 10 a.m. or after 6 p.m. **Special comments** A Disney standard.

Thumbs Up for the Whole Family

Duration of ride 7½ minutes. **Average wait in line per 100 people ahead of you** 3½ minutes. **Assumes** 10 boats operating. **Loading speed** Moderate–slow.

DESCRIPTION AND COMMENTS On this boat ride through jungle waterways, passengers encounter elephants, lions, hostile natives, and a menacing hippo. It's a long-enduring Disney favorite with the boatman's spiel adding measurably to the fun.

As more technologically advanced attractions have been added to the park over the years, the Jungle Cruise has, by comparison, lost some of its luster. Though still a good attraction, it offers few thrills and no surprises for Disneyland Park veterans, many of whom can rattle off the ride's narration right along with the guide. For park first-timers, however, the Jungle Cruise continues to delight.

TOURING TIPS This ride loads slowly, and long lines form as the park fills. To compound problems, guests exiting Indiana Jones tend to head for the Jungle Cruise. Go early, or during a parade or *Fantasmic!* Be forewarned that the Jungle Cruise has an especially deceptive line: just when you think that you are about to board, you are shunted into yet another queuing maze (not visible outside the ride). Regardless of how short the line *looks* when you approach the Jungle Cruise, inquire about the length of the wait—at least you will know what you are getting into. If the second floor of the queue building is in use, you're in for at least a 20-minute wait. When the queue splits before the loading dock, the left lane is often quicker. Finally, many readers consider the Jungle Cruise much better at night.

DISNEY DISH WITH JIM HILL

FROM DANCING NATIVES TO DANCING ON BROADWAY You wouldn't expect to find many musical theater fans out here in the jungle. But there must be at least one musical fan who handles the props for this Adventureland attraction. If you look closely as your tramp steamer moves from the Hippo Pool to the Dancing Natives, you should see a series of shields on the ground behind those animatronic tribesmen who are chanting and dancing in a circle. Do you see the one with the stylized lion head on it? Does the image on that shield look familiar? It should. It's the logo for Disney's long-running hit Broadway musical *The Lion King*.

Tarzan's Treehouse ★★★

APPEAL BY AGE	PRESCHOOL ★★★★	GRADE SCHOOL ★★★★	TEENS ★★½
YOUNG ADULTS ★★★		OVER 30 ★★★	SENIORS ★★½

What it is Walk-through tree house exhibit. **Scope and scale** Minor attraction. **When to go** Anytime. **Special comments** Requires climbing a lot of stairs; a very creative exhibit. **Duration of tour** 8–12 minutes. **Average wait in line per 100 people ahead of you** 7 minutes.

Thumbs Up for the Whole Family

DESCRIPTION AND COMMENTS Inspired by Disney's 1999 animated film *Tarzan,* Tarzan's Treehouse replaced the venerable Swiss Family Treehouse that had been an Adventureland icon for 37 years. To enter the attraction, you climb a rustic staircase and cross a suspension bridge. From there, as they say, it's all downhill. Pages from Jane's sketchbook scattered about tell the Tarzan story and provide insights into the various rooms and levels of the tree house. At the base of the tree is an interactive play area where characters from Disney's *Tarzan* drop in for photos and autographs.

TOURING TIPS This self-guided, walk-through tour involves a lot of climbing up and down stairs but with no ropes or ladders or anything fancy. People stopping during the walk-through to look extra-long or to rest sometimes create bottlenecks that slow crowd flow. We recommend visiting this attraction in the late afternoon or early evening if you are on a one-day tour schedule.

NEW ORLEANS SQUARE

ACCESSIBLE VIA ADVENTURELAND AND FRONTIERLAND, New Orleans Square is one of three "lands" that does not emanate from the central hub. The architecture and setting are Caribbean Colonial, like New Orleans itself, with exceptional attention to detail.

Disneyland Railroad

DESCRIPTION AND COMMENTS The Disneyland Railroad stops in New Orleans Square on its circle tour around the park. See the description on pages 222–223 for additional details regarding the sights en route.

TOURING TIPS This is a pleasant and feet-saving way to commute to Mickey's Toontown/Fantasyland, Tomorrowland, or Main Street. Be advised, however, that the New Orleans Square Station is usually the most congested.

The Haunted Mansion ★ ★ ★ ★

APPEAL BY AGE	PRESCHOOL ★ ★ ★	GRADE SCHOOL ★ ★ ★ ★	TEENS ★ ★ ★ ★ ½
YOUNG ADULTS ★ ★ ★ ★ ½		OVER 30 ★ ★ ★ ★ ½	SENIORS ★ ★ ★ ★

What it is Indoor haunted-house ride. **Scope and scale** Major attraction. **When to go** Before 11:30 a.m. or after 6:30 p.m. **Special comments** Not to be missed; frightens some small children; some of Disneyland's best special effects. **Duration of ride** 5½-minute ride plus a 2-minute preshow. **Average wait in line per 100 people ahead of you** 2½ minutes. **Assumes** Both stretch rooms operating. **Loading speed** Fast.

Dark   Scary

DESCRIPTION AND COMMENTS The Haunted Mansion is a fun attraction more than a scary one. An ingenious preshow serves as a vehicle to deliver guests to the ride's boarding area, where they board "doom buggies" for a ride through the mansion's parlor, dining room, library, halls, and attic before descending to an uncommonly active graveyard. Disney employs almost every special effect in its repertoire in The Haunted Mansion, making it one of the most inventive and different of all Disney attractions. Be warned that some youngsters build a lot of anxiety concerning what they think they will see. The actual attraction scares almost nobody. Though this mansion is the original, the ride is somewhat shorter and lacks the high-tech interactive upgrades of the Walt Disney World version.

The Haunted Mansion is one of veteran Unofficial Guide writer Eve Zibart's favorite attractions. She warns:

Don't let the childishness of the old-fashioned Haunted Mansion put you off: this is one of the best attractions [in the park]. It's jam-packed with visual puns, special effects, hidden Mickeys, and really lovely Victorian-spooky sets. It's not scary, except in the sweetest of ways, but it will remind you of the days before ghost stories gave way to slasher flicks.

Each September, The Haunted Mansion substitutes a special holiday version of the attraction that runs through early January. Inspired by Tim Burton's 1993 stop-motion musical *The Nightmare Before Christmas,* the overlay features characters such as Jack Skellington and Oogie Boogie cavorting among the familiar mansion haunts to songs from Danny Elfman's classic score. Though The Haunted Mansion is not normally a Fastpass attraction, the holiday version is usually included in the Fastpass lineup. Be aware that the attraction will be closed for several weeks before and after the holiday season to install and remove the overlay.

TOURING TIPS This attraction would be more at home in Fantasyland, but no matter—it's Disney at its best: another not-to-be-missed attraction. Because The Haunted Mansion is in an especially high-traffic corridor (between Pirates of the Caribbean and Splash Mountain), it stays busy all day. Try to see The Haunted Mansion before 11:30 a.m., after 6:30 p.m., or during a parade. In the evening, crowds for *Fantasmic!* gather in front of The Haunted Mansion, making it very difficult to access.

Pirates of the Caribbean ★★★★★

APPEAL BY AGE   PRESCHOOL ★★★½   GRADE SCHOOL ★★★★½   TEENS ★★★★½
YOUNG ADULTS ★★★★½   OVER 30 ★★★★½   SENIORS ★★★★★

What it is A Disney indoor-adventure boat ride. **Scope and scale** Major attraction. **When to go** Before 11:30 a.m. or after 4:30 p.m. **Special comments** Frightens some small children; our pick as one of Disneyland's very best. **Duration of ride** Approximately 14 minutes. **Average wait in line per 100 people ahead of you** 3 minutes. **Assumes** 42 boats operating. **Loading speed** Fast.

Dark   Loud   Scary

DESCRIPTION AND COMMENTS Another boat ride, this time indoors, takes you through a series of sets depicting a pirate raid on an island settlement, from the bombardment of the fortress to the debauchery that follows the victory. Pirates of the Caribbean was the target of a much-publicized political-correctness controversy relating to the objectification of women and the "boys will be boys" way in which the pirates' debauchery was depicted. Ultimately, Disney was pressured into revamping the attraction (though not much). More recently, the attraction underwent an extensive rehab that included the addition of characters (Jack Sparrow and Barbossa in animatronic form, and a high-tech mist projection of Davy Jones and Blackbeard) from the *Pirates of the Caribbean* movies.

TOURING TIPS Another not-to-be-missed attraction. Undoubtedly one of the most elaborate and imaginative attractions in Disneyland Park. Though engineered to move large crowds, this ride sometimes gets overwhelmingly busy in the early and midafternoon. Try to ride before noon or while a parade or *Fantasmic!* is in progress. If you have only experienced the Walt Disney World version of Pirates, don't bypass Disneyland's version thinking that it's more of the same: the original ride is far longer, more detailed, and better maintained than its Floridian cousin.

█ CRITTER COUNTRY

CRITTER COUNTRY, situated at the end of a cul-de-sac and accessible via New Orleans Square, sports a pioneer appearance not unlike that of Frontierland.

Davy Crockett's Explorer Canoes *(open seasonally)* ★★★

APPEAL BY AGE	PRESCHOOL ★★	GRADE SCHOOL ★★★½	TEENS ★★★★½
YOUNG ADULTS ★		OVER 30 ★★½	SENIORS ★

What it is Scenic canoe ride. **Scope and scale** Minor attraction. **When to go** As soon as it opens, usually 11 a.m. **Special comments** Skip if the lines are long; closes at sunset. **Special comments** Most fun way to see Rivers of America. **Duration of ride** 8–10 minutes, depending on how fast you paddle. **Average wait in line per 100 people ahead of you** 12½ minutes. **Assumes** 6 canoes operating. **Loading speed** Slow.

DESCRIPTION AND COMMENTS Paddle-powered ride (you do the paddling) around Tom Sawyer Island and Fort Wilderness. Runs the same route with the same sights as the steamboat and the sailing ship. According to newspaper accounts, when the entire 9-million-gallon river was drained in 2010 for refurbishment, workers found half a canoe, scores of Mickey Mouse ears, and hundreds of cell phones at the bottom. The lesson here is to always keep a tight grip on your canoe. The canoes operate only on busier days and close at sunset. The sights are fun and the ride is a little different in that the patrons paddle the canoe. Those with tender rotator cuffs be warned: the trip can give your shoulders quite a workout, unless you slack off and let your fellow passengers handle the hard rowing. We think that this is the most fun of any of the various river trips. Long lines from about 11 a.m. on reflect the popularity of this attraction.

TOURING TIPS The canoes represent one of three ways to see the same waterways. Because the canoes are slower in loading, we usually opt for the larger steamboat or sailing ship. If you are not up for a boat ride, a different view of the same sights can be had by hoofing around Tom Sawyer Island. Try to ride at 11 a.m. or shortly thereafter. The canoes operate on selected days and seasonal periods only. If the canoes are a big deal to you, call ahead to make sure that they are operating.

The Many Adventures of Winnie the Pooh ★★★½

APPEAL BY AGE	PRESCHOOL ★★★★★	GRADE SCHOOL ★★★★	TEENS ★★★½
YOUNG ADULTS ★★★½		OVER 30 ★★★½	SENIORS ★★★½

What it is Indoor track ride. **Scope and scale** Minor attraction. **When to go** Before 11 a.m. or the late afternoon or evening. **Duration of ride** About 3 minutes. **Average wait in line per 100 people ahead of you** 5 minutes. **Loading speed** Moderate.

Thumbs Up for the Whole Family

DESCRIPTION AND COMMENTS Pooh is sunny, upbeat, and fun—more in the image of Peter Pan's Flight or Splash Mountain. You ride a "hunny pot" through the pages of a huge picture book into the Hundred Acre Wood, where you encounter Pooh, Eeyore, Owl, Rabbit, Tigger, Kanga, Roo, and Piglet too as they contend with a blustery day. There's even a dream sequence with Heffalumps and Woozles, a favorite of this 30-something couple from Lexington, Massachusetts, who think Pooh has plenty to offer adults:

> The attention to detail and special effects on this ride make it worth seeing even if you don't have children in your party. The Pooh dream sequence was great!

TOURING TIPS Though well done, The Many Adventures of Winnie the Pooh is not wildly popular. There is rarely more than a 15-minute wait, and it's typically less than 5. The only exceptions are on supercrowded days or when Splash Mountain is temporarily closed, which then causes crowds to swarm Winnie the Pooh.

Splash Mountain *(Fastpass)* ★★★★½

APPEAL BY AGE   PRESCHOOL †   GRADE SCHOOL ★★★★½   TEENS ★★★★★   YOUNG ADULTS ★★★★½   OVER 30 ★★★★½   SENIORS ★★★★

† Many preschoolers are too short to meet the height requirement, while others are intimidated by watching the ride while standing in line. Of those preschoolers who actually ride, most give the attraction high marks; ★★★½.

What it is Water-flume adventure boat ride. **Scope and scale** Headliner. **When to go** Before 9:45 a.m. or use Fastpass. **Special comments** A wet winner, not to be missed; must be 40" tall to ride; those age 7 or younger must ride with an adult; switching-off option provided (see page 149). **Duration of ride** About 10 minutes. **Average wait in line per 100 people ahead of you** 3½ minutes. **Assumes** Operation at full capacity. **Loading speed** Moderate.

Scary   Lose Things   Queasy   Muss Your 'Do

DESCRIPTION AND COMMENTS Splash Mountain is a Disney-style amusement park flume ride. The ride combines steep chutes with a variety of Disney's best special effects. Covering more than 0.5 mile, the ride splashes through swamps, caves, and backwoods bayous before climaxing in a 52-foot plunge and Br'er Rabbit's triumphant return home. The entire ride is populated by more than 100 Audio-Animatronics, including Br'er Rabbit, Br'er Bear, and Br'er Fox, all regaling riders with songs, including "Zip-A-Dee-Doo-Dah."

TOURING TIPS This is the most popular ride in Disneyland Park for patrons of all ages—happy, exciting, and adventuresome all at once. Though eclipsed somewhat by newer attractions, Splash Mountain nevertheless builds crowds quickly during the morning, and waits of more than two hours are not uncommon once Disneyland Park fills up on a busy day. Lines persist throughout the day until a few minutes before closing.

There are five ways to experience Splash Mountain without a long wait. The first is to be on hand when the park opens and to sprint over and get in line before anyone else. The second way is to allow the initial mob of Splash cadets to be processed through and to arrive at Splash Mountain about 20–40 minutes after the park opens or after riding Peter Pan and/or Space Mountain. A third strategy is to get in line for Splash Mountain during a parade and/or a performance of *Fantasmic!* Be advised, however, that huge crowds gathering along the New Orleans Square and Frontierland waterfronts for *Fantasmic!* make getting to Splash Mountain very difficult (if not impossible) just before, during, and just after performances. Fourth, use Fastpass, and fifth, use the single-rider line by entering through the exit.

Disneyland veteran Ken Warhola offers this suggestion:

> *Use Fastpass to experience Splash. Using Fastpass lets you visit non-Fastpass, slow-loading attractions in the golden early morning. Also, who wants to get wet first thing in the morning?*

A Suffolk, Virginia, mom contends that there are more important considerations than beating crowds:

> *The only recommendation I do have is to definitely wait to do Splash Mountain at the end of the day. We were seated in the front of the ride, and needless to say we were drenched to the bone. If we had ridden the ride [first thing in the morning] according to your plan, I personally would have been miserable for the rest of the day. Parents, beware! It says you will get wet, not drowned.*

It is almost a certainty that you will get wet, though probably not drenched, riding Splash Mountain. During the summer months, the water jets are cranked up to 11, practically guaranteeing that you'll get soaked. If you visit on a cool day, you may want to carry a plastic garbage bag. By tearing holes in the bottom and sides, you can fashion a sort of raincoat. Be sure to tuck the bag under your bottom. Though you can get splashed regardless of where you sit, riders in the front seat generally get the worst of it. If you have a camera, either leave it with a nonriding member of your party or wrap it in a plastic bag.

One final word: This is not just a fancy flume ride—it is a full-blown Disney adventure. The scariest part by far is the big drop into the pool (visible from the sidewalk in front of Splash Mountain), and even this plunge looks worse than it really is. Despite reassurances, however, many children wig out after watching it from the sidewalk. A Grand Rapids, Michigan, mother recalls her kids' rather unique reaction:

> *We discovered after the fact that our children thought they would go underwater after the five-story drop and tried to hold their breath throughout the ride in preparation. They were really too preoccupied to enjoy the clever Br'er Rabbit story.*

Flash Mountain

What it is Water-flume adventure strip show. **Scope and scale** Eyepopper. **When to go** Spring break; weekend nights. **Special comments** A liberating experience. **Duration of show** About 2 seconds.

DESCRIPTION AND COMMENTS It was reported by the Associated Press that certain female Splash Mountain riders (though we're sure that male riders, not to be outdone, will soon follow their female compatriots in similar fashion) are behaving in a most un–Disney-like manner by "flinging their blouses open" as they plummet down the climactic plunge at the end of the ride. (Fully visible, we might add, to dozens of guests waiting in line in front of the attraction.)

Indeed, automatic cameras shooting souvenir photographs of participants have documented an astounding array of feminine anatomy in free fall. The practice is apparently too spontaneous for Disneyland, which reports that it "has no plans at this time to change the theme of the attraction." Though, ever mindful of guest safety, management has concerns about "undue congestion" in front of the ride and the "possibility of guests catching cold." Some years ago, Disney initiated what it called its "nipple policy," which decreed that photos of offending guests were vaporized immediately. Thanks to budget cuts, the cast members who formerly spent their days screening snapshots for contraband skin have been reassigned, leaving the images free for all to enjoy again. This development has been roundly applauded by nearly everyone except the reassigned employees, some of whom had collected veritable scrapbooks of the floating strippers.

TOURING TIPS During spring break or weekend nights, spectators should stand on the walkway directly in front of Splash Mountain. Be sure to bring a sign denouncing such unchaste exhibitionist behavior, or, depending on your point of view, a camera with a telescopic lens. If you are a participant, you will have approximately 2 minutes following the big plunge to get yourself back together before you arrive at the unloading area.

FRONTIERLAND

FRONTIERLAND ADJOINS NEW ORLEANS SQUARE as you move clockwise around the theme park. The focus here is on the Old West, with log stockades and pioneer trappings. In addition to the attractions listed below, there is the Big Thunder Ranch—featuring pungent pygmy petting goats and Miss Chris's cabin of coloring activities and equestrian Disney memorabilia—on the walkway to Fantasyland.

Big Thunder Mountain Railroad *(Fastpass)* ★★★★

| APPEAL BY AGE | PRESCHOOL ★★★½ | GRADE SCHOOL ★★★★½ | TEENS ★★★★½ |
| YOUNG ADULTS ★★★★★ | | OVER 30 ★★★★½ | SENIORS ★★★★ |

What it is Tame roller coaster with exciting special effects. **Scope and scale** Headliner. **When to go** Before 10:30 a.m., after 6:30 p.m., or use Fastpass. **Special comments** Great effects, though a relatively tame ride; must be 40" tall to ride; those age 8 and younger must ride with an adult; switching-off option provided (see page 149). **Duration of ride** 3½ minutes. **Average wait in line per 100 people ahead of you** 3 minutes. **Assumes** 5 trains operating. **Loading speed** Moderate–fast.

Scary   Lose Things   Queasy   Rough   Muss Your 'Do

DESCRIPTION AND COMMENTS A roller coaster through and around a Disney "mountain." The idea is that you are on a runaway mine train during gold rush days. Along with the usual thrills of a roller coaster (about a 5 on a "scary scale" of 10), the ride showcases some first-rate examples of Disney creativity: lifelike scenes depicting a mining town, falling rocks, and an earthquake, all humorously animated.

In 2013 Disneyland gave Big Thunder Mountain a massive makeover, replacing the aging track and trains and reconstructing the ramshackle Rainbow Ridge buildings, which dated back to 1956. The track layout and vehicle styling remain the same, so the upgrade may seem superficial to the casual guest, but frequent visitors should appreciate the refreshed visuals and smoother ride.

TOURING TIPS A superb Disney experience but not too wild a roller coaster. The emphasis here is much more on the sights than on the thrill of the ride itself. Regardless, it's a not-to-be-missed attraction. Finally, give Big Thunder a try after dark. The lighting gives the attraction a whole new feel.

As an example of how differently guests experience Disney attractions, consider this letter that we received from a reader in Brookline, Massachusetts:

> Being in the senior citizens' category and having limited time, my friend and I confined our activities to those attractions rated as 4 or 5 stars for seniors. Because of your recommendation and because you listed it as "not to be missed," we waited for one hour to board the Big Thunder Mountain Railroad, which you rated a 5 on a scary scale of 10. After living through 3½ minutes of pure terror, I will rate that attraction a 15 on a scary scale of 10. We were so busy holding on and screaming and even praying for our safety that we did not see any falling rocks, a mining town, or an earthquake. In our opinion it should not be recommended for seniors or preschool children.

A woman from New England discovered that there's more to consider about Big Thunder than being scared:

> I won't say it warranted a higher scare rating, but it was much higher on the lose-your-lunch meter. One more sharp turn and the kids in front of me would have needed a dip in Splash Mountain!

Frontierland Shootin' Exposition ★★

APPEAL BY AGE	PRESCHOOL ★★★	GRADE SCHOOL ★★★★	TEENS ★★★
YOUNG ADULTS ★★★½	OVER 30 ★★★½		SENIORS ★★★★★

What it is Electronic shooting gallery. **Scope and scale** Diversion. **When to go** Whenever convenient. **Special comments** Costs extra; a nifty shooting gallery.

Thumbs Up for the Whole Family

DESCRIPTION AND COMMENTS A very elaborate electronic shooting gallery that costs $1 to play. One of the few attractions in Disneyland Park not included in the admission pass.

TOURING TIPS Good fun for those who like to shoot, but definitely not a place to blow time if you are on a tight schedule. Try it on your second day if time allows.

The Golden Horseshoe ★★★★½

APPEAL BY AGE   PRESCHOOL ★★★½   GRADE SCHOOL ★★★★   TEENS ★★★½
YOUNG ADULTS ★★★★½   OVER 30 ★★★★½   SENIORS ★★★★★

What it is Western dance-hall stage show. **Scope and scale** Minor attraction. **When to go** Catch a show and lunch at the same time. **Special comments** Delightfully zany show; food is available. **Duration of show** 30 minutes.

DESCRIPTION AND COMMENTS   The Golden Horseshoe has always offered a decent show, hearty snacks, and a nice air-conditioned respite from the sun. A while back, however, either intentionally or accidentally, Disney signed up an act so good that it turned the humble venue into one of the best attractions in either park. The talent, the unfortunately named Billy Hill and the Hillbillies, consists of a quartet of master bluegrass fiddlers who also happen to be born comics. The show is double-over funny, zany, and totally engaging. And did we mention that the fiddling is phenomenal? At the end of the show, we noticed something that we've never seen at any Disney stage production—the audience refused to leave. Instead, they stood clapping and cheering like at a rock concert, trying to bring back the performers for an encore. They stayed at it so long that the fiddlers were forced to return and take a second bow (though they didn't perform another song). Still the audience lingered, departing only reluctantly after many minutes. We rate the Golden Horseshoe ★★★★½ and classify it as not to be missed. The Hillbillies have occasionally bounced around to other venues (primarily the festival arena behind Big Thunder Ranch), but their popularity keeps bringing them back to the Horseshoe. If you are a superfan, you can find their album *The Billys—Live!* on Amazon and iTunes.

TOURING TIPS   The Golden Horseshoe has first-come, first-serve seating. Find performance times in the daily *Times Guide*. An interactive comedy troupe performs here when the Hillbillies are elsewhere. We recommend arriving 30 minutes early if you want to find a table and grab some grub. Food service can be slow; look for the shortest of three service lines, usually on the far left. Absurdly oversize safety railings now ruin sight lines from the balcony (curse you, OSHA!), so the best view is from the floor front and center, but Walt liked the opera box seats best.

Mark Twain Riverboat ★★★

APPEAL BY AGE   PRESCHOOL ★★★½   GRADE SCHOOL ★★★½   TEENS ★★★
YOUNG ADULTS ★★   OVER 30 ★★★½   SENIORS ★★★★½

What it is Scenic boat ride. **Scope and scale** Minor attraction. **When to go** 11 a.m.–5 p.m. **Special comments** Provides an excellent vantage point; suspends operation at sunset. **Duration of ride** About 14 minutes. **Average wait to board** 10 minutes. **Assumes** Normal operations. **Loading method** En masse.

Thumbs Up for the Whole Family

DESCRIPTION AND COMMENTS   This large-capacity paddle-wheel riverboat navigates the waters around Tom Sawyer Island and Fort Wilderness. A beautiful craft, the riverboat provides a lofty perch from which to see Frontierland

and New Orleans Square. The *Mark Twain,* Sailing Ship *Columbia,* and Davy Crockett's Explorer Canoes travel through the Rivers of America, which was refurbished in 2010. The show scenes were updated to include a home for Mike Fink (and one of his keelboats, a former Disneyland attraction) and 26 new audio-animatronic animals, and the audio spiel now includes a musical nod to the New Orleans–set *The Princess and the Frog.*

TOURING TIPS One of three boat rides that survey the same real estate. Because the Explorer Canoes are slower in loading and the *Columbia* operates seasonally, we think the riverboat makes more efficient use of touring time. If you are not in the mood for a boat ride, many of the same sights can be seen by hiking around Tom Sawyer Island.

Pirate's Lair on Tom Sawyer Island ★★★

APPEAL BY AGE PRESCHOOL ★★★★ GRADE SCHOOL ★★★★½ TEENS ★★★★
YOUNG ADULTS ★★★★ OVER 30 ★★★½ SENIORS ★★★

What it is Walk-through exhibit and rustic playground. **Scope and scale** Minor attraction. **When to go** Midmorning–late afternoon. **Special comments** The place for rambunctious kids; closes at sunset.

DESCRIPTION AND COMMENTS Pirate's Lair on Tom Sawyer Island manages to impart something of a sense of isolation from the rest of the park. It has hills to climb, a cave and a tree house to explore, tipsy bridges to cross, paths to follow, and a "rock-climbing" play area. It's a delight for adults but a godsend for children who have been in tow all day.

As an aside, a mother of four from Duncan, South Carolina, found Tom Sawyer Island as much a refuge as an attraction, writing:

> I do have one tip for parents. In the afternoon, when the crowds were at their peak, the weather was hottest, and the kids started lagging behind, our organization began to suffer. We then retreated over to Tom Sawyer Island, which proved to be a true haven. My husband and I found a secluded bench and regrouped. Meanwhile, the kids were able to run freely in the shade. Afterward, we were ready to tackle the park again refreshed and with direction once more.

The island has sets from the *Pirates of the Caribbean* films, such as William Turner's blacksmith shop, and story artifacts, such as Elizabeth Swann's love letters, tucked into every nook and cranny. Kids exploring the caverns of Dead Man's Grotto will encounter spooky voices, ghostly apparitions, and buried treasure. Elsewhere, a sunken chest can be discovered by operating a hoist.

Evidently, you can't have a pirate's lair without a bunch of gore. A pop-up head and moving skeletal arm are just the beginning. There's also a "bone cage" and, our favorite, a treasure chest containing Davy Jones's beating heart. If your child doesn't have a playmate, don't worry. There's usually a gang of itinerant pirates on hand to administer the "pirate oath" and, somewhat incongruously, lead sing-alongs.

TOURING TIPS Pirate's Lair on Tom Sawyer Island is not one of Disneyland Park's more celebrated attractions, but it's certainly one of the most well done. Attention to detail is excellent, and kids particularly revel in its adventuresome atmosphere. We think it's a must for families with children ages 5–15. If your party has only adults, visit the island on your second day, or stop by on your first day if you have seen the attractions you most wanted to see. We like the island from about noon until the island closes at sunset. Access is by raft from Frontierland, and you may have to stand in line to board both coming and going. Two or three rafts operate simultaneously, however, and the round-trip is usually pretty time efficient. Tom Sawyer Island takes about 30 minutes or so to see, but many children could spend a whole day there.

Raft to and from Tom Sawyer Island

What it is Transportation ride to Tom Sawyer Island. **Scope and scale** Minor attraction. **Duration of ride** A little more than 1 minute one way. **Average wait in line per 100 people ahead of you** 4½ minutes. **Assumes** 3 rafts operating. **Loading speed** Moderate.

Sailing Ship *Columbia* (open seasonally) ★★★½

APPEAL BY AGE	PRESCHOOL ★★★½	GRADE SCHOOL ★★★½	TEENS ★★
YOUNG ADULTS ★★★★	OVER 30 ★★★★		SENIORS ★★★½

What it is Scenic boat ride. **Scope and scale** Minor attraction. **When to go** 11 a.m.–5 p.m. **Special comments** Pirates on extremely busy days; a stunning piece of workmanship. **Duration of ride** About 14 minutes. **Average wait to board** 10 minutes. **Assumes** Normal operations. **Loading method** En masse.

Thumbs Up for the Whole Family

DESCRIPTION AND COMMENTS The *Columbia* is a stunning replica of a three-masted 18th-century merchant ship. Both its above and below decks are open to visitors, with below decks outfitted to depict the life and work environment of the ship's crew in 1787. The *Columbia* operates only on busier days and runs the same route as the canoes and the riverboat. As with the other rivercraft, the *Columbia* suspends operations at sunset.

TOURING TIPS The *Columbia,* along with the *Mark Twain* Riverboat, provides a short-wait, high-carrying-capacity alternative for cruising the Rivers of America. We found the beautifully crafted *Columbia* by far the most aesthetically pleasing and historically interesting of any of the three choices of boat rides on the Rivers of America. If you have time to be choosy, ride aboard the *Columbia.* After boarding, while waiting for the cruise to begin, tour below deck. Once the ride begins, come topside and stroll the deck, taking in the beauty and complexity of the rigging.

The *Columbia* does not usually require a long wait, which makes it a good bet during the crowded afternoon hours.

FANTASYLAND

TRULY AN ENCHANTING PLACE, spread gracefully like a miniature alpine village beneath the towers of Sleeping Beauty Castle, Fantasyland is the heart of the park. Fantasyland is the backbone of the Magic

Mornings early-entry program, with nine rides open. If your group consists of older kids and adults, ride Peter Pan's Flight first during the early-entry period, followed by Matterhorn Bobsleds. If you have younger children in your group, start with Peter Pan and then ride Dumbo. Take note that certain Fantasyland attractions close for fireworks and may not reopen until the fire marshal gives the all clear, as this Calgary dad discovered:

> A significant number of Disneyland's Fantasyland attractions close before fireworks, and of these, some reopen several minutes later while others remain closed for the night. We arrived at Fantasyland immediately after the fireworks and found very little open.

Alice in Wonderland ★★★½

APPEAL BY AGE	PRESCHOOL ★★★★	GRADE SCHOOL ★★★½	TEENS ★★★½
YOUNG ADULTS ★★★★	OVER 30 ★★★½		SENIORS ★★★★

What it is Track ride in the dark. **Scope and scale** Minor attraction. **When to go** Before 11 a.m. or after 5 p.m. **Special comments** Good characterization and story line; do not confuse with Mad Tea Party ride. **Duration of ride** Almost 4 minutes. **Average wait in line per 100 people ahead of you** 12 minutes. **Assumes** 16 cars operating. **Loading speed** Slow.

DESCRIPTION AND COMMENTS This attraction recalls the story of *Alice in Wonderland* with some nice surprises and colorful effects. Guests ride nifty caterpillar cars in this Disney spook-house adaptation. Though not a spring chicken, Alice is a third-generation Disney dark ride with more vibrant, evocative, and three-dimensional sets and characters than Pinocchio's Daring Journey or Mr. Toad's Wild Ride. This is also the only two-story Disney dark ride with an outdoor section.

TOURING TIPS This is a very well-done ride in the best Disney tradition, with familiar characters, good effects, and a theme you can follow—too bad it loads very slowly. Do not confuse it with the Mad Tea Party ride.

Bibbidi Bobbidi Boutique

This pricey beauty salon for little girls is located in Sleeping Beauty Castle. Here, Fairy Godmothers–in-training make would-be princesses look like prom queens (or vice versa). A range of packages are offered, including everything from hair styling and makeup to princess gowns and accessories (cha-ching). If you have the bucks, the girls love it. For reservations, call ☎ 714-781-7895. A Winston, Oregon, mom thinks highly of Bibbidi Bobbidi:

> Bibbidi Bobbidi Boutique is a must if traveling with little girls. Our party had three girls ages 4, 4, and 6, and this was their favorite and most memorable event of the trip. Even though we traveled during the off-season, it was hectic and a little unorganized. We made reservations and still had to wait around for 30 minutes, but once the girls were matched up with their Fairy Godmother–in-training, we were absolutely pleased with the service. It is a little spendy (I think around $50 for a princess hairdo, even more if you want the full

service), but it was completely worth it. The hair survived the rest of the day and looked perfect when they put their princess gowns on at night for the fireworks.

Casey Jr. Circus Train   ★★½

APPEAL BY AGE   PRESCHOOL ★★★★   GRADE SCHOOL ★★★★   TEENS ★★
YOUNG   ADULTS   ★★½   OVER 30   ★★★½   SENIORS   ★★½

What it is Miniature-train ride. **Scope and scale** Minor attraction. **When to go** Before 11 a.m. or after 5 p.m. **Special comments** A quiet, scenic ride. **Duration of ride** A little under 4 minutes. **Average wait in line per 100 people ahead of you** 12 minutes. **Assumes** 2 trains operating. **Loading speed** Slow.

DESCRIPTION AND COMMENTS A long-standing attraction and a pet project of Walt Disney, Casey Jr. circulates through a landscape of miniature towns, farms, and lakes. Visible from this ride are some stunning bonsai specimens, as well as some of the most manicured landscaping you are ever likely to see.

TOURING TIPS This ride covers the same sights as the Storybook Land Canal Boats but does it faster and with less of a wait. Accommodations for adults, however, are less than optimal on this ride, with some passengers having to squeeze into diminutive caged cars (after all, it is a circus train). If you do not have children in your party, you can enjoy the same sights more comfortably by riding the Storybook Land Canal Boats, which also benefit from live narration instead of Casey Jr.'s canned soundtrack.

A father of two toddlers from Menlo Park, California, explains that issues of redundancy were not uppermost in his children's minds.

Contrary to your advice, the Casey Jr. Train and Storybook Land Canal Boats are totally different experiences—if you are 4 or younger. Hey, one is a boat and one is a train! Seems obvious to the mind of a 4-year-old! We did both, and the kids loved both, and we loved it because they loved it.

Disneyland Railroad

DESCRIPTION AND COMMENTS The Disneyland Railroad stops in Fantasyland/Mickey's Toontown on its circuit around the park. The station is located to the left of It's a Small World, next to the Fantasyland Theatre. From this boarding point, transportation is available to Tomorrowland, Main Street, and New Orleans Square.

Dumbo the Flying Elephant   ★★½

APPEAL BY AGE   PRESCHOOL ★★★★½   GRADE SCHOOL ★★★★   TEENS ★★
YOUNG   ADULTS   ★★★½   OVER 30   ★★★½   SENIORS   ★★★

What it is Disney-fied midway ride. **Scope and scale** Minor attraction. **When to go** Before 10 a.m. or during late evening parades, fireworks, or *Fantasmic!* performances. **Special comments** An attractive children's ride. **Duration of ride** 1⅔ minutes. **Average wait in line per 100 people ahead of you** 12 minutes. **Assumes** Normal staffing. **Loading speed** Slow.

DESCRIPTION AND COMMENTS A nice, tame, happy children's ride based on the lovable Disney flying elephant. An upgraded rendition of a ride that can be found at state fairs and amusement parks across the country. Shortcomings notwithstanding, Dumbo is the favorite Disneyland Park attraction of most preschoolers. A lot of readers take us to task for lumping Dumbo in with state-fair midway rides. These comments from a reader in Armdale, Nova Scotia, are representative:

I think you have acquired a jaded attitude. I know [Dumbo] is not for everybody, but when we took our oldest child (then just 4), the sign at the end of the line said there would be a 90-minute wait. He knew and he didn't care, and he and I stood in the hot afternoon sun for 90 blissful minutes waiting for his 90-second flight. Anything that a 4-year-old would wait for that long and that patiently must be pretty special.

TOURING TIPS This is a slow-loading ride that we recommend you bypass unless you are on a very relaxed touring schedule. If your kids are excited about Dumbo, try to get them on the ride before 10 a.m., during the parades or *Fantasmic!*, or just before the park closes. Also, consider this advice from an Arlington, Virginia, mom:

Grown-ups, beware! Dumbo is really a tight fit with one adult and two kids. My kids threw me out of their Dumbo and I had to sit in a Dumbo all by myself. Pretty embarrassing, and my husband got lots of pictures.

Fantasy Faire

DESCRIPTION AND COMMENTS Once a sleepy corner off the Main Street hub, mainly known since the 1950s for weekend swing-dancing parties, the Carnation Plaza Gardens was given a pink-and-purple princess makeover in 2013 and emerged as the Fantasy Faire. Purists may bemoan the loss of history and liberal application of eye-popping pastels, but don't bother telling that to the kids running to meet their royal role models. Even if you aren't enamored of the princess marketing craze, you can't help but admire the loving details applied throughout this mini-land, from a snoozing animatronic Figaro kitty and crank-operated Clopin music box to the twinkling hair on the courtyard's *Tangled*-inspired tower. (Boogie and jive fans, don't get jumpy: the weekend swing-dancing parties have relocated to a stage in Downtown Disney and return to Disneyland, on its original dance floor, which was preserved during the renovation, on select summer nights.)

The two main components of the Fantasy Faire are the Royal Hall and the Royal Theatre. Royal Hall is an indoor meet and greet with three princesses always on duty (usually Ariel, Aurora, and Cinderella). The usual Disneyland queue (mercifully mostly shaded) must be endured to meet and be photographed, but while the queue at the former Fantasy Faire location regularly reached a 45- to 60-minute wait at the peak of the day, this new incarnation typically sees somewhat shorter waits. The trick is that the Royal Hall's intimate wood-paneled interior actually houses two identical meeting areas with duplicate trios of princesses (perhaps the product of an Epcot cloning experiment?) for double the greeting capacity.

Royal Theatre, which once hosted jazz greats such as Dizzy Gillespie, now houses a rotating pair of 20-minute stage shows dramatizing the tales of *Tangled* and *Beauty and the Beast*. The *Tangled* show is usually performed at the first three showtimes of the day, with *Beauty and the Beast* typically taking the stage for the remainder. If you can pick, *Tangled* has the better script.

Rapunzel (with Flynn Ryder) and Belle join in their respective reenactments, accompanied by narrators Mr. Smyth and Mr. Jones, milkmaid stagehands, and a live pianist. Rather than straightforward retellings, these fast-paced comic condensations capture the anarchic slapstick of a Renaissance fair trunk show. Witty enough to keep adults, who are far outside the target demographic, awake, the Royal Theatre's shows are the sleeper hits of Fantasy Faire. The theater only seats a little more than 200 (with room for 50 kids on the floor up front), so you may want to line up 30 or more minutes before showtime. Stick around after the curtain falls for an autograph session with the stars.

In addition to the theater and hall, you'll find the Fairytale Treasures shop, stocked with princess outfits and accessories, and Maurice's Treats snack cart (see page 177). Passageways from the courtyard connect to Frontierland (through Rancho del Zocalo) and Fantasyland.

TOURING TIPS Little girls love the Fantasy Faire, as do boys age 6 and younger. Incidentally, you won't believe how many of the kids come in costume. If you do everything, you'll spend about an hour, not counting shopping time. On busy days, you may be barred from bringing your stroller into Fantasy Faire, unless your child is asleep in it, so teach your kid to play dead on command if you don't want to park.

Fantasyland Theatre

DESCRIPTION AND COMMENTS Originally installed as a teen nightspot called Videopolis, this venue has been converted into a sophisticated amphitheater where concerts and elaborate stage shows are performed according to the daily entertainment schedule. Better productions that have played the Fantasyland Theatre stage include *Beauty and the Beast Live, Snow White,* and *The Spirit of Pocahontas,* all musical stage adaptations of the respective Disney-animated features.

After a half decade of serving as a shopping center for precocious princesses, the Fantasyland Theatre was returned to service as a stage in 2013. *Mickey and the Magic Map,* the debut production in the reborn venue, involves apprentice Mickey's accidental adventure into sorcerer Yen Sid's mysterious dream-controlling map. This 25-minute musical adventure combines new songs and classic tunes in a newly recorded score that skips from India to Hawaii, with a stopover under the sea. Rapunzel, Pocahontas, Mulan, King Louie, Sebastian, and Stitch are among the Disney icons who appear, along with a platoon of dancing paintpots and brushes, but the show is stolen by a mischievous animated paint splotch (brought to life through high-tech video effects).

The opening number is less than memorable, and the computer-generated animation of Yen Sid is disappointingly chunky. On the whole, however, this is easily the best new musical production that Disneyland's parks have mounted in a decade. Live singing and energetic choreography influenced by drum corps enliven the somewhat overfamiliar songs, and a gospel-flavored riverboat finale (complete with streamers shot over the audience) brings down the house. Well worth watching once you've experienced the headliners, or on your second day at Disneyland.

TOURING TIPS Performance schedules are listed in the *Times Guide.* Arrive up to an hour early for optimal seating. Good views can be found anywhere in the center section, but side seats distort the image on the slanted screen.

It's a Small World ★★★½

APPEAL BY AGE	PRESCHOOL ★★★★½	GRADE SCHOOL ★★★★
TEENS ★★★ YOUNG ADULTS ★★★½ OVER 30 ★★★★ SENIORS ★★★★½		

What it is World brotherhood–themed indoor boat ride. **Scope and scale** Major attraction. **When to go** Anytime except after a parade. **Special comments** A pleasant change of pace. **Duration of ride** 14 minutes. **Average wait in line per 100 people ahead of you** 2½ minutes. **Assumes** Busy conditions with 56 boats operating. **Loading speed** Fast.

Thumbs Up for the Whole Family

DESCRIPTION AND COMMENTS A happy and upbeat attraction with a world-brotherhood theme and a catchy tune that will stick in your head for weeks. Small boats convey visitors on a tour around the world, with singing and dancing dolls showcasing the dress and culture of each nation. Almost everyone enjoys It's a Small World (well, there are those jaded folks who are put off by the dolls' homogeneous appearance, especially in light of the diversity theme), but it stands, along with the *Enchanted Tiki Room,* as an attraction that some could take or leave but that others consider one of the real masterpieces of

Disneyland Park. In 2009 Disney inserted more than 20 new figures of Disney and Pixar characters into the classic attraction, over the vocal objections of some serious Disney fans. Tastefully crafted in the style of original artist Mary Blair, the additions don't detract from the ride, except in the tacky U.S.A. tribute tacked onto the end. In any event, a woman from Holbrook, New York, wrote with this devilish suggestion for improvement:

> Small World would be much better if each person got a few softballs on the way in!

A mom from Castleton, Vermont, added this:

> It's a Small World at Fantasyland was like a pit stop in the Twilight Zone. They were very slow unloading the boats, and we were stuck in a line of about six boats waiting to get out while the endless chanting of that song grated on my nerves. I told my husband that I was going to swim for it just to escape one more chorus.

From November through New Year's, the attraction receives an annual holiday overlay inside the attraction as well as outside, featuring "Jingle Bells" and "Deck the Halls" instead of the usual earworm soundtrack. We particularly enjoy the light show and projection effects outside the attraction that happen every 15 minutes.

TOURING TIPS Totally renovated and upgraded in 2009 with a deeper flue to accommodate today's heavier guests, It's a Small World is a fast-loading ride that's usually a good bet during the busier times of the day. The boats are moved along by water pressure, which increases as boats are added. Thus, the more boats in service when you ride (up to a maximum total of 60), the shorter the duration of the ride (and wait). Small World is taken off-line in mid-October and reopened in November with a special Christmas holiday theme. Removal of the overlay also keeps the ride closed for several weeks after the holiday season. Two notes: While the loading can be very quick when there are many boats running, the unloading can be very slow. Second, the attraction has two loading zones, one that has wheelchair access and one without. Unless you need wheelchair access, we recommend using the loading zone on the far side of the entrance by choosing the right side of the queue when it splits.

King Arthur Carrousel ★ ★ ★

APPEAL BY AGE	PRESCHOOL ★ ★ ★ ★ ½	GRADE SCHOOL ★ ★ ★ ★	TEENS ★ ★ ★ ½
YOUNG ADULTS ★ ★ ★ ½		OVER 30 ★ ★ ★ ½	SENIORS ★ ★ ★

What it is Merry-go-round. **Scope and scale** Minor attraction. **When to go** Before 11:30 a.m. or after 5 p.m. **Special comments** A showpiece carousel; adults enjoy the beauty and nostalgia of this ride. **Duration of ride** A little more than 2 minutes. **Average wait in line per 100 people ahead of you** 8 minutes. **Assumes** Normal staffing. **Loading speed** Slow.

DESCRIPTION AND COMMENTS A merry-go-round to be sure, but certainly one of the most elaborate and beautiful you will ever see, especially when lit at night. For the 50th anniversary in 2005, a special horse was added in tribute to Julie Andrews and her iconic role in *Mary*

Poppins. It is a white horse with bells all over, hence her name, Jingles. She is the horse closest to the handicapped ramp.

TOURING TIPS Unless there are small children in your party, we suggest that you appreciate this ride from the sidelines. If your children want to ride, try to get them on before 11:30 a.m. or after 5 p.m. While nice to look at, the carousel loads and unloads very slowly.

Mad Tea Party ★★

APPEAL BY AGE PRESCHOOL ★★★★½ GRADE SCHOOL ★★★★½
TEENS ★★★★ YOUNG ADULTS ★★★★ OVER 30 ★★★½ SENIORS ★½

What it is Midway-type spinning ride. **Scope and scale** Minor attraction. **When to go** Before 11 a.m. or after 5 p.m. **Special comments** You can make the teacups spin faster by turning the wheel in the center of the cup; fun but not worth the wait. **Duration of ride** 1½ minutes. **Average wait in line per 100 people ahead of you** 8 minutes. **Assumes** Normal staffing. **Loading speed** Slow.

Queasy Muss Your 'Do

DESCRIPTION AND COMMENTS Well done in the Disney style, but still just an amusement-park ride. *Alice in Wonderland's* Mad Hatter provides the theme, and patrons whirl around feverishly in big teacups. A rendition of this ride, sans Disney characters, can be found at every local carnival and fair.

TOURING TIPS This ride, besides not being particularly special, loads notoriously slowly. Skip it on a busy schedule if the kids will let you. Ride in the morning of your second day if your schedule is more relaxed. A warning for parents who have not given this ride much thought: Teenagers like to lure an adult onto the teacups and then turn the wheel in the middle (which makes the cup spin faster) until the adults are plastered against the side of the cup and are on the verge of throwing up.

Matterhorn Bobsleds ★★★½

APPEAL BY AGE PRESCHOOL ★★★† GRADE SCHOOL ★★★★
TEENS ★★★★ YOUNG ADULTS ★★★★ OVER 30 ★★★★ SENIORS ★★★

† Some preschoolers loved Matterhorn Bobsleds; others were frightened.

What it is Roller coaster. **Scope and scale** Major attraction. **When to go** During the first 90 minutes the park is open or during the hour before it closes. **Special comments** Fun ride but not too scary; must be 42" tall to ride. **Duration of ride** 2½ minutes. **Average wait in line per 100 people ahead of you** 13 minutes. **Assumes** Both tracks operating with 10 sleds per track with 23-second dispatch intervals. **Loading speed** Moderate.

Scary Lose Things Queasy Rough Muss Your 'Do

DESCRIPTION AND COMMENTS The Matterhorn is the most distinctive landmark on the Disneyland scene, visible from almost anywhere in the park. Open since 1959, the Matterhorn maintains its popularity and long lines year in and year out. The Matterhorn Bobsleds is a roller coaster with an alpine motif. On the scary scale, the ride ranks about 6 on a scale of 10. The special effects cannot compare to Space Mountain, but they do afford a few surprises. In 2012 the Matterhorn completed its first top-to-bottom overhaul since the 1970s, receiving rehabilitated tracks and a more-realistic exterior paint job. More controversially, the old four-passenger vehicles with straddle seats were replaced by three-passenger cars with individual seats (similar to Florida's Space Mountain) and seat belts. Future children will be robbed of the traditional thrill of riding nestled between their parent's legs, and thankful fathers will be spared the traditional bruising of their family jewels. The new configuration also increased the minimum height from 35" to 42" and reduced the theoretical hourly capacity, though an added single-rider line helps move things along. The revamped vehicles are also unfriendly to the long-legged. Tall riders are advised to ask for the middle or back rows, which have marginally more room, and slide their feet forward into the snug footwells on either side of the seat ahead. A Richboro, Pennsylvania, dad disagrees with our scary rating of the Matterhorn:

> *My biggest disappointment was the Matterhorn. I understand it's iconic, but the notion that it could rate as a 6 out of 10 on the scare factor is pure insanity. I'd rate it as a 1! After the steep climb in the dark, you basically just go down in circles until you are left baffled that the "roller coaster" ride is over.*

TOURING TIPS Lines for the Matterhorn form as soon as the gates open and persist throughout the day. Ride first thing in the morning or just before the park closes. If you are a roller coaster person, ride Space Mountain and then hurry over and hop on the Matterhorn. If roller coasters are not the end-all for you, we recommend choosing one of the other coasters or saving one for a second day. The Matterhorn's poorly marked single-rider line, which can save you an hour in the queue, is currently one of the park's best-kept secrets. Ask an employee at the Fantasyland side exit how to take advantage of it.

One of the things we like about the Matterhorn is that the entire queuing area is visible. This makes the lines look more oppressive than they actually are and also provides an opportunity to closely approximate the time of your wait. If the line extending toward Tomorrowland reaches a point across from the Photo Spot, your wait to ride the Matterhorn Bobsleds will be about 16 minutes. Most people stay to the left when the queue splits, often leaving the right loading station with a shorter line. Though the two sides are similar, they are not identical; veterans say the Tomorrowland track is faster, while the Fantasyland side is slightly longer with sharper turns.

Mr. Toad's Wild Ride ★★½

APPEAL BY AGE PRESCHOOL ★★★   GRADE SCHOOL ★★★★   TEENS ★★★½
YOUNG ADULTS ★★★★   OVER 30 ★★★½   SENIORS ★★★★

Dark

What it is Track ride in the dark. **Scope and scale** Minor attraction. **When to go** Before 11 a.m. **Special comments** Past its prime. **Duration of ride** Almost 2 minutes. **Average wait in line per 100 people ahead of you** 9 minutes. **Assumes** 12 cars operating. **Loading speed** Slow.

DESCRIPTION AND COMMENTS Mr. Toad's Wild Ride is a twisting, curving ride in the dark that passes two-dimensional sets and props. There are a couple of clever effects, but basically it's at the technological basement of the Disney attraction mix. Its sister attraction at Disney World was scrapped in 1999. Though Mr. Toad doesn't compare well with newer high-tech attractions, many Disneyland veterans appreciate it because it's one of a handful of attractions remaining from the park's beginning.

TOURING TIPS Not a great but certainly a popular attraction. Lines build early in the day and never let up. Catch Mr. Toad before 11 a.m.

Peter Pan's Flight ★★★★

APPEAL BY AGE PRESCHOOL ★★★★½ GRADE SCHOOL ★★★★½ TEENS ★★★½
YOUNG ADULTS ★★★★½ OVER 30 ★★★★½ SENIORS ★★★★½

What it is Indoor fantasy-adventure ride. **Scope and scale** Minor attraction. **When to go** Before 10 a.m. or after 6 p.m. **Special comments** Happy and mellow. **Duration of ride** Just over 2 minutes. **Average wait in line per 100 people ahead of you** 11 minutes. **Assumes** 13 ships operating. **Loading speed** Slow.

Thumbs Up for the Whole Family

DESCRIPTION AND COMMENTS Although it is not considered one of Disneyland Park's major attractions, Peter Pan's Flight is superbly designed and absolutely delightful, with a happy theme, a reunion with some unforgettable Disney characters, beautiful effects, and charming music. Tiny pirate ships suspended from an overhead track launch you from Wendy's window to fly over nighttime London and on to Never Land and an encounter with Captain Hook, Mr. Smee, and the ubiquitous crocodile.

TOURING TIPS Though not a major feature of Disneyland Park, we nevertheless classify it as the best attraction in Fantasyland. Try to ride before 10 a.m. or after 6 p.m., during the afternoon or evening parade(s), or during a performance of *Fantasmic!*

Pinocchio's Daring Journey ★★½

APPEAL BY AGE PRESCHOOL ★★★ GRADE SCHOOL ★★★½ TEENS ★★★½
YOUNG ADULTS ★★★½ OVER 30 ★★★½ SENIORS ★★★★

What it is Track ride in the dark. **Scope and scale** Minor attraction. **When to go** Before noon or after 3:30 p.m. **Special comments** A big letdown. **Duration of ride** Almost 3 minutes. **Average wait in line per 100 people ahead of you** 8 minutes. **Assumes** 15 cars operating. **Loading speed** Slow.

Dark

DESCRIPTION AND COMMENTS This is another twisting, curving track ride in the dark, this time tracing the adventures of Pinocchio as he tries to find his way home. The action is hard to follow, and it lacks continuity. Although the sets are three-dimensional and more visually compelling than, say, Mr. Toad, the story line is dull and fails to engage the guest. In the ride's defense, it features some deliciously trippy Pleasure Island imagery, a clever vanishing Blue Fairy effect, and almost always an empty queue.

TOURING TIPS The word must be out about Pinocchio because the lines are seldom very long. Still, the longest waits occur 11:30 a.m.–4:30 p.m.

Sleeping Beauty Castle ★★★

APPEAL BY AGE   PRESCHOOL ★★★½   GRADE SCHOOL ★★★   TEENS ★★½
YOUNG ADULTS ★★★½   OVER 30 ★★★½   SENIORS ★★★½

What it is Walk-through exhibit. **Scope and scale** Minor attraction. **When to go** Anytime. **Special comments** Must be able to climb up and down two flights of stairs. **Duration of exhibit** Varies; about 10 minutes. **Average wait** Usually none.

DESCRIPTION AND COMMENTS Disneyland Park's most famous icon, Sleeping Beauty Castle is at the heart of Disneyland and serves as a stage for shows and special events. For the non-claustrophobic, the Sleeping Beauty Castle walk-through exhibit is a miniature 3-D series, arranged along a narrow passage inside the castle, that tells the story of Sleeping Beauty. Originally opened on April 29, 1957, to "preview" the upcoming 1959 movie *Sleeping Beauty,* and then closed for most of a decade after 9/11, the attraction reopened in November 2008 with new dioramas reflecting the style of artist Eyvind Earle, who gave *Sleeping Beauty* its distinctive design. In this version there are animated scenes, interactive elements, and Pepper's Ghost projection effects (as also seen in the Haunted Mansion).

DISNEY DISH WITH JIM HILL

FERAL CATS CAUSE IMAGINEERS TO FLEA . . . ER . . . FLEE When Disneyland Park was originally being built in late 1954, Walt didn't have enough money to install an attraction inside of Sleeping Beauty Castle. So the iconic structure stood empty until the fall of 1956, when the theme park had better cash flow. But when a design team arrived to begin taking measurements for the soon-to-be-built Sleeping Beauty Castle walk-through, they discovered that someone had moved into this structure ahead of Princess Aurora— a family of feral cats. To make matters worse, the castle was now so badly infested with fleas from these cats that—after spending just a few minutes inside—the Imagineers were forced to retreat, itching and scratching all the way. It took several weeks to capture and then relocate the cats, not to mention thoroughly fumigate the enormous structure, which is why the grand opening of Disneyland's Sleeping Beauty walk-through was pushed back to late April 1957.

TOURING TIPS The entrance is on the Fantasyland side of the castle near the passageway to Plaza Gardens and Frontierland. The exhibit allows for one-way traffic only. It can get a bit crowded inside, but there should rarely be a line outside the attraction. For those guests unable to handle stairs, a small alcove is to the left of the bridge to Tomorrowland. Inside you will find a collection of the animations, as well as music, allowing you to experience the attraction's elements without walking. The viewing location runs on a loop, so you might have to watch it out of order.

Snow White's Scary Adventures ★★★

What it is Track ride in the dark. **Scope and scale** Minor attraction. **When to go** Before 11 a.m. or after 5 p.m. **Special comments** Quite intimidating for preschoolers; worth seeing if the wait is not long. **Duration of ride** Almost 2 minutes. **Average wait in line per 100 people ahead of you** 9 minutes. **Assumes** 10 cars operating. **Loading speed** Slow.

  DESCRIPTION AND COMMENTS Here, you ride in a mining car in the dark through a series of sets drawn from *Snow White and the Seven Dwarfs*. The attraction has a *Perils of Pauline* flavor and features Snow White as she narrowly escapes harm at the hands of the wicked witch. The action and effects are a cut above Mr. Toad's Wild Ride but not as good as Peter Pan's Flight. This ride is more condensed and less coherent compared to its now-closed Orlando cousin, but it does boast new high-tech projection effects enhancing the magic mirror and rainstorm scenes.

TOURING TIPS Enjoyable but not particularly compelling. Experience it if the lines are not too long or on a second-day visit. Ride before 11 a.m. or after 5 p.m. if possible. Also, don't take the "scary" part too seriously. The witch looks mean, but most kids take her in stride. Or maybe not. A mother from Knoxville, Tennessee, commented:

> *The outside looks cute and fluffy, but inside, the evil witch just keeps coming at you. My 5-year-old, who rode Space Mountain three times [and took other scary rides] right in stride, was near panic when our car stopped unexpectedly twice during Snow White. [After Snow White] my 6-year-old niece spent a lot of time asking, "Will a witch jump out at you?" before other rides. So I suggest that you explain a little more what this ride is about. It's tough on preschoolers who are expecting forest animals and dwarfs.*

In point of fact, we receive more mail from parents about this ride than about all other Disneyland Park attractions combined. The bottom line is that it really punches the buttons of the 6-and-under crowd, when other more traditionally scary rides don't. Many kids, once frightened by Snow White's Scary Adventures, balk at trying any other attractions that go into the dark, regardless of how benign they are.

Storybook Land Canal Boats ★★★

What it is Scenic boat ride. **Scope and scale** Minor attraction. **When to go** Before 10:30 a.m. or after 5:30 p.m. **Special comments** Pretty, tranquil, and serene. **Duration of ride** 6½ minutes. **Average wait in line per 100 people ahead of you** 16 minutes. **Assumes** 7 boats operating. **Loading speed** Slow.

Thumbs Up for the Whole Family

DESCRIPTION AND COMMENTS Guide-operated boats wind along canals situated beneath the same miniature landscapes visible from the Casey Jr. Circus Train. This ride, offering stellar examples of bonsai cultivation, selective pruning, and miniaturization, is a must for landscape-gardening enthusiasts. The landscapes include scenes from more recent Disney features, in addition to those from such classics as *The Wind in the Willows* and *The Three Little Pigs*.

TOURING TIPS The boats are much more comfortable than the train, the view of the miniatures is better, and the pace is more leisurely. On the downside, the lines are long and, if not long, definitely slow moving. The ride itself also takes a lot of time. Our recommendation is to ride Casey Jr. if you have children or are in a hurry. Take the boat if your party is all adults or your pace is more leisurely. Best of all, the boats' pilots deliver live narration that (depending on the driver) can be delightfully droll. If you ride the boats, try to get on before 10:30 a.m. If the queue isn't prohibitive, this ride is especially appealing after sunset, when the creative lighting adds a whole new dimension. It's closed during parades.

MICKEY'S TOONTOWN

MICKEY'S TOONTOWN IS SITUATED across the Disneyland Railroad tracks from Fantasyland. Its entrance is a tunnel that opens into Fantasyland just to the left of It's a Small World. As its name suggests, Toontown is a fanciful representation of the wacky cartoon community where all of the Disney characters live. Mickey's Toontown was inspired by the Disney animated feature *Who Framed Roger Rabbit?*, in which humans were able to enter the world of cartoon characters.

Mickey's Toontown consists of a colorful collection of miniature buildings, all executed in exaggerated cartoon style with rounded edges and brilliant colors. Among the buildings are Mickey's and Minnie's Houses, both open to inspection inside and out.

If you want to see characters, Mickey's Toontown is the place to go. In addition to Mickey, who receives guests all day (except during parades) in his dressing room, and Minnie, who entertains in her house, you are likely to bump into such august personages as Goofy and Pluto lurking around the streets. It would be a rare event to visit Toontown without bumping into a few characters. From time to time, horns sound and whistles blow atop the Toontown City Hall, followed by a fanfare rendition of the Mickey Mouse Club theme song. This indicates, as a mom from Texas explained to us, that "some characters are fixin' to come out." And there you have it.

Mickey's Toontown is rendered with masterful attention to artistic humor and detail. The colorful buildings each have a story to tell or a gag to visit upon an unsuspecting guest. There is an explosion at the Fireworks Factory every minute or so, always unannounced. Across the street, the sidewalk is littered with crates containing strange contents addressed to exotic destinations. If you pry open the top of one of the crates (easy to do), the crate will emit a noise consistent with its contents. A box of "train parts," for example, broadcasts the sound of a racing locomotive when you lift the top.

Everywhere in Mickey's Toontown are subtleties and absurdities to delight the imagination. Next to Goofy's Playhouse is a Goofy-shaped impact crater marking the spot where he missed his swimming pool while high diving. A sign in front of the local garage declares, "If we can't fix it, we won't."

While adults will enjoy the imaginative charm of Mickey's Toontown, it will quickly become apparent that there is not much for them to do there. Most of the attractions in Mickey's Toontown are for kids, specifically smaller children. Attractions open to adults include a dark ride drawn from *Who Framed Roger Rabbit?* (sort of a high-tech rendition of Mr. Toad's Wild Ride) and a diminutive roller coaster.

In many ways, Mickey's Toontown is a designer playground, a fanciful cousin to Tom Sawyer Island in Frontierland, where it's OK for the kids to run, climb, and let off steam. What distinguishes Mickey's Toontown is that the play areas are specially designed for smaller children; it's also much cleaner than Tom Sawyer Island (that is, no dirt—though this does not guarantee a dirt-free child upon leaving the area). Finally, in the noblest Disney tradition, you must wait in line for virtually everything.

Also, be forewarned that Mickey's Toontown is not very large, especially in comparison with neighboring Fantasyland. A tolerable crowd in most of the other lands will seem like Times Square on New Year's Eve in Mickey's Toontown. Couple this congestion with the unfortunate fact that none of the attractions in Mickey's Toontown are engineered to handle huge crowds, and you come face-to-face with possibly the most attractive traffic jam the Disney folks have ever created.

Mickey's Toontown opens one hour after the rest of the park. If you're touring with younger children, hit the Fantasyland attractions during the first hour the park is open, and then head for Mickey's Toontown.

Finally, be aware that all of Toontown, including the Roger Rabbit ride, will close early before every nighttime fireworks show. It seems that rockets are launched from a building behind the land, showering Mickey's city with fiery embers, which might prove inconvenient for anyone standing below.

Chip 'n Dale Treehouse ★★

APPEAL BY AGE	PRESCHOOL ★★★½	GRADE SCHOOL ★★★	TEENS ★
YOUNG ADULTS ★★	OVER 30 ★★		SENIORS ★½

What it is Imaginative children's play area. **Scope and scale** Diversion. **When to go** Anytime. **Special comments** Good exercise for the small fry.

DESCRIPTION AND COMMENTS The play area consists of a tree house with slides.

TOURING TIPS Located in the most remote corner of Mickey's Toontown and obscured by the crowd waiting to ride the roller coaster next door, the tree house is frequently overlooked. Of all the attractions in Mickey's Toontown, this is the easiest one to get the kids into without much of a wait. Most any child who can fit is allowed to rummage around in the tree house.

Disneyland Railroad

DESCRIPTION AND COMMENTS Mickey's Toontown and Fantasyland share a station on the Disneyland Railroad's route around the perimeter of the park. This station becomes fairly crowded on busy days. If you are interested primarily in getting there, it may be quicker to walk.

Gadget's Go Coaster ★★

APPEAL BY AGE PRESCHOOL ★★★★ GRADE SCHOOL ★★★★ TEENS ★★★
YOUNG ADULTS ★★★ OVER 30 ★★★ SENIORS ★★★

What it is Small roller coaster. **Scope and scale** Minor attraction. **When to go** Before 10:30 a.m., during the parades or *Fantasmic!* in the evening, or just before the park closes. **Special comments** Great for little ones but not worth the wait for adults; must be 35" to ride; expectant moms shouldn't ride. **Duration of ride** About 50 seconds. **Average wait in line per 100 people ahead of you** 10 minutes. **Assumes** Normal staffing. **Loading speed** Slow.

Rough

Lose Things

DESCRIPTION AND COMMENTS Gadget's Go Coaster is a very small roller coaster, the idea of which is that you are miniaturized and riding around in an acorn shell. The zippy ride is over so quickly that you hardly know that you've been anywhere. In fact, of the 52 seconds the ride is in motion, 32 seconds are consumed in exiting the loading area, being ratcheted up the first hill, and braking into the off-loading area. The actual time you spend careening around the track is a whopping 20 seconds.

TOURING TIPS Gadget's Go Coaster, a beginner roller coaster for young children, is the perfect attraction to gauge the pluckiness of your little ones before tossing them to the coyotes on Big Thunder Mountain Railroad. The coaster cars are not very comfortable for adults, and you can expect a fair amount of whiplash, but as noted, the ride takes less than a minute. The coaster is both slow-loading and visually attractive, so you can expect long waits except during the first 30 minutes that Mickey's Toontown is open.

Goofy's Playhouse ★★½

APPEAL BY AGE PRESCHOOL ★★★★½ GRADE SCHOOL ★★★½ TEENS ★★
YOUNG ADULTS ★★½ OVER 30 ★★½ SENIORS ★★★

What it is A whimsical children's play area. **Scope and scale** Diversion. **When to go** Anytime.

DESCRIPTION AND COMMENTS Goofy's Playhouse is a small but nicely themed play area for the under-6 set. Usually not crowded, the playhouse is a pleasant place to let preschoolers ramble and parents relax while older sibs enjoy more adventurous attractions.

TOURING TIPS There's not a lot of shade, so visit early or late in the day.

Mickey's House and Meet Mickey ★★★

APPEAL BY AGE PRESCHOOL ★★★★½ GRADE SCHOOL ★★★★ TEENS ★★★½
YOUNG ADULTS ★★★ OVER 30 ★★★★ SENIORS ★★★½

What it is Walk-through tour of Mickey's House and Movie Barn, ending with a personal visit with Mickey. **Scope and scale** Minor attraction and character-greeting opportunity. **When to go** Before 10:30 a.m. or after 5:30 p.m. **Special comments** Well done. **Duration of tour** 15–30 minutes (depending on the crowd). **Average wait in line per 100 people ahead of you** 20 minutes. **Assumes** Normal staffing. **Touring speed** Slow.

DESCRIPTION AND COMMENTS Mickey's House is the starting point of a self-guided tour that winds through the famous mouse's house, into his backyard, and past Pluto's doghouse, and then into Mickey's Movie Barn. This last stop harks back to the so-called "barn" studio where Walt Disney created a number of the earlier Mickey Mouse cartoons. Once in the Movie Barn, guests watch vintage Disney cartoons while awaiting admittance to Mickey's Dressing Room.

In small groups of one or two families, guests are ultimately conducted into the dressing room where Mickey awaits to pose for photos and sign autographs. The visit is not lengthy (2–4 minutes), but there is adequate time for all of the children to hug, poke, and admire the star.

TOURING TIPS The cynical observer will discern immediately that Mickey's House, backyard, Movie Barn, and so on are no more than a cleverly devised queuing area to deliver guests to Mickey's Dressing Room for the mouse encounter. For those with some vestige of child in their personalities, however, the preamble serves to heighten anticipation while providing the opportunity to get to know the corporate symbol on a more personal level. Mickey's House is well conceived and contains a lot of Disney memorabilia. You will notice that children touch everything as they proceed through the house, hoping to find some artifact that is not welded or riveted into the set (an especially tenacious child during one of our visits was actually able to rip a couple of books from a bookcase).

Meeting Mickey and touring his house are best done during the first two hours the park is open or, alternatively, in the evening during *Fantasmic!* If meeting Mickey is at the top of your child's list, you might consider taking the Disneyland Railroad from Main Street to the Toontown/Fantasyland Station as soon as you enter the park. Some children are so obsessed with seeing Mickey that they cannot enjoy anything else until they get Mickey in the rearview mirror.

Minnie's House ★★½

APPEAL BY AGE PRESCHOOL ★★★★★ GRADE SCHOOL ★★★★½ TEENS ★★★
YOUNG ADULTS ★★★ OVER 30 ★★★½ SENIORS ★★★½

What it is Walk-through exhibit. **Scope and scale** Minor attraction and character-greeting opportunity. **When to go** Before 11:30 a.m. or after 4:30 p.m. **Special comments** OK but not great. **Duration of tour** About 10 minutes. **Average wait in line**

per 100 people ahead of you 12 minutes. **Touring speed** Slow.

DESCRIPTION AND COMMENTS Minnie's House consists of a self-guided tour through the various rooms and backyard of Mickey Mouse's main squeeze. Similar to Mickey's House, only predictably more feminine, Minnie's House likewise showcases some fun Disney memorabilia. Among the highlights of the short tour are the fanciful appliances in Minnie's kitchen. Like Mickey, Minnie is usually present to receive guests.

TOURING TIPS The main difference between Mickey's House and Minnie's House is that Minnie's House cannot accommodate as many guests. See Minnie early and before Mickey to avoid waiting outdoors in a long queue. (Neither Mickey nor Minnie is available during parades.)

Miss Daisy, Donald's Boat   ★★

APPEAL BY AGE	PRESCHOOL ★★★★	GRADE SCHOOL ★★★★	TEENS ★½
YOUNG ADULTS ★★½	OVER 30 ★★½		SENIORS ★★

What it is Creative play area with a boat theme. **Scope and scale** Diversion. **When to go** Before 10:30 a.m. or after 4:30 p.m.

DESCRIPTION AND COMMENTS Another children's play area, this time with a tugboat theme. Children can climb nets, ring bells, survey Toontown from the captain's bridge, and scoot down slides. The idea is that Donald Duck (who, as everyone knows, lives in Duckburg) is visiting Toontown.

TOURING TIPS Kids more or less wander on and off of the *Miss Daisy,* and usually there is not any sort of organized line or queuing area. Enjoy this play area at your leisure and stay as long as you like.

Roger Rabbit's Car Toon Spin *(Fastpass)*   ★★★

APPEAL BY AGE	PRESCHOOL ★★★½	GRADE SCHOOL ★★★★	TEENS ★★★½
YOUNG ADULTS ★★★★	OVER 30 ★★★½		SENIORS ★★★½

What it is Track ride in the dark. **Scope and scale** Major attraction. **When to go** Before 10:30 a.m. or after 6:30 p.m. **Special comments** Ride with your kids, if you can stomach it. **Duration of ride** A little more than 3 minutes. **Average wait in line per 100 people ahead of you** 7 minutes. **Assumes** Full-capacity operation. **Loading speed** Moderate.

Dark   Rough   Queasy

DESCRIPTION AND COMMENTS A so-called dark ride where guests become part of a cartoon plot. The idea is that you are renting a taxicab for a tour of Toontown. As soon as your cab gets under way, however, weasels throw a slippery glop (known as dip) on the road, sending the cab into a more or less uncontrollable spin. This spinning continues as the cab passes through a variety of sets populated by cartoon and audio-animatronic characters and punctuated by simulated explosions. As a child of the 1960s put it, "It was like combining Mr. Toad's Wild Ride with the Mad Tea Party while tripping on LSD." The ride features an elaborate indoor queue, and the best effects of any Disneyland cartoon dark ride, climaxing in a head-scratchingly effective "portable hole" gag that holds up under repeated viewing.

The main problem with the Car Toon Spin is that, because of the spinning, you are often pointed in the wrong direction to appreciate (or even see) many of the better visual effects. Furthermore, the story line is loose. The attraction lacks the continuity and humor of Splash Mountain or the suspense of The Haunted Mansion or Snow White's Scary Adventures.

The spinning, incidentally, can be controlled by the guests. If you don't want to spin, you don't have to. If you do elect to spin, you still will not be able to approach the eye-popping speed attainable on the teacups at the Mad Tea Party. Sluggish spinning aside, our advice for those who are at all susceptible to motion sickness is not to get near this ride if you are touring with anyone under 21 years of age.

A reader from Milford, Michigan, echoed our sentiments, lamenting:

The most disappointing ride to me was Roger Rabbit's Car Toon Spin. I stood 45 minutes for a fun house ride, and the wheel was so difficult to operate that I spent most of my time trying to steer the bloody car and missed the point of the ride.

TOURING TIPS The ride is popular for its novelty, and it is one of the few Mickey's Toontown attractions that parents (with strong stomachs) can enjoy with their children. Because the ride stays fairly thronged with people all day long, ride before 10:30 a.m., during parades or *Fantasmic!*, or in the hour before the park closes. The best move is to obtain Fastpasses before 10:30 a.m., when the return time is an hour or less away, and then let your children enjoy the other Toontown attractions until it's time to ride.

■■ TOMORROWLAND

LOCATED DIRECTLY TO THE RIGHT of the central hub is Tomorrowland. This themed area is a futuristic mix of rides and experiences that relates to technological development and what life will be like in the years to come.

Before its 2000 renovation, Tomorrowland's 40-year-old buildings more resembled 1970s motel architecture than anyone's vision of the future. Tomorrowland's current design is more enduring, reflecting a nostalgic vision of the future as imagined by dreamers and scientists in the 1920s and 1930s. Frozen in time, Tomorrowland conjures up visions of Buck Rogers (whom nobody under age 60 remembers), fanciful mechanical rockets, and metallic cities spread beneath towering obelisks. Disney refers to Tomorrowland as the "Future That Never Was." *Newsweek* has dubbed it "retro-future."

Astro Orbitor ★★

APPEAL BY AGE	PRESCHOOL ★★★★	GRADE SCHOOL ★★★★	TEENS ★★★½
YOUNG ADULTS ★★★½		OVER 30 ★★★	SENIORS ★★½

What it is Very mild midway-type thrill ride. **Scope and scale** Minor attraction. **When to go** Before 10 a.m. or during the hour before the park closes. **Special**

comments Not worth the wait. **Duration of ride** 1½ minutes. **Average wait in line per 100 people ahead of you** 13 minutes. **Assumes** Normal staffing. **Loading speed** Slow.

DESCRIPTION AND COMMENTS The Astro Orbitor is a visually appealing midway-type ride involving small rockets that rotate on arms around a central axis. Be aware that the Astro Orbitor flies higher and faster than Dumbo and that it frightens some small children.

Queasy

Thumbs Up for the Whole Family

TOURING TIPS Astro Orbitor is slow to load and expendable on any schedule. If you want to take a preschooler on this ride, place your child in the seat first and then sit down yourself.

Autopia *(Fastpass)* ★★½

APPEAL BY AGE	PRESCHOOL ★★★★½	GRADE SCHOOL ★★★★
TEENS ★★★½	YOUNG ADULTS ★★★	OVER 30 ★★★ SENIORS ★★½

What it is Drive-'em-yourself miniature cars. **Scope and scale** Minor attraction. **When to go** Before 10 a.m., after 5 p.m., or use Fastpass. **Special comments** Boring for adults; great for preschoolers; must be at least 32" tall to ride, and at least one guest in car must be 54". **Duration of ride** Approximately 4½ minutes. **Average wait in line per 100 people ahead of you** 6 minutes. **Assumes** 35 cars operating on each track. **Loading speed** Slow.

DESCRIPTION AND COMMENTS An elaborate miniature freeway with gasoline-powered cars that will travel at speeds of up to 7 miles per hour. The attraction design, with its sleek cars, auto noises, highway signs, and even an "off-road" section, is quite alluring. In fact, however, the cars poke along on a track that leaves the driver with little to do. Pretty ho-hum for most adults and teenagers, but at least it's much more visually stimulating than the unthemed Magic Kingdom version.

TOURING TIPS This ride is appealing to the eye but definitely expendable on a schedule for adults. Preschoolers, however, love it. If your preschooler is too short to drive, place the child behind the wheel and allow him or her to steer (the car runs on a guide rail) while you work the foot pedal.

A mom from North Billerica, Massachusetts, writes:

> I was truly amazed by the number of adults in the line. Please emphasize to your readers that these cars travel on a guided path and are not a whole lot of fun. The only reason I could think of for adults to be in line was an insane desire to go on absolutely every ride. The other feature about the cars is that they tend to pile up at the end, so it takes almost as long to get off as it did to get on. Parents riding with their preschoolers should keep the car going as slow as it can without stalling. This prolongs the preschooler's joy and decreases the time you will have to wait at the end.

Be aware that Fastpass is only offered on busier days and doesn't work very well at Autopia. It's typical for the wait in the Fastpass return line to exceed 20 minutes. If Autopia ranks high on your pop chart, you might be better off riding the first hour the park is open and using the standby line.

Buzz Lightyear Astro Blasters ★★★★

APPEAL BY AGE　PRESCHOOL ★★★★　GRADE SCHOOL ★★★★½
TEENS ★★★★　YOUNG ADULTS ★★★★　OVER 30 ★★★★　SENIORS ★★★★

What it is Space-travel interactive dark ride. **Scope and scale** Major attraction.
When to go Before 10:30 a.m. or after 6 p.m. **Special comments** A real winner!
Duration of ride About 4½ minutes. **Average wait in line per 100 people ahead
of you** 3 minutes. **Loading speed** Fast.

DESCRIPTION AND COMMENTS This attraction is based on the space-commando character Buzz Lightyear from *Toy Story*. The marginal story line has you and Buzz Lightyear trying to save the universe from the evil Emperor Zurg. The indoor ride is interactive to the extent that you can spin your car and shoot simulated laser cannons at Zurg and his minions.

A similar attraction at the Magic Kingdom at Walt Disney World opened with little fanfare in 1998 but immediately became one of the most popular attractions in the park. The Disneyland version, situated across from Star Tours, is much the same except mobile guns allow more accurate aiming. Don't forget to smile! There is an in-ride photo that you can actually e-mail to yourself for free from kiosks at the exit.

Praise for Buzz Lightyear is almost universal. This comment from a Massachusetts couple is typical:

> Buzz Lightyear was the surprise hit of our trip! My husband and I enjoyed competing for the best score so much that we went on this ride several times during our stay. Definitely a must, especially when there's no wait.

TOURING TIPS Each car is equipped with two laser cannons and a score-keeping display. Each score-keeping display is independent, so you can compete with your riding partner. A joystick allows you to spin the car to line up the various targets. Each time you pull the trigger, you'll release a red laser beam that you can see hitting or missing the target. Most folks' first ride is occupied with learning how to use the equipment (fire off individual shots as opposed to keeping the trigger depressed) and figuring out how the targets work. The next ride (as with certain potato chips, one is not enough), you'll surprise yourself by how much better you do. Unofficial Guide readers are unanimous in their praise of Buzz Lightyear. Some guests, in fact, spend several hours on the attraction, riding again and again. See Buzz Lightyear after riding Space Mountain and Star Tours first thing in the morning.

Captain EO ★★★

APPEAL BY AGE　PRESCHOOL ★★★　GRADE SCHOOL ★★★½　TEENS ★★★
YOUNG ADULTS ★★★½　OVER 30 ★★★½　SENIORS ★★★½

What it is 3-D film with special effects. **Scope and scale** Major attraction. **When to
go** Before noon or after 4 p.m. **Special comments** Adults should not be put off by

the sci-fi theme or rock music. The loud, intense show with tactile effects frightens some young children. **Duration of show** Approximately 17 minutes. **Preshow** 8 minutes. **Probable waiting time** 15 minutes (at suggested times).

Loud   Scary

DESCRIPTION AND COMMENTS In response to pop music star Michael Jackson's death in 2009, Disney brought back Jackson's 3-D space-themed rock music video, *Captain EO*, for a limited engagement in its theme parks. *Captain EO* originally ran in Epcot 1986–1994. There's no telling how long it'll last on its second run in Disneyland, but showings have been sparsely attended during our recent visits, so it's possible that Disney may posthumously pull the plug on the King of Pop at any point. The film has an exceptionally loud soundtrack and a propensity to frighten small children.

Captain EO is sort of the ultimate music video. Starring Jackson and directed by Francis Coppola, this 3-D space fantasy is more than a film; it's a happening. Action on the screen is augmented by in-theater lighting and hydraulic moving seats that enforce involuntary audience participation, though the original laser and fog effects have sadly not returned. There's not much of a story, but there's plenty of music and dancing performed by some of the most unlikely creatures ever to shake a tail feather. If nothing else, *Captain EO* reminds us that music videos once contained more than young urbanites dancing in clubs or five ill-dressed, unshaven guys whining onstage. Unfortunately, the 70-millimeter film looks fuzzy and faded compared to modern projection methods, and the aggressive bouncing with every bass beat grows bothersome.

TOURING TIPS Shows usually begin every 20 minutes. The sound level is earsplitting, frightening some young children. Many adults report that the loud soundtrack is distracting, even uncomfortable. Avoid seats in the first several rows; if you sit too close to the screen, the 3-D images don't focus properly. If the bouncing floor bothers you, ask for a stationary seat in the last row.

Disneyland Monorail System ★★★

APPEAL BY AGE PRESCHOOL ★★★½ GRADE SCHOOL ★★★★ TEENS ★★★½
YOUNG ADULTS ★★★★   OVER 30 ★★★½   SENIORS ★★★★

What it is Scenic transportation. **Scope and scale** Major attraction. **When to go** During the hot, crowded period of the day (11:30 a.m.–5 p.m.). **Special comments** Nice, relaxing ride with some interesting views of the park; take the monorail to Downtown Disney for lunch. **Duration of ride** 12–15 minutes round-trip. **Average wait in line per 100 people ahead of you** 10 minutes. **Assumes** 3 monorails operating. **Loading speed** Moderate–fast.

Thumbs Up for the Whole Family

DESCRIPTION AND COMMENTS The monorail is a futuristic transportation ride that affords the only practical opportunity for escaping the park during the crowded lunch period and early afternoon. Boarding at the Tomorrowland monorail station, you can commute to the Disneyland Resort hotels and Downtown Disney complex, where it's possible to have a nice lunch without fighting the crowds. For those not interested in lunch, the monorail provides a tranquil trip with a nice view of Downtown Disney, Disney California Adventure theme park, Fantasyland, and Tomorrowland. The new Mark VII monorails have a sleek, retro look but can get quite hot inside during the summer (no air-conditioning!).

TOURING TIPS We recommend using the monorail to commute to Downtown Disney for a quiet, relaxing lunch away from the crowds and the heat. If you only want to experience the ride, go whenever you wish; the wait to board is usually 15–25 minutes except in the two hours before closing when everyone tries to leave at once. Also note that during busy times you may be required to disembark and then queue up to reboard at Downtown Disney. The monorail does not provide service during the evening fireworks at Disneyland Park and ceases to bring guests into the park 30 minutes before closing.

DISNEY DISH WITH JIM HILL

MAKING ROOM FOR A MARVEL-OUS TOMORROWLAND EXPANSION On the heels of Marvel's *The Avengers* and *Iron Man 3* each earning over $1 billion at the worldwide box office in 2012 and 2013 respectively (not to mention how enthusiastic Disneyland visitors have been about the "Iron Man Tech Presented by Stark Industries" exhibit at Innoventions), the Imagineers are now finally getting serious about adding some Marvel-themed attractions to Disneyland. But what may surprise some is the lengths that Imagineers are apparently willing to go to create room for these proposed rides and shows. At least one version of this ambitious plan calls for the monorail route through Tomorrowland to be simplified and the PeopleMover tracks to be removed entirely. That would open up a huge chunk of property that Disneyland's Motor Boat Cruise used to occupy for development, which the Imagineers hope to use as the site of a cutting-edge thrill ride that would pay tribute to the Marvel Universe.

Disneyland Railroad

DESCRIPTION AND COMMENTS The Disneyland Railroad makes a regular stop at the Tomorrowland Railroad Station. Usually the wait to board here is short.

Finding Nemo Submarine Voyage ★★★★

APPEAL BY AGE	PRESCHOOL ★★★★	GRADE SCHOOL ★★★★	TEENS ★★★½
YOUNG ADULTS ★★★★		OVER 30 ★★★½	SENIORS ★★★

What it is Simulated submarine ride. **Scope and scale** Headliner. **When to go** Before 10 a.m. or during evening parades or fireworks. **Duration of ride** 11½ minutes. **Average wait in line per 100 people ahead of you** 7½ minutes. **Assumes** All 8 subs operating. **Loading speed** Slow–moderate.

DESCRIPTION AND COMMENTS The Finding Nemo Submarine Voyage ride is based on the story line of the hit Disney-Pixar animated feature *Finding Nemo.* Here you board a submarine in a loading area situated below the Disneyland monorail station in Tomorrowland. After a quick lap of the open-air lagoon, the sub passes through a waterfall and inside to follow the general *Finding Nemo* story. Special effects center on a combination of traditional Audio-Animatronics and, once you're inside the dark interior of the building, what appear to be rear-projection screens, underwater, at a distance of 3–10 feet from the sub's windows. Encased in rock and shipwrecks, the screens are natural looking and allow the animated characters to appear three-dimensionally in the undersea world. Other elements include traveling through a minefield and a sea of jellyfish (very cool) and entering the mouth of a whale. The onboard sound system allows the story to "travel" from front to back of the sub, and the visual experience is different depending on what seat you're in.

The attraction is well done. You don't have to be a Nemo fan to be impressed by the scale and effects. It's not fast-paced but, rather, leisurely in the way that Pirates of the Caribbean is.

TOURING TIPS Finding Nemo Submarine Voyage is a theatrical and technical success but in many ways an engineering failure. By lengthening the duration of the voyage, by failing to provide adequate loading facilities, and by being slowed down due to a technical dispatching constraint, the Imagineers have reduced the attraction's capacity to about 900 guests per hour, a shockingly small capacity for a headliner attraction. Further, owing to the low carrying capacity, the subs are not a good candidate for Fastpass (all Fastpasses would be gone before noon).

Although Finding Nemo isn't as immensely popular as when it first opened, a sizable percentage of the guests on hand at park opening head straight for the subs—only if you are literally among the first 70 people to enter the park and arrive at the subs will you be rewarded with a short wait. But here's the kicker: Adding the time it takes to reach the subs, wait to board, ride, and disembark, you will invest 35–70 minutes to ride Finding Nemo first thing in the morning, sacrificing in the process the most crowd-free touring period of the day for the other popular attractions.

We've determined that, taking the day as a whole, you make much better use of your time enjoying Space Mountain, Splash Mountain, Peter Pan's Flight, and other popular attractions during the first hour the park is open and saving the subs for later, when a parade, fireworks show, or *Fantasmic!* has siphoned a large number of guests from the line. Incidentally, arriving 15 minutes before a parade or other presentation is not an arbitrary suggestion—during this time window, the Finding Nemo line (or lines at other popular attractions) will be its shortest. The last 30 minutes before park closing is another good time to get in line.

Claustrophobes may not be comfortable with the experience, even though the sub doesn't actually submerge (we saw one 30-ish woman who started hyperventilating before the sub left the dock). Children may be scared of the same thing, or of the encounter with sharks (they keep their distance). The sharks here are a bit less menacing than in the movie too.

The bright-yellow subs, revived from the previous attraction, have been reengineered with electric power to minimize noise and pollution. The subs fit 40 people. It's not easy to get 40 aboard, however, because the seats are narrow and a few guests take up two. Ideally, large guests should aim to be in one of the four seats at the front or back, but this may be difficult to negotiate. Wheelchair-bound guests or those who can't get down the spiral staircase into the sub can view the experience from a special topside viewing room (seats about six able-bodied persons plus two wheelchairs). With the exception of one small animated effect, the visual is identical (perhaps faster), but despite a large monitor the creatures appear smaller than when viewing them through a real porthole. The wait for the alternate viewing area is usually brief (ask a cast member how to bypass the standby line), and there are Mickeys hidden in the dive lockers inside.

A reader from Sydney, Australia, disagrees with our Finding Nemo rating, writing:

> The ride that was the most overrated was Finding Nemo. Perhaps it would rate high for the under 8-year-olds, but for our group it was one of the worst rides. It was boring, had rushing water, moved slowly, and creaked with age. What made it worse was that it had a high rating and this raised expectations.

Innoventions ★★★

APPEAL BY AGE	PRESCHOOL ★	GRADE SCHOOL ★★★	TEENS ★★
YOUNG ADULTS ★★★	OVER 30 ★★½		SENIORS ★★★½

What it is Multifaceted attraction featuring static and hands-on exhibits relating to products and technologies of the near future. **Scope and scale** Major diversion. **When to go** On your second day or after you have seen all the major attractions. **Special comments** Most exhibits demand time and participation to be rewarding; not much gained here by a quick walk-through; very commercial but well presented.

DESCRIPTION AND COMMENTS Modeled after a similar attraction at Epcot in Walt Disney World, Innoventions was part of the 1996–2000 Tomorrowland renovation. In 2008 Disney scrapped the trade show–like collection of high-tech gizmos and games and borrowed a page from the park's ancient past. One of the most beloved and often remembered attractions of Disneyland's early years was the Monsanto House of the Future, a stand-alone building with a curved spaceship-style exterior and rooms outfitted with furniture and appliances forecast to be in everyone's home before the millennium. This time around, sans Monsanto, it's the Dream Home, located in the middle of the ground floor of Innoventions. Surrounding the Dream Home are rooms from equally futuristic "neighbors'" homes, complete with actors playing the neighbors. Between the neighbors and a member of the Dream Home family, you are guided on a tour of the home's wondrous rooms and the technology within them. A grand piano in the great room is networked to a music teacher across the country. In the dining room, touch screens in the dinner table allow the family to assemble a scrapbook. A 100-inch television dominates the family room. The kitchen, which will remind you of the bridge of the Starship *Enterprise,* is of course the mother lode: among its many amazements is a computer that reads RFID (radio-frequency identification) "smart" labels on food packages and warns you if you're about to chug a glass of milk past its expiration date; the same computer will alert you if you don't have an ingredient on hand for a recipe you're making. A story line concerning the Dream Home family, the Eliases, sort of ties everything together. On the second floor you'll find an entertaining 15-minute show demonstrating Honda's ASIMO, an impressive humanoid robot capable of walking autonomously, climbing stairs, and kicking soccer balls. Also upstairs are some Xbox 360 Kinect video game consoles, Siemens's Project Tomorrow simulations (as also seen at Epcot's Spaceship Earth), and St. Joseph Hospital's interactive health-living play area.

In 2013 Disney temporarily turned a corner of Innoventions over to "Stark Industries" for interactive exhibitions of Iron Man's armored suits. The "advertraction" for the superhero film franchise, which allowed guests to simulate using Tony Stark's explosive outerwear, marked the first appearance of a Marvel Comics character (now owned by Disney) inside Disneyland.

A reader from Washington state likes the Dream Home but sees it as a Band-Aid:

> Innoventions seems a little more coherent than it was, now that the model house has been installed, but I don't get the whole point. It still strikes me as filling up room until the Disney people figure out what "real" attraction they're going to put in there.

TOURING TIPS The Dream Home creates order and continuity at Innoventions, where previously there was an almost random assemblage of games, gadgets, and imponderables. It also provides structure, with the house tour regimenting the way you view the exhibit and probably extending the amount of time you would have spent there otherwise. A brief Iron Man–driven attendance bump aside, crowds are rarely an issue at this attraction. Puzzlingly, Disney recently reversed this attraction's crowd flow, eliminating the Tom Morrow animatronic introduction and forcing guests to climb the former exit ramp and enter on the second story. Lately, the building's carousel structure hasn't been rotating, lending credence to rumors that this location might not have a long future.

We recommend that you spend time at Innoventions on your second day. If you have only one day, visit sometime during the evening if you have the time and endurance. Be forewarned that when you return home, your wife will want to remodel the kitchen.

Incidentally, Innoventions is a great place to hide out during inclement weather.

Be aware that this attraction usually opens one hour after the rest of the park and shuts its doors to new entrants two hours before the official closing time.

Jedi Training Academy   ★ ★ ★ ½

APPEAL BY AGE	PRESCHOOL ★★★★½	GRADE SCHOOL ★★★★½	TEENS ★★★½
YOUNG ADULTS ★★★½	OVER 30 ★★★★		SENIORS ★★★★

What it is Live entertainment where young audience members are trained to be Jedis. **Scope and scale** Major diversion. **When to go** See *Times Guide* for performance times. **Duration of show** 25 minutes.

DESCRIPTION AND COMMENTS Staged at the Tomorrowland Terrace Theater, the *Jedi Training Academy* recruits 30 young volunteers and trains them to fight with a light saber (an elegant, if plastic, weapon). The training consists of practicing a surprisingly long set of fencing-style moves while the audience gets to enjoy the minimal comprehension by some of the youngest Jedis. Just when the training ends, Darth Vader and Darth Maul arrive with a couple of Stormtroopers, and the young recruits meet them in "battle," with each Jedi getting his or her turn to take a whack at a Darth. All volunteers are awarded a *Jedi Training Academy* diploma. It's a great photo op for parents and a major hoot for everyone else. For a London, England, mother, Jedi boot camp was a highlight of the trip:

> My 8-year-old son literally cried with joy after participating in the Jedi experience in Tomorrowland. You advise sitting in the front two rows to be picked, but actually, they picked my son only after my husband launched him onto his shoulders to draw their attention. I noticed that they especially picked other kids on their parents' shoulders.

TOURING TIPS There are two prime viewing locations: standing room on the show floor underneath the overhang, and seating at the Terrace counter-service restaurant. There are only 10–20 tables with decent views of the show, so make sure to stake them out early. Otherwise, there is plenty of standing room space around the sides of the stage.

To be chosen to participate, arrive 20–30 minutes early and seat your child in the first couple of rows surrounding the stage. Jedis look for energetic and excited children to recruit; wearing a *Star Wars* T-shirt helps, but don't bring your own light saber because those are supplied.

Space Mountain *(Fastpass)* ★★★★½

APPEAL BY AGE	PRESCHOOL ★★★	GRADE SCHOOL ★★★★	TEENS ★★★★★
YOUNG ADULTS ★★★★★		OVER 30 ★★★★½	SENIORS ★★★★

What it is Roller coaster in the dark. **Scope and scale** Super-headliner. **When to go** Right after the park opens or use Fastpass. **Special comments** Much improved; must be 40" tall to ride. **Duration of ride** 2¾ minutes. **Average wait in line per 100 people ahead of you** 3½ minutes. **Loading speed** Moderate.

Dark Scary Lose Things Queasy Rough Muss Your 'Do

DESCRIPTION AND COMMENTS Space Mountain is an indoor roller coaster with a theme of high-speed interstellar travel. Roller coaster aficionados will tell you (correctly) that Space Mountain is a designer version of the Wild Mouse, a midway ride that's been around for at least 50 years. There are no long drops or swooping hills as there are on a traditional roller coaster—only quick, unexpected turns and small drops. Disney's contribution essentially was to add a space theme to the Wild Mouse and put it in the dark. And this does indeed make the Mouse seem wilder.

The most surprising thing about the new Space Mountain is its aesthetic beauty. No, we're not kidding. The vistas of the solar system and the stars, the distant galaxies, and passing comets are intoxicating and very realistic. Because you cannot see the ride's infrastructure, Space Mountain is no longer simply a roller coaster in a dimly lit building with some Buck Rogers planets and meteors projected on the ceiling. Because you can't see the track or anticipate where your vehicle will go, your eyes are free to feast on the rich visuals. Since 2009, Disney has transformed Space Mountain into Ghost Galaxy for Halloween, adding atmospheric audio and video projections of an angry space ghost (no, not that Space Ghost) chasing you through the cosmos. The interstellar specter is more goofy than genuinely scary, but it makes a fun novelty for the spooky season. Nighttime video projections, which make the iconic conical building look like it's crumbling to dust or crackling with electricity, are the most impressive element of the overlay.

TOURING TIPS Space Mountain is one of the park's most popular attractions. Experience it immediately after the park opens or use Fastpass.

Starcade

DESCRIPTION AND COMMENTS Starcade is nothing more than a moderately sized electronic-games arcade. Since the second floor was sealed off and much of the floor space was given over to sci-fi souvenirs, the most interesting items in here are a handful of vintage arcade machines such as *TRON* and *Pac-Man.* Note the full-size versions of *Fix It Felix Jr.,* the fictional coin-op from *Wreck-It Ralph.*

TOURING TIPS Enjoy your time in the area with a pocket full of quarters.

Star Tours: The Adventures Continue *(Fastpass)* ★★★★½

**APPEAL BY AGE   PRESCHOOL ★★★★   GRADE SCHOOL ★★★★½
TEENS ★★★★★   YOUNG ADULTS ★★★★½   OVER 30 ★★★★½   SENIORS ★★★★★**

What it is Space-flight simulation ride. **Scope and scale** Headliner. **When to go** Before 11 a.m. or use Fastpass. **Special comments** A blast; not to be missed; frightens many small children; expectant mothers are also advised against riding; must be 40" tall to ride. **Duration of ride** Approximately 7 minutes. **Average wait in line per 100 people ahead of you** 6 minutes. **Assumes** 4 simulators operating. **Loading speed** Moderate.

Scary   Queasy   Rough

DESCRIPTION AND COMMENTS When Disney's first modern flight simulator ride debuted in 1987, guests lined up for hours for their hyperspace voyage into a galaxy far, far away. But time and technology march on, and because George Lucas is never finished tinkering with the *Star Wars* universe, Star Tours received a top-to-bottom overhaul in 2011. The original StarSpeeder 3000 cabins (retro-christened as the model 1000) have been upgraded with cutting-edge digital 3-D screens (the sharpest and clearest that we've ever seen) and new in-cabin audio-animatronic figures of C-3P0, your golden droid pilot. During your inevitably turbulent travels, you'll bump, twist, and dive into a who's who of *Star Wars* icons, with heroes Master Yoda and Admiral "It's A Trap!" Akbar on your side, and villains Darth Vader and Boba Fett on your back. Jedi junkies will want to know that the refreshed ride takes place between episodes III and IV, so you'll be visiting planets from both the classic trilogy—such as icy Hot and arid Tatooine—and the not-so-classic prequels, including Geonosis (home of the dreaded Death Star) and Naboo (home of the equally dreaded Jar Jar Binks).

The big twist is that the six possible cosmic destinations and five celebrity cameos are randomly combined into 54 different story variations, giving the attraction unprecedented re-ridability (though you may see all 11 potential ride elements in as few as three voyages). Fans of the former ride will be thrilled to find a wealth of references (along with hidden Disney characters and *Star Wars* inside jokes) inside the detailed queue, and those made uncomfortable by the old ride's jerkiness will be surprised at how smooth and well-synchronized the reprogrammed experience now is.

TOURING TIPS Disney has a galactic-size smash on its hands with the refreshed Star Tours. With only two-thirds the carrying capacity of Walt Disney World's version, Disneyland's Star Tours has seen multihour waits, so grab a Fastpass as early in the morning as possible. If you have young children (or anyone) who are apprehensive about this attraction, ask the attendant about switching off (see page 149).

LIVE ENTERTAINMENT *and* SPECIAL EVENTS

LIVE ENTERTAINMENT IN THE FORM OF BANDS, Disney character appearances, parades, singing and dancing, and ceremonies further enliven and add color to Disneyland Park on a daily basis. For specific information about what's happening on the day you visit, check the daily entertainment schedule in the *Times Guide*. Be forewarned, however, that if you are on a tight schedule, it is impossible to both see the park's featured attractions and take in the numerous and varied live performances offered. In our one-day touring plans, starting on page 365, we exclude the live performances in favor of seeing as much of the park as time permits. This is a tactical decision based on the fact that the parades and *Fantasmic!*, Disneyland Park's river spectacular, siphon

The Smith family from East Wimple stakes out their viewing spot for Fantasmic!

crowds away from the more popular rides, shortening waiting lines.

The color and pageantry of live events around the park are an integral part of the Disneyland Park entertainment mix and a persuasive argument for second-day touring. Though live entertainment is varied, plentiful, and nearly continuous throughout the day, several productions are preeminent.

Fantasmic! ★★★★★

Loud   Scary

DESCRIPTION AND COMMENTS *Fantasmic!* is a mixed-media show presented one or more times each evening that the park is open late (10 p.m. or later). Staged at the end of Tom Sawyer Island opposite the Frontierland and New Orleans Square waterfronts, *Fantasmic!* is far and away the most extraordinary and ambitious outdoor spectacle ever attempted in any theme park. Starring Mickey Mouse in his role as the sorcerer's apprentice from *Fantasia,* the production uses lasers, images projected on a shroud of mist, fireworks, lighting effects, and music in combinations so stunning that you can scarcely believe what you have seen.

Incidentally, if you invested in the Glow with the Show light-up ears that synchronize with DCA's *World of Color* show (see page 316), you'll find that they interact with *Fantasmic!* as well. At times, an exclusive viewing area may be offered for hat holders, intensifying the impact of the illumination effects.

The plot is simple: good versus evil. The story gets lost in all the special effects at times, but no matter—it is the spectacle, not the story line, that is so overpowering. While *beautiful, stunning,* and *powerful* are words that immediately come to mind, they fail to convey the uniqueness of this presentation. In recent years, the production has been upgraded with brighter high-definition projectors and a 45-foot-tall full-bodied fire-breathing dragon (nicknamed Murphy) for the finale. It could be argued, with some validity, that *Fantasmic!* alone is worth the price of Disneyland Park admission. Needless to say, we rate *Fantasmic!* as not to be missed.

TOURING TIPS It is not easy to see *Fantasmic!* For the first show particularly, guests begin staking out prime viewing spots along the edge of the New Orleans Square and Frontierland waterfronts as much as four hours in advance. Similarly, good vantage points on raised walkways and terraces are also grabbed up early. A mom from Lummi Island, Washington, dismantled her Disney stroller to make a nest:

> We used the snap-off cover on the rental stroller to sit on during Fan-tasmic! *since the ground was really cold.*

Along similar lines, a middle-aged New York man wrote, saying:

> *Your excellent guidebook also served as a seat cushion while seated on the ground waiting for the show to begin. Make future editions thicker for greater comfort.*

The best seats in the house are at the water's edge. For adults, it is really not necessary to have an unobstructed view of the staging area because most of the action is high above the crowd. Children standing in the closely packed crowd, however, are able to catch only bits and pieces of the presentation. The best elevated view can be had from the bridge over the Pirates of the Caribbean queue.

Probably the most painless strategy for seeing *Fantasmic!* is to attend the second show. Usually, the second performance follows the first by about 90 minutes. At the second *Fantasmic!* fewer people are in the park and viewing conditions are less crowded. If you let the crowd for the first show clear out and then take up your position, you should be able to find a good vantage point, as a Salt Lake City reader found:

> During the first showing, I perused the shops in New Orleans Square and then found a place to sit for awhile. When the show was almost over, I worked my way to Pirates and stationed myself in front of the entrance. When the show was over and the crowd started to disperse, I worked my way down to the riverfront and into prime seating where I was able to watch the fireworks and the second showing of Fantasmic!

Another good strategy is to board the train as the first show is concluding and disembark in New Orleans Square.

Rain and wind conditions sometimes cause *Fantasmic!* to be canceled. Unfortunately, Disney officials usually do not make a final decision about whether to proceed or cancel until just before showtime. We have seen guests wrapped in ponchos sit stoically in rain or drizzle for more than an hour with no assurance that their patience and sacrifice would be rewarded. Unless you can find a covered viewing spot, we do not recommend staking out vantage points on rainy or especially windy nights. On nights like these, pursue your own agenda until 10 minutes or so before showtime, and then head to the waterfront to see what happens.

You can view *Fantasmic!* from a special reserved viewing area located near the Tom Sawyer Island raft dock. To make reservations, call ☎ 714-781-4400. The price for the dock-viewing area runs $59 for adults and $49 for children ages 3–9. A dessert box is included, but be aware of this Petaluma, California, family's experience:

> We did the reserved seating for Fantasmic!, and that was pretty much a waste of money. After picking up our tickets earlier in the day, we stood in line at the designated spot at 7:50 p.m. for the 8 p.m. opening of first-come, first-serve seating. Somehow every seat was taken by the time we got to the front of the line at 8:15 p.m., except for four seats in the very back. When the show began at 9 p.m., we had a terrible view of the show between the light pole and people's heads in front of us. Note that they serve hot coffee/chocolate and give a dessert box, but bring your own treats for the kids—the dessert box is full of fancy desserts that no child recognizes or wants to eat.

However, a multigenerational Seattle family called it the "highlight of the trip":

> Because we had a large party (8), we opted to pay for the dessert package for Fantasmic! Everyone thought it was well worth it, especially since our trip only coincided with one showing. I would HIGHLY

recommend the dessert package, especially if you have seniors in your touring group. Being able to sit in a chair was worth the price alone!

Finally, make sure to hang on to children during *Fantasmic!* and to give them explicit instructions for regrouping in the event that you are separated. Be especially vigilant when the crowd disperses after the show.

PARADES

DISNEY THEME PARKS ARE FAMOUS THE WORLD OVER for their parades. Currently, there is a parade every day in late afternoon or early evening. On days when the park closes late (10 p.m.–midnight), the parade runs twice.

The parades are full-blown Disney productions with some combination of floats, huge inflated balloons of the characters, marching bands, old-time vehicles, dancers, and, of course, literally dozens of costumed Disney characters. Themes for the parades vary from time to time, and a special holiday parade is always produced for Christmas. Mickey's Soundsational Parade, Disneyland's latest daytime processional, premiered in 2011. It features a whimsical marching band theme with brand-new floats dedicated to *The Princess and the Frog, The Little Mermaid,* and a Keith Moon–channeling Drummer Mickey. The new parade is a big improvement over Disneyland's previous street party, and well worth watching from the stick-twirling drum-line kickoff to the *Mary Poppins* finale.

Parades always draw thousands of guests from the attraction lines. We recommend, therefore, watching from the departure point. With this strategy you can enjoy the parade, and then while the parade is continuing on its route, take advantage of the diminished lines at the attractions. Watching a parade that begins in Fantasyland from Small World Mall affords the greatest mobility in terms of accessing other areas of the park when the parade has passed.

Main Street is the most crowded area from which to watch a parade when the route begins at Town Square. The opposite is true when the parade begins in Fantasyland. The upper platform of the Main Street train station affords the best viewing perspective along the route. The best time to get a position on the platform is when the parade begins in Fantasyland. When this happens, good spots on the platform are available right up to the time the parade begins. When you are at the end of the parade route, you can assume that it will take the parade 15–18 minutes to get to you. Some recent Disney parades have included show stops, meaning that the floats freeze in place for a few minutes while the cast dances in the streets. When this occurs, show stop viewing spots will be marked on the park map. There are usually three locations (two on Main Street and one in Fantasyland), with the Small World Mall providing the best perspective.

Keep an eye on your children during parades and give them explicit instructions for regrouping in the event that you get separated. Children constantly jockey for better viewing positions. A few wiggles this way and a few wiggles the other, and presto, they are lost in the

Disneyland Parade Route

Fantasyland

Frontierland

New Orleans
Square

Parade Route

Parade Route

crowd. Finally, be especially vigilant when the crowd starts dispersing after the parade. Thousands of people suddenly strike out in different directions, creating a perfect situation for losing a child or two.

LIVE ENTERTAINMENT THROUGHOUT THE PARK

PARADES AND FANTASMIC! MAKE UP only a part of the daily live-entertainment offerings at Disneyland Park. The following is an incomplete list of other performances and events that are scheduled with some regularity and that require no reservations.

DISNEY CHARACTER APPEARANCES Disney characters appear at random throughout the park but are routinely present in Mickey's Toontown, in Fantasyland, and on Main Street. Merida, still riding high on the popularity of 2012's *Brave,* draws long lines at her meet and greet in Fantasyland. An irregularly used greeting area that sometimes features Aladdin and Jasmine is located at Aladdin's Oasis in Adventureland (see the *Times Guide*). Disney princesses are on call daily at the Fantasy Faire (see page 241). Subsequent to the release of the *Tinker Bell* animated feature, pixies and fairies are all the rage (and have been in LA for years, but that's another story). An elaborate character-greeting area, Pixie Hollow, situated on the path connecting the Matterhorn Bobsleds to the central hub, accumulates substantial wait times to meet Tink and a squad of her buddies. Princess Tiana can usually be found in New Orleans Square's Court of Angels.

DISNEY CHARACTER BREAKFASTS AND DINNERS Disney characters join guests for breakfast each morning until 11 a.m. at the **Plaza Inn** on Main Street and **Storytellers Café** at the Grand Californian Hotel. Disney characters also join guests for breakfast and dinner at **Goofy's Kitchen** at the Disneyland Hotel and **Disney's PCH Grill** at Paradise Pier Hotel. **Ariel's Grotto** at Disney California Adventure serves breakfast and lunch with Ariel and friends.

DISNEY ROCK GROUPS High-energy Disney rock groups perform seasonally in Tomorrowland according to the *Times Guide*.

FIREWORKS *REMEMBER . . . DREAMS COME TRUE* Since it debuted in 2005, *Remember* has been the go-to fireworks show in between seasonal varieties and is a particular favorite among locals. The show runs the full gamut of special effects: a rousing score, spectacular firework effects, castle lighting, lasers, and an impressive flight from the fairy Tinker Bell. Julie Andrews narrates this pyrotechnic tribute to classic Disneyland attractions—featuring a pirate cannon assault on Sleeping Beauty Castle and audio from Adventure Thru Inner Space—with music from Walt Disney World's popular *Wishes* fireworks. We rate this show as five stars and not to be missed.

unofficial **TIP**
If you plan to leave the park after the fireworks, the second-floor platform of the Main Street train station affords one of the best views you'll find.

During the summer season, *Remember* is replaced by *Magical.* Tinker Bell is your host and kicks it off with a zany flight path that makes you wonder what she's on besides pixie dust. *Magical* features an array of Disney's most magical characters, including Peter Pan, Mary Poppins, and the three good fairies from *Sleeping Beauty*. Dumbo (in the form of a giant puppet) joins Tink in flight and steals the show. Broadway singer Eden Espinosa belts out the theme song, and the program also features sentimental classic Disney tunes such as "Baby Mine" from *Dumbo* and "So This Is Love" from *Cinderella*.

Two other first-rate fireworks shows—*Halloween Screams* and *Believe . . . In Holiday Magic*—are only performed seasonally and may require paid admission to an after-hours party. The summer and holiday fireworks displays also now synchronize with Glow with the Show hats; reserved viewing sections are occasionally offered as an incentive to hat wearers.

Without a doubt, the central hub is the best vantage point for watching fireworks. Unfortunately, every guest in the park won't fit in the hub at the same time. The next-best positions are at any open (that is, not canopied by trees) spots facing Sleeping Beauty Castle. We've stood between the castle and the Matterhorn, for example, and found the view just gorgeous. If those spots are taken, try any open spot without something really big, such as a Disney mountain, in the way. Concerning the latter, you'll be able to see the fireworks fine but will miss Tinker Bell. Other interesting (and less crowded) viewing angles can be found in Tomorrowland, near It's a Small World, and along the Rivers of America.

GOLDEN HORSESHOE—LAUGHING STOCK CO. The Laughing Stock Company is a Frontierland comedy show that performs inside the Golden Horseshoe Saloon on days when Billy Hill is not on the stage, and outside the building (sometimes on the second floor!) when he is. Each show is different and includes a set of zany Wild West–style characters. A particular favorite of ours is the "find a suitor," where three unsuspecting members of the crowd are selected to answer questions from the Mayor of Frontierland's less-than-handsome daughter (played by a man).

The showtimes are in the *Times Guide* as well as our Lines app, and we recommend showing up just 1 or 2 minutes before the show. They don't perform daily, but when they do perform, they can have up to eight shows throughout the late morning until late afternoon.

RETREAT CEREMONY Daily at around sunset in Town Square, an honor guard lowers the flag as the Disneyland marching band plays patriotic tunes. Members of the armed forces are encouraged to participate in this respectful ceremony and are called up to be honored by branch.

STREET ENTERTAINMENT Various bands, singers, comics, and strolling musicians entertain in spontaneous (that is, unscheduled) street performances throughout the park. Musical styles include banjo, Dixieland, steel drum, marching, and fife and drum. You'll often find the Bootstrappers, a roving band of musical pirates, roaming the waterfront near New Orleans Square. For a respite from the rides, grab a snack and listen to the ragtime piano player outside the Refreshment Corner on Main Street. You don't want to miss the Dapper Dans, a slapstick barbershop quartet that has been performing on Main Street, U.S.A. in Disneyland since 1959. While the cast changes on a regular basis, the Dans really liven up the street.

UNHERALDED TREASURES *at* DISNEYLAND PARK

UNHERALDED TREASURES are special features found in all of the Disney theme parks that add texture, context, beauty, depth, and subtlety to your visit. Generally speaking, unheralded treasures are nice surprises that should be accorded a little time. Lani Teshima, Unofficial Guide friend and writer for **mouseplanet.com,** knows them all. Her list follows.

TREASURE Snow White's Grotto and Wishing Well
LOCATION The front right of Sleeping Beauty Castle

A SLOW STROLL AROUND THE SLEEPING BEAUTY CASTLE can be romantic, but sitting quietly to its right is Snow White's Grotto and Wishing Well. If you stop for a few moments, you can hear the voice of Snow White singing "I'm Wishing" in the area. The grotto includes a trickling waterfall framing statues of Snow White and the Seven Dwarfs, placed on three tiers in such a way as to make Snow White appear to be off in the distance in an optical illusion that masks the fact that her statue is the same height as those of the dwarfs. Next to the grotto is a wishing well, where you can toss a coin and make a wish. This area is a popular place for Snow White to appear for photos, so don't be surprised to see a group of people milling around.

TREASURE Disneyland Railroad | **LOCATION** Stations in Main Street, U.S.A.; New Orleans Square; Toontown/Fantasyland; and Tomorrowland

AFTER A LONG DAY, the Disneyland Railroad offers a nice way to get from one end of the park to another. But trains held a special place in Walt Disney's heart, and the railroad offers much more than just a ride back to the park gates. Pause and turn around before you enter Main Street Station for a beautiful view of the entire length of Main Street, U.S.A. Inside the station, you can enjoy looking at model trains and other little exhibits. If you get off at the New Orleans Square Station, stop and listen—that beeping sound you hear is Walt Disney's 1955 Disneyland Park opening speech in landline telegraphic code. And don't forget to ride from Tomorrowland back to Main Street so you can enjoy an unexpected treat: two large indoor dioramas inside the train tunnel, one depicting the Grand Canyon and another depicting a primeval world, complete with large-scale dinosaurs!

TREASURE Windows on Main Street | **LOCATION** Main Street, U.S.A.

DO YOU EVER WONDER IF THE NAMES ON ALL THOSE WINDOWS on Main Street mean anything? The names represent very special people who have had a profound influence on the park in some way, and they are like guardian angels looking over everyone who walks through the park. The names are also often associated with "professions" related to what the person used to do when he or she worked for Disney. For example, the inscription for a window dedicated to the person who modeled Disneyland's waterways reads, "Decorative Fountains and Watercolor by Fred Joerger." Disneyland still occasionally bestows this window honor in official dedication ceremonies in the park.

TREASURE Frontierland Shootin' Exposition | **LOCATION**

SMACK IN THE MIDDLE OF FRONTIERLAND is the shooting gallery where cowpokes can close an eye and squeeze the trigger to try to get their target to ping, ting, move, or light up. Don't discount the Frontierland Shootin' Exposition as just another arcade gimmick. Everything about this well-themed attraction is dusty and rustic—except the laser-powered guns, which are both safe and cause little wear on the targets—and about the only things missing are blowing tumbleweeds and Clint Eastwood.

TREASURE Edible Plants | **LOCATION** Tomorrowland

DON'T BE SO SURE THAT ALL YOU CAN FIND in Disneyland is junk food. The Disney theme parks are known for their magnificent landscaping, but did you know that many of the plants in Tomorrowland are edible, emphasizing the practicality of a future where the garden plants do double-duty as your vegetable garden? For example, the entryway to Tomorrowland is lined with orange trees, and the bushes along the walkways are planted with leafy vegetables such as lettuce, kale, and rhubarb, as well as herbs such as sage, chives, rosemary, and basil.

TREASURE Flag Retreat Ceremony | **LOCATION** Main Street Square

EVERY DAY IN THE AFTERNOON, THE DISNEYLAND BAND or Dapper Dans vocal group marches to the front of Main Street to perform a number of Americana tunes. Park security guards then lower the American flag as the band plays "The Star-Spangled Banner" in this very respectful ceremony.

TREASURE *Partners* statue | **LOCATION** Central Hub

AT THE CASTLE END OF MAIN STREET, in the center of the circular hub, is a bronze statue of Walt Disney holding the hand of Mickey Mouse. The statue, simply called *Partners,* pays homage to the two original ambassadors of Disneyland. If you stand in front of the statue, you can get a nice shot of it with Sleeping Beauty Castle in the background. The spot is encircled by a bench, and it's a great place to meet should your family decide to split off to visit different lands. Smaller statues of other popular Disney figures such as Dumbo, Goofy, and Pluto form a ring around this garden oasis in the middle of the park.

QUIET PLACES AT DISNEYLAND PARK

PEACE AND QUIET ARE ANYTHING BUT THE NORM at Disneyland. Yet sometimes when you're overwhelmed by it all, a place to decompress is worth a lot, as a reader from Culver City, California, points out:

> I confess that I can't tolerate the hyperstimulation as well as my husband and kids. Sometimes when I'm on my ninth nerve, I'd give anything to put myself in time-out and just collapse for a while. Are there any nice out-of-the-way places in the park where this is possible?

Actually, there are a few. There's a **pier** with a canopy and benches opposite the Matterhorn Bobsleds loading area. Created for a long-departed boat ride, the pier overlooks a quiet pool. There's still ambient noise, of course, but the pier is far enough removed from the action to afford both tranquillity and a lovely setting. The **Hungry Bear Restaurant** in Critter Country offers upper and lower covered outdoor decks overlooking the Rivers of America. In between major feeding periods, the decks are decidedly low-key. **Snow White's Grotto and Wishing Well,** described on page 272, is also very pleasant, though there is a modest but continuous flow of pedestrian traffic there. Finally, the alfresco dining area of **Troubadour Tavern,** adjacent to Fantasyland Theatre, is very relaxing between shows.

TRAFFIC PATTERNS *at* DISNEYLAND PARK

WHEN WE BEGAN our research on Disneyland, we were very interested in traffic patterns throughout the park, specifically these issues:

1. WHAT ATTRACTIONS AND WHICH SECTIONS OF THE PARK DO VISITORS HEAD FOR WHEN THEY FIRST ARRIVE? When guests are admitted to the various lands, the flow of people to Tomorrowland (Space Mountain, Buzz Lightyear, and Finding Nemo Submarine Voyage) is heaviest. The next most crowded land is Fantasyland, though the crowds are distributed over a large number of attractions. Critter Country is likewise crowded with its small area and only two attractions (Splash Mountain and The Many Adventures of Winnie the Pooh). Adventureland, Frontierland, and New Orleans Square fill more slowly, with Mickey's Toontown not really coming alive until later in the morning. As the park fills, visitors appear to head for specific favored attractions that they wish to ride before the lines get long. This, more than any other factor, determines traffic patterns in the mornings and accounts for the relatively equal distribution of visitors throughout Disneyland.

ATTRACTIONS HEAVILY ATTENDED IN EARLY MORNING
ADVENTURELAND Indiana Jones Adventure | Jungle Cruise
CRITTER COUNTRY Splash Mountain
FANTASYLAND Alice in Wonderland | Dumbo the Flying Elephant Matterhorn Bobsleds | Peter Pan's Flight
TOMORROWLAND Buzz Lightyear Astro Blasters | Finding Nemo Submarine Voyage Space Mountain | Star Tours: The Adventures Continue

2. HOW LONG DOES IT TAKE FOR THE PARK TO REACH PEAK CAPACITY FOR A GIVEN DAY? HOW ARE THE VISITORS DISPERSED THROUGHOUT THE PARK? There is a surge of early birds who arrive before or around opening time but are quickly dispersed throughout the empty park. After the initial onslaught is absorbed, there is a bit of a lull that lasts until about an hour after opening. Following the lull, the park is inundated with arriving guests for about two hours, peaking 10–11 a.m. Guests continue to arrive in a steady but diminishing stream until around 2 p.m. Sampled lines reached their longest length noon–3 p.m., indicating more arrivals than departures in the early afternoon. For general touring purposes, most attractions develop substantial lines 9:30–11 a.m. In the early morning, Tomorrowland, Critter Country, and Fantasyland fill up first. By late morning and into early afternoon, attendance is fairly equally distributed throughout all of the "lands." Mickey's Toontown, because it is comparatively small, stays mobbed from about 11:30 a.m. on. By midafternoon, however, we noted a concentration of visitors in Fantasyland, New Orleans Square, and Adventureland, and a slight decrease of visitors in Tomorrowland.

In the late afternoon and early evening, attendance continues to be more heavily distributed in Tomorrowland, Critter Country, and Fantasyland. Though Space Mountain, Buzz Lightyear, Splash Mountain, and Star Tours remain inundated throughout the day, most of the other attractions in Tomorrowland and Critter Country have reasonable lines. In New Orleans Square, The Haunted Mansion, Pirates of the Caribbean, and the multitudes returning from nearby Critter Country keep traffic brisk. Frontierland and Adventureland (except the Indiana Jones ride) become less congested as the afternoon and evening progress.

3. HOW DO MOST VISITORS GO ABOUT TOURING THE PARK? IS THERE A DIFFERENCE IN THE TOURING BEHAVIOR OF FIRST-TIME VISITORS AND REPEAT VISITORS? Many first-time visitors accompany friends or relatives who are familiar with Disneyland and who guide their tour. These tours sometimes do and sometimes do not proceed in an orderly (clockwise or counterclockwise) touring sequence. First-time visitors without personal touring guidance tend to be more orderly in their touring. Many first-time visitors, however, are drawn to Sleeping Beauty Castle on entering the park and thus commence their rotation from Fantasyland. Repeat visitors usually proceed directly to their favorite attractions or to whatever is new.

4. WHAT EFFECT DO SPECIAL EVENTS SUCH AS PARADES, FIREWORKS, AND *FANTASMIC!* HAVE ON TRAFFIC PATTERNS? Special events such as parades, fireworks, and *Fantasmic!* pull substantial numbers of visitors from the lines for rides. Unfortunately, however, the left hand taketh what the right hand giveth. A parade or *Fantasmic!* snarls traffic flow throughout Disneyland so much that guests find themselves captive wherever they are. Attraction lines in Tomorrowland, Mickey's Toontown, Adventureland, and Fantasyland (behind the castle) diminish dramatically, making Space Mountain, Finding Nemo Submarine Voyage, Buzz Lightyear, Star Tours, the Jungle Cruise, Indiana Jones Adventure, Peter Pan's Flight, and Snow White's Scary Adventures particularly good choices during the evening festivities. The remainder of the park (Critter Country, New Orleans Square, Frontierland, Main Street, and Small World Plaza in Fantasyland) is so congested with guests viewing the parade or *Fantasmic!* that it's almost impossible to move.

5. WHAT ARE THE TRAFFIC PATTERNS NEAR TO AND AT CLOSING TIME? On our sample days, which were recorded in and out of season, park departures outnumbered arrivals beginning in midafternoon, with a substantial number of guests leaving after the afternoon parade. Additional numbers of visitors departed during the late afternoon as the dinner hour approached. When the park closed early, there were steady departures during the two hours preceding closing, with a mass exodus of remaining visitors at closing time.

When the park closed late, departures were distributed throughout the evening hours, with waves of departures following the evening parade(s), fireworks, and *Fantasmic!* Though departures increased exponentially as closing time approached, a huge throng was still on hand when the park finally shut down. The balloon effect of this last throng at the end of the day generally overwhelmed the shops on Main Street, the parking lot, trams, and the hotel shuttles, and the exits onto adjoining Anaheim streets. In the hour before closing in the lands other than Main Street, touring conditions were normally uncrowded except at Indiana Jones in Adventureland and Splash Mountain in Critter Country.

DISNEYLAND PARK TOURING PLANS

THE DISNEYLAND PARK TOURING PLANS are step-by-step plans for seeing as much as possible with a minimum of time wasted standing in line. They are designed to assist you in avoiding crowds and bottlenecks on days of moderate to heavy attendance. On days of lighter attendance (see "Selecting the Time of Year for Your Visit," page 24), the plans will still save you time but will not be as critical to successful touring.

Choosing the Right Touring Plan

Six different touring plans are presented:

- One-Day Touring Plan for Adults
- Author's Select One-Day Touring Plan
- Dumbo-or-Die-in-a-Day Touring Plan for Adults with Small Children
- Two-Day Touring Plan for Adults with Small Children
- Two-Day Touring Plan A, for Daytime Touring or for When the Park Closes Early (before 8 p.m.)
- Two-Day Touring Plan B, for Morning and Evening Touring or for When the Park Is Open Late (after 8 p.m.)

If you have two days to spend at Disneyland Park, the two-day touring plans are by far the most relaxed and efficient. The Two-Day Touring Plan A takes advantage of early-morning touring, when lines are short and the park has not yet filled with guests. This plan works well all year and is particularly recommended for days when Disneyland Park closes before 8 p.m. On the other hand, Two-Day Touring Plan B combines the efficiencies of early-morning touring on the first day with the splendor of Disneyland Park at night on the second day. This plan is perfect for guests who wish to sample both the attractions and the special magic of Disneyland Park after dark, including *Fantasmic!,* parades, and fireworks. The Two-Day Touring Plan for Adults with Small Children spreads the experience over two more-relaxed days and incorporates more attractions that both children and parents will enjoy.

For readers who have requested a Three-Day Park Hopper Touring Plan, we recommend using the Two-Day Disneyland Park Touring Plan of your choice and mixing it with the One-Day Disney California Adventure Touring Plan as you see fit. Enter Disneyland Park first, and then when DCA opens, send a runner across the Esplanade with your entire group's tickets. Because the Fastpass systems of the two parks are disconnected, you can collect Fastpasses for World of Color, Radiator Springs Racers, and a third DCA attraction simultaneously with any you've already claimed in Disneyland Park (such as Space or Splash Mountains). Just keep an eye on your return windows when juggling cross-park Fastpasses, as attendants will enforce the expiration times.

If you have only one day but wish to see as much as possible, use the One-Day Touring Plan for Adults. This plan will pack as much into a single day as is humanly possible, but it is pretty exhausting. If you prefer a more relaxed visit, try the Author's Select One-Day Touring Plan. This plan features the best that Disneyland Park has to offer (in the author's opinion), eliminating some of the less impressive attractions.

If you have small children, you may want to use the Dumbo-or-Die-in-a-Day Touring Plan for Adults with Small Children. This plan includes most of the children's rides in Fantasyland and Toontown and omits roller coasters and other attractions that small children cannot ride (because of Disney's age and height requirements), as well as rides and shows that are frightening for small children. Because this plan calls for adults to sacrifice many of the better Disney attractions, it is not recommended unless you are touring Disneyland Park primarily for the benefit of your children. In essence, you pretty much stand around, sweat, wipe noses, pay for stuff, and watch the children have fun. It's great.

An alternative to the Dumbo plan is the One-Day Touring Plan for Adults or the Author's Select One-Day Touring Plan, taking advantage of switching off, a technique whereby children accompany adults to the loading area of rides with age and height requirements but do not actually ride (see page 149). Switching off allows adults to enjoy the wilder rides while keeping the whole group together.

Park-Opening Procedures

Your progress and success during your first hour of touring will be affected by the particular opening procedure the Disney people use that day.

A. All guests are held at the turnstiles until the park opens (which may or may not be at the official opening time). On admittance, all "lands" are open. If this is the case on the day you visit, blow right past Main Street and head for the first attraction on whatever touring plan you are following.

B. Guests are admitted to Main Street 30 minutes to one hour before the remaining "lands" open. Access to the other lands is blocked by a rope barrier at the central-hub end of Main Street on these days. On admittance, move to the rope barrier and stake out a position as follows:

(1) If you are going to Indiana Jones or Splash Mountain first, take up a position in front of Plaza Pavilion at the central-hub end of Main Street on the left. Wait next to the rope barrier blocking the walkway to Adventureland. When the rest of the park opens, proceed quickly to Adventureland for Indiana Jones, or Critter Country by way of Adventureland and New Orleans Square for Splash Mountain.

(2) If you are going to Finding Nemo Submarine Voyage, Star Tours, or Space Mountain first, wait on the right at the central-hub end of Main Street. When the rope drops at opening time, bear right and zip into Tomorrowland.

(3) If you are going to Fantasyland or Frontierland first, proceed to the end of Main Street and line up at the rope, right of center.

PRELIMINARY INSTRUCTIONS FOR ALL DISNEYLAND PARK TOURING PLANS

ON DAYS OF MODERATE to heavy attendance, follow the touring plans exactly, deviating only when you do not wish to experience a listed show or ride. For instance, the touring plan may direct you to go next to Big Thunder Mountain, a roller coaster. If you do not like roller coasters, simply skip that step and proceed to the next activity.

1. Buy your admission in advance (see "Admission Options" on page 19).

2. Call ☎ 714-781-7290 the day before you go for the official opening time.

3. Become familiar with the park-opening procedures (described on page 277) and read over the touring plan of your choice so that you will have a basic understanding of what you are likely to encounter as you enter the park.

DISNEYLAND PARK ONE-DAY TOURING PLAN FOR ADULTS *(page 365)*

FOR Adults without small children.

ASSUMES Willingness to experience all major rides (including roller coasters) and shows.

If you have only one day but wish to see as much as possible, use this touring plan. It packs as much into a single day as is humanly possible, but it is pretty exhausting. Be forewarned that this plan requires a lot of walking and some backtracking; this is necessary to avoid long waits in line. A little extra walking coupled with some hustle in the morning will save you 2–3 hours of standing in line. Note that you might not complete the tour. How far you get will depend on the size of your group, how quickly you move from ride to ride, how many times you pause for rest or food, how quickly the park fills, and what time the park closes.

ABOUT EARLY ENTRY If you are eligible for early entry, arrive at the turnstiles 45–60 minutes before the early-entry period begins on Tuesday, Thursday, or Saturday (days subject to change) with admission in hand. Upon admission to the park, experience (1) Peter Pan's Flight, (2) Matterhorn Bobsleds, (3) Star Tours, and (4) Finding Nemo Submarine Voyage, and then obtain Fastpasses for Space Mountain (in that order). If you're not able to enjoy all of the above during the early-entry hour, see as many as you can. When the park opens to the general public, join the touring plan at Step 7 and proceed from there.

If you are not eligible for early entry, use the plan on a non-early-entry day (currently Sunday, Monday, Wednesday, or Friday). Do not attempt to use the plan on an early-entry day—Disneyland Park will be packed with early-entry guests before you even make it past the turnstiles. If you wish to tour on an early-entry day but are not eligible for early entry, visit DCA and save Disneyland Park for a non-early-entry day.

Note: The success of the touring plan hinges on you entering the park when it first opens. Arrive at the entrance 40 minutes before official opening time.

AUTHOR'S SELECT DISNEYLAND PARK ONE-DAY TOURING PLAN *(page 366)*

FOR Adults touring without small children.
ASSUMES Willingness to experience all major rides (including roller coasters) and shows.

This touring plan is selective, including only attractions that, in the author's opinion, represent the best that Disneyland Park has to offer.

Be forewarned that this plan requires a lot of walking and some backtracking; this is necessary to avoid long waits in line. A little extra walking coupled with some hustle in the morning will save you two to three hours of standing in line. Note that you might not complete this tour. How far you get will depend on the size of your group, how quickly you move from ride to ride, how many times you pause for rest or food, how quickly the park fills, and what time the park closes. With a little zip and some luck, it is possible to complete the touring plan even on a busy day when the park closes early.

ABOUT EARLY ENTRY If you are eligible for early entry, arrive at the turnstiles 45–60 minutes before the early-entry period begins on Tuesday, Thursday, or Saturday (days subject to change) with admission in hand. Upon admission to the park, experience (1) Peter Pan's Flight, (2) Matterhorn Bobsleds, (3) Star Tours, and (4) Buzz Lightyear Astro Blasters, in that order. If you're not able to enjoy all of the above during the early-entry hour, see as many as you can. When the park opens to the general public, join the touring plan at Step 5 and proceed from there.

If you are not eligible for early entry, use the plan on a non-early-entry day (currently Sunday, Monday, Wednesday, or Friday). Do not attempt to use the plan on an early-entry day—Disneyland Park will be packed with early-entry guests before you even make it past the turnstiles. If you wish to tour on an early-entry day but are not eligible for early entry, visit DCA and save Disneyland Park for a non-early-entry day.

Note: The success of the touring plan hinges on your entering the park when it first opens. Arrive at the entrance 40 minutes before official opening time.

DUMBO-OR-DIE-IN-A-DAY TOURING PLAN FOR ADULTS WITH SMALL CHILDREN *(page 367)*

FOR Parents with children under age 7 who feel compelled to devote every waking moment to the pleasure and entertainment of their small children.

ASSUMES Periodic stops for rest, restrooms, and refreshment.

The name of this touring plan notwithstanding, this itinerary is not a joke. Regardless of whether you are loving, guilty, masochistic, truly selfless, insane, or saintly, this touring plan will provide a small child with about as perfect a day as is possible at Disneyland Park.

If this description has intimidated you somewhat or if you have concluded that your day at Disneyland Park is as important as your children's, use the One-Day Touring Plan for Adults, making use of the switching-off option (see page 149) at those attractions that impose height or age restrictions.

Because the children's attractions in Disneyland Park are the most poorly engineered in terms of handling large crowds, this touring plan is the least efficient of our touring plans. It does represent the best way to experience most of the child-oriented attractions in one day, if that is what you hope to do. We do not make recommendations in this plan for meals. If you can, try to hustle along as quickly as is comfortable until about noon. After noon, it won't make much difference if you stop to eat or take it a little easier.

ABOUT EARLY ENTRY Do not attempt to use the plan on an early-entry day if you're not eligible for early entry—Disneyland Park will be packed with early-entry guests before you even make it past the turnstiles. If you wish to tour on an early-entry day but are not eligible for early entry, visit DCA and save Disneyland Park for a non-early-entry day.

If you are eligible for early entry, experience (1) Peter Pan's Flight, (2) Dumbo, and (3) Alice in Wonderland, in that order, followed by the other Fantasyland attractions through Step 9.

Note: The success of this touring plan hinges on you being among the first to enter the park when it opens. Arrive at the entrance 40 minutes before official opening time.

DISNEYLAND PARK TWO-DAY TOURING PLAN
FOR ADULTS WITH SMALL CHILDREN *(pages 368–369)*

FOR Parents with children under age 7 who wish to spread their Disneyland Park visit over two days.

ASSUMES Frequent stops for rest, restrooms, and refreshments.

This touring plan represents a compromise between the observed tastes of adults and the observed tastes of younger children. Included in this touring plan are many of the midway-type rides that your children may have the opportunity to experience at local fairs and amusement parks. These rides at Disneyland Park often require long waits in line, and they consume valuable touring time that could be better spent experiencing the many rides and shows found only at a Disney theme park and which best demonstrate the Disney genius. This touring plan is heavily weighted toward the tastes of younger children. If you want to balance it a bit, try working out a compromise with your kids to forgo some of the carnival-type rides (such as Mad Tea Party, Dumbo, King Arthur Carrousel, and Gadget's Go Coaster) or such rides as Autopia. All of the attractions are appropriate for children 40 inches and shorter.

Another alternative is to use one of the other two-day touring plans and take advantage of the switching-off option (see page 149). This technique allows small children to be admitted to rides such as Space Mountain, Indiana Jones, Big Thunder Mountain Railroad, Star Tours, and Splash Mountain. The children wait in the loading area as their parents ride one at a time, the nonriding parent waits with the children.

TIMING This two-day touring plan takes advantage of early-morning touring. On each day you should complete the structured part of the plan by 3 p.m. or so. We highly recommend returning to your hotel by midafternoon for a nap and an early dinner. If the park is open in the evening, come back to the park by 7:30 or 8 p.m. for the evening parade, fireworks, and *Fantasmic!*

ABOUT EARLY ENTRY Do not attempt to use the touring plan on early-entry days if you are not eligible for early entry—Disneyland Park will be packed with early-entry guests before you even make it past the turnstiles. Do day one of the plan on a non-early-entry day. The next day will be an early-entry day, so visit DCA on that day. Come back to Disneyland Park on the following non-early-entry day and proceed with day two.

If you are eligible for early entry, experience (1) Peter Pan's Flight, (2) Mr. Toad's Wild Ride, and (3) Dumbo, in that order, followed by the other Fantasyland attractions. At the end of the early-entry hour, begin the touring plan, skipping any attractions called for in the touring plan that you experienced during early entry.

Note: Because the needs of small children are so varied, we have not built specific instructions for eating into the touring plan. Simply stop for refreshments or a meal when you feel the urge. For best results, however, try to keep moving in the morning. In the afternoon, you can eat, rest often, and adjust the pace to your liking.

DISNEYLAND PARK TWO-DAY TOURING PLAN A, FOR DAYTIME TOURING OR FOR WHEN THE PARK CLOSES EARLY *(pages 370–371)*

FOR Parties wishing to spread their Disneyland Park visit over two days and parties preferring to tour in the morning.

ASSUMES Willingness to experience all major rides (including roller coasters) and shows.

TIMING This two-day touring plan takes advantage of early-morning touring and is the most efficient of all the touring plans for comprehensive touring with the least time lost waiting in line. On each day you should complete the structured part of the plan by 3 p.m. or so. If you are visiting Disneyland Park during a period of the year when the park is open late (after 8 p.m.), you might prefer our Two-Day Touring Plan B, which offers morning touring on one day and late afternoon and evening touring on the other day. Another highly recommended option is to return to your hotel around midafternoon for a well-deserved nap and an early dinner, and to come back to the park by 7:30 or 8 p.m. for the evening parade, fireworks, and live entertainment.

ABOUT EARLY ENTRY Do not attempt to use the plan on early-entry days if you are not eligible for early entry—Disneyland Park will be packed with early-entry guests before you even make it past the turnstiles. Do day one of the plan on a non-early-entry day. The next day will be an early-entry day, so visit DCA on that day. Come back to Disneyland Park on the following non-early-entry day and proceed with day two.

If you're eligible for early entry, experience (1) Peter Pan's Flight, (2) Mr. Toad's Wild Ride, (3) Matterhorn Bobsleds, and (4) Space Mountain, in that order. If you're not able to enjoy all of the above during the early-entry hour, ride as many as you can. When the park opens to the general public, continue the sequence until you've experienced all four. At that point, begin the touring plan, skipping any attractions you've already seen.

DISNEYLAND PARK TWO-DAY TOURING PLAN B, FOR MORNING AND EVENING TOURING OR FOR WHEN THE PARK IS OPEN LATE *(pages 372–373)*

FOR Parties who want to enjoy Disneyland Park at different times of day, including evenings and early mornings.

ASSUMES Willingness to experience all major rides (including roller coasters) and shows.

TIMING This two-day touring plan is for those visiting Disneyland Park on days when the park is open late (after 8 p.m.). The plan offers morning touring on the first day and late afternoon and evening touring on the other day. If the park closes early, or if you prefer to do all of your touring during the morning and early afternoon, use the Two-Day Touring Plan A, for Daytime Touring or for When the Park Closes Early.

ABOUT EARLY ENTRY If you are not eligible for early entry, do not try to use day one of the plan on an early-entry day. Disneyland Park will be packed with early-entry guests before you even get past the turnstiles.

If you are eligible for early entry and want to use day one of the plan on an early-entry day, experience (1) Peter Pan's Flight, (2) Matterhorn Bobsleds, (3) Space Mountain, and (4) Finding Nemo Submarine Voyage, in that order. If you're not able to enjoy all of the above during the early-entry hour, ride as many as you can. When the park opens to the general public, continue the sequence until you've experienced all four. At that point, begin the touring plan, skipping any attractions you've already seen.

THE DISNEYLAND NO RIDES, NO QUEUES, NO STRESS ANTI-TOURING PLAN

MOST OF OUR READERS are interested in touring plans to get them through as many attractions as possible in the most efficient manner. But, like the authors, some of you may have siblings, spouses, or other companions who are congenitally opposed to queuing for anything clanking or claustrophobic. What can Disney do to occupy your Aunt Gertie, who is dead set against standing in a line, or sitting in anything with a lap bar?

Disneyland Park is one of the few places where you can experience a full day of entertainment without getting on a ride faster than the railroad, and without waiting more than 15 minutes or so, even during the busiest season.

Yes, you can get your money's worth at Disneyland without sprinting to Space Mountain or spinning in a teacup. You just have to adjust your expectation of what constitutes an attraction. (A handful of sedate activities are available at Disney California Adventure, such as Disney Animation, the winery, and the bakery tour, but not enough to justify a full-price pass.)

Because this "anti-touring" plan is designed to eliminate stress, there is no strict order to follow the steps in, nor instructions to arrive before rope drop (though it doesn't hurt). Simply tour the park as your feet take you, skipping any suggested experiences that don't interest you. If there is more than a 15–20 minute wait for anything you want to do, simply move along and check back later. Most important, take a break after four or five hours and leave the park for a nap, meal, or swim. The key is to take your time and (literally) stop to smell the roses.

Main Street, U.S.A.

- Ride one of the vintage vehicles up Main Street to the hub, and then take a different one back.
- Look at the memorabilia in the Main Street train station, and then ride the rails for a round-trip or two around the park.
- Explore the Disneyana shop's collectible artwork inside the old Bank of Main Street.

- See *Great Moments with Mr. Lincoln,* arriving early enough to see the Steve Martin preshow and the lobby's Disney Gallery historical displays.
- Watch the classic short films inside the Main Street Cinema.
- Snoop on the antique party line telephones inside the Market House, and then sit outside at a table on Center Street, listening to the amusing sounds emanating from the windows above.
- Check out the primitive 3-D movie viewers in the Penny Arcade.
- Watch the chefs in the candy store whip up a batch of sweets.
- Catch a performance or three of the Dapper Dans, Main Street Marching Band, or Coke Corner ragtime pianist. The daily flag retreat ceremony is not to be missed.
- Try to identify the names of Disney legends and Imagineers honored on Main Street's windows.
- Stop and watch some artisans work, such as the silhouette cutters, glass sculptors, and watch painters.
- Ask the prestidigitators at the Magic Shop to demonstrate some tricks for you, and stare at the creepy optical illusion in the window.
- On the right side of the street next to the silhouette shop, sit in the chairs on the porch.
- Take a picture with the *Partners* statue in the central hub, and appreciate the surrounding flora and fauna.

Adventureland

- See the *Enchanted Tiki Room,* arriving in time to buy a Dole Whip and watch the preshow.
- Jungle Cruise is gentle fun if the line isn't long.
- If stairs aren't an issue, climb Tarzan's Treehouse, or at least enter through the exit and watch the kids going wild on the playground.
- Consider walking through the Indiana Jones queue at least once, even if you aren't interested in riding; it's an impressive (if exhausting) example of scenic design. When the posted wait time is more than 15 minutes, get a Fastpass to skip the boring exterior line. Before you climb the stairs near the loading bay, you can simply tell a cast member that you want to exit. If you are brave but impatient, Indy's single-rider line often has little to no wait.

New Orleans Square

- Haunted Mansion and Pirates of the Caribbean both move guests through quickly even on busy days, and neither is likely to disturb any but the most delicate constitutions.
- Seek out the jazz and pirate bands that play in the area.

- Poke around the lovingly detailed alleyways around the Pirates of the Caribbean exit.
- Sit outside at Café Orléans with a plate of *pommes frites* and watch the crowds go by.

Critter Country

- Stand on the bridge near Splash Mountain and watch riders take the plunge. If you dare to get damp, the single-rider wait is usually bearable.
- Feed the ducks from the porch behind the Hungry Bear Restaurant.

Frontierland

- Take a raft to Tom Sawyer Island. Explore the caves.
- Sail on the Sailing Ship *Columbia, Mark Twain,* or both. You can usually step on board just before departure time without standing in line, or board early for the best seat at the top front.
- Don't miss Billy Hill and the Hillbillies at the Golden Horseshoe. Show up early to grab a box seat and some chili. If the Hillbillies have the day off, the Laughing Stock comics are a fun diversion.
- Get to know the pygmy goats, pardoned turkeys, and other animals at the Big Thunder Ranch petting zoo. Explore the decor inside Miss Chris's cabin.
- Look for the petrified tree that was an anniversary gift from Walt to his wife; she donated it to the park. Also try to spot the jumping fish and railroad tunnel remains from Mine Train Through Nature's Wonderland, across from Big Thunder Mountain.
- Pump some quarters into the Frontierland shooting gallery.
- Walk through the Rancho del Zocalo patio, especially when decorated for Dia de Los Muertos.

Fantasyland

- Go through the Sleeping Beauty Castle walk-through, or watch the alternative experience video.
- Toss a wish into Snow White's well in front of the castle, and gaze at her grotto of handcrafted sculptures.
- Cruise Storybook Land or It's a Small World if lines are short.
- Try on some mouse ears in the Mad Hatter chapeau shop.
- Take a break with a vendor treat (such as an ear of corn) on the benches at the old motorboat dock across from the Matterhorn.
- Stick your head in the Fantasy Faire if a show is scheduled, but don't bother with the massive queue to meet a princess.
- The elevated mall near It's a Small World is a convenient spot to stand for the parade or fireworks show.
- Enjoy the stage musical inside the Fantasyland Theatre.

286 PART 5 DISNEYLAND PARK

Mickey's Toontown

- Play with the interactive doodads dotted around the building facades.
- Take a tour of Mickey's and Minnie's homes, but bail on the meet and greet if the line is out the door.
- Walk though the cleverly decorated children's playgrounds, being wary of bouncing babes.

Tomorrowland

- Take the monorail to Downtown Disney for a bite or a drink, and then return (remember your park ticket!).
- Watch young Padawans battle Sith Lords on Tomorrowland Terrace in the *Jedi Training Academy* show. Check the schedule for other entertainment on this stage.
- Explore both levels of the Innoventions building, leaving time to take in the ASIMO robot demonstration upstairs.
- Experience *Captain EO* if you can endure the rock-concert volume. Ask for a nonmoving seat in the back to avoid bouncing.
- The line for Buzz Lightyear moves swiftly, and almost everyone of all ages loves it.
- Browse the unique *Star Wars* merchandise (including build-your-own light sabers and droid action figures) in Star Traders with a life-size X-Wing overhead.
- Search for imaginatively groomed edible plants along the Tomorrowland walkways.
- Play an old-school 1980s arcade game in the Starcade.

PART SIX

DISNEY CALIFORNIA ADVENTURE

We enjoyed DCA much more than Disneyland. More fun, less strollers and little kids, more adventurous people. Just a different feeling all the way around.

—Mom from Bend, Oregon

A MOST ANTICIPATED SEQUEL

DISNEY CALIFORNIA ADVENTURE held its grand opening on February 8, 2001. Now known as DCA among Disneyphiles, the park is a bouquet of contradictions conceived in Fantasyland, starved in utero by corporate Disney, and born into a hostile environment of Disneyland loyalists who believed they'd been handed a second-rate theme park. Its parts are stunningly beautiful yet come together awkwardly, failing to compose a handsome whole. And perhaps most lamentable of all, the California theme is impotent by virtue of being all-encompassing. But despite the long odds, just a decade after its inauspicious debut, DCA has emerged from a billion-dollar metamorphosis that has finally made it an honorable companion to its storied older sibling across the Esplanade.

The history of the park is another of those convoluted tales found only in Robert Ludlum novels and corporate Disney. Southern California Disney fans began clamoring for a second theme park shortly after Epcot opened at Walt Disney World in 1982. Although there was some element of support within the Walt Disney Company, the Disney loyal had to content themselves with rumors and half-promises for two decades while they watched new Disney parks go up in Tokyo, Paris, and Florida. For years, Disney teasingly floated the "Westcot" concept, a California version of Epcot that was always just about to break ground. Whether it was a matter of procrastination or simply pursuing better opportunities elsewhere, the Walt Disney Company sat on the sidelines while the sleepy community of Anaheim became a sprawling

Disney California Adventure

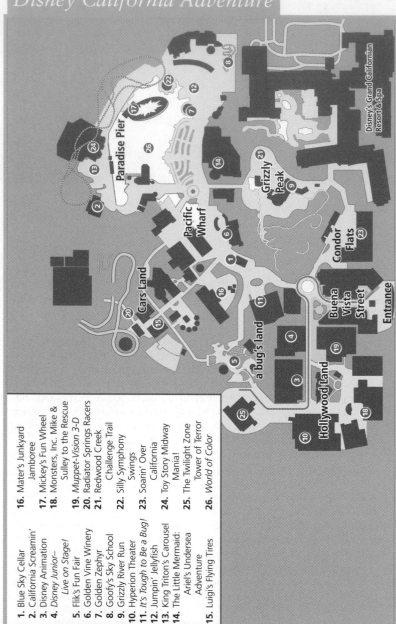

1. Blue Sky Cellar
2. California Screamin'
3. Disney Animation
4. Disney Junior–
   Live on Stage!
5. Flik's Fun Fair
6. Golden Vine Winery
7. Golden Zephyr
8. Goofy's Sky School
9. Grizzly River Run
10. Hyperion Theater
11. It's Tough to Be a Bug!
12. Jumpin' Jellyfish
13. King Triton's Carousel
14. The Little Mermaid:
    Ariel's Undersea
    Adventure
15. Luigi's Flying Tires
16. Mater's Junkyard
    Jamboree
17. Mickey's Fun Wheel
18. Monsters, Inc. Mike &
    Sulley to the Rescue
19. Muppet-Vision 3-D
20. Radiator Springs Racers
21. Redwood Creek
    Challenge Trail
22. Silly Symphony
    Swings
23. Soarin' Over
    California
24. Toy Story Midway
    Mania!
25. The Twilight Zone
    Tower of Terror
26. World of Color

city and property values skyrocketed. By the time Disney emerged from its Westcot fantasy and began to get serious about a second California park, the price tag—not to mention the complexity of integrating such a development into a mature city—was mind-boggling.

Westcot had been billed as a $2- to $3-billion, 100-plus-acre project, so that was what the Disney faithful were expecting when Disney California Adventure was announced. What they got was a park that cost $1.4 billion (slashed from an original budget of about $2.1 billion), built on 55 acres, including a sizable piece carved out for the Grand Californian Hotel. It's quite a small park by modern theme park standards, but $1.4 billion, when lavished on 55 acres, ought to buy a pretty good park.

Then there's the park's theme. Although flexible, California Adventure came off like a default setting, lacking in imagination, weak in concept, and without intrinsic appeal, especially when you stop to consider that two-thirds of Disneyland guests come from Southern California. As further grist for the mill, before the arrival of Cars Land, there was precious little new technology at work in Disney's newest theme park. Of the headliner attractions, only two—Soarin' Over California, a simulator ride, and Toy Story Midway Mania!, a "virtual dark ride"—broke new ground. All the rest are recycled, albeit popular, attractions from the Animal Kingdom and Disney's Hollywood Studios. When you move to the smaller-statured second half of the attraction batting order, it gets worse. Most of these attractions are little more than off-the-shelf midway rides spruced up with a Disney story line and facade.

From a competitive perspective, Disney California Adventure was an underwhelming shot at Disney's three Southern California competitors. The Hollywood section of DCA takes a hopeful poke at Universal Studios Hollywood, while Paradise Pier offers midway rides à la Six Flags Magic Mountain. Finally, the whole California theme has for years been the eminent domain of Knott's Berry Farm. In short, there's not much originality in DCA, only Disney's now-redundant mantra that "whatever they can do, we can do better."

Finally, after more than eight years of basically being in denial about Disney California Adventure, the Walt Disney Company seemed willing to admit that this theme park (which pulled in only about a third of Disneyland's attendance annually) needed some help. On June 15, 2012, the mouse held a grand reopening to celebrate the completion of a $1.1-billion effort, originally announced in 2007, to address DCA's problems. And that's only one portion of the $10 billion Disney has budgeted over 10 years for an extreme makeover of the entire Disneyland Resort.

Starting at the park entrance, the Imagineers have scoured every inch of DCA, injecting charm, character, and ride capacity wherever they could. A new entryway embraces the legacy of Disneyland's founder with a nostalgic re-creation of 1920s Los Angeles. That freshly poured-on theming flows all the way to Paradise Pier, where the tacky seaside amusements have been softened with new-old Victorian-era stylings. An original family-friendly dark ride based on a popular Piscean princess has been added, and the central lagoon now sports a Vegas-quality water show designed expressly to keep crowds in DCA after dark. The final element of DCA's transformation fell into place with 2012's opening of Cars Land, an entire area dedicated to the best-selling Pixar property. Cars Land has shaped up to be the biggest project to hit theme parks since Universal Orlando's Wizarding World of Harry Potter, and appears to be the final puzzle piece needed to rehabilitate DCA's poor reputation. While the park spent its first decade as a punch line, DCA is now a legitimate destination in its own right and finally rivals its older brother for turnstile entry bragging rights on busy days—something that was once almost unimaginable.

Mind you, the rest of Disneyland Resort is experiencing its own gussying up. Look for Downtown Disney to increase in size, adding new shops, clubs, and restaurants to its lineup. Likewise, Disneyland Hotel completed a face-lift in 2012, which folded festive new furnishings and up-to-date amenities into the then-56-year-old resort. Disneyland Park is also rumored to see an expansion in time for its 60th anniversary, now that the major work on DCA is done. There's also at least one new hotel on the drawing boards, plus a Disney Vacation Club property. According to the rumor mill, there might even be a third theme park in the works, possibly to be built on the Disneyland employee parking lot.

Meanwhile, as the Disneyholics churn up cyberspace debating DCA's theme and worrying whether expensive additions and patched-on personality can compensate for a flawed foundation, the rest of us will have some fun enjoying the park that is.

ARRIVING *and* GETTING ORIENTED

THE ENTRANCE TO Disney California Adventure faces the entrance to Disneyland Park across a palm-shaded pedestrian plaza called the **Esplanade.** If you arrive by tram from one of the Disney parking lots, you'll disembark at the Esplanade. Facing east toward Harbor Boulevard, Disneyland Park will be on your left and DCA will be on your right. In the Esplanade are ticket booths, the group sales office, and resort information.

Seen from overhead, Disney California Adventure is roughly arrayed in a fan shape around the park's central visual icon, **Grizzly Peak.** At ground level, however, the park's layout is not so obvious.

There are seven themed "lands" at DCA, not including **Buena Vista Street.** A left turn at the hub leads you to **Hollywood Land,** celebrating California's history as the film capital of the world. **Condor Flats, Grizzly Peak,** and **Pacific Wharf** (formerly known collectively as the Golden State land) are a trio of separate themed areas that showcase

California's architecture, agriculture, industry, history, and natural resources. You'll find Condor Flats by taking the first right as you approach the hub. Grizzly Peak will likewise be to your right, though you must walk two-thirds of the way around the mountain to reach its attractions. Pacific Wharf, the remaining Golden State–themed area, is situated along a kidney-shaped lake and can be accessed by following the walkway emanating from the hub at 7 o'clock and winding around Grizzly Peak. A fifth land, **a bug's land,** is situated opposite the Golden Vine Winery and can be reached by taking the same route. The sixth land, **Paradise Pier,** recalls seaside amusement parks of the Victorian era. It is situated in the southwest corner of the park, around the large lake. **Cars Land** is the seventh land, claiming a former parking lot behind the Pacific Wharf and Hollywood Land, with its primary entrance across from the Golden Vine Winery.

SINGLE-RIDER LINES

YOU CAN OFTEN SAVE TIME WAITING in line by taking advantage of single-rider lines, a separate line for people who are alone or don't mind riding alone or with a stranger. The objective of single-rider lines is to fill odd spaces left by groups who don't quite fill the entire ride vehicle. Because there aren't many singles and most groups aren't willing to split up, single-rider lines are usually much shorter than the regular line. Five attractions at DCA offer single-rider lines: California Screamin', Goofy's Sky School, Grizzly River Run, Radiator Springs Racers, and Soarin' Over California.

PARK-OPENING PROCEDURES

DISNEYLAND RESORT HOTEL GUESTS get a one-hour jump on the public four or more mornings each week through the Extra Magic Hours program (see page 27). You'll be required to show a hotel key card before being allowed through. This entrance is often overwhelmed, especially on early-entry days, so you may save time by walking to the front gate. All other guests will be allowed through the main entrance onto Buena Vista Street up to one hour early and held at Carthay Circle until after a brief "rope drop" musical fanfare at the official opening time. A queue for Radiator Springs Racers Fastpasses will form stretching through Hollywood Land as soon as visitors are allowed in the gates, and the crowd will be walked toward Cars Land at the appointed hour to avoid a stampede.

BUENA VISTA STREET

FROM THE ESPLANADE, where huge block letters spelling CALIFORNIA originally stood, you now pass through a new Streamline Modern entrance facade, designed after Los Angeles's fabled Pan Pacific Auditorium. (If it looks familiar, that's because it can also be recognized as the entrance to Disney's Hollywood Studios park in Florida.)

Once past the turnstiles, you'll find yourself on **Buena Vista Street,** a re-creation of 1920s Hollywood as Walt saw it when he first arrived. Immediately upon entering, to your left you'll find **Oswald's Filling Station** (a souvenir shop with a snazzy antique car parked outside) and the **Chamber of Commerce** (concealing Guest Services and First Aid). To your right you'll see lockers, restrooms, an ATM, and phones. The street leading to the central plaza is lined on both sides with a variety of shops and eateries with backstories referring to Disney's early biography. Among the shops on the east side are **Elias & Company Department Store** (the park's largest shop, named after Walt's father), **Los Feliz Five and Dime** (hats and shirts), and **Big Top Toys.** The west side of the street features an indoor shopping arcade that leads to **Kingswell Camera Shop** (a PhotoPass printing location), **Julius Katz & Sons** (kitchen items), **Atwater Ink & Paint** (collectibles), and the **Trolley Treats** candy shop (check out the Big Rock Candy Mountain model in the window). **Fiddler, Fifer & Practical Café** and adjoining **Clarabelle's Hand-Scooped Ice Cream Parlor** round out the street's retail district.

NOT TO BE MISSED AT DISNEY CALIFORNIA ADVENTURE
A BUG'S LAND *It's Tough to Be a Bug!*
CARS LAND Radiator Springs Racers
GRIZZLY PEAK Grizzly River Run | Soarin' Over California
HOLLYWOOD LAND Hyperion Theater | *Muppet-Vision 3-D* The Twilight Zone Tower of Terror
PARADISE PIER California Screamin' | Toy Story Midway Mania! | *World of Color*

The original hub area, called Sunshine Plaza, was dominated by a an arresting metal sculpture of the sun. In its place now stands Carthay Circle, home to the *Storytellers* statue (depicting a young Walt Disney with an early version of Mickey Mouse) and a replica of the **Carthay Circle Theater,** where *Snow White and the Seven Dwarfs* premiered in 1937; in this incarnation, it encloses an upscale restaurant and bar.

Winding past the new shops and facades, the **Red Car Trolley** transports guests from the park entrance to the Twilight Zone Tower of Terror and back again along freshly laid tracks.

Together, Buena Vista Street and Carthay Circle don't simply serve as a point of departure for the park's other various themed areas. They bring much-needed charm and warmth to DCA's opening act, forming a fantastic improvement over the flat cartoon-postcard facades that framed the former entryway.

Red Car Trolleys ★★½

What it is Scenic in-park transportation. **Scope and scale** Minor attraction. **When to go** The first or last 2 hours the park is open. **Duration of ride** About 11 minutes. **Average wait in line per 100 people ahead of you** 12 minutes. **Loading speed** Very slow.

DESCRIPTION AND COMMENTS Much like the vintage vehicles that travel up and down Main Street, U.S.A., at Disneyland Park, these trolley cars add visual interest to DCA's entrance area but not much entertainment value. Modeled after the Pacific Electric Railway that served the Los Angeles area in the 1920s and 1930s (as seen in *Who Framed Roger Rabbit?*), the trolleys boast authentic details such as narrating conductors who share historical tidbits during your travels, retro-styled interior advertisements, and realistic overhead power lines—unelectrified, as the new eco-friendly cars are actually battery-powered. More transportation than attraction, the Red Car Trolleys ferry guests on a one-way trip between Buena Vista Street near the park entrance and the Tower of Terror (or back the other way), making stops in Carthay Circle and Hollywood Land along the way.

TOURING TIPS It is usually faster to walk the route than to wait for the next Red Car Trolley, but if you wish to experience this nostalgic transportation, do so in the morning. Hop on at the station near the Tower of Terror exit; it should be less crowded than the station on Buena Vista Street near the park entrance.

The Red Car briefly stops serving guests several times daily so it can be commandeered as a stage for the Red Car News Boys show (see show schedule for details).

HOLLYWOOD LAND

HOLLYWOOD LAND OFFERS attractions and shopping that are inspired by California's (and Disney's) contribution to television and cinema. Visually, the land is themed as a studio back lot with sets, including an urban street scene, soundstages, and a central street with shops and restaurants that depict Hollywood's golden age.

As with most of DCA, Hollywood Land (originally known as Hollywood Pictures Backlot) has not been immune to refurbishment. The new red trolleys run from Buena Vista Street to here, and a host of further enhancements are on the drawing board.

Disney Animation ★★★½

APPEAL BY AGE	PRESCHOOL ★★★½	GRADE SCHOOL ★★★★
TEENS ★★★★	YOUNG ADULTS ★★★★½	OVER 30 ★★★★ SENIORS ★★★★½

What it is Behind-the-scenes look at Disney animation. **Scope and scale** Major attraction. **When to go** Anytime. **Special comments** Quite amusing, though not very educational. **Duration of experience** 35–55 minutes. **Probable waiting time** 5 minutes.

Thumbs Up for the Whole Family

DESCRIPTION AND COMMENTS The Disney Animation building houses a total of 10 shows, galleries, and interactive exhibits that collectively provide a sort of crash course in animation. Moving from room to room and exhibit to exhibit, you follow the Disney animation process from concept to finished film, with a peek at each of the steps along the way. Throughout, you are surrounded by animation, and sometimes it's even projected above your head and under your feet!

Because DCA's Animation building is not a working studio, the attraction does not showcase artists at work on real features, and the interactive exhibits are more whimsical than educational. "Sorcerer's Workshop," for example, is an interactive exhibit where you can act and sing with various cartoon scenes through a touch screen computer interface.

The Animation Academy, hosted by a Disney cartoonist, teaches you how to draw a Disney character; if you have any artistic inclination, you may consider it DCA's best-kept secret and find yourself taking the class repeatedly, as a Salt Lake City reader suggests:

> *[Animation Academy] turned out to be one of my absolute favorite things. I did it four times in a row and would have gone more if I wasn't starving. I plan to devote quite a bit of time to it on my next trip. I don't think you give it enough credit in your book.*

And from a Sammamish, Washington, mom:

> *I agree with the reader comment that you do not give enough emphasis to the Animation Academy drawing classes. I took three, and they were the highlight of the trip. I have no drawing ability whatsoever, but following along with the instructor I was able to make a pretty decent Donald, a passable Mickey, and a Pooh Bear, although he looked like he was in a car accident. My 4-year-old loved drawing along, my husband loved it, and my 2-year-old loved scribbling on her paper and drawing board. It was fun for the whole family.*

Both "Sorcerer's Workshop" and Animation Academy provide a good foundation on the animation process and will enhance your appreciation of the other exhibits. *Turtle Talk with Crush* is also located here (see page 298). Finally, for a WOW! moment, be sure to check out the amazing zoetrope (no, don't worry, it's not that thing that the urologist threatened you with).

TOURING TIPS On entering the Animation building, you'll step into a lobby where signs mark the entrances of the various exhibits. Look up in the lobby for a moment at the oversize projections of animations in process, including Pixar's latest hits. It takes 40–55 minutes to do all the interactive stuff and see everything. You probably won't experience much of a wait for the Disney Animation offerings except on weekends and holidays. Even then, the Animation building clears out considerably by late afternoon.

Disney Junior—Live on Stage! ★★★★

APPEAL BY AGE	PRESCHOOL ★★★★★	GRADE SCHOOL ★★★★	TEENS ★★★★
YOUNG ADULTS ★★★	OVER 30 ★★★½		SENIORS ★★★★

What it is Live show for children. **Scope and scale** Minor attraction. **When to go** Per the daily entertainment schedule. **Special comments** Audience sits on the floor. A must for families with preschoolers. **Duration of show** 20 minutes. **Probable waiting time** 25 minutes.

DESCRIPTION AND COMMENTS The show features characters from the Disney Channel's *Sofia the First, Mickey Mouse Clubhouse, Jake and the Never Land Pirates,* and *Doc McStuffins,* plus other Disney Channel characters. Refreshed in 2013, *Disney Junior* uses elaborate puppets instead of live characters on stage. A simple plot serves as the platform for singing, dancing, some great puppetry, and a great deal of audience participation. The characters, who ooze love and goodness, rally throngs of tots and preschoolers to sing and dance along with them. All the jumping, squirming, and high-stepping is facilitated by having the audience sit on the floor so that kids can spontaneously erupt into motion when the mood strikes. Even for adults without children, it's a treat to watch the tykes rev up. However, solo adults might feel creepy amid this extremely youthful exuberance, especially if they lack familiarity with any of the characters. If you have a younger child in your party, all the better: just stand back and let the video roll.

For preschoolers, *Disney Junior* will be the highlight of their day, as a Thomasville, North Carolina, mom attests:

> *[It] was fantastic! My 3-year-old loved it. The children danced, sang, and had a great time.*

Disney Junior is the second iteration of the stage show since 2007. Both versions replaced live characters with puppets, a fact that has left some parents less than enthralled. These comments from a Virginia Beach, Virginia, couple are typical:

> *We were disappointed with the newly updated [show]. This did not consist of live characters, and I think the level of excitement from the kids was lower because of this. I mean, the kids enjoyed it, but you would think they would be more excited when it's a show with some of their favorite characters.*

TOURING TIPS The show is headquartered in what was formerly the ABC Soap Opera Bistro restaurant to the right of the entrance to the Hollywood Land. It now has a new Art Deco marquee. Because the tykes just can't get enough, it has become a hot ticket. Arrive earlier on Sundays, when all showings sometimes fill to capacity. If you arrive to find a line that extends out of the main queuing area and onto the sidewalk, you might not get into the show. Count two palm trees to the left of the theater entrance; if the line extends to the left of the second palm, you probably won't make the cut. If the line hasn't extended past the second palm tree, go ahead and get in line—chances are about 90% that you'll be admitted to the next show. Once inside, pick a spot on the floor and take a breather until the performance begins.

Hyperion Theater ★★★★

APPEAL BY AGE	PRESCHOOL ★★★★	GRADE SCHOOL ★★★★½	TEENS ★★★★½
YOUNG ADULTS ★★★★★		OVER 30 ★★★★½	SENIORS ★★★★½

What it is Venue for live shows. **Scope and scale** Major attraction. **When to go** After experiencing DCA's rides. **Special comments** Great venue; not to be missed. **Duration of show** 50 minutes. **Probable waiting time** 30 minutes.

Thumbs Up for the Whole Family

DESCRIPTION AND COMMENTS This 2,000-seat theater is DCA's premier venue for live productions, many of which are based on Disney-animated films and feature Disney characters. Shows exhibit Broadway quality in every sense, except duration of the presentation, and alone are arguably worth the price of park admission. In 2011 the Hyperion was supposed to debut *Toy Story—The Musical,* an adaptation of the first Pixar film crafted for Disney's cruise ships. That plan hasn't happened yet, nor have rumors of an indoor lobby replacing the theater's current false front. For now, *Aladdin—A Musical Spectacular* is continuing its run as the most elaborate show staged at any stateside Disney theme park. A breezy stage version of the *Aladdin* story, it features familiar film tunes ("Friend Like Me" and "Prince Ali") plus one newly written ballad, along with jaw-dropping overhead flying carpet effects. If *Aladdin* is still running when you visit, we rate it not to be missed, thanks largely to the actors playing the Genie, who are given remarkably long leashes to ad lib up-to-the-minute pop-culture references that sail right over younger audience members' heads. In the evening the Hyperion is sometimes used as a stage for separate-admission concerts and special events.

TOURING TIPS The lavish productions hosted by the Hyperion Theater are rightly very popular and commonly sell out on busier days. Presentations are described, and showtimes listed, in the park *Times Guide.* The theater is multilevel. Though all the seats provide a good line of sight, we recommend that you sit on the ground level relatively close to the entrance doors (if possible) to facilitate an easy exit after the performance. Finally, be forewarned that the sound volume for Hyperion Theater productions would give heavy metal concerts a good run for the money.

Monsters, Inc. Mike & Sulley to the Rescue ★ ★ ★ ½

APPEAL BY AGE	PRESCHOOL ★★★★	GRADE SCHOOL ★★★★	TEENS ★★★★
YOUNG ADULTS ★★★★		OVER 30 ★★★½	SENIORS ★★★★

What it is Dark ride. **Scope and scale** Major attraction. **When to go** Before 11 a.m. **Special comments** Disney's best dark ride in years. **Duration of ride** 3¾ minutes. **Average wait in line per 100 people ahead of you** 4 minutes. **Loading speed** Moderate.

Dark

DESCRIPTION AND COMMENTS Based on characters and the story from the Disney-Pixar film *Monsters, Inc.,* the ride takes you through child-phobic Monstropolis as Mike and Sulley try to return baby Boo safely to her bedroom. If you haven't seen the film, the story line won't make much sense. In a nutshell, a human baby gets loose in a sort of parallel universe populated largely by amusing monsters. Good monsters Mike and Sulley try to return Boo to her home before the bad monsters get their hands on her.

The Disney Imagineers did a very good job on the Monsters, Inc. ride, re-creating the humor, characters, and setting of the film in great detail. The section of the attraction where you ride through the door warehouse with all of its lifts and conveyors is truly inspired. Special effects are first-rate, and lots of subtle and not-so-subtle jokes are worked into the whole experience. As in the Tower of Terror, you'll have to ride several times to catch them all. Before disembarking, be sure to banter with sluglike supervisor Roz, an animatronic "living character" that can see and interact with riders.

TOURING TIPS The attraction was very popular when it first opened, but today you can usually ride without too much of a wait. Because it's near several theater attractions, the ride is subject to experiencing a sudden deluge of guests when the theaters disgorge their audiences.

Monsters, Inc. is an iffy attraction for preschoolers: some love it and some are frightened. Increase your odds for a positive experience by exposing your little ones to the movie before leaving home.

DISNEY DISH WITH JIM HILL

MOVIN' RIGHT ALONG—TO BROADWAY?! Over the past two years, DCA has regularly cancelled daily presentations of *Muppet-Vision 3-D,* so that the Muppet Theater could be used to promote upcoming Walt Disney Pictures' releases such as *Frankenweenie, Oz The Great and Powerful,* and *The Lone Ranger.* So it should probably not surprise you to hear that the Imagineers are now considering cutting Kermit & Co.'s run at this theater short to make room for a new *Monsters, Inc.*–themed coaster. But Miss Piggy fans shouldn't despair. You see, Disney Theatrical (the division of the Mouse House that creates all of Disney's long-running productions for the stage) recently held a workshop for a live stage production modeled on the old *Muppets* TV show. And if all goes according to plan, it could be "time to make the music" as early as Broadway's 2015-2016 season.

Muppet-Vision 3-D ★★★★½

APPEAL BY AGE	PRESCHOOL ★★★★½	GRADE SCHOOL ★★★★½	TEENS ★★★½
YOUNG ADULTS ★★★★	OVER 30 ★★★★		SENIORS ★★★★

What it is 3-D movie featuring the Muppets. **Scope and scale** Major attraction. **When to go** Before noon or after 4 p.m. **Special comments** Must see; 3-D effects and loud noises frighten many preschoolers. **Duration of show** 17 minutes. **Probable waiting time** 20 minutes.

Thumbs Up for the Whole Family

DESCRIPTION AND COMMENTS *Muppet-Vision 3-D* provides a total sensory experience, with wild 3-D action augmented by auditory, visual, and tactile special effects. If you're tired and hot, this show will make you feel brand-new. Arrive early to catch the subversively snarky preshow.

TOURING TIPS Although popular, this attraction handles crowds exceedingly well. Your wait should not last longer than 20 minutes except on days when the park is jam-packed. Special effects and loud noises may frighten some preschoolers.

Lately, the Muppets have frequently been preempted in favor of 4-D feature film previews promoting Disney's latest potential franchise, such as *Frankenweenie* and *Oz: The Great and Powerful*. Check it out if you are interested in a supersized trailer of an upcoming movie, accompanied by bursts of wind and water.

Turtle Talk with Crush ★ ★ ★ ★

APPEAL BY AGE PRESCHOOL ★ ★ ★ ★ ½ GRADE SCHOOL ★ ★ ★ ★ ★ TEENS ★ ★ ★ ½
YOUNG ADULTS ★ ★ ★ ★   OVER 30 ★ ★ ★ ★   SENIORS ★ ★ ★ ★ ½

What it is An interactive animated film. **Scope and scale** Minor attraction. **When to go** After you see the other attractions in the Animation building. **Duration of show** 17 minutes. **Probable waiting time** 10–20 minutes.

DESCRIPTION AND COMMENTS *Turtle Talk with Crush* is an interactive theater show starring the 153-year-old surfer-dude turtle from *Finding Nemo*. Although it starts like a typical Disney theme park movie, *Turtle Talk* quickly turns into a surprise interactive encounter as the on-screen Crush begins to have actual conversations with guests in the audience. Real-time computer graphics are used to accurately move Crush's mouth when forming words.

A mom from Henderson, Colorado, has a crush on Crush:

> Turtle Talk with Crush *is a must-see. Our 4-year-old was picked out of the crowd by Crush, and we were just amazed by the technology that allowed one-on-one conversation. It was adorable and enjoyed by everyone from Grammy and Papa to the 4-year-old!*

TOURING TIPS The animation is brilliant, and guests of all ages list *Crush* as their favorite Animation building feature. By late afternoon, the building has usually cleared out. Save this for your last stop there.

The Twilight Zone Tower of Terror (*Fastpass*) ★ ★ ★ ★ ½

APPEAL BY AGE PRESCHOOL ★ ★ ★ ★ GRADE SCHOOL ★ ★ ★ ★ TEENS ★ ★ ★ ★ ★
YOUNG ADULTS ★ ★ ★ ★ ½   OVER 30 ★ ★ ★ ★ ½   SENIORS ★ ★ ★ ★

What it is Sci-fi–themed indoor thrill ride. **Scope and scale** Super-headliner. **When to go** The first hour the park is open or use Fastpass. **Special comments** Not to be missed; must be 40" tall to ride; switching-off option provided (see page 149). **Duration of ride** About 4 minutes plus preshow. **Average wait in line per 100 people ahead of you** 4 minutes. **Assumes** All elevators operating. **Loading speed** Moderate.

Dark   Scary   Rough   Lose Things   Queasy   Muss Your 'Do

DESCRIPTION AND COMMENTS The Twilight Zone Tower of Terror is a unique species of Disney thrill ride, though it borrows elements of The Haunted Mansion at Disneyland Park. The story is that you're touring a once-famous Hollywood hotel gone to ruin. As at Star Tours, the queuing area integrates guests into the adventure as they pass through the hotel's once-opulent public rooms. From the lobby, guests are escorted into the hotel's library, where Rod Serling, speaking on an old black-and-white television, greets the guests and introduces the plot.

The Tower of Terror is a whopper at 13-plus stories tall. It breaks tradition in terms of visually isolating themed areas. The entire park is visible from the top, but you have to look quickly! The ride vehicle, one of the hotel's service elevators, takes guests to see the haunted hostelry. The tour begins with a startling fiber-optic star field effect, and from there things quickly get seriously weird. You have entered The Twilight Zone. Guests are subjected to a full range of special effects as they encounter unexpected horrors and optical illusions. The climax of the adventure occurs when the elevator reaches the 13th floor and the cable snaps.

DCA's Tower of Terror is very similar to the Walt Disney World version, but they are definitely not clones. In Florida, you start by slowly approaching the tower through mood-setting decayed gardens, while in DCA you simply step off the street and through the hotel's front door. From there, the adventure begins the same way—you pass through the hotel lobby and into the library for the preshow, after which you enter the boarding area. DCA's boiler room is much bigger with colorful (that is, less creepy) lighting, and it's decorated with additional insider nods to the original TV series.

Once you're on the elevator, however, the two attractions really part company. In the Disney World version, the elevator stops at a couple of floors to reveal some eerie visuals, but then actually moves out of the shaft onto one of the floors. The effects during this brief sojourn are remarkable, and more remarkable still is that you don't know that you've reentered the shaft until the elevator speeds skyward. In the DCA Tower of Terror, the elevator never leaves the shaft. The visuals and special effects are equally compelling, especially the unique ghostly mirror not found in Orlando, but there's never that feeling of disorientation that distinguishes the Florida attraction. The DCA Tower of Terror is more straightforward, and consequently a little less mysterious. Once the elevator dropping ensues, both versions are similar, but Florida features multiple randomized drop profiles, making each re-ride a surprise, while every stay in DCA's hotel is the same. Regardless of which version you try, unless you're already fanatically familiar with the superior original, you're unlikely to be disappointed.

The Tower has great potential for terrifying young children and rattling more mature visitors. If you have teenagers in your party, use them as experimental probes—if they report back that they really, really liked it, run as fast as you can in the opposite direction. Seriously, avoid assuming that this attraction isn't for you. A senior from the United Kingdom tried The Tower of Terror and liked it very much, writing:

> I was thankful I read your review of The Tower of Terror, or I would certainly have avoided it. As you say, it is so full of magnificent detail that it is worth riding, even if you don't fancy the drops involved.

TOURING TIPS Because of its height, the tower is a veritable beacon, visible from outside the park and luring curious guests as soon as they enter. Because of the attraction's popularity with schoolkids, teens, and young adults, you can count on a footrace to get there when the park opens. The tower used to be mobbed most of the day, but newer attractions such as Toy Story Midway Mania! and Cars Land have siphoned away some of the lines.

To access The Tower of Terror, bear left from the park entrance into Hollywood Land. Continue straight to the Hyperion Theater and then turn right. To save time, when you enter the library waiting area, stand in the far back corner across from the door where you entered and at the opposite end of the room from the TV. When the doors to the loading area open, you'll be one of the first admitted.

A BUG'S LAND

THIS LAND IS DISNEY'S RESPONSE to complaints that DCA lacked appeal for younger children. A bug's land incorporates the vestiges of Bountiful Valley Farm, which celebrated California's agribusiness, into a bug's-eye world of giant objects, children's rides, and the *It's Tough to Be a Bug!* attraction.

Flik's Fun Fair   ★ ★ ★ ½

APPEAL BY AGE	PRESCHOOL ★ ★ ★ ★ ½	GRADE SCHOOL ★ ★ ★ ½	TEENS ★ ★
YOUNG ADULTS ★ ★ ★		OVER 30 ★ ★ ★	SENIORS ★ ★

What it is Children's rides and play areas. **Scope and scale** Minor attraction. **When to go** Before 11:30 a.m. for the rides; anytime for the play areas. **Special comments** Preschool heaven. **Duration of tour** About 50 minutes for a comprehensive visit.

DESCRIPTION AND COMMENTS Flik's Fun Fair is a children's park as seen through the eyes of an insect. Children can wander among 20-foot-tall blades of grass, tunnel-size garden hoses, an enormous anthill, and the like. Princess Dot's Puddle Park is a kid's water-maze play area fashioned from giant-size garden sprinklers (we're not making this up). Kiddie rides include Flik's Flyers, with a balloon-ride theme; a drive-it-yourself car ride called Tuck and Roll's Drive 'Em Buggies; Heimlich's Chew Chew Train, a miniature train ride; and a mini–Mad Tea Party ride titled Francis' Ladybug Boogie, where you can spin your own "ladybug."

TOURING TIPS Though they're colorful and magnetically alluring to the under-8 crowd, all of the rides are low capacity, slow loading, and ridiculously brief. Our advice is to ride them before 11 a.m. if you visit on a weekend or during the summer. The play areas can be enjoyed anytime, but then you're faced with the prospect of the kids caterwauling to get on the rides. Following is the relevant data on the kiddie rides (note that waiting times are per 50 people ahead of you as opposed to the usual 100 people):

FLIK'S FLYERS *(suspended "baskets" swing around a central axis)*
   RIDE TIME Almost 1½ minutes
   AVERAGE WAIT IN LINE PER 50 PEOPLE AHEAD OF YOU 6 minutes

FRANCIS' LADYBUG BOOGIE *(adaptation of the Mad Tea Party)*
   SPECIAL COMMENTS Unlike most teacup-style rides, turning the center wheel won't spin you faster. Instead, squeeze together on one side of the car and lean your weight into the turns.

RIDE TIME 1 minute
AVERAGE WAIT IN LINE PER 50 PEOPLE AHEAD OF YOU 8 minutes

HEIMLICH'S CHEW CHEW TRAIN (train ride)
SPECIAL COMMENTS Adults as well as children can ride and should enjoy the surreal narration and scent effects.
RIDE TIME Almost 2 minutes
AVERAGE WAIT IN LINE PER 50 PEOPLE AHEAD OF YOU 5 minutes

TUCK AND ROLL'S DRIVE 'EM BUGGIES (bumper cars)
SPECIAL COMMENTS Adults as well as children can ride. Cars are much slower than on normal bumper car rides.
RIDE TIME Almost 2 minutes
AVERAGE WAIT IN LINE PER 50 PEOPLE AHEAD OF YOU 12 minutes

It's Tough to Be a Bug! ★ ★ ★ ★

APPEAL BY AGE	PRESCHOOL ★ ★ ★	GRADE SCHOOL ★ ★ ★ ★	TEENS ★ ★ ★ ★
YOUNG ADULTS ★ ★ ★ ★	OVER 30 ★ ★ ★ ★		SENIORS ★ ★ ★ ★

What it is 3-D movie. **Scope and scale** Major attraction. **When to go** After experiencing DCA's better rides. **Special comments** 3-D effects and loud noises frighten many preschoolers. **Duration of show** 8½ minutes. **Probable waiting time** 20 minutes.

Dark   Scary   Loud

DESCRIPTION AND COMMENTS *It's Tough to Be a Bug!* is an uproarious 3-D film about the difficulties of being a very small creature and features some of the characters from the Disney-Pixar film *a bug's life. It's Tough to Be a Bug!* is similar to *Captain EO* at Disneyland Park in that it combines a 3-D film with an arsenal of tactile and visual special effects. In our view, the special effects are a bit overdone and the film somewhat disjointed. Even so, we rate the *Bug* as not to be missed.

TOURING TIPS Because it's situated in one of the sleepier themed areas, *Bug* is not usually under attack from the hordes until late morning. This should make *It's Tough to Be a Bug!* the easiest of the park's top attractions to see.

Be advised that *It's Tough to Be a Bug!* is very intense and that the special effects will do a number on young children as well as anyone who is squeamish about insects. Check out the following comments from readers who saw *It's Tough to Be a Bug!* at Walt Disney World. First, from a mother of two from Mobile, Alabama:

> It's Tough to Be a Bug! *was too intense for any kid. Our boys are 5 and 7 [years old], and they were scared to death. They love bugs, and they hated this movie. All of the kids in the theater were screaming and crying. I felt like a terrible mother for taking them into this movie. It is billed as a bug movie for kids, but nothing about it is for kids.*

But a Williamsville, New York, woman had it even worse:

> *We almost lost the girls to any further Disney magic due to the 3-D movie* It's Tough to Be a Bug! *It was their first Disney experience, and almost their last. The story line was nebulous and difficult to follow— all they were aware of was the torture of sitting in a darkened theater*

being overrun with bugs. Total chaos, the likes of which I've never experienced, was breaking out around us. The 11-year-old refused to talk for 20 minutes after the fiasco, and the 3½-year-old wanted to go home—not back to the hotel, but home.

Most readers, however, loved the movie, including this mom from Brentwood, Tennessee:

It's intense like Honey, I Shrunk the Audience *but mostly funny. The bugs are cartoonlike instead of realistic and icky, so I can't understand what all the fuss is about. Disney has conditioned us to think of rodents as cute, so kids think nothing of walking up to a mouse the size of a portable toilet but go nuts over some cartoon bugs. Get a grip!*

 # PARADISE PIER

WRAPPED AROUND THE SOUTHERN SHORE of the kidney-shaped lake, Paradise Pier is Disney's version of a seaside amusement park from the Victoria era. It covers about one-third of Disney California Adventure and contains almost one-third of the attractions.

Paradise Pier was the focal point during the early phases of the refurbishment activity recently completed at DCA. The biggest addition was Disney's *World of Color Nighttime Spectacular,* an evening show complete with more than a thousand water fountains shooting water hundreds of feet into the sky, synchronized to music and Disney film clips. A new Little Mermaid–themed dark ride, as well as the removal or retheming of several existing attractions and restaurants, rounded out the rehabilitation of an area that was once widely considered an eyesore.

Paradise Pier's original tacky mid-20th-century theme at DCA was ironic, and in a perverse way it brought the story of Walt Disney and Disneyland full circle. Walt, you see, created Disneyland Park as an alternative to parks such as this—parks with a carnival atmosphere, simple midway rides, carny games, and amply available wine, beer, and liquor. Amazingly, corporate Disney had made just such a place the centerpiece of Disneyland's sister park, slaughtering in effect one of the last of Walt's sacred cows. The refurb's clapboard buildings and retro carnival games gave the area much-needed charm, but not everything is perfect in Paradise; the now-removed Maliboomer tower was supposed to become a lush park, but it turned out to be a few benches on concrete and a patch of green behind barricades to gaze at longingly. The foregoing notwithstanding, Paradise Pier is spotlessly clean, exciting during the day, and eye-popping in the evening with all its colorful lights.

Incidentally, those aforementioned carnival games aren't as avaricious as their unfair fair ancestors. If you and a companion play together, you can win a modest stuffed animal for only $5 (less than you'd pay in the park's gift shops). Some games let you combine multiple wins for an impressive prize. The fishing and racehorse games seem easiest to win.

Note: Most of the attractions (except Toy Story Midway Mania!) in Paradise Pier will close early for *World of Color* performances.

California Screamin' *(Fastpass)* ★ ★ ★ ★

What it is Big, bad roller coaster. **Scope and scale** Super-headliner. **When to go** Ride first thing in the morning, or use Fastpass. **Special comments** Long and smooth; may induce motion sickness; must be 48" tall to ride; switching-off option provided (see page 149). **Duration of ride** 2½ minutes. **Loading speed** Moderate–fast.

Scary Lose Things Queasy Muss Your 'Do

DESCRIPTION AND COMMENTS This apparently antiquated wooden monster is actually a modern steel coaster, and at 6,072 feet, it's the second longest in the United States. California Screamin' gets off to a 0-to-55-mph start by launching you up the first hill like a jet fighter plane off the deck of a carrier (albeit with different technology). From here you will experience tight turns followed by a second launch that sends you over the crest of a 110-foot hill with a 107-foot drop on the far side. Next, you bank and complete an elliptical loop. A diving turn followed by a series of camelbacks brings you back to the station. Speakers play a synchronized soundtrack complete with recorded canned screaming and a carnival barker cameo by actor Neil Patrick Harris.

We were impressed by the length of the course and the smoothness of the ride. From beginning to end, the ride is about 2½ minutes, with 2 minutes of actual ride time. En route the coaster slows enough on curves and on transition hills to let you take in the nice view. On the scary-o-meter, Screamin' is certainly worse than Space Mountain but doesn't really compare with some of the steel coasters at nearby Magic Mountain. What Screamin' loses in fright potential, however, it makes up for in variety. Along its course, Disney has placed every known curve, hill, dip, and loop in roller coaster design.

A Carlsbad, California, woman found the roller coaster to be a smooth operator:

> California Screamin' was WONDERFUL, and I am a 57-year-old mom, not an adrenaline-crazed young adult! It was my first ever upside-down ride, but it was so smooth and quick [that] I only felt a gentle pressure pushing me into the seat. It was so fun [that] I went again! Don't miss this one, at any age!

A Texas woman agrees, writing:

> I hate roller coasters, and I love California Screamin'. Very smooth.

TOURING TIPS California Screamin' is a serious coaster, a coaster that makes Space Mountain look like Dumbo. Secure any hats, cameras, eyeglasses, or anything else that might be ripped from your person during the ride. Stay away completely if you're prone to motion sickness.

Engineered to run several trains at once, California Screamin' does a better job than any roller coaster we've seen at handling crowds, at least when the attraction is running at full capacity. The coaster is sometimes shut down two or more times a day for technical problems. Early in the morning, however, it's usually easy to get two or three rides under your belt in about 15 minutes. Ride in the first hour the park is open or use Fastpass or the single-rider line (enter up the ramp to the left of the queue).

Golden Zephyr ★★

APPEAL BY AGE PRESCHOOL ★★★★ GRADE SCHOOL ★★★½ TEENS ★★★
YOUNG ADULTS ★★½   OVER 30 ★★★   SENIORS ★★★

What it is Zephyrs spinning around a central tower. **Scope and scale** Minor attraction. **When to go** The first 90 minutes the park is open or just before closing. **Special comments** Totally redundant; can't operate on breezy days. **Duration of ride** About 2½ minutes. **Loading speed** Slow.

Queasy

DESCRIPTION AND COMMENTS First, a *zephyr* is a term often associated with blimps. On this attraction, the zephyrs look like open-cockpit rockets. In any event, each zephyr holds about a dozen guests and spins around a central axis with enough centrifugal force to lay the zephyr partially on its side. As it turns out, the Golden Zephyrs are very touchy, as zephyrs go: they can't fly in a wind exceeding about 5 miles per hour. Needless to say, the attraction is shut down much of the time.

TOURING TIPS A colorful, beautiful attraction, it is another slow-loading cycle ride. Go during the 90 minutes the park is open or prepare for a long wait.

Goofy's Sky School *(Fastpass)* ★★★

APPEAL BY AGE PRESCHOOL ★★★★½ GRADE SCHOOL ★★★★½ TEENS ★★★★½
YOUNG ADULTS ★★★★   OVER 30 ★★★½   SENIORS ★★★★

What it is Disney's version of a Wild (or Mad) Mouse ride. **Scope and scale** Major attraction. **When to go** During the first hour the park is open. **Special comments** Space Mountain with the lights on; may induce motion sickness; a retheming of Mulholland Madness, the previous ride in this location; must be 42" tall to ride; switching-off option provided (see page 149). **Duration of ride** About 1½ minutes. **Loading speed** Slow–moderate.

Scary   Lose Things   Queasy   Muss Your 'Do

DESCRIPTION AND COMMENTS Themed as Goofy teaching a bunch of new pilots how to fly, Goofy's Sky School is a designer Wild Mouse (sometimes also called a Mad Mouse). If you're not familiar with the genre, it's a small, convoluted roller coaster where the track dips and turns unexpectedly, presumably reminding its inventor of a mouse tearing through a maze. To define it more in Disney terms, the ride is similar to Space Mountain, only outdoors and therefore in the light. Goofy's Sky School is an off-the-shelf midway ride in which Disney has invested next to nothing in spiffing up. In other words, fun but nothing special.

TOURING TIPS A fun ride but also a slow-loading one, and one that breaks down frequently. Ride during the first hour that the park is open, or use Fastpass or the single-rider line (when open).

Jumpin' Jellyfish ★★

APPEAL BY AGE	PRESCHOOL ★★★★½	GRADE SCHOOL ★★★½	TEENS ★★
YOUNG ADULTS ★★★	OVER 30 ★★½		SENIORS ★★½

What it is Parachute ride. **Scope and scale** Minor attraction. **When to go** The first 90 minutes the park is open or just before closing. **Special comments** All sizzle, no meat; can't operate on breezy days; must be 40" tall to ride. **Duration of ride** About 45 seconds. **Loading speed** Slow.

DESCRIPTION AND COMMENTS On this ride, you're raised on a cable to the top of the tower and then released to gently parachute back to earth. Mostly a children's ride, Jumpin' Jellyfish is paradoxically off limits to those who would most enjoy it because of its 40-inch minimum-height restriction. For adults, the attraction is a real snore. Oops, make that a real bore—the paltry 45-second duration of the ride is not long enough to fall asleep.

TOURING TIPS The Jellyfish, so called because of a floating jellyfish's resemblance to an open parachute, is another slow-loading ride of very low capacity. Get on early in the morning or prepare for a long wait.

King Triton's Carousel ★★★

APPEAL BY AGE	PRESCHOOL ★★★★½	GRADE SCHOOL ★★★½	TEENS ★★★½
YOUNG ADULTS ★★★½	OVER 30 ★★★½		SENIORS ★★★★

What it is Merry-go-round. **Scope and scale** Minor attraction. **When to go** Before noon. **Special comments** Beautimus. **Duration of ride** A little less than 2 minutes. **Loading speed** Slow.

DESCRIPTION AND COMMENTS On this elaborate and stunningly crafted carousel, dolphins, sea horses, seals, and the like replace the standard prancing horses.

TOURING TIPS Worth a look even if there are no children in your party. If you have kids who want to ride, try to get them on before noon.

The Little Mermaid: Ariel's Undersea Adventure ★★★½

APPEAL BY AGE	PRESCHOOL ★★★★½	GRADE SCHOOL ★★★★	TEENS ★★★½
YOUNG ADULTS ★★★★	OVER 30 ★★★½		SENIORS ★★★★

What it is Track ride in the dark. **Scope and scale** Headliner. **When to go** First thing in the morning or after 4 p.m. **Duration of ride** 6¼ minutes. **Loading speed** Fast.

DESCRIPTION AND COMMENTS The Palace of Fine Arts dome (former home of the Whoopi Goldberg–hosted *Golden Dreams* film) has been incorporated into an impressive new lagoon-facing facade modeled on early-20th-century aquariums. The seafoam-trimmed building, which is topped by a statue of King Triton, conceals Disney's newest old-school attraction. Opened in 2011, the basics of The Little Mermaid: Ariel's Undersea Adventure are similar to Disneyland's Haunted Mansion: a continuously loading ride system transports you through a series of elaborately themed, darkened scenes with sophisticated special effects. In this case, the Little Mermaid attraction takes you to the bottom of the ocean in clam shell cars, where the ride recaps Ariel's journey from her father's undersea kingdom to marrying Prince Eric. After Scuttle the seagull recaps the backstory for you, your vehicle descends backward beneath the simulated sea surface with a spritz of cool air. Assuming that you haven't drowned, you'll then meet a cutting-edge animatronic Ariel (featuring "floating" hair and synchronized lips); party down "Under the Sea" with Sebastian the crab; and be menaced by a 12-foot-wide, 7½-foot-tall undulating figure of Ursula, the evil sea witch. The adventure is all set to newly orchestrated versions of Alan Menken and Howard Ashman's classic songs, and original animator Glen Keane and actress Jodi Benson both returned to lend their talents.

Unfortunately, though the ride is colorful and kinetic, it suffers from shortchanged storytelling and several sections that feel unfinished. While it's a welcome addition to DCA's short roster of kid-friendly indoor rides, anyone expecting a modern-day classic to compete with Haunted Mansion and Pirates of the Caribbean (as the reported $100-million budget might suggest) will come away sorely disappointed.

TOURING TIPS As one of the park's newest attractions and one that's suitable for most small children, The Little Mermaid can attract long lines as soon as the park opens on peak days. (On a positive note, this should reduce some of the early-morning demand for Toy Story Midway Mania! and Cars Land.) This attraction does not have Fastpass. However, the Omnimover ride system is capable of efficiently handling more than 2,000 guests per hour, keeping lines moving swiftly even on busy days. If you find the line prohibitive, check back in the late afternoon, when you will often be able to walk on with little wait.

Mickey's Fun Wheel ★★

APPEAL BY AGE	PRESCHOOL ★★★	GRADE SCHOOL ★★★½	TEENS ★★★★
YOUNG ADULTS ★★★½		OVER 30 ★★★	SENIORS ★★½

What it is Ferris wheel. **Scope and scale** Major attraction. **When to go** The first 90 minutes the park is open or just before closing. **Special comments** The world's largest chicken coop; may induce motion sickness. **Duration of ride** 2 minutes. **Loading speed** Slow.

Queasy

DESCRIPTION AND COMMENTS Higher than the Matterhorn attraction at Disneyland Park, this whopper of a Ferris wheel tops out at 150 feet. Absolutely spectacular in appearance, with an enormous Mickey in the middle of its wheel, the aptly named Mickey's Fun Wheel offers stunning views in all directions. Unfortunately, however, the view is severely compromised by the steel mesh that completely encloses the passenger compartment. In essence, Disney has created the world's largest revolving chicken coop. As concerns the ride itself, some of the passenger buckets move laterally from side to side across the Fun Wheel in addition to rotating around with the wheel. Because it feels like your bucket has become unattached from the main structure, this lateral movement can be a little disconcerting if you aren't expecting it. If the movement proves too disconcerting, motion sickness bags are thoughtfully provided in each swinging car.

TOURING TIPS Ferris wheels are the most slow loading of all cycle rides. Thus, we were very curious to see how the loading and unloading of the Fun Wheel is engineered. The Fun Wheel has a platform that allows three compartments to be loaded at once. The lateral sliding buckets are loaded from the two outside platforms, while the stationary compartments are loaded from the middle platform. Loading the entire wheel takes about 6½ minutes, following which the Fun Wheel rotates for a 2-minute ride. And speaking of the ride, the Fun Wheel rotates so slowly that the wonderful rising and falling sensations of the garden-variety Ferris wheel are completely absent. For our money, the Fun Wheel is beautiful to behold but terribly boring to ride. If you decide to give it a whirl, ride the first hour the park is open or in the hour before the park closes.

Silly Symphony Swings ★★★

APPEAL BY AGE PRESCHOOL ★★★★½ GRADE SCHOOL ★★★★ TEENS ★★★★
YOUNG ADULTS ★★★½   OVER 30 ★★★½   SENIORS ★★★

What it is Swings rotating around a central tower. **Scope and scale** Minor attraction. **When to go** The first 90 minutes the park is open or just before closing. **Special comments** Simple but fun; must be 40" tall to ride (48" tall to ride solo). **Duration of ride** Less than 1½ minutes. **Loading speed** Slow.

Lose Things   Queasy   Muss Your 'Do

DESCRIPTION AND COMMENTS Originally opened as the Orange Stinger, with guests seated in swings flying around a giant citrus fruit, the ride was redone in 2009 as part of the DCA refurbishment and expansion. The new theme pays tribute to the 1935 Mickey Mouse cartoon *The Band Concert,* the first color Mickey cartoon released to the public, but the net effect is still the same. In the scary department, it's a wilder ride than Dumbo, but SSS is still just swings going in circles. A number of tandem swings are available to allow children 40–48 inches to ride with a parent; look for a separate tandem line to the left as you approach the attraction.

TOURING TIPS This is a fun and visually appealing ride, but it's also one that loads slowly and occasions long waits unless you ride during the first hour or so the park is open. Be aware that it's possible for the swing chairs to collide when the ride comes to a stop—the author once picked up a nice bruise when an empty swing smacked him during touchdown.

Toy Story Midway Mania! ★★★★½

APPEAL BY AGE   PRESCHOOL ★★★★½   GRADE SCHOOL ★★★★½
TEENS ★★★★½ YOUNG ADULTS ★★★★½ OVER 30 ★★★★½ SENIORS ★★★★½

What it is 3-D ride through indoor shooting gallery. **Scope and scale** Headliner. **When to go** First thing after the park opens. **Special comments** Not to be missed. **Duration of ride** About 6½ minutes. **Average wait in line per 100 people ahead of you** 4½ minutes. **Loading speed** Fast.

DESCRIPTION AND COMMENTS Toy Story Midway Mania! ushers in a whole new generation of Disney attractions: virtual dark rides. Since

Disneyland opened in 1955, ride vehicles have moved past two- and three-dimensional sets often populated by Audio-Animatronics (AA). Designed by the Imagineers and constructed by skilled craftsmen, these amazingly detailed sets and robotic figures literally defined the Disney creative genius in attractions such as Pirates of the Caribbean, The Haunted Mansion, and Peter Pan's Flight. Now for Toy Story Midway Mania!, the elaborate sets and endearing AA characters are gone. Imagine long corridors, totally empty, covered with reflective material. There's almost nothing there . . . until you put on your 3-D glasses. Instantly, the corridor is full and brimming with color, action, and activity, thanks to projected computer-graphic imagery (CGI).

Conceptually, this is an interactive shooting gallery much like Buzz Lightyear Astro Blasters (see page 257), but in Toy Story Midway Mania!, your ride vehicle passes through a totally virtual midway, with booths offering such games as ring tossing and ball throwing. You use a cannon on your ride vehicle to play as you move along from booth to booth. Unlike the laser guns in Buzz Lightyear, however, Toy Story Midway Mania's pull-string cannons take advantage of CGI technology to toss rings, shoot balls, and even throw eggs and pies. Each game booth is manned by a *Toy Story* character who is right beside you in 3-D glory cheering you on. In addition to 3-D imagery, you experience various smells, vehicle motion, wind, and water spray. The ride begins with a training round to familiarize you with your cannon and the nature of the games and then continues through a number of "real" games in which you compete against your riding mate. The technology has the ability to self-adjust the level of difficulty so that every rider is challenged, and there are plenty of easy targets for small children to reach. *Tip:* Let the pull-string retract all the way back into the cannon before pulling it again. If you don't, the cannon won't fire.

Finally, and also of note, a new generation of "living character" AA figures was introduced in the preshow queuing area of Toy Story Midway Mania! A 6-foot-tall Mr. Potato Head breaks new ground for an AA character by interacting with and talking to guests in real time.

TOURING TIPS Much of the queuing area for Toy Story Midway Mania! is across the pedestrian walkway from the attraction's entrance. The queuing is covered, which is good, but it's not air-conditioned, which is very bad, with temperatures escalating into the 90s and higher. Not roasting in this oven is a great incentive to experience Toy Story Midway Mania! in the early morning, before it gets crowded.

As you might expect, Toy Story Midway Mania! is addictive, and though it's great fun right off the bat, it takes a couple of rides before you really get the hang of the pull-string cannon and the way the targets are presented. To rack up a high score, you must identify and shoot at high-value targets: low-value targets are larger and easier to hit, while high-value targets are small and often moving. Toward the end of the ride, the top score of the day and the top scores of the month are posted.

If you're a newbie and you'd like to ride several times to gain experience and get your skill level up, consider making the attraction your first stop after the park opens.

The challenge of seeing Toy Story Midway Mania! without a horrendous wait was a hot topic among *Unofficial Guide* readers. But since Cars

Land's debut, waits have become much more manageable, especially in the early morning. Still, you should make this a priority after securing Radiator Springs Racers Fastpasses. If you've experienced the extreme waits that always accompany the Orlando clone of this ride, rest assured that Anaheim's operations keep the line here moving much more swiftly.

CARS LAND

CARS LAND IS THE CROWNING CAPSTONE on DCA's transformation, and the first major "land" in an American Disney theme park devoted solely to a single film franchise. Tucked in the park's southeast corner on 12 acres of repurposed parking lot, Cars Land's main entrance is across from the Golden Vine Winery, though there are secondary gateways in a bug's land and in Pacific Wharf (the vista through the latter's stone archway entrance is especially scenic). A massive mountainous backdrop topped with 125-foot-high peaks patterned after 1950s Cadillac Pinnacle tail fins, known as the Cadillac Range, cradles Ornament Valley, home to a screen-accurate re-creation of Radiator Springs. That's the sleepy single-stoplight town along Route 66 populated by Pixar's anthropomorphized automobiles. Along its main drag, in addition to three rides, you find eateries themed to the film's minor characters, such as **Fillmore's Taste-in,** serving fruit drinks and snacks; **Cozy Cone Motel,** with chili, ice cream, and popcorn, all served in conical containers; and **Flo's V8 Café,** serving creative takes on classic comfort food with a Southwestern twist for breakfast, lunch, and dinner. Souvenir shops include **Radiator Springs Curios** (collectible pins and Route 66 postcards), **Ramone's House of Body Art** (car-themed artwork and clothes), and **Sarge's Supply Hut** (*Cars*-branded toys and games).

Cars Land represents a considerable investment in capital and creativity for the Disney company, resulting in a rare example of complete entertainment immersion. Walking through the aesthetically astounding area is uncannily like stepping into the cinematic universe, and well worth the wait even if you weren't particularly enamored of the merchandise-moving movies. Since opening, the area has attracted massive crowds all day and has dramatically increased DCA's overall attendance. As striking as Cars Land is by daylight, it is even more stunning after sunset; the nightly neon-lighting ceremony set to the doo-wop classic "Life Could Be a Dream" is a magical must-see (showtimes are not publicized and vary seasonally, so ask a Cars Land cast member and arrive early).

Luigi's Flying Tires ★★★

APPEAL BY AGE	PRESCHOOL ★★★★	GRADE SCHOOL ★★★★	TEENS ★★★½
YOUNG ADULTS ★★★½		OVER 30 ★★★½	SENIORS ★★★½

What it is Bumper cars meets human air hockey. **Scope and scale** Minor attraction. **When to go** The first 30 minutes the park is open. **Special comments** Must be 32" tall to ride; more fun to watch than ride. **Duration of ride** 2 minutes. **Average wait in line per 100 people ahead of you** 12 minutes. **Loading speed** Very slow.

DESCRIPTION AND COMMENTS Unless you are over the age of 50, you're unlikely to remember Disneyland Park's Flying Saucers, a Tomorrowland attraction that lasted five years in the early 1960s. But Imagineers have retreaded the concept of hovercraft bumper cars as the basis for a tribute to the Radiator Springs resident Ferrari fanatic. You first queue inside the Casa Della Tires shop (where memorabilia from Luigi's and Guido's careers is on display), and then pass through a garden of automotive-inspired topiaries, before boarding your own supersize tire. Using a system similar to an air hockey table, your two-passenger vehicle (up to three with a child) lifts up on a thin cushion of air. You then get about 2 minutes to scoot around the arena, trying to bump against other riders. Actor Tony Shalhoub sings a soundtrack of Italian American standards, adding to the *festa Italia* fun.

Luigi's Flying Tires may be an example of nostalgia being better than reality; the tires accelerate gradually and can be tricky for first-time riders to control (see our tips below). With the epic wait times this glacially loading attraction attracts, riding enough times to become an expert driver appears an unrealistic prospect for all but the most avid Annual Pass holders. However, hovering is a blast once you get the hang of it, and most guests get off giggling even if they spent much of the short ride stalled on the sidelines.

TOURING TIPS Luigi's is a slow-loading cycle ride under the best circumstances. Expect long lines all day. Your only hope for a reasonable wait is to be among the first people in the queue upon opening. If you don't want to ride, loiter near the exit and enjoy watching other guests getting jostled.

To steer, first shift your body weight to find your tire's center point of balance, so that it sits evenly on the air cushion. Then gradually lean your body weight in the direction that you want to move, without going so far that the tire's leading edge drags on the floor. Single riders may initially find it easier to get the feel of balancing and steering. To reach maximum velocity, try to aim for an open corner away from the crowd.

DISNEY DISH WITH JIM HILL

WILL LUIGI'S FLYING TIRES BE RETIRED? Ever since it opened in June 2012, Cars Land at Disney California Adventure has been considered a smashing success—with the notable exception of Luigi's Flying Tires. This slow-to-load, low-capacity ride hasn't exactly been wowing the tens of thousands of Disneyland guests who visit Radiator Springs daily. So the Imagineers are now reportedly toying with the idea of replacing this underwhelming attraction (which drew its inspiration from Disneyland's Flying Saucers, a Tomorrowland ride from the 1960s) with a new *Cars*-themed dark ride, something similar in style and scale to Mr. Toad's Wild Ride, that would fill a niche that Radiator Springs Racers and Mater's Junkyard Jamboree don't.

Mater's Junkyard Jamboree ★★★

APPEAL BY AGE PRESCHOOL ★★★★½ GRADE SCHOOL ★★★★½ TEENS ★★★★
YOUNG ADULTS ★★★★ OVER 30 ★★★★ SENIORS ★★★½

What it is Midway-type whip ride. **Scope and scale** Minor attraction. **When to go** The first 30 minutes the park is open. **Special comments** Must be 32" tall to ride. **Duration of ride** About 1½ minutes. **Average wait in line per 100 people ahead of you** 8 minutes. **Loading speed** Slow.

Queasy

DESCRIPTION AND COMMENTS On the outskirts of town sits the junkyard home of Mater, the redneck tow truck voiced by Larry the Cable Guy. In his yard sit 22 baby tractors, each towing an open-air two-seater trailer. While Mater's voice emerges from a jury-rigged jukebox singing one of seven specially composed square-dancing tunes (plus one hilarious hidden song that plays only once per hour), the tractors travel in overlapping figure eight patterns along interlocking turntables. The vehicles are transferred from one revolving turntable to another, creating near-miss moments much like Francis' Ladybug Boogie. The difference is that Mater's trailers swing freely from side to side, creating a centripetal snapping sensation similar to vintage whip carnival rides. Mater's may look like a simple kiddie ride, but it supplies an unexpected kick that draws us back for repeated spins.

TOURING TIPS Mater is the breakout hit character of the *Cars* franchise, and his namesake ride is visually attractive but slow loading. Still, it typically has the shortest queue of the three Cars Land attractions.

Radiator Springs Racers *(Fastpass)* ★★★★★

What it is Automotive dark ride with high-speed thrills. **Scope and scale** Super-headliner. **When to go** The first 30 minutes the park is open or use Fastpass. **Special comments** Must be 40" tall to ride; switching-off option provided (see page 149). Not to be missed. **Duration of ride** About 4 minutes. **Average wait in line per 100 people ahead of you** 4 minutes. **Loading speed** Moderate–fast.

Dark   Scary   Lose Things   Muss Your 'Do

DESCRIPTION AND COMMENTS To the right of the Radiator Springs Courthouse at the end of Route 66 lies the entrance to the most ambitious attraction built at Disneyland Resort in more than a decade.

Disney's Imagineers have wedded an enhanced version of the high-speed slot cars developed for Epcot's Test Track with immersive sets and elaborate animatronics. The ride, which covers nearly 6 of Cars Land's 12 acres, mixes slow indoor sections with thrilling open-air acceleration in a way that appeals to every end of the demographic spectrum.

You begin your road trip by walking through Stanley's Oasis, the town's original 1909 settlement, and end up in a cavernous loading station. There you board a six-passenger convertible, each with a smiling face on its front grill, and you're off on a scenic tour of stunning Ornament Valley, on your way to compete in today's big race.

After a leisurely drive past massive rock formations and a majestic waterfall, you enter the show building for a series of indoor scenes depicting the residents of Radiator Springs. These environments don't quite match the awe-inspiring scale of scenes in Pirates of the Caribbean or Indiana Jones, but they are a big step up from the old-fashioned

Fantasyland dark rides and feature movie-accurate animatronics with impressively expressive eyes and mouths (achieved through a combination of digital projections and practical effects). Along your tour, you'll be sidetracked by a tractor-tipping expedition with Mater, which leads to a run-in with an angry harvester. Before reaching the starting line, you'll need some new tires or a fresh coat of paint. Then it's time to line up alongside another carload of guests as you await Luigi's countdown. The last third of the ride is a flat-out race over camelback hills, under outcrops, and around banked curves, with a randomly chosen car crossing the finish line first. Radiator Springs Racers's top speed of 40 miles per hour falls short of Test Track's 60-plus peak, but the winding turns and airtime-inducing humps supply an exhilarating rush. After a final swing past the glowing stalactites of Tail Light Cavern and some parting praise from Lightning McQueen and Mater, you'll exit your vehicle and inspect your obligatory on-ride photo.

TOURING TIPS As the $200 million, 800-pound gorilla of DCA's makeover, Radiator Springs Racers is a massive draw from the minute the park opens every day. With a carrying capacity of about 1,500 riders per hour, the attraction regularly sees standby waits of two to three hours, and Fastpasses may all be claimed for the day within an hour of opening; even the single-rider queue can run 45 minutes or more. Your best options are to line up for a Fastpass at least 30 minutes before the park *officially* opens (see page 291), or step into the standby queue shortly before closing. If time permits, try to ride once by day and again after dark; evening illumination makes the outdoor portions especially enchanting.

Note that Fastpasses for Radiator Springs Racers are distributed outside of Cars Land proper, near *It's Tough to Be Bug!* You may be tempted to rush to the standby queue at rope drop instead of getting a Fastpass, but be warned that the ride regularly opens late due to daily maintenance, potentially wasting your valuable morning touring time. This attraction's Fastpasses (like *World of Color*'s) are disconnected from the rest of the system, meaning that you can hold a ticket for here and another ride at the same time.

█ CONDOR FLATS

SITUATED JUST TO THE RIGHT of the central hub, Condor Flats pays homage to California aviation. The pedestrian walkway is marked like a runway, and all of the buildings look like airplane hangars. Condor Flats is the home of one of the park's super-headliner attractions, **Soarin' Over California.**

Soarin' Over California *(Fastpass)*　★★★★½

APPEAL BY AGE	PRESCHOOL ★★★★½		GRADE SCHOOL ★★★★★
TEENS ★★★★½	YOUNG ADULTS ★★★★½	OVER 30 ★★★★★	SENIORS ★★★★★

What it is Flight-simulation ride. **Scope and scale** Super-headliner. **When to go** The first 30 minutes the park is open, or use Fastpass. **Special comments** The park's best ride for the whole family; must be 40" tall to ride; switching-off option provided (see page 149). **Duration of ride** 4½ minutes. **Loading speed** Moderate.

Thumbs Up for the Whole Family

DESCRIPTION AND COMMENTS Once you enter the main theater, you're secured in a seat not unlike the ones used on inverted roller coasters (in which the coaster is suspended from above). Once everyone is in place, you are suspended with your legs dangling. Thus hung out to dry, you embark on a hang glider tour of California with IMAX-quality images projected below you, and with the simulator moving your seat in sync with the movie. The immersive images are well chosen and slapdab beautiful, though scene transitions are jarringly abrupt, and the once-pristine film has lately become scratched and dirty. Special effects include wind, sound, and even olfactory stimulation. The ride itself is thrilling but perfectly smooth, exciting, and relaxing simultaneously. We think Soarin' Over California is a must-see for guests of any age who meet the 40-inch minimum-height requirement. And yes, seniors we interviewed were crazy about it.

TOURING TIPS Aside from being a true technological innovation, Soarin' Over California also happens to be located near the entrance of the park, thus ensuring heavy traffic all day. Soarin' should be your very first attraction in the morning after experiencing Cars Land, or, alternatively, use Fastpass or the single-rider line. If you arrive later and elect to use Fastpass, obtain your Fastpass before noon. Later than noon you're likely to get a return period in the hour before the park closes, or worse, find that the day's supply of Fastpasses is gone. Interestingly, while this ride is virtually identical to Soarin' at Epcot, the line for DCA's version moves much more efficiently.

PACIFIC WHARF

THIS LAND INCORPORATES a Cannery Row–inspired eatery area adjacent to Paradise Bay with a diminutive winery, situated at the base of Grizzly Peak and across from a bug's land, making it the smallest of the Golden State–themed areas. It would be a stretch to call it an attraction, much less a themed area. You'll also find the Boudin Bakery Tour, a walk-through exhibit where you can watch Rosie O'Donnell explain the bread-making process while snacking on some free sourdough; even on the busiest days, you should be able to enter without a wait. Next door is the new Ghirardelli's Soda Fountain and Chocolate Shop, where you can indulge in diabetes-inducing ice cream sundaes.

Golden Vine Winery and Blue Sky Cellar ★★½

APPEAL BY AGE PRESCHOOL ★★★½ GRADE SCHOOL ★★★★½ TEENS ★★★½
YOUNG ADULTS ★★★★ OVER 30 ★★★★ SENIORS ★★★★

What it is Exhibit of attraction concept art. **Scope and scale** Minor attraction; exhibit. **When to go** Anytime. **Duration of film** 6½ minutes. **Probable waiting time** 10 minutes for film.

DESCRIPTION AND COMMENTS This Mission-style complex, squeezed into the side of Grizzly Peak, offers a demonstration vineyard. The rest of the facility, predictably, is occupied by a tasting room and restaurant. Also located at the winery is the Walt Disney Imagineering Blue Sky Cellar preview center, a fantastic stop for the huge Disney fans in your group. It usually showcases concept art, models, and promotional videos about the latest expansion underway at the Disneyland Resort; most recently, the construction of Fantasy Faire was featured. In between preview exhibits, the collection is cast as Radiator Springs's "historical museum" with manufactured memorabilia and an amusing Pixar-produced short film fleshing out the burg's backstory.

TOURING TIPS The Blue Sky Cellar is a great way to kill 15–30 minutes. Make time to see this when you have some downtime, perhaps after a meal, while on the way back to Paradise Pier, or before watching Disney's *Aladdin—A Musical Spectacular*. Save the Golden Vine Winery for the end of the day.

GRIZZLY PEAK

GRIZZLY PEAK, a huge mountain shaped like the head of a bear, is home to **Grizzly River Run**, a whitewater raft ride, and the **Redwood Creek Challenge Trail**, an outdoor playground that resembles an obstacle course.

Grizzly River Run *(Fastpass)* ★★★★½

APPEAL BY AGE	PRESCHOOL ★★★½	GRADE SCHOOL ★★★★½	TEENS ★★★★½
YOUNG ADULTS ★★★★½	OVER 30 ★★★★½		SENIORS ★★★★

What it is Whitewater raft ride. **Scope and scale** Super-headliner. **When to go** First hour the park is open, or use Fastpass. **Special comments** Not to be missed; you are guaranteed to get wet, and possibly soaked; must be 42" tall to ride. **Duration of ride** 5½ minutes. **Average wait in line per 100 people ahead of you** 5 minutes. **Loading speed** Moderate.

Scary   Wet   Lose Things   Rough   Muss Your 'Do

DESCRIPTION AND COMMENTS Whitewater raft rides have been a hot-weather favorite of theme park patrons for almost 20 years. The ride consists of an unguided trip down a man-made river in a circular rubber raft, with a platform mounted on top seating six to eight people. The raft essentially floats free in the current and is washed downstream through rapids and waves. Because the river is fairly wide with numerous currents, eddies, and obstacles, there is no telling exactly where the raft will go. Thus, each trip is different and unpredictable. The rafts are circular and a little smaller than those used on most rides of the genre. Because the current can buffet the smaller rafts more effectively, the ride is wilder and wetter.

What distinguishes Grizzly River Run from other theme park raft rides is Disney's trademark attention to visual detail. Where many raft rides essentially plunge down a concrete ditch, Grizzly River

Run winds around and through Grizzly Peak, the park's foremost visual icon, with the great rock bear at the summit. Featuring a 50-foot climb and two drops—including a 22-footer where the raft spins as it descends—the ride flows into dark caverns and along the mountain's precipitous side before looping over itself just before the final plunge. As part of DCA's makeover, the ride's original extreme sports elements have been eliminated in favor of period-appropriate props supporting the new midcentury national parks theme.

When Disney opened the Kali River Rapids raft ride at the Animal Kingdom theme park at Walt Disney World, it was roundly criticized (and rightly so) for being a wimpy ride. Well, we're here to tell you that Disney learned its lesson. Grizzly River Run is a heart thumper, one of the best of its genre anywhere. And at 5½ minutes from load to unload, it's also one of the longest. The visuals are outstanding, and the ride is about as good as it gets on a man-made river. While it's true that theme park raft rides have been around a long time, Grizzly River Run has set a new standard, one we don't expect to be equaled for some time.

TOURING TIPS This attraction is hugely popular, especially on hot summer days. Ride the first hour the park is open, after 4:30 p.m., or use Fast-pass or the single-rider line. Make no mistake—you will certainly get wet on this ride. Our recommendation is to wear shorts to the park and bring along a jumbo-size trash bag, as well as a smaller plastic bag. Before boarding the raft, take off your socks and punch a hole in your jumbo bag for your head. Though you can also cut holes for your arms, you will probably stay drier with your arms inside the bag. Use the smaller plastic bag to wrap around your shoes. If you are worried about mussing your hairdo, bring a third bag for your head.

A Shaker Heights, Ohio, family who adopted our garbage-bag attire, however, discovered that staying dry on a similar attraction at Walt Disney World is not without social consequences:

> I must tell you that the Disney cast members and the other people in our raft looked at us like we had just beamed down from Mars. Plus, we didn't cut armholes in our trash bags because we thought we'd stay drier. Only problem was that once we sat down, we couldn't fasten our seat belts. The Disney person was quite put out and asked sarcastically whether we needed wet suits and snorkels. After a lot of wiggling and adjusting and helping each other, we finally got belted in and off we went looking like sacks of fertilizer with little heads perched on top. It was very embarrassing, but I must admit that we stayed nice and dry.

If you forget your plastic bag, ponchos are available at the adjacent Rushin' River Outfitters. Since the summer of 2010, the Grizzly River Run Fastpass booths have been partially taken over by *World of Color* Fastpass distribution. Depending on the day, all or half of the Fastpass booths are taken up by *World of Color*. The booths then slowly return to becoming Grizzly River Run booths as the *World of Color* Fastpasses have been fully distributed. The effect of *World of Color* has generally made Grizzly River Run more popular of an attraction, as well as getting a Fastpass a generally harder position, especially earlier in the day.

Redwood Creek Challenge Trail and Wilderness Explorer Camp ★★★½

APPEAL BY AGE PRESCHOOL ★★★★   GRADE SCHOOL ★★★★   TEENS ★★★★
YOUNG ADULTS ★★★½   OVER 30 ★★★½   SENIORS ★★★★½

What it is Elaborate playground and obstacle course. **Scope and scale** Minor attraction. **When to go** Anytime. **Special comments** Very well done; must be 42" tall. Plan to spend about 20 minutes here.

DESCRIPTION AND COMMENTS An elaborate maze of rope bridges, log towers, and a cave, the Redwood Creek Challenge Trail is a scout camp combination of elements from Tarzan's Treehouse and Tom Sawyer Island. Built into and around Grizzly Peak, the Challenge Trail has eye-popping appeal for young adventurers. A mom from Salt Lake City writes:

> Most underrated . . . If this were a city park, it would be packed every day. In Disneyland it seems to be the least popular thing. The kids just loved it, young and older. The adults were able to run for Fastpasses, change diapers, get snacks for all the kids, and sit down while the kids had a great time.

Russell and Dug from Pixar's *Up* appear here daily to lead kids in a short but sweet Wilderness Explorer ceremony. Grab a map near the entrance and complete the self-guided activities to earn your own merit badge sticker.

TOURING TIPS The largest of several children's play areas in the park, and the only one that is dry (for the most part) and relatively shady, the Challenge Trail is the perfect place to let your kids cut loose for a while. Though the Challenge Trail will be crowded, you should not have to wait to get in. Experience it after checking out the better rides and shows. Be aware, however, that the playground is quite large, and that you will not be able to keep your children in sight unless you tag along with them.

PARADES *and* LIVE ENTERTAINMENT

Disney's World of Color Nighttime Spectacular (Fastpass) ★★★★½

APPEAL BY AGE PRESCHOOL ★★★★   GRADE SCHOOL ★★★★   TEENS ★★★★
YOUNG ADULTS ★★★★½   OVER 30 ★★★★½   SENIORS ★★★★½

Muss Your 'Do

DESCRIPTION AND COMMENTS The 1,200 high-pressure water nozzles installed under the surface of DCA's Paradise Bay are the infrastructure for Disney's $75-million attempt to keep guests in the park (and spending money) until closing time. If you've seen or heard about the spectacular fountain show at the Bellagio in Las Vegas, *World of Color* is similar but larger, with more special effects and themed to Disney movies. The show includes a new musical score and incorporates dozens of Disney films and characters in its 27-minute performance. The show's backdrop includes Mickey's Fun Wheel, which was fitted with special lighting effects for use in the show. Giant projection surfaces sculpted by sprayed water—even larger than those used in *Fantasmic!*—display custom-made animations, and flame-throwers spew almost enough heat to dry off guests standing in the splash zones. What's most remarkable about the show is how the flashing colored lights and pulsating fountains combine to look like low-level fireworks. The effects are astounding, the colors are vibrant and deep, and the music includes some of Disney's best songs without being overloaded by overly sentimental ballads. You can even invest $25 in Glow with the Show mouse ear hats that illuminate in sync with the show; better yet, stand toward the rear and freeload by eyeballing others who bought them. But while *World of Color* is aesthetically entrancing, dramatically speaking it's a bit of a dud. Disney spectacles have never needed especially strong story lines, but *World of Color* is so plotless that it makes *Fantasmic!* next door look like a Russian novel. The show is essentially a 30-minute montage of movie moments with awkwardly edited segues straining to tie them together. Despite the show's titular association with Uncle Walt's 1960s NBC TV show, and the retro theme of DCA's overall rebranding, there's precious little vintage Disney referenced in *World of Color*. Aside from a brief cameo by 1937's *The Old Mill*, almost all the featured films are drawn from the last quarter century, with lots of mist-screen time given to modern Pixar heroes such as Buzz Lightyear and Wall-E, and footage from the fourth *Pirates of the Caribbean* film. From time to time, a sequence will be temporarily added to the show in celebration of a holiday or to promote a new Disney product; for example, a Christmas season preshow features elves from Pixar's "Prep and Landing" shorts, and a *Brave*-based montage was inserted during the film's summer 2012 debut. There's also a handful of obscurities mysteriously tossed in: was there a fan club somewhere clamoring for more of *Fantasia 2000*'s flying whales? Ultimately, there's enough dazzling eye candy to overwhelm any underlying emotional emptiness in the narrative. Finally, *World of Color* has more false finales than the last *Lord of the Rings* film, so stay put until you're absolutely sure that the show is over.

TOURING TIPS Entertainment value aside, *World of Color* is an operational nightmare. The effects were expressly designed to be viewed from Paradise Park, the tiered area along the lagoon in front of The Little Mermaid attraction. Unfortunately, only about 4,500 people—less than a quarter of the park's average daily attendance—are permitted to stand there for each show. Though demand has slacked somewhat since its opening season, getting a decent view for *World of Color* still requires time, planning, and/or money, and therefore can almost seem to be more trouble to see than it's worth, but we still consider it not to be missed. A couple from San Jose writes:

> Although the [World of Color] *Fastpass line was horrible and waiting for the show was horrible, the show itself was simply amazing.*

A California mom adds the following:

We recently saw the World of Color *show at DCA. It is by far the best Disney show we have seen and worth keeping the kids up for. . . . This seems like a show that you want to sit toward the back to see everything. We were in the last row and still got wet from the fountains. I can only imagine what the front row must be like!*

An Austin, Texas, mom found *World of Color* challenging:

World of Color *was fantastic but hard for kids and shorter adults to see unless they are standing right in front facing Mickey's Wheel. My son could not see the preshow at all, and I had to put him on my shoulders for the 26-minute production. My back has not recovered. They need amphitheater reserved seating. We arrived 1½ hours prior to DCA opening to get a Fastpass and waited 1½ hours for the show to start when admitted.*

If you want anything approaching a decent view of *World of Color*, you'll need a special Fastpass, the securing of which can be an annoying adventure in and of itself. Here are your options for obtaining Fastpasses, beginning with the easiest (and most expensive) method.

Guests staying at Disney's three on-site hotels are eligible to enter DCA an hour before the general public on Extra Magic Hour mornings (currently Sunday, Monday, Wednesday, and Friday), during which time *World of Color* Fastpasses are distributed near Grizzly River Run. No other Fastpasses are distributed during early-entry hours.

World of Color meal packages are offered by Wine Country Trattoria and Ariel's Grotto. The fixed-price dinner runs $42 per adult ($22 for kids) and includes an appetizer, your choice of entrée, dessert, and nonalcoholic beverage. Lunch (only at Wine Country Trattoria) is $30 ($19 for kids) from a more limited menu. Dining reservations are a must, especially during busy seasons (see Part 4 for dining details). All lunch and dinner patrons at Carthay Circle Restaurant who order both an entrée and an appetizer or dessert are eligible for VIP *World of Color* viewing at no additional cost. After your meal, you'll receive special Fastpasses for each member of your party, permitting entry into a VIP Preferred Viewing area reserved for dining package patrons. Note that you don't actually watch the show from the restaurant, so you'll want to eat early enough to make it to the viewing area. Though expensive, this is the only way to be guaranteed a central viewing spot with minimal crowding. On nights when there are multiple *World of Color* performances, early eaters receive passes to the first show, while those eating later get tickets to the later viewing.

You can also watch *World of Color* from the Cove Bar. The view of the projections is less than ideal, but no reservations are required, and you can sit down with an adult beverage during the show.

Free Fastpasses are distributed on a first-come, first-serve basis from the Grizzly River Run Fastpass machines. Make sure that you get passes for your whole party at once, or you may end up in different sections or showings. These machines are disconnected from the rest of the park's Fastpasses system, so your *World of Color* ticket won't interfere with other attractions. On busy days they may all be claimed by early afternoon. If seeing the first *World of Color* show of the night is a priority for you, we suggest getting a Fastpass within the first 30 minutes the park is open. When a second show is scheduled, Fastpasses for the late performance can often be had well into the afternoon.

Once you have your Fastpass, you'll notice that you've been assigned one of two color-coded sections. Yellow is the most central viewing area and stretches to the right side (near the Golden Zephyr), and blue includes the left side and bridge. A special section is available upon request for disabled guests, and a prime area in the middle is reserved for VIPs and dining package purchasers.

Your Fastpass also includes a return time window. You won't be allowed into Paradise Park before the start time, but the best viewing spots will all be claimed shortly after opening, so don't be surprised to see people lining up an hour before the area opens. Once inside the viewing area, try to move to the front of an elevated area. You're best off at the front of an elevated tier farther back, rather than at the rear of a lower section, as these readers from Langley, British Columbia, discovered:

> World of Color *was great, but even with Fastpass it was hard for me to see (wearing flat shoes and being 5'5"). My husband, who is 6'4", also found himself bobbing around trying to see. When we got there, we had good line of sight, but as people stood up and put their kids on their shoulders, it became difficult.*

If you stand close to the railing, pay attention to the splash zone signs; on a calm night, you'll be seriously spritzed, and if the wind blows the wrong way, you'll get soaked.

If all else fails, it's theoretically possible to view the show from various points around the park, but employees with flashlights will vigorously shoo you away from all the obvious vantage points. The best ticketless viewing spot is next to the Golden Zephyr, to the right of the yellow section. Unticketed viewing is also available immediately in front of The Little Mermaid attraction. You can see many of the fountain and lighting effects from the opposite side of Paradise Pier, near the bases of Mickey's Fun Wheel and Silly Symphony Swings, but the mist projections are illegible from that angle, so we can't recommend it for first-time viewers. On nights when there are multiple performances, you have better odds finding a good spot for the last show.

After the show, if you are headed to the hotels or Downtown Disney, you can bypass the crowd at the main entrance by exiting through the Grand Californian.

This family from South Jordan, Utah, seems to have found a sensible strategy:

> *We didn't want to waste time waiting for* World of Color. *We got our Fastpasses in the morning for the blue section. We entered the section about one minute before it started, stood at the bottom of an upper tier, and watched a great show. We were right by the exit and got to leave quickly. We spent our time on Toy Story Midway Mania and Little Mermaid before the show [and] didn't have a lot of wait since all the crowds were anxiously trying to stake out their spots for* World of Color. *Take advantage of as many rides as you can and then just swing by the* World of Color *at the last minute.*

AFTERNOON AND EVENING PARADES Pixar Play Parade features characters from *a bug's life; Cars; Finding Nemo; Monsters, Inc.; The Incredibles;* and *Toy Story.* Lively, very funny, and as varied as the Pixar characters, Pixar Play Parade should be on your must-see list.

The parade route runs from a gate to the left of Boardwalk Pizza & Pasta at Paradise Pier, through The Bay Area, around a bug's land side of Grizzly Peak, and on to Buena Vista Street, where it takes a lap around the fountain toward Hollywood Land and then disappears backstage near Tower of Terror. On days when the crowds are light, any place along the parade route will suffice. On days of heavy attendance, try to score a viewing spot on the elevated courtyard or steps of the Golden Vine Winery. The upstairs Alfresco Lounge offers an excellent bird's-eye perspective.

Several times a day, Phineas and Ferb (from the hit Disney Channel cartoon of the same name) ride a parade float through Paradise Pier and for an interactive Rockin' Rollin' Dance Party, certain to please their pint-size fans (and nonplus uninitiated adults).

MINNIE'S FLY GIRLS Clearly inspired by the *Mad Men*–sparked boom in mod nostalgia, this modest but charming stage show features a trio of Pan Am–style stewardesses singing aviation-themed tunes from the 1940s–1960s. The soaring Frank Sinatra standard "Come Fly with Me" starts the song list, which also includes a medley of international anthems from Ireland to Israel, a musical tribute to Rosie the Riveter, and a retrospective of flight-related Disney songs such as "Let's Go Fly a Kite" from *Mary Poppins*. Minnie herself comes in for a landing at the climax, dressed in a snazzy pilot suit; the character costume is one of those newfangled models that can blink and lip-synch in an eerily lifelike way. The dialogue isn't Shakespearean, but it is peppered with welcome references to Walt Disney as an actual person (not just a corporate icon). A wonderful upgrade from the tween-centric Disney Channel shows that used to dominate, this is the kind of entertainment that grandparents and grandkids alike can get into.

MAD T PARTY Since the summer of 2010, Disney California Adventure has been turning Hollywood Land over to high-energy dance parties on select evenings. Originally called Glow Fest and tied to the debut of *World of Color,* the event quickly evolved into ElecTRONica, which proved more popular than the 2010 cinematic *TRON* sequel that inspired it. The latest version, which kicked off in the summer of 2012, is a Mad T Party that takes stylistic cues from Tim Burton's take on *Alice in Wonderland.* All incarnations of this soirée center on house techno-spinning DJs (many with authentic club cred) and exclusive (read: overpriced) alcoholic beverages in collectible cups. The giant Recognizer prop and vintage video arcade that were a highlight of ElecTRONica are gone; instead, there's a "rabbit hole" entry portal and a live band clad in garishly "hip" garb loosely based on *Wonderland* characters. Whether you find the change an improvement or not depends largely on your love for Burton's profitable but tonally problematic pass on Alice and Co. Between the Day-Glo human slinky contorting on the side stage and the neon Nok-Hockey tables in the streets, the aesthetic resembles an over-the-top Bar Mitzvah party on acid. If you really want to get into the psychedelic spirit, the Glow with the Show ears introduced for *World of Color* will also blink in sync with the Mad T Party's light display. If you're looking to get your dance and drink on without heading out to Downtown Disney, look no further. And if you aren't, the custom carnival games and oversize armchairs may provide comfort.

HYPERION THEATER A state-of-the-art theater that hosts the best of DCA's live shows as well as special concerts and events. Check the daily entertainment schedule in the handout park map to see what's playing and for showtimes.

HOLLYWOOD BACKLOT STAGE This open-air stage that features small productions and Disney characters is one of our favorite venues in the park. Recently, visiting school bands have used this stage. Check the *Times Guide* to see what's playing.

STREET ENTERTAINMENT You'll frequently find a period-appropriate klezmer, Irish, or other ethnic band playing outside the Paradise Garden Grill. On Buena Vista Street, a gang of singing **Red Car News Boys** (and one newsgirl), loosely inspired by the cult film and Tony-winning Broadway musical *Newsies,* use the Red Car Trolleys as a roving stage for exuberant song-and-dance performances (look for the high-tech talking Mickey Mouse to make an extended cameo appearance), and the **Five and Dime** musical sextet (accompanied by a zoot suit–clad Goofy) sings jazz standards of the 1920s and 1930s such as "Toot, Toot, Tootsie," "Red, Red Robin," and "Bye, Bye, Blackbird"; this is one of the best street shows in Disney's repertoire. You may also bump into interactive improvisation actors portraying police officers, bicycle messengers, or other eccentric **Citizens of Buena Vista,** a troupe similar to the popular Streetmosphere characters at Disney's Hollywood Studios in Orlando. Along Cars Land's main drag, **Red the Firetruck** shows up in the morning with sirens blazing to spray down the crowds, and **DJ's Dance and Drive** features the "ultimate party car" hosting afternoon oldies dance parties with the help of interactive carhop waitresses. Maestro Goofy gets into the act over at Paradise Bay by conducting a water fountain ballet titled *Instant Concert . . . Just Add Water!*

DISNEY CHARACTERS Character appearances are listed in the daily *Times Guide.* In addition, Flik and Atta can usually be found at a bug's land, Russell and Dug from Pixar's *Up!* hang out around the Redwood Creek Challenge Trail, the Incredibles make appearances in Hollywood Land, and Ariel's Grotto restaurant at Paradise Pier offers character dining featuring Ariel and her princess friends. Duffy the Disney Bear (a marketing creation imported from Tokyo DisneySea) greets guests across from Ariel's Grotto. Mater and Lightning take turns posing for photos near the Cozy Cone Motel; these life-size vehicles can deliver quips recorded by the original voice actors to grinning guests.

DISNEY DISH WITH JIM HILL

KIND OF A SORE-CEROR'S SUBJECT Since early 2012, visitors to Walt Disney World have been enjoying Sorcerers of the Magic Kingdom, an interactive role-playing game where guests use magic spell cards to defeat various Disney villains. Disneyland fans have been asking when Sorcerers will be showing up at their theme park, and the answer is that it won't. Most of the streets inside of Disneyland Park are so narrow (coupled with the tens of thousands of people who visit this theme park every day) that it just wouldn't be smart or safe to set up a questing game like this inside of "The Happiest Place on Earth." But Disney California Adventure, with its ridiculously wide performance corridors, would be the ideal setting for this sort of role-play-your-way-around-a-theme-park interactive entertainment. The Imagineers are already hard at work designing a DCA-specific role-playing game, which should go live in in late 2014 or early 2015, just in time for the kickoff of the Disneyland Resort's 60th anniversary celebration.

UNHERALDED TREASURES *at* DCA

TREASURE: Cove Bar | **LOCATION:** On the bridge to Paradise Pier

ARIEL'S GROTTO IS A FIXED-PRICE character-meal restaurant on the span connecting Paradise Pier to the Golden State area. Instead of heading downstairs to the restaurant from the entrance, though, go around the walkway. There, you'll find the Cove Bar, where you can enjoy a full-service bar and a small selection of food. For some, the thought of a cocktail at the end of a long day might be enticement enough, but this is a good spot even for teetotalers—it's one of the best places to enjoy the view. It's a bit too sunny during the day, but as the sun sets and the evening lights come on, the Cove turns into a mellow hideaway where you can enjoy a beautiful view of Paradise Pier. In the background, you hear music, laughter, and the occasional sounds of a roller coaster. You look out and see the small waves lapping against the pier that houses a brightly lit carousel—enough to make you forget that you're sitting in the middle of a completely artificial environment.

TREASURE: Redwood Creek Challenge Trail | **LOCATION:** Opposite Grizzly Peak

MAYBE A VISIT TO A THEME PARK was your kid's idea, and you prefer going on a quiet walk in the woods or enjoying a hike in a national park. If you just want to take a break from the hectic rush of a trip to DCA, hop over to the Redwood Creek Challenge Trail. Looking at the park map, you probably assume that this is just a playground designed for little kids, but the area is actually a good representation of a wilderness park. OK, so you don't really need to bring your bird-watching book, but there are various nooks and crannies, as well as a few "ranger buildings," that are very well themed (down to the wildlife books on the shelves). You could easily spend a portion of your day just enjoying the decidedly rustic feel of Redwood Creek.

TRAFFIC PATTERNS
at DISNEY CALIFORNIA
ADVENTURE

ONE OF THE PROBLEMS that Disney had at DCA early on was that there was no traffic to create patterns. Attendance figures were far less than projected, though guests on hand did stack up daily at Soarin' Over California and Grizzly River Run. On the relatively few crowded days (mostly weekends), the park didn't handle crowds particularly well. If Disney's gate projections had panned out, the park would have been in gridlock much of the time.

If you happen to hit DCA on a day of high attendance, here's what to expect. The majority of the crowd will likely sprint to the Cars Land, grabbing Fastpasses for Radiator Springs Racers and quickly overwhelming the two low-capacity attractions found there. Because Cars Land is such a draw, wait times at the park's former see-first attractions, including Toy Story Midway Mania! and Soarin' Over California, have moderate waits for the first hour the park is open.

Some guests also head to Tower of Terror, but the rest of Hollywood Land, as well as Pacific Wharf and a bug's land, are deserted until midmorning. Unless the day starts off unusually warm, lines don't develop at Grizzly River Run until just before lunchtime.

The crowd begins working its way into Paradise Pier an hour or two after the park is open. The super-headliner Toy Story Midway Mania! is the big draw here, followed by California Screamin'. Although they're not popular, the slow-loading cycle rides at Paradise Pier will begin to develop lines a bit later. There's rarely a long wait for the Little Mermaid attraction, though, at any time of day.

The crowds redistribute to the park's shows around lunchtime. *Disney Junior, Muppet-Vision,* and the Hyperion Theater each draw good-size crowds. By 2 p.m., the whole park is fairly socked in with guests, and even minor attractions and displays, such as the sourdough bread demonstration, build lines.

Park departures begin around 3 p.m. when families with small children start heading home. What's interesting, however, is that 9-to-5 workers start coming into the park around 6 p.m. and will generally stay for the evening. It's common to see waits hold steady or even rise from early evening until the park closes, undoubtedly because of Cars Land and *World of Color.*

Guests with *World of Color* Fastpasses will begin queuing in the Pacific Wharf, Grizzly Peak, and Paradise Pier walkways an hour or more before showtime. The largest wave of departing guests occur at the end of *World of Color.* Just before closing, crowd levels are thin except, of course, at Cars Land, Soarin' Over California, and The Tower of Terror.

CALIFORNIA ADVENTURE TOURING PLANS

PRELIMINARY INSTRUCTIONS FOR ALL DISNEY CALIFORNIA ADVENTURE TOURING PLANS

ON DAYS OF MODERATE to heavy attendance, follow the touring plans exactly, deviating only when you do not wish to experience a listed show or ride.

1. Buy your admission in advance (see "Admission Options" on page 19).
2. Call ☎ 714-781-7290 the day before you go for the official opening time.
3. Become familiar with the park-opening procedures (described on page 291) and read over the touring plan of your choice so that you will have a basic understanding of what you are likely to encounter as you enter the park.

DCA ONE-DAY TOURING PLAN FOR ADULTS
(page 374)

FOR Adults without small children.
ASSUMES Willingness to experience all rides and shows.

Height and age requirements apply to many attractions. If you have kids who aren't eligible to ride, try switching off (see page 149) or use the One-Day Touring Plan for Parents with Small Children. This touring plan includes most of the amusement park rides on Paradise Pier. If you're short on time or wish to allocate more of the day to DCA's theatrical attractions, forgo a few of the rides in a bug's land. Crowds are smaller at DCA on Tuesday, Thursday, and Saturday when Disneyland Park has early entry.

ABOUT EARLY ENTRY If you are eligible for early entry, experience Luigi's Flying Tires and Mater's Junkyard Jamboree, in that order, followed by Tower of Terror and/or Soarin' Over California (time permitting). Get in the exclusive early-entry queue for Radiator Springs Racers Fastpasses at least 10 minutes before the official park opening. Pick up the plan with step 5, and return to ride Radiator Springs Racers once your Fastpass window starts.

DCA normally hosts early entry on Sunday, Monday, Wednesday, and Friday. This may expand to seven days a week, depending on demand. Unlike Disneyland, DCA's early entry is strictly for hotel guests only; Magic Morning ticket holders may not enter early. If you are not eligible for early entry, try not to use the plan on an early-entry day. Cars Land will be packed with early-entry guests before you even get past the turnstiles.

DCA ONE-DAY TOURING PLAN FOR ADULTS WITH SMALL CHILDREN *(page 375)*

FOR Adults with small children who wish to experience all major rides and shows.

ASSUMES Willingness to experience all rides and shows.

Height and age requirements apply to many attractions. If you have kids who aren't eligible to ride, try switching off (see page 149). This touring plan includes most of the amusement park rides on Paradise Pier. If you're short on time or wish to allocate more of the day to DCA's theatrical attractions, forgo a few of the rides in a bug's land. Crowds are smaller at DCA on Tuesday, Thursday, and Saturday when Disneyland Park has early entry.

ABOUT EARLY ENTRY If you are eligible for early entry, experience Luigi's Flying Tires and Mater's Junkyard Jamboree, in that order, followed by Tower of Terror and/or Soarin' Over California (time permitting). Get in the exclusive early-entry queue for Radiator Springs Racers Fastpasses at least 10 minutes before the official park opening. Pick up the plan with step 5, and return to ride Radiator Springs Racers once your Fastpass window starts.

DCA normally hosts early entry on Sunday, Monday, Wednesday, and Friday. This may expand to seven days a week, depending on demand. Unlike Disneyland, DCA's early entry is strictly for hotel guests only; Magic Morning ticket holders may not enter early. If you are not eligible for early entry, try not to use the plan on an early-entry day. Cars Land will be packed with early-entry guests before you even get past the turnstiles.

PART SEVEN

UNIVERSAL STUDIOS HOLLYWOOD

UNIVERSAL STUDIOS HOLLYWOOD was the first film and TV studio to turn part of its facility into a modern theme park. By integrating shows and rides with behind-the-scenes presentations on moviemaking, Universal Studios Hollywood created a new genre of theme park, stimulating a number of clone and competitor parks. First came the Disney-MGM Studios (now Disney's Hollywood Studios) at Walt Disney World, followed shortly by Universal Studios Florida, also near Orlando. Where Universal Studios Hollywood, however, evolved from an established film and TV venue, its cross-country imitators were launched primarily as theme parks, albeit with some production capability on the side. Disney is also challenging Universal in California with Disney California Adventure. While DCA does not have production facilities, one of its themed areas focuses on Hollywood and the movies.

Located just off US 101 north of Hollywood, Universal Studios operates on a scale and with a quality standard rivaled only by Disney, SeaWorld, and Busch Gardens parks. Unique among American theme parks for its topography, Universal Studios Hollywood is tucked on top of, below, and around a tall hill. The studios consist of an open-access area and a controlled-access area. The latter contains the working soundstages, back lot, wardrobe, scenery, prop shops, postproduction facility, and administration offices. Guests can visit the controlled-access area by taking the Studio Tour. The open-access area, which contains the park's rides, shows, restaurants, and services, is divided into two sections. The main entrance provides access to the upper section, the Upper Lot, on top of the hill. Five theater shows and two rides, as well as the loading area for the Studio Tour, are located in the Upper Lot. The Lower Lot, at the northeastern base of the hill, is accessible from the Upper Lot via escalators. There are three rides and a walk-through exhibit in the Lower Lot. All attractions, including rides, shows, and tours, are profiled in this chapter.

In 2013 Universal received governmental approval to implement its ambitious Evolution plan, which will dramatically reshape its complex over the next decade. Two 500-room on-site hotels are planned, and CityWalk will expand into the current front entryway, accompanied by new parking structures. Inside the park, several new attractions are proposed for the Upper Lot, and three additional points of interest will be installed along the tram tour. And all of that is in addition to a West Coast annex of the wildly popular Wizarding World of Harry Potter found at Orlando's Islands of Adventure park. At press time, official details—including what rides might be included or an opening date—are scarcer than muggles in Hogsmeade. But you can count on a clone of the fantastic Forbidden Journey dark ride, plus opportunities to go broke on exclusive merchandise and food, such as wands and delicious Butterbeer. Our crystal balls point to Hogwarts Castle opening in 2015 or 2016, but look for construction walls to go up before long. To accommodate all this activity, some old friends will say farewell; the disused Wild West arena has already been transformed into a multipurpose plaza, and the Special Effects Stage, *WaterWorld* show, and Gibson Amphitheatre are on the chopping block.

The park offers all standard services and amenities, including stroller and wheelchair rental, lockers, diaper-changing and nursing facilities, car assistance, and foreign-language assistance. Most of the park is accessible to disabled guests, and TDDs are available for the hearing impaired. Almost all services are in the Upper Lot, just inside the main entrance.

GATHERING INFORMATION

THE MAIN UNIVERSAL STUDIOS information number is ☎ 818 622-3801. Calling this number, however, often results in up to 20 minutes of holding time or about 7 minutes on hold followed by a disconnect. To short-circuit the operating-hours litany, dial 3. If you have problems, try calling ☎ 818-622-3735 or 818-622-3750. Universal Studios' website, **universalstudioshollywood.com,** is easy to navigate.

WHAT MAKES UNIVERSAL STUDIOS
HOLLYWOOD DIFFERENT

WHAT MAKES UNIVERSAL STUDIOS HOLLYWOOD different is that the attractions, with a couple of exceptions, are designed to minimize long waits in line. The centerpiece of the Universal Studios experience is the Studio Tour. While on the tram, you experience an earthquake, are attacked by the killer shark from *Jaws,* and endure a simulated rain shower and a flash flood, among other things. In other parks, including Universal's sister park in Florida, each of these spectacles is presented as an individual attraction, and each has its own long queue. At Universal Studios Hollywood, by contrast, you suffer only one very manageable wait to board the tram and then experience all of these events as part of the tour.

In addition to the time saving and convenience provided by the tram tour, most of the live shows at Universal Studios Hollywood

Universal Studios Hollywood

1. Despicable Me: Minion Mayhem
2. Jurassic Park—The Ride
3. The NBC Universal Experience
4. Revenge of the Mummy–The Ride

5. *Shrek 4-D*
6. The Simpsons Ride
7. Special Effects Stage
8. Studio Tour

9. Transformers—The Ride
10. *Universal's Animal Actors*
11. Universal's House of Horrors
12. *WaterWorld*

are performed in large theaters or stadiums. Instead of standing in line outside, guests are usually invited to enter the theater and wait in seated comfort for the production to begin.

TIMING *Your* VISIT

CROWDS ARE LARGEST IN THE SUMMER (Memorial Day–Labor Day) and during specific holiday periods during the rest of the year. Christmas Day–New Year's Day is extremely busy, as are Thanksgiving weekend, the week of Washington's birthday, spring break for schools and colleges, and the two weeks bracketing Easter. The least busy time is from after Thanksgiving weekend until the week before Christmas. The next slowest times are September through the weekend preceding Thanksgiving, January 4 through the first week of March, and the week following Easter to Memorial Day weekend.

SELECTING THE DAY OF THE WEEK FOR YOUR VISIT

WEEKENDS ARE MORE CROWDED than weekdays year-round. Saturday is the busiest day. Sunday, particularly Sunday morning, is the best bet if you have to go on a weekend, but it is still extremely busy. During the summer, Friday is very busy; Monday, Wednesday, and Thursday are usually less so; Tuesday is normally the slowest of all. During the off-season (September–May, holidays excepted), Tuesday is usually the least-crowded day, followed by Thursday.

HOW MUCH TIME TO ALLOCATE

ALTHOUGH THERE'S A LOT TO SEE and do at Universal Studios Hollywood, you can (unlike at Disneyland) complete a comprehensive tour in one day. If you follow our touring plan, which calls for being on hand at park opening, you should be able to check out everything by mid- to late afternoon, even on a crowded day.

Never mind that Universal Studios Hollywood claims to cover 400 acres; the area you will have to traverse on foot is considerably smaller. In fact, you will do much less walking and, miracle of miracles, much less standing in line at Universal Studios than at Disneyland.

UNIVERSAL STUDIOS HOLLYWOOD
FOR YOUNG CHILDREN

WE DO NOT RECOMMEND UNIVERSAL STUDIOS HOLLYWOOD for preschoolers. Of 10 major attractions, all but 2 (*Universal's Animal Actors* and *Shrek 4-D*) have the potential for flipping out sensitive little ones. See the Small-Child Fright-Potential Chart on page 343.

COST

ONE-DAY TICKETS ARE AVAILABLE for about $85 for persons more than 48 inches tall and $77 for those shorter than 48 inches. A pass that allows you to skip to the front of the line at all attractions and attend behind-the-scenes cast member question-and-answer sessions after select shows runs $150 ($170 during peak season) for both adults and children. Annual passes cost $109 (with blackout dates) or $139 (without blackout dates) for all patrons over age 3 (add $40 for a pass with parking). Admission is free for those under age 3. By purchasing tickets online at **universal studioshollywood.com,** at times you can buy two days' admission for the price of one day. Additionally, Universal almost always has some ticket special going online and at the park's ticket booths. You can print your tickets for $1 fee at the Universal website.

For Hollywood-happy high rollers, USH now offers a $299 VIP Experience that includes escorted queue-cutting at all attractions, off-tram walking tours of sets and soundstages, gourmet breakfast and lunch, and amenities such as ponchos and bottled water. If you have the spare dough, it's undoubtedly a better deal than Disney's pay-per-hour VIP guides. Reservations are required; call ☎ 818-622-1141 to book.

In addition to the website discounts, admission discounts are sometimes offered in area freebie publications available in hotels. Admission discounts are also periodically offered to AAA members. Vacation packages including lodging and park admission are available from Hilton and Sheraton hotels, both of which offer accommodations nearby.

In a groundbreaking initiative, Universal Studios Hollywood will issue you a rain check good for 30 days if it rains more than one-eighth of an inch by 2 p.m. They'll also keep you warm with complimentary coffee and cocoa.

THE SHUTTLE

UNIVERSAL CITY is on the Red Line of **Los Angeles Metro Rail,** which makes it relatively easy to commute by light rail from downtown LA and many other places, though not from Anaheim. Across the street from the subway station and the bus stop, at Lankershim Boulevard and Universal Terrace Parkway, is a free shuttle bus that will conveniently take you to the main entrances of Universal Studios Hollywood and Universal CityWalk Hollywood. The bus runs daily, beginning at 7 a.m., with pickups about every 10–15 minutes; service continues until about two hours after the theme park closes. Refer to the posted times at each shuttle stop for information on the last departing shuttle. For rail and bus schedules and additional public transportation information, call MTA at ☎ 800-COMMUTE or 213-626-4455, or visit **metro.net.**

ARRIVING *and*
GETTING ORIENTED

MOST FOLKS ACCESS UNIVERSAL STUDIOS by taking US 101, also called the Hollywood Freeway, and following the signs to the park. If the freeway is gridlocked, you can also get to the Studios by taking Cahuenga Boulevard and then turning north toward Lankershim

Boulevard. If you are coming from Burbank, take Barham Boulevard toward US 101, and then follow the signs.

Universal Studios has a big, multilevel parking garage at the top of the hill. Signs directing you to the garage are a bit confusing, so pay attention and stay to the far right when you come up the hill. Even after you have made it to the pay booth and shelled out $15 to park ($25 for premium parking, $17 if your RV is more than 15 feet long, and $10 after 3 p.m.), it is still not exactly clear where you go next. Drive slowly, follow other cars proceeding from the pay booths, and avoid turns onto ramps marked EXIT. You may become a bit disoriented, but ultimately you will blunder into the garage. Once parked, make a note of your parking level and the location of your space.

Walk toward the opposite end of the garage from where you entered and exit into Universal CityWalk, a shopping, dining, and entertainment complex (no admission required) situated between the parking structure and the main entrance of the park. As an aside, City-Walk is much like Downtown Disney at Disneyland. Some of Universal's better restaurants and more interesting shops are at CityWalk, and it's so close to the theme park entrance that you can conveniently pop out of the park to grab a bite (don't forget to have your hand stamped for reentry).

Universal Studios' ticket booths and turnstiles are about 100 yards from the main parking garage. If you need cash, an ATM is outside and to the right of the main entrance. There is also an ATM inside the park next to the Cartooniversal store. Nearby is a guest-services window. As you enter the park, be sure to pick up a park map and a daily entertainment schedule.

THE UPPER LOT

THE UPPER LOT is essentially a large, amorphous pedestrian plaza. In-park signage (which is inordinately confusing) references street names such as New York Street and Baker Street and place names such as Cape Cod and Moulin Rouge, but on foot these theme distinctions are largely lost and placement of buildings appears almost random. In other words, do not expect the sort of thematic integrity that you find at Disneyland.

Inside the main entrance, stroller and wheelchair rentals are on the right, as are rental lockers. Straight ahead is a TV Audience Ticket Booth, where you can obtain free tickets to join the audience for any TV shows that are taping during your visit (subject to availability).

Attractions in the Upper Lot are situated around the perimeter of the plaza. Near The Simpsons Ride (straight ahead) are the escalators and stairs that lead to the Lower Lot. The Upper Lot attractions are described in detail on the following pages.

THE LOWER LOT

THE LOWER LOT IS ACCESSIBLE ONLY via the escalators and stairs descending from the back left section of the Upper Lot. Configured roughly in the shape of the letter T, the Lower Lot is home to

Transformers, Jurassic Park, and Revenge of the Mummy, all headliner attractions at Universal Studios Hollywood. The Lower Lot attractions are described beginning on page 338 following the Upper Lot attractions.

UNIVERSAL STUDIOS HOLLYWOOD ATTRACTIONS

UPPER LOT ATTRACTIONS

Despicable Me: Minion Mayhem ★ ★ ★ ★

APPEAL BY AGE   PRESCHOOL ★ ★ ★ ★   GRADE SCHOOL ★ ★ ★ ★ ★   TEENS ★ ★ ★ ★ ★
YOUNG ADULTS ★ ★ ★ ★   OVER 30   ★ ★ ★ ★   SENIORS   ★ ★ ★

What it is Motion simulator with 3-D projection. **Scope and scale** Major attraction. **When to go** The first hour the park is open or after 4 p.m. **Special comments** Must be 40" to ride in motion seats; nonmoving seats are available. **Duration of ride** 5 minutes, plus 10-minute preshow. **Average wait time per 100 people ahead of you** 7 minutes. **Loading speed** Moderate–slow.

DESCRIPTION AND COMMENTS Despicable Me: Minion Mayhem is a 3-D motion simulator ride similar to Universal's The Simpsons Ride and Star Tours at Disneyland. The idea is that you're seated in a ride vehicle that faces a large video screen, on to which the attraction's story is projected. When the story calls for you to drop down the side of a mountain, your ride vehicle tilts forward as if you were falling; when you need to swerve left or right, your ride vehicle tilts the same way. The main difference between Minion Mayhem and other simulators is that most other simulators usually provide one video screen per ride vehicle, while Minion Mayhem arranges all of its eight-person vehicles in front of one large IMAX-size video screen. The ride vehicles are set on raised platforms, which get slightly higher toward the back of the theater, affording good views for all guests.

The preshow area is inside the home of adorably evil Gru (voiced by Steve Carell), where you see his unique family tree and other artifacts. The premise of the ride is that you're turned into one of Gru's chattering yellow minions. Once converted you must navigate the minion training grounds, where your "speed, strength, and ability not to die" is tested. Something soon goes amiss, though, and your training turns into a frenetic rescue operation.

The ride is a fast-paced series of dives, climbs, and tight turns through Gru's Rube Goldberg–esque machines. Like The Simpsons Ride, there are more sight gags and interesting things to see here than anyone possibly could in a single ride. Guests exiting the ride may find the opportunity for a short dance with one of the minions.

TOURING TIPS Minion Mayhem, a hit import from Universal Studios Florida, arrives in Hollywood during 2014, replacing the long-running *Terminator 2* show. Because the ride is new and based on a popular franchise, lines are sure to be long during its debut season. Ride it immediately after experiencing the Lower Lot attractions, or first thing if you are skipping the bigger thrill rides. If the line for Despicable Me exceeds 30 minutes, try late afternoon or the hour before the park closes. Adjacent to the exit, a Super Silly Fun Land playground area (with wet and dry activities and a simple spinning carnival ride) should help small tykes burn off some steam.

Shrek 4-D ★★★★

APPEAL BY AGE	PRESCHOOL ★★★★	GRADE SCHOOL ★★★★½	TEENS ★★★★½
YOUNG ADULTS ★★★★½		OVER 30 ★★★★½	SENIORS ★★★★

What it is 3-D theater show. **Scope and scale** Headliner. **When to go** The first hour the park is open or after 4 p.m. **Duration of show** About 20 minutes. **Preshow** 5-minute video. **Probable waiting time** About an hour.

DESCRIPTION AND COMMENTS *Shrek 4-D* is based on characters from the hit movie *Shrek*. A preshow presents the villain from the movie, Lord Farquaad, as he appears on various screens to describe his posthumous plan to reclaim his lost bride, Princess Fiona, who married Shrek. Lord Farquaad died in the movie, and it's his ghost making the plans, but never mind. Guests then move into the main theater, don their 3-D glasses, and recline in seats equipped with "tactile transducers" and "pneumatic air propulsion and water-spray nodules." As the 3-D film plays, guests are also subjected to smells relevant to the on-screen action (oh boy).

Technicalities aside, *Shrek* is a real winner. It's irreverent, frantic, laugh-out-loud funny, and iconoclastic. Concerning the latter, the film takes a good poke at Disney with Pinocchio, the Three Little Pigs, and Tinker Bell (among others) all sucked into the mayhem. The film quality and 3-D effects are great, and like the feature film, it's sweet without being sappy. Plus, in contrast to Disney's *It's Tough to Be a Bug!*, *Shrek 4-D* doesn't generally frighten children under 7 years of age.

TOURING TIPS Universal claims that they can move 2,400 guests an hour through *Shrek 4-D*. If true, that should keep things moving efficiently. Still, expect big crowds. Try to see *Shrek* before noon.

The Simpsons Ride ★★★★

APPEAL BY AGE	PRESCHOOL ★★★½	GRADE SCHOOL ★★★★	TEENS ★★★★
YOUNG ADULTS ★★★★		OVER 30 ★★★★	SENIORS ★★★½

What it is Mega-simulator ride. **Scope and scale** Super-headliner. **When to go** After the Lower Lot rides and Despicable Me. **Special comments** Must be 40" tall to ride; not recommended for pregnant women or people prone to motion sickness. Switching-off option provided (see page 149). **Duration of ride** 4⅓ minutes, plus preshow. **Average wait time per 100 people ahead of you** 5 minutes. **Loading speed** Moderate.

Queasy

DESCRIPTION AND COMMENTS In spring 2007 this ride, based on the Fox animated series that is TV's longest-running sitcom, opened. Featuring the voices of Dan Castellaneta (Homer), Julie Kavner (Marge), Nancy Cartwright (Bart), Yeardley Smith (Lisa), and other cast members, the attraction takes a wild and humorous poke at thrill rides, dark rides, and live shows "that make up a fantasy amusement park dreamed up by the show's cantankerous Krusty the Clown."

Two preshows involve Simpsons characters speaking sequentially on different video screens around the line area. Their comments help define the characters for guests who are unfamiliar with the TV show. The attraction is a simulator ride similar to Star Tours at Disneyland Park, but with a larger IMAX-type screen more like that of Soarin' at DCA.

The story line has the conniving Sideshow Bob secretly arriving at Krustyland, the aforementioned amusement park, and plotting his revenge on Krusty and Bart, who, in a past *Simpsons* episode, revealed that Sideshow Bob had committed a crime for which he'd framed Krusty. Sideshow Bob gets even by making things go wrong with the attractions that the Simpsons (and you) are riding.

Like the show on which it's based, The Simpsons Ride definitely has an edge, and more than a few wild hairs. There will be jokes and visuals that you'll get but will fly over your children's heads—and most assuredly vice versa. A mom from Huntington, New York, had this to say:

> The ride is lots of fun and suitable for all guests. I'm not a fan of wild motion [simulators], but I was fine on this ride. The field of vision makes it very engrossing, like Soarin'.

TOURING TIPS You can expect large crowds all day. We recommend arriving at the park before opening and making the ride your first stop after experiencing the Lower Lot attractions. Though not as rough and jerky as its predecessor, it's a long way from being tame. Several families we interviewed found the humor a little too adult for their younger children. Don't miss the neighboring Kwik-E-Mart gift shop for more snarky Simpsons sight gags, and look for other Springfield-inspired eateries to appear in 2014.

Special Effects Stage ★ ★ ★

APPEAL BY AGE	PRESCHOOL ★ ★ ½	GRADE SCHOOL ★ ★ ★	TEENS ★ ★ ★ ½
YOUNG ADULTS ★ ★ ★ ½	OVER 30 ★ ★ ★		SENIORS ★ ★ ★ ½

What it is A theater presentation on special effects. **Scope and scale** Major attraction. **When to go** Anytime. **Special comments** Predictable but still interesting; may frighten young children. **Duration of show** 30 minutes. **Probable waiting time** 15 minutes.

DESCRIPTION AND COMMENTS Guests view a fast-paced presentation on special effects, with elements borrowed from both the old Special Effects Stages (formerly on the park's Lower Lot) and the *Horror Make-up* and *Disaster!* attractions found in Universal Studios Florida. Audience members participate in demonstrations of green screens, computer-generated imagery (CGI), and motion capture. For the finale, a volunteer is apparently attached to a flying rig (left over from the short-lived *Creature of the Black Lagoon* musical that once occupied this space) and sent sailing above the crowd. The educational content will already be familiar to anyone who has ever watched a DVD making-of documentary, and the thin through-line about a youthful digital-era director upstaging an aging analog artist may mildly offend viewers who still appreciate old-fashioned films that don't look like video games.

TOURING TIPS The best seats seem to be in the center of the theater, not directly up front. Or try the seats to the left of the stage.

Studio Tour including *King Kong 360/3-D*   ★★★★★

What it is Indoor-outdoor tram tour of soundstages and back lot. **Scope and scale** Headliner. **When to go** After experiencing the other rides. **Duration of tour** About 42 minutes. **Loading speed** Fast.

Loud

Scary

DESCRIPTION AND COMMENTS The Studio Tour is the centerpiece of Universal Studios Hollywood and is one of the longest attractions in American theme parks. The tour departs from the tram boarding facility to the *right* of The Simpsons Ride and down the escalator. (Note that there's also an escalator to the left of The Simpsons Ride, so don't get confused.)

The tour circulates through the various street scenes, lagoons, special-effects venues, and storage areas of Universal's back lot. The tram passes several soundstages where current films and TV shows such as *CSI* are in production and actually enters three soundstages where action inspired by *Earthquake, The Mummy,* and *King Kong* is presented. The Studio Tour was improved in 2006 with a robotic car chase from *The Fast and the Furious: Tokyo Drift* and the addition of sets and filmmaking demonstrations from *War of the Worlds.* Other famous sets visited include those from *Psycho, Jaws,* and *The Grinch Who Stole Christmas.* A simulated flash flood, long a highlight of the tour, was enhanced by increasing the volume of water used. A 2008 fire destroyed the New York Street section of the back lot, including the huge animatronic King Kong, the courthouse square from *Back to the Future,* and much of the contents of a video-archive storage vault. The back lot was restored more or less to its original appearance, but when King Kong returned in 2010, it was in a very different form. Instead of rebuilding the classic banana-breathing robotic monkey based on the 1976 version, the award-winning new *King Kong 360/3-D* is a virtual experience inspired by Peter Jackson's 2005 remake. Guests enter a darkened tunnel where tram-length curved projection screens transform into the jungles of Skull Island. A family of hungry V-Rexes decide to dine on your tour, and Kong himself swings to save you, with hydraulic lifts under the cars simulating the sensations of their tug-of-war. The experience is visceral and visually stunning, especially when seen from the middle of a row (sitting on the outside exposes the top of the screen, spoiling the illusion). At only about 90 seconds, *King Kong* is too short to be a satisfying stand-alone attraction, but it's a terrific addition to the overall tour.

As a great enhancement, all trams are equipped with high-definition monitors showing clips from actual movies that demonstrate how the various sets and soundstages were used in creating the films. In 2011 talk show host and former *Saturday Night Live* star Jimmy Fallon became the tour's prerecorded host. (We dare you to get Fallon's "Tram-Tastic" tune out of your head.)

The great thing about the Studio Tour is that you see everything without leaving the tram—essentially experiencing four or five major attractions with only one wait.

TOURING TIPS Though the wait to board might appear long, do not be discouraged. Each tram carries several hundred people and departures are frequent, so the line moves quickly. We recommend taking the tram tour after experiencing the other rides.

Including your wait to board and the duration of the tour, you will easily invest an hour or more at this attraction. Remember to take a restroom break before queuing up. Though the ride as a whole is gentle, some segments may induce vertigo or motion sickness—especially The Curse of the Mummy's Tomb, inspired by *The Mummy* and adapted from the old avalanche-effect section of the tour. Finally, be aware that several of the scenes may frighten small children.

Universal's Animal Actors ★ ★ ★ ½

APPEAL BY AGE	PRESCHOOL ★ ★ ★ ½	GRADE SCHOOL ★ ★ ★ ★	TEENS ★ ★ ★ ½
YOUNG ADULTS ★ ★ ★ ½	OVER 30 ★ ★ ★ ½		SENIORS ★ ★ ★ ½

What it is Trained animals stadium performance. **Scope and scale** Major attraction. **When to go** After you have experienced all rides. **Special comments** Warm and delightful. **Duration of show** 20 minutes. **Probable waiting time** 15 minutes.

Thumbs Up for the Whole Family

DESCRIPTION AND COMMENTS *Universal's Animal Actors* features various critters, including some rescued from shelters, demonstrating behaviors that animals often perform in the making of motion pictures. The live presentation is punctuated by clips from films and TV shows. Of course, the animals often exhibit an independence that frustrates their trainers while delighting the audience.

TOURING TIPS Presented five or more times daily, the program's schedule is in the daily entertainment guide. Go when it's convenient for you; queue about 20 minutes before showtime.

Universal's House of Horrors ★ ★ ★

APPEAL BY AGE	PRESCHOOL –	GRADE SCHOOL ★ ★ ★	TEENS ★ ★ ★ ½
YOUNG ADULTS ★ ★ ★ ½	OVER 30 ★ ★ ★		SENIORS ★ ★ ½

What it is A fun house–style walk-through of scenes based on classic Universal horror films, incorporating robotics, hydraulics, real people, smoke, and mirrors. **Scope and scale** Minor attraction. **When to go** Anytime. **Special comments** Not suitable for children age 10 and younger. Switching-off option provided (see page 149). **Probable waiting time** 3–5 minutes.

Dark   Loud   Scary

DESCRIPTION AND COMMENTS This attraction is an extremely elaborate horror maze. It's quite similar to the walk-through haunted houses you see around Halloween. Basically, you walk in near darkness through the tight, winding corridors of Dracula's castle, occasionally coming upon a large set from the *Van Helsing* vampire-killing film (including a 50-foot bridge overlooking Frankenstein's monster while he enjoys a little electroshock therapy) or a more modern maniac such as Chucky or Leatherface. As you pick your way through the dark, there are lots of gruesome sights, disorienting devices such as mirrors, and worst of all, live people springing out of dark corners to startle you. If you don't like being startled but really want to see the attraction, follow some teenage girls through. The leaping, growling, menacing ghouls will expend lots of extra energy on the girls and be in a state of relative depletion when you pass through.

TOURING TIPS House of Horrors is located very near the main entrance to the park. It doesn't take long to tour (as the length of the experience depends on how badly you want out), and it can be gotten out of the way quickly.

WaterWorld ★ ★ ★ ★

APPEAL BY AGE	PRESCHOOL ★ ★	GRADE SCHOOL ★ ★ ★ ★	TEENS ★ ★ ★ ★
YOUNG ADULTS ★ ★ ★ ★		OVER 30 ★ ★ ★ ½	SENIORS ★ ★ ★ ½

What it is Arena show featuring simulated stunt-scene filming. **Scope and scale** Major attraction. **When to go** After experiencing all of the rides and the tram tour. **Duration of show** 15 minutes. **Probable waiting time** 15 minutes.

Thumbs Up for the Whole Family

DESCRIPTION AND COMMENTS Drawn from the film *WaterWorld,* this outdoor theater presentation features stunts and special effects performed on and around a small man-made lagoon. The action involves various watercraft and, of course, a lot of explosions and falling from high places into the water. Fast-paced and well adapted to the theater, the production is in many ways more compelling than the film that inspired it.

TOURING TIPS Wait until you have experienced all of the rides and the tram tour before checking out *WaterWorld.* Because the show is located near the main entrance, most performances are sold out. Arrive at the theater about 30 minutes before the showtime listed in the daily entertainment schedule. Be careful where you sit; when this show says "splash zone," they mean it.

LOWER LOT ATTRACTIONS

Jurassic Park—The Ride ★ ★ ★ ★

APPEAL BY AGE	PRESCHOOL ★ ★	GRADE SCHOOL ★ ★ ★ ★ ½	TEENS ★ ★ ★ ★ ½
YOUNG ADULTS ★ ★ ★ ★		OVER 30 ★ ★ ★ ★	SENIORS ★ ★ ★ ★

What it is Indoor-outdoor adventure ride based on the movie *Jurassic Park*. **Scope and scale** Super-headliner. **When to go** Before 10:30 a.m. **Special comments** Must be 46" tall to ride. Switching-off option provided (see page 149). **Duration of ride** 6 minutes. **Loading speed** Fast.

Scary   Lose Things   Queasy   Rough

DESCRIPTION AND COMMENTS Guests board boats for a water tour of Jurassic Park. Everything is tranquil as the tour begins; the boat floats among large herbivorous dinosaurs such as apatosaurus and stegosaurus. Then word is received that some of the carnivores have escaped their enclosure, and the tour boat is accidentally diverted into Jurassic Park's water-treatment facility. Here the boat and its riders are menaced by an assortment of hungry meat-eaters led by the ubiquitous *T. rex.* At the climactic moment, the boat and its passengers escape by dropping over a waterfall.

Jurassic Park is impressive in its scale, but the number of dinosaurs is a little disappointing. The big herbivores are given short shrift to set up the plot for the carnivore encounter, which leads to floating around in what looks like a brewery. When the carnivores make their appearance, however, they definitely get your attention. The final drop down a three-story flume to safety is a dandy, though not as impressive as its Orlando sibling.

TOURING TIPS You can get very wet on this ride, and extra jets enabled during hot weather practically ensure a soaking. Once the ride is under way, there's a little splashing but nothing major until the big drop at the end. When you hit the bottom, enough water will cascade into the boat to extinguish a three-alarm fire. Bring along an extra-large garbage bag and (cutting holes for your head and arms) wear it like a sack dress. If you forget to bring a garbage bag, you can purchase a poncho at the park for about $8.

Young kids must endure a double whammy. First, they are stalked by giant, salivating reptiles and then are catapulted over the falls. Wait until your kids are fairly stalwart before you spring Jurassic Park on them.

Jurassic Park stays jammed most of the day. Ride early in the morning after Revenge of the Mummy.

The NBC Universal Experience ★★★

APPEAL BY AGE	PRESCHOOL ★	GRADE SCHOOL ★★	TEENS ★★★
YOUNG ADULTS ★★★	OVER 30 ★★★		SENIORS ★★★

What it is Interactive walk-through exhibit. **Scope and scale** Diversion. **When to go** Anytime. **Duration of tour** 15–40 minutes. **Probable waiting time** None.

DESCRIPTION AND COMMENTS This exhibit features authentic props and costumes from many of Universal's most famous films—*Gladiator, To Kill a Mockingbird, Jurassic Park, E.T., The Sting, Psycho,* and *Coraline,* just to name a few. Cinephiles will love it. Recently added highlights include artifacts from the Oscar-winning musical *Les Misérables* and the time-traveling DeLorean used in the *Back to the Future* trilogy.

TOURING TIPS Never crowded—visit after you've experienced all of rides.

Revenge of the Mummy—The Ride ★★★½

APPEAL BY AGE	PRESCHOOL –	GRADE SCHOOL ★★★½	TEENS ★★★★½
YOUNG ADULTS ★★★★½	OVER 30 ★★★★		SENIORS ★★★½

What it is High-tech dark ride. **Scope and scale** Super-headliner. **When to go** The first hour the park is open or after 4 p.m. **Special comments** Must be 48" to ride. Switching-off option provided (see page 149). **Duration of ride** About 2 minutes. **Loading speed** Slow.

Dark

Scary

Lose Things

Queasy

Rough

DESCRIPTION AND COMMENTS It's kind of hard to wrap your mind around the actual attraction, but it pretty much lives up to the Universal press release, though the press release is generally incomprehensible. Here, quoting that press release, are some of the things you can look forward to: "authentic Egyptian catacombs;

high-velocity show immersion system [we think this has something to do with very fast baptism]; magnet-propulsion launch wave system; and canopic jars containing grisly remains."

Of course the art of the press release is to create allure and excitement without actually spilling the beans. Actually, Revenge of the Mummy is an indoor dark ride based on the *Mummy* flicks, where guests fight off "deadly curses and vengeful creatures" while flying through Egyptian tombs and other spooky places on a high-tech roller coaster.

The queuing area serves to establish the story line: you're in a group touring a 1944 archeological dig of an Egyptian tomb when evil Imhotep decides to make another comeback. The theming includes authentic hieroglyphics as the queue makes its way to the loading area, where you board a somewhat clunky, jeep-looking vehicle. The ride begins as a slow, elaborate dark ride passing through various chambers, including one where golden treasures are offered in exchange for your soul. Suddenly the aforementioned "magnet-propulsion launch wave system" comes in. In more ordinary language, this means that you're shot at high speed straight forward into a minute of pitch-black hills and tight curves, dead-ending in an encounter with leg-tickling scarab beetles. We don't want to divulge too much, but the roller coaster part of the ride has no barrel rolls or any upside-down stuff.

After an all-too-brief backward section, the attraction anti-climaxes in a darkened dome, where the mummy moans and then blinds you with a strobe. Compared to Universal Studios Florida's ride of the same name, this abbreviated attraction severely disappoints with shorter drops, simpler animatronics, and no "Brain-Fire" pyrotechnics.

TOURING TIPS Revenge of the Mummy has a very low riders-per-hour capacity for one of the park's top draws. Your only prayer for a tolerable wait is to be on hand when the park opens and sprint to the Mummy immediately after riding Transformers. If you can ride Space Mountain without getting sick, you should be fine on this.

Transformers—The Ride 3-D ★ ★ ★ ★ ★

APPEAL BY AGE PRESCHOOL ★ ★ ★ GRADE SCHOOL ★ ★ ★ ★ ★ TEENS ★ ★ ★ ★ ★
YOUNG ADULTS ★ ★ ★ ★ ★ OVER 30 ★ ★ ★ ★ ★ SENIORS ★ ★ ★ ★

What it is Multisensory 3-D dark ride. **Scope and scale** Super-headliner. **When to go** The first 30 minutes the park is open or after 4 p.m. **Special comments** Must be 40" to ride; single-rider line is available. **Duration of ride** 4½ minutes. **Loading speed** Moderate–fast.

Dark   Loud   Scary   Rough

DESCRIPTION AND COMMENTS Hasbro's Transformers—those toy robots from the 1980s that you turned and twisted into trucks and planes—have been around long enough to go from commercial to kitsch to cool and back again. Thanks to director Michael Bay's recent movie trilogy, "Robots in Disguise" are again a blockbuster global franchise, and in 2012, Transformers fans finally received a theme park attraction befitting their pop-culture idols. Recruits to this cybertronic war enlist by entering the N.E.S.T. Base (headquarters of the heroic Autobots and their human allies) beneath a massive dimensional mural depicting Optimus Prime and his nemesis Megatron locked in mortal metal combat. Inside an extensive, elaborately detailed queue, video monitors catch you up on the backstory. Basically, the Decepticon baddies are after the Allspark, source of cybernetic sentience. We're supposed to safeguard the shard by hitching a ride aboard our friendly Autobot ride vehicle EVAC, presumably without getting "smooshed" like a Lincoln in a souvenir penny press when he shifts into android form. Needless to say, Megatron and his pals Starscream and Devastator won't make things easy, but you'll have Sideswipe and Bumblebee (sadly, the modern Camaro version instead of an old-school VW Beetle) backing you up. For the ride's 4½ minutes, you play human Ping-Pong ball in an epic battle between these Made in Japan behemoths. To do justice to this Bay-splosion–packed war of good versus evil, Universal has harnessed the same ride system behind Islands of Adventure's Amazing Adventures of Spider-Man ride. That's good news since Spidey, which broke ground by blending motion simulation and live effects with 3-D, was already acclaimed as one of the best attractions anywhere.

Transformers ups the ante with photo-realistic high-definition imagery, boosted by dichroic 3-D glasses (the same kind used in the upgraded Star Tours) that produce remarkably sharp, vivid visuals. The plot amounts to little more than a giant game of keep-away, and the uninitiated will likely be unable to tell one meteoric mass of metal from another, but you'll be too dazzled by the debris whizzing by to notice. Fanboys will squeal with delight at hearing original cartoon actors Peter Cullen and Frank Welker voicing the pugilistic protagonists, and then spill into the post-ride gift shop to purchase armloads of exclusive merchandise, while the rest of us might need a bench on which to take a breather afterward. We'll admit slight disappointment at not getting to see an actual four-story-tall animatronic transform, but the ride's mix of detailed (though largely static) set pieces and video projections was likely a much more maintenance-friendly solution for bringing these colossi to life. Either way, this is one of the most intense, immersive thrill rides found in any theme park and makes a credible claim on the title "best attraction in California." If you visit Universal and only ride this and the Tram Tour, you'll get your money's worth.

TOURING TIPS This is the most ambitious attraction that Universal Studios Hollywood has built in more than a decade and could prove a game changer for the park's attendance. Transformers draws heavy crowds to the Lower Lot from the moment the park opens, so ride immediately upon park opening. The single-rider entrance will often let you walk on the attraction, even when the standby wait is an hour, but its queue lacks any theming, so be sure to take at least one trip through the regular line. It can be difficult for your eyes to focus on the fast-moving imagery from the front row; center seats in the second and third rows provide the best perspective. And be sure to say hello to the towering robots posing for photos outside the entrance.

LIVE ENTERTAINMENT *at* UNIVERSAL STUDIOS HOLLYWOOD

THE THEATER AND AMPHITHEATER ATTRACTIONS operate according to the entertainment schedule available with handout park maps. The number of daily performances of each show varies from as few as 3 a day during less busy times of year to as many as 10 a day during the summer and holiday periods. Blues Brothers impersonators offer a high-energy show in the Upper Lot near the front entrance. The instrumental track is prerecorded, but the show is a spirit lifter nonetheless. Look for the Doo Wop Singers belting out 1950s and 1960s harmonies near Mel's Diner.

DINING *at* UNIVERSAL STUDIOS HOLLYWOOD

THE COUNTER-SERVICE FOOD at Universal Studios runs the gamut from burgers and hot dogs to pizza, fried chicken, crêpes, and Mexican specialties. We rank most selections marginally better than fast food. Prices are comparable to those at Disneyland.

If you are looking for full-service dining, try **Wolfgang Puck Bistro, Buca di Beppo, Wasabi,** or the **Hard Rock Cafe** in the Universal CityWalk just outside the park entrance. Our favorites in the park are the gourmet sandwiches at **International Cafe, Doc Brown's Fancy Chicken,** and the **Hollywood Grill** burger joint across from *WaterWorld*. If you leave the park for lunch, be sure to have your hand stamped for reentry.

UNIVERSAL STUDIOS HOLLYWOOD ONE-DAY TOURING PLAN *(page 376)*

THIS PLAN IS FOR GROUPS OF ALL SIZES and ages and includes thrill rides that may induce motion sickness or get you wet. If the plan calls for you to experience an attraction that does not interest you, proceed to the next step. The plan calls for minimal backtracking.

Before You Go

1. Call ☎ 818-622-3801 the day before your visit for the official opening time. If you can't get through, call ☎ 818-622-3735 or 818-622-3750. On all numbers, press 3 for a live attendant.

2. If you have young children in your party, consult the Universal Studios Hollywood Small-Child Fright-Potential Chart on the opposite page.

Universal Studios Hollywood Small-Child Fright-Potential Chart

DESPICABLE ME: MINION MAYHEM Loud with some intense 3-D effects. Stationary seats are available.

JURASSIC PARK—THE RIDE Intense water-flume ride. Potentially terrifying for people of any age.

REVENGE OF THE MUMMY—THE RIDE Scares guests of all ages.

SHREK 4-D Special effects may frighten preschoolers.

THE SIMPSONS RIDE Motion simulator too intense for many children age 7 and younger tall enough to ride.

SPECIAL EFFECTS STAGE Some intense special effects. Shows how bloody fake wounds are created.

STUDIO TOUR Certain parts of the tour are too frightening and too intense for many preschoolers.

TRANSFORMERS—THE RIDE 3-D Too intense for children younger than age 7, and potentially terrifying for visitors of any age.

UNIVERSAL'S ANIMAL ACTORS Not frightening in any way.

UNIVERSAL'S HOUSE OF HORRORS Frightens guests of all ages.

WATERWORLD Fighting, gunplay, and explosions may frighten children age 4 and younger.

APPENDIX

READERS' QUESTIONS
to the AUTHORS

QUESTION:

When you do your research, are you admitted to the park for free? Do the Disney people know you are there?

ANSWER:

We pay the regular admission, and usually the Disney people do not know we are on-site. Both in and out of Disneyland, we pay for our own meals and lodging.

QUESTION:

How often is The Unofficial Guide to Disneyland *revised?*

ANSWER:

We publish a new edition once a year but make corrections every time we go to press.

QUESTION:

I have an older edition of The Unofficial Guide to Disneyland. *How much of the information in it is still correct?*

ANSWER:

Veteran travel writers will acknowledge that 5%–8% of the information in a guidebook is out of date by the time it comes off the press! Disneyland is always changing. If you are using an old edition of *The Unofficial Guide to Disneyland,* the descriptions of attractions existing when the guide was published should still be generally accurate. Many other things, however—particularly the touring plans and the hotel and restaurant reviews—change with every edition. Finally, and obviously, older editions of *The Unofficial Guide to Disneyland* do not include new attractions or developments.

QUESTION:

Do you write each new edition from scratch?

ANSWER:

We do not. With a destination the size of Disneyland, it's hard enough keeping up with what is new. Moreover, we put great effort into communicating the most salient and useful information in the clearest possible language. If an attraction or hotel has not changed, we are very reluctant to tinker with its coverage for the sake of freshening up the writing.

QUESTION:

Do you stay at Disneyland hotels? If not, where do you stay?

ANSWER:

We do stay at Disneyland-area hotels from time to time, usually after a renovation or management change. Since we began writing about Disneyland in 1984, we have stayed in more than 50 different properties in various locations around Anaheim.

QUESTION:

How many people have you interviewed or surveyed for your age-group ratings on the attractions?

ANSWER:

Since the publication of the first edition of the *Unofficial Guide* in 1985, we have interviewed or surveyed more than 19,000 Disneyland patrons.

QUESTION:

How are your age-group ratings determined? I am 42 years old. During Star Tours, I was quite worried about hurting my back. If the senior citizens rating is determined only by those brave enough to ride, it will skew the results.

ANSWER:

The reader makes a good point. Unfortunately, it's impossible to develop a rating unless the guest (of any age group) has actually experienced the attraction. So yes, all age-group ratings are derived exclusively from members of that age group who have experienced the attraction. Health problems, such as a bad back, however, can affect guests of any age, and Disney provides more-than-ample warnings on attractions that warrant such admonitions. But if you are in good health, our ratings will give you a sense of how much others your age enjoyed the attraction.

QUESTION:

I have heard that when there are two lines to an attraction, the left line is faster. Is this true?

ANSWER:

In general, no. We have tested this theory many times and usually have not gained an advantage of even 90 seconds by getting in one line versus another. The few rare exceptions are noted in the ride descriptions. What *does* occasionally occur, however, is that after a second line has *just been opened*, guests ignore the new line and persist in standing in the established line. Generally, if you encounter a two-line waiting configuration with no barrier to entry for either and one of the lines is conspicuously less populated than the other, get in it.

AND FINALLY . . .

To end on a high note, consider this compliment from a Redding, California, reader:

> *Thanks to your book, this trip turned out much better than our last, so much in fact that I required only half as much Valium.*

And so it goes . . .

ACCOMMODATION INDEX

Note: Page numbers in **bold face** type indicate profiles.

RESTAURANT INDEX

Note: Page numbers in **bold face** type indicate a profile.

SUBJECT INDEX

Note: Attractions at California Adventure and Universal Studios Hollywood theme parks are designated (DCA) and (USH), respectively; all others are Disneyland Park.

One-Day Plan for Adults

Disneyland Park

Mickey's Toontown

Fantasyland

Critter Country

Frontierland

Tomorrowland

New Orleans Square

Adventureland

Main Street, U.S.A.

1. As soon as the park opens, ride Peter Pan's Flight in Fantasyland.
2. Experience the Matterhorn Bobsleds in Fantasyland.
3. Ride Star Tours in Tomorrowland.
4. Try Buzz Lightyear Astro Blasters.
5. Obtain Fastpasses for Space Mountain.
6. Take the Finding Nemo Submarine Voyage.
7. Ride It's a Small World in Fantasyland.
8. Return to Tomorrowland and ride Space Mountain using the Fastpasses obtained earlier.
9. Obtain Fastpasses for the Indiana Jones Adventure in Adventureland.
10. Take the Jungle Cruise.
11. Check the daily entertainment schedule for the next performance at the Golden Horseshoe. If possible, eat lunch while watching the show.
12. Return to Tomorrowland and see *Captain EO*.
13. See *Enchanted Tiki Room* in Adventureland.
14. Experience the Indiana Jones Adventure using the Fastpasses obtained earlier.
15. Experience Pirates of the Caribbean in New Orleans Square.
16. Explore Tarzan's Treehouse nearby.
17. Obtain Fastpasses for Big Thunder Mountain Railroad in Frontierland.
18. See The Haunted Mansion in New Orleans Square.
19. Take a round-trip on the Disneyland Railroad from the New Orleans Square station.
20. Ride Big Thunder Mountain in Frontierland, using the Fastpasses obtained earlier.
21. Experience the Sailing Ship *Columbia* or the *Mark Twain* Riverboat.
22. See *The Disneyland Story,* presenting *Great Moments with Mr. Lincoln,* on Main Street.
23. Obtain Fastpasses for Splash Mountain in Critter Country.
24. Eat dinner.
25. See The Many Adventures of Winnie the Pooh in Critter Country.
26. Ride Splash Mountain using the Fastpasses obtained earlier.
27. Tour Mickey's Toontown if you have kids and time permits.
28. Visit any attractions you may have missed earlier.
29. Check the *Times Guide* for parades, fireworks, and *Fantasmic!*

Author's Select One-Day Plan

Disneyland Park

Mickey's Toontown
23

7

Fantasyland

13

Critter Country

14 21

19 22

Frontierland

17

1

2

6

Tomorrowland

4

3

18

New Orleans Square

20

12

11

15

10

Adventureland

Main Street, U.S.A.

8

5

9

16

1. As soon as the park opens, ride Peter Pan's Flight in Fantasyland.
2. Experience the Matterhorn Bobsleds.
3. Ride Star Tours in Tomorrowland.
4. Try Buzz Lightyear Astro Blasters.
5. Obtain Fastpasses for Space Mountain.
6. Take the Finding Nemo Submarine Voyage.
7. Ride It's a Small World in Fantasyland.
8. Return to Tomorrowland and see *Captain EO.*
9. Ride Space Mountain using the Fastpasses obtained earlier.
10. Obtain Fastpasses for the Indiana Jones Adventure in Adventureland.
11. Check the daily entertainment schedule for the next performance at the Golden Horseshoe. If possible, eat lunch while watching the show.
12. Experience Pirates of the Caribbean in New Orleans Square.
13. See The Many Adventures of Winnie the Pooh in Critter Country.
14. Obtain Fastpasses for Splash Mountain.
15. Experience the Indiana Jones Adventure using the Fastpasses obtained earlier.
16. See *The Disneyland Story,* presenting *Great Moments with Mr. Lincoln,* on Main Street.
17. Experience the Sailing Ship *Columbia* or the *Mark Twain* Riverboat.
18. See The Haunted Mansion in New Orleans Square.
19. Obtain Fastpasses for Big Thunder Mountain Railroad in Frontierland.
20. Take a round-trip on the Disneyland Railroad from the New Orleans Square station.
21. Ride Splash Mountain using the Fastpasses obtained earlier.
22. Ride Big Thunder Mountain using the Fastpasses obtained earlier.
23. Tour Mickey's Toontown if you have kids and time permits.
24. Visit any attractions you may have missed earlier.
25. Check the *Times Guide* for parades, fireworks, and *Fantasmic!*

Dumbo-or-Die-in-a-Day Plan

Disneyland Park

Mickey's Toontown

Fantasyland

Critter Country

Frontierland

Tomorrowland

New Orleans Square

Adventureland

Main Street, U.S.A.

1. As soon as the park opens, ride Peter Pan's Flight in Fantasyland.
2. Ride Dumbo the Flying Elephant.
3. Ride Alice in Wonderland.
4. Ride the King Arthur Carrousel.
5. Take Pinocchio's Daring Journey.
6. Ride the Casey Jr. Circus Train.
7. Take a spin on the Mad Tea Party.
8. Ride the Storybook Land Canal Boats.
9. In Toontown, ride Roger Rabbit's Car Toon Spin. Obtain Fastpasses if the wait exceeds 30 minutes.
10. Tour Mickey's House.
11. Ride Gadget's Go Coaster.
12. Tour Minnie's House.
13. Let the kids blow off some steam at Goofy's Playhouse.
14. Take the It's a Small World boat ride.
15. Experience the Disney Princess Royal Walk.
16. In Tomorrowland, ride the Autopia.
17. Ride Buzz Lightyear Astro Blasters.
18. See *Enchanted Tiki Room* in Adventureland.
19. Ride Pirates of the Caribbean in New Orleans Square.

20. Eat lunch.
21. If you're visiting between mid-September and New Year's, and Haunted Mansion has Fastpasses available, obtain Fastpasses for Haunted Mansion now. Otherwise, skip this step.
22. Take The Many Adventures of Winnie the Pooh ride in Critter Country.
23. Take a raft to explore the Pirate's Lair on Tom Sawyer Island.
24. See The Haunted Mansion.
25. Take a round-trip on the Disneyland Railroad from the New Orleans Square station.
26. If time permits, ride the *Mark Twain* Riverboat.
27. Explore Tarzan's Treehouse in Adventureland.
28. If time permits, let the kids play at Donald's Boat and the Chip 'n Dale Treehouse in Mickey's Toontown.
29. Visit any attractions you may have missed earlier.
30. Check the *Times Guide* for parades, fireworks, and *Fantasmic!*

Two-Day Plan for Adults with Children: Day One

1. Arrive at the entrance 40 minutes before official opening time.
2. As soon as the park opens, ride the Indiana Jones Adventure in Adventureland.
3. Take the Jungle Cruise, also in Adventureland.
4. Try Splash Mountain in Critter Country.
5. Ride The Many Adventures of Winnie the Pooh, also in Critter Country.
6. Experience the Disney Princess Royal Walk in Fantasyland.
7. In Toontown, tour Mickey's House.
8. Ride Gadget's Go Coaster.
9. Let the kids blow off some steam at Goofy's Playhouse.
10. Try Roger Rabbit's Car Toon Spin. Obtain Fastpasses if the wait exceeds 30 minutes.
11. In Fantasyland, ride It's a Small World.
12. Ride Pirates of the Caribbean in New Orleans Square.
13. See The Haunted Mansion. If you're visiting between mid-September and New Year's, and Haunted Mansion is distributing Fastpasses, obtain Fastpasses if the wait exceeds 30 minutes.
14. Eat lunch and take the Disneyland Railroad from New Orleans Square to Toontown.
15. In Mickey's Toontown, see Minnie's House.
16. Try the Chip 'n Dale Treehouse and Donald's Boat, also in Mickey's Toontown.
17. Obtain Fastpasses for Autopia in Tomorrowland.
18. If time permits, take a round-trip on the Disneyland Monorail in Tomorrowland.
19. See *Captain EO* in Tomorrowland.
20. Ride the Autopia using the Fastpasses obtained earlier.
21. Eat dinner.
22. Visit any attractions you may have missed earlier.
23. Check the *Times Guide* for parades, fireworks, and *Fantasmic!*

Two-Day Plan for Adults with Children: Day Two

1. Arrive at the entrance 40 minutes before official opening time.
2. As soon as the park opens, ride Peter Pan's Flight in Fantasyland.
3. Take Mr. Toad's Wild Ride.
4. Experience Dumbo the Flying Elephant.
5. Ride Alice in Wonderland.
6. Try the Storybook Land Canal Boats.
7. Take a spin on the Mad Tea Party.
8. In Tomorrowland, send one member of your party to obtain Fastpasses for Star Tours: The Adventures Continue.
9. Ride Space Mountain.
10. Take the Finding Nemo Submarine Voyage.
11. Ride Buzz Lightyear Astro Blasters, also in Tomorrowland.
12. In Fantasyland, ride Pinocchio's Daring Journey.

13. Take a spin on the King Arthur Carrousel.
14. Ride Big Thunder Mountain in Frontierland.
15. See *Enchanted Tiki Room* in Adventureland.
16. Ride Star Tours in Tomorrowland, using the Fastpasses obtained earlier.
17. Eat lunch.
18. Take a raft to Tom Sawyer Island, and let the kids run around the island's Pirate's Lair.
19. Explore Tarzan's Treehouse.
20. If time permits, try the Sailing Ship *Columbia* or the *Mark Twain* Riverboat.
21. Visit any attractions you may have missed earlier.
22. Check the *Times Guide* for parades, fireworks, and *Fantasmic!*

Two-Day Plan A: Day One

Disneyland Park

Mickey's Toontown

Fantasyland ⑥

④ ③
⑤ ②
⑦
⑧
Critter Country ⑰
⑯ ⑲
⑰ Frontierland
⑮
Tomorrowland
⑩
⑪
New Orleans
Square ⑱ ⑬
Adventureland

Main Street, U.S.A.

⑫ ⑨

⑭

①

1. Arrive at the entrance 40 minutes before official opening time.
2. As soon as the park opens, ride Peter Pan's Flight in Fantasyland.
3. Take Mr. Toad's Wild Ride.
4. Take Pinocchio's Daring Journey.
5. Ride Snow White's Scary Adventures.
6. Ride the Storybook Land Canal Boats.
7. Experience the Matterhorn Bobsleds.
8. In Tomorrowland, take the Finding Nemo Submarine Voyage.
9. Obtain Fastpasses for Space Mountain.
10. Ride Buzz Lightyear Astro Blasters.
11. Eat lunch and work in a show at the Golden Horseshoe.
12. Return to Tomorrowland and ride Space Mountain using the Fastpasses obtained earlier.
13. See *Enchanted Tiki Room* in Adventureland.
14. See *The Disneyland Story,* presenting *Great Moments with Mr. Lincoln.*
15. Ride the Sailing Ship *Columbia* or the *Mark Twain* Riverboat, whichever is boarding first.
16. Send one member of your party to obtain Fastpasses for Big Thunder Mountain Railroad in Frontierland.
17. Take a raft to the Pirate's Lair on Tom Sawyer Island.
18. Climb through Tarzan's Treehouse in Adventureland.
19. Ride Big Thunder Mountain Railroad using the Fastpasses obtained earlier.
20. Eat dinner.
21. Visit any attractions you may have missed earlier.
22. Check the *Times Guide* for parades, fireworks, and *Fantasmic!*

Two-Day Plan A: Day Two

1. Arrive at the entrance 40 minutes before official opening time.
2. As soon as the park opens, ride Star Tours: The Adventures Continue in Tomorrowland.
3. Take the Indiana Jones Adventure in Adventureland.
4. In Mickey's Toontown, visit Mickey's House.
5. See Minnie's House.
6. Try Roger Rabbit's Car Toon Spin. Use Fastpasses if the wait exceeds 30 minutes.
7. Ride Alice in Wonderland in Fantasyland.
8. Ride It's a Small World.
9. Take the Jungle Cruise in Adventureland.
10. Ride The Haunted Mansion.
11. Experience The Many Adventures of Winnie the Pooh in Critter Country.
12. Obtain Fastpasses for Splash Mountain, also in Critter Country.
13. Take a round-trip on the Disneyland Railroad from the New Orleans Square station.
14. Ride Pirates of the Caribbean.
15. Eat lunch.
16. Ride Splash Mountain using the Fastpasses obtained earlier.
17. In Tomorrowland, see *Captain EO*.
18. See the *Jedi Training Academy*.
19. Revisit any favorite attractions or visit any attractions you may have missed earlier.
20. Check the *Times Guide* for parades, fireworks, and *Fantasmic!*

Two-Day Plan B: Day One

Disneyland Park

Mickey's Toontown

Fantasyland

Critter Country

Frontierland

Tomorrowland

New Orleans Square

Adventureland

Main Street, U.S.A.

1. Arrive at the entrance 40 minutes before official opening time.
2. As soon as the park opens, ride Peter Pan's Flight in Fantasyland.
3. Try the Matterhorn Bobsleds, also in Fantasyland.
4. Ride Space Mountain in Tomorrowland.
5. Take the Finding Nemo Submarine Voyage, also in Tomorrowland.
6. Ride Buzz Lightyear Astro Blasters.
7. Obtain Fastpasses for the Indiana Jones Adventure in Adventureland.
8. Ride Pirates of the Caribbean in New Orleans Square.
9. See The Haunted Mansion.
10. Obtain Fastpasses for Splash Mountain in Critter Country.
11. Check the daily entertainment schedule for the next performance at the Golden Horseshoe. If possible, eat lunch while watching the show.
12. Ride The Many Adventures of Winnie the Pooh in Critter Country.
13. Experience Splash Mountain using the Fastpasses obtained earlier.
14. Obtain Fastpasses for Big Thunder Mountain in Frontierland.
15. Ride the *Mark Twain* Riverboat or Sailing Ship *Columbia,* whichever boards first.
16. Ride the Indiana Jones Adventure using the Fastpasses obtained earlier.
17. Ride Big Thunder Mountain Railroad using the Fastpasses obtained earlier.
18. In Tomorrowland, see *Captain EO.*
19. On Main Street, see *The Disneyland Story,* presenting *Great Moments with Mr. Lincoln.*
20. Revisit any favorite attractions or visit any attractions you may have missed earlier.
21. Check the *Times Guide* for parades, fireworks, and *Fantasmic!*

Two-Day Plan B: Day Two

1. Arrive at the entrance around 5 p.m.
2. Ride Star Tours: The Adventures Continue in Tomorrowland.
3. Ride Alice in Wonderland in Fantasyland.
4. Obtain Fastpasses for Roger Rabbit's Car Toon Spin in Mickey's Toontown.
5. See It's a Small World in Fantasyland.
6. Ride Roger Rabbit's Car Toon Spin using the Fastpasses obtained earlier.
7. See *Enchanted Tiki Room* in Adventureland.
8. Take the Jungle Cruise.
9. Explore Tarzan's Treehouse.
10. Take a round-trip on the Disneyland Railroad from New Orleans Square.
11. If time permits, try Mr. Toad's Wild Ride in Fantasyland.
12. Revisit any favorite attractions or visit any attractions you may have missed earlier.
13. Check the *Times Guide* for parades, fireworks, and *Fantasmic!*

One-Day Plan for Adults

Disney California Adventure

1. Arrive at the entrance 40 minutes before official opening time.
2. As soon as the park opens, obtain Fastpasses for Radiator Springs Racers in Cars Land.
3. Ride Mater's Junkyard Jamboree.
4. Ride Luigi's Flying Tires.
5. Ride Radiator Springs Racers using the Fastpasses obtained earlier. If your passes are not yet valid, leave Cars Land now, and break from the plan to return at the printed time.
6. Obtain Fastpasses for Soarin' Over California.
7. Obtain Fastpasses for *World of Color.* Fastpasses are distributed near the entrance to Grizzly River Run.
8. Try Toy Story Midway Mania! in Paradise Pier.
9. Ride Goofy's Sky School in Paradise Pier.
10. Try the Silly Symphony Swings.
11. Check the daily entertainment schedule for the next showing of Disney's *Aladdin—A Musical Spectacular.* Work in this show either before or after lunch.
12. Send one member of your party to obtain Fastpasses for California Screamin' in Paradise Pier.

13. Ride Soarin' Over California using the Fastpasses obtained earlier.
14. See *It's Tough to Be a Bug!*
15. Ride California Screamin' using the Fastpasses obtained earlier.
16. Obtain Fastpasses for The Twilight Zone Tower of Terror in Hollywood Land.
17. Ride Monsters, Inc. Mike & Sulley to the Rescue!
18. See *Muppet-Vision 3-D.*
19. Ride The Twilight Zone Tower of Terror, using the Fastpasses obtained earlier.
20. Ride The Little Mermaid—Ariel's Undersea Adventure.
21. If time permits, take the bakery tour in the Pacific Wharf.
22. See the Disney Animation exhibit, including the Animation Academy and *Turtle Talk with Crush.*
23. Eat dinner.
24. Ride Grizzly River Run.
25. Repeat any favorite attractions or see any missed attractions.
26. Check your daily entertainment schedule for parades, and check your *World of Color* Fastpass for the performance time.

One-Day Plan for Adults with Small Children

Disney California Adventure

1. Arrive at the entrance 40 minutes before official opening time.
2. As soon as the park opens, obtain Fastpasses for Radiator Springs Racers in Cars Land.
3. Ride Mater's Junkyard Jamboree.
4. Ride Luigi's Flying Tires.
5. Ride Radiator Springs Racers using the Fastpasses obtained earlier. If your passes are not yet valid, leave Cars Land now, and break from the plan to return at the printed time.
6. Obtain Fastpasses for Soarin' Over California.
7. Obtain Fastpasses for World of Color. Fastpasses are distributed near the entrance to Grizzly River Run.
8. Ride Francis' Ladybug Boogie in a bug's land.
9. Ride Tuck and Roll's Drive 'Em Buggies, also in a bug's land.
10. Experience Flik's Flyers.
11. Check the daily entertainment schedule for the next showing of Disney's Aladdin—A Musical Spectacular. Work in this show either before or after lunch.
12. See the Disney Animation exhibit, including the Animation Academy and Turtle Talk with Crush.
13. Ride Soarin' Over California using the Fastpasses obtained earlier.
14. Try the Silly Symphony Swings in Paradise Pier.
15. Ride Toy Story Midway Mania!
16. Experience King Triton's Carousel in Paradise Pier.
17. Explore the Redwood Creek Challenge Train in Grizzly Peak.
18. Obtain Fastpasses for The Twilight Zone Tower of Terror in Hollywood Land.
19. Ride Monsters, Inc. Mike & Sulley to the Rescue!
20. See Muppet-Vision 3-D.
21. Experience Disney Junior.
22. Ride The Tower of Terror using the Fastpasses obtained earlier.
23. Eat dinner.
24. Ride The Little Mermaid—Ariel's Undersea Adventure.
25. Repeat any favorite attractions or see any missed attractions.
26. Check your daily entertainment schedule for parades, and check your World of Color Fastpass for the performance time.

Universal Studios One-Day Touring Plan

1. Arrive 20 minutes before opening time.
2. Ride Transformers in the Lower Lot.
3. Ride Revenge of the Mummy.
4. Check out Jurassic Park.
5. Ride Despicable Me: Minion Mayhem.
6. In the Upper Lot, experience The Simpsons Ride.
7. See Shrek 4-D.
8. See the Special Effects Stage.
9. Check out daily entertainment schedule for a) *WaterWorld* and b) *Universal's Animal Actors* showtimes.
10. Eat lunch and take the Studio Tour. Allocate an hour and 10 minutes for the tour.
11. Return to the Lower Lot and check out The NBC Universal Experience.
    Return to the Upper Lot.
12. Check out a) Universal's House of Horrors and b) *The Blues Brothers* show.
13. Revisit your favorites or see attractions you missed. Check your daily entertainment schedule for live performances that interest you.